Enter the Era of Empowerment
Self-Sovereignty in a Complex World

J ohn J ones

Enter the Era of Empowerment: Self-Sovereignty in a Complex World Copyright © 2013 John Jones

Published by Karmic Communications, LLC

First Edition 2012
Second Edition 2016

Edition 2 Editors: John Jones, Betty Alamo, Cheryl Koenigbauer
Original Book Cover and Typesetting: Ja-lene Clark
Author Photo: Geoffrey Baris, Miami, Florida
Graphics Creation and Editing: Ja-Lene Clark, John Jones, and Douglas Gobel of GobelDesign.com

PRINTED IN USA

Dedication

*This book is dedicated to each self-sovereign person who is living in the midst of these times of powerful change, and doing their best to make sense of it all;
I wish you all the best and only the best.*

A quote by Blaise Pascal sums up our species current situation:

"All of humanity's problems stem from man's inability
to sit quietly in a room alone."

TABLE OF CONTENTS

Chapter One
Entering the Age of Individual Power

WE ARE ALL ENDOWED WITH PERSONAL POWER, WHETHER we realize it or not. We are meant to own and consciously wield our personal power in the world and achieve heightened understanding through doing so. Yet wisely mastering this power is challenging, thus it is precisely why we are here, so that the essence of who and what we are can be expressed in willful actions. Through this life process we eventually learn and understand who we truly are as individuals. We experience and learn from the results of experimenting with our expressions of our personal power, which is how we ultimately achieve wisdom and enlightenment. This process of personal evolution is quite often messy, confusing and emotional pain producing. It is also vital to the fulfillment of our potential. In effect the only way out is through.

I have written this book to provide the requisite self-awareness, understanding, perspective and tools to set readers on the path to personal em*power*ment and **self-sovereignty** (this term will be defined later in the text). Yet for us to arrive at the destination we desire, we must first understand where we are now as individuals, and as a meaningful part of humanity.

Simply stated, owning our power means that we make our choices with total personal accountability and awareness of their implications. From that vantage point of understanding the nature of our power we learn how to consciously choose to form our life intentions and then act upon our intentions, rather than merely reacting to our life experiences. This requires that we consistently look at all aspects of our lives with an unflinching, compassionately observant eye, and consciously choose who we will become, and then earnestly work to become our chosen vision. We came here to creatively learn and in every moment of our lives we are learning. Each choice we make, whether seemingly good or bad, serves us as we continually refine our decision-making strategies. By doing so we evolve our consciousness, and fine-tune ourselves to the point at which we attain wisdom, discipline and discernment.

We have been vested with all the power necessary to accomplish our goals, dreams and desires in this lifetime, and only we as individuals can choose to accomplish this. Consistent and determined application of our personal freewill can move us toward what we want. Our freewill is a fundamental ability and power, and we each have the God-given right to decide for ourselves what is good, right and best for us from moment-to-moment.

No one can take our freewill away; no government, no rule, no law nor any external power. It is always our free-will choice how we choose to respond to these external influences. Although there are always results or even consequences derived from the use of our freewill, there are no limits to it. We do not "have to" do anything at all, not even eat or breathe if we choose not to. Still many of us live in an "I have to" mindset. (i.e. "I have to meet other's expectations", or "I have to do what others want me to do" or "I have to follow my family's or my culture's traditions").

The truth of our total freedom of free-will was evidenced by Mahatma Gandhi when he endured a long hunger strike to free the country of India from British rule. In this way, he demonstrated the true power of the individual. Choosing to believe that any of us "have to" do anything in life means that we then assume that we do not have free will choice and personal power in all moments of our lives. This blinding assumption denies our freewill, our personal power and directly limits our creativity. Feeling or believing in any part of ourselves that "I have to", generates a limitation in our understanding of our own power. It also creates an extremely unconscious attachment to our achieving socially expected results or states of being. If someone tells you that you have to do anything they are in effect saying you have no free will in the matter, which is never true. If you tell yourself you have to do anything, you get the same limiting result. Any extreme attachment to any specific life goal or result creates an imbalance in our systems, in our decision-making processes, and then in our lives. Setting and achieving intentions is wonderful, doing so in an unbalanced way causes suffering, stress, limitation and dysfunction.

Defining our present state of power as individuals is a necessary beginning to the achievement of mapping and navigating our way to where to go and who we most want to be. We must first be willing to acknowledge and truly understand the basic nature of our current life challenges and situations, as seen from both individual and global perspectives. Otherwise we cannot hope to define precise and effective solutions for them and at the same time define our path to greater personal power. If we are unable to accurately perceive the nuances of our own conscious and subconscious basic nature and their influence on our life results, how can we hope to effectively transcend them? In this endeavor the degree of developmental and transformational efficiency we apply to the process is a significant determinant of our results.

You may have heard the expression that "every cloud has a silver lining". I would say that it is effective and constructive to hold this statement in mind when reviewing the variety of issues discussed in this book. Truly there are many challenges in our world, yet I believe that in the long run these challenges are all facilitating humankind's development. So, in the process of reviewing these issues it is necessary that we be willing to suspend judgments of all of our life situations, and every problematic world situation, in order to see things from the most constructive and positive vantage point possible. To get full benefit from reading "Enter the Era of Empowerment", I ask that you be willing to set aside many of the ways you might have previously looked at life and relationships in order to be open to different and possibly more self-empowering approaches to these topics. When we are well-balanced and objective, then we become optimally empowered to transcend any life challenge. We are disempowered when we lose ourselves in criticism, being judgmental, blame, emotional reactions or polarizing black-and-white interpretations of life. In these situations, we lose perspective, balance and clarity in our interpretive, emotional and decision-making processes.

The fact that the world and everyone in it are rapidly changing at this moment is common knowledge and can be the sparking point for heated discussions. These changes span the spectrum from the gross to the extremely subtle, and everyone on the planet is to some extent aware of and affected by them. The environment in which we live, work and create families is the result of our choices, it is also a process of our adapting to the results of our ongoing individual choices. (i.e. Learning from our choices and results). I would argue that all the changes we are experiencing are both necessary and for the better. Some of these changes are obviously positive, and signal the potential for a great and positive world future. I would also say that we must be willing to look at the overall history of humanity in order to be able to appreciate how far we have come and what we have accomplished as a species.

Today, in most developed countries of the world, the standard of living is far better than it has ever been. In the United States, even the poor often have better food, shelter and medical care than most of humanity has enjoyed prior to the last century. For example, just 150 years ago only 10% of the adult population of the world could read and write; UNESCO estimated in 2010 that 84.1% of adults worldwide could read and write at some minimal level.

(See http:// www.uis.unesco.org/literacy/Documents/fs20-literacy-day-2012-en-v3.pdf.)

This is an unprecedented and incredibly empowering social transformation. Additionally, the great scourge of government-supported slavery, with us since the dawn of recorded history, has at last been outlawed across the globe, and new awareness has been brought to the problem of slavers who still operate outside the law. The other great menace of communicable diseases such as leprosy, polio and smallpox have been so reduced in outbreaks that they barely register in our current consciousness. Technological advances such as electricity, refrigeration and the unsung miracle of improved sanitation have freed many of us from the need to spend all our time on basic survival issues. This has in turn given us the historical luxury to consider our purpose in life.

Our world has the potential to be a veritable paradise as technology now rapidly solves many problems that have previously plagued humanity. I believe we would all benefit from being patient with humanity's development for just a little longer as well as retaining our hope and faith.

In the next several pages we will go deeper into areas where major positive developmental changes are occurring around the world.

Global Social, Political and Economic Awareness:

We are currently experiencing major shifts in the political systems of several Middle Eastern countries toward some form of democracy, in spite of massive terrorist disruptions. I am not, by saying this, suggesting that democracy is the best or most acceptable political system. In fact, all the world's political systems are feeding the overall development of human political understanding. I am saying that at this time some form of democracy appears to be the general chosen direction of many nations. In addition, political systems in historically violent or oppressive locations are making some progress in learning to establish and implement human rights principles. These evolving situations are and will continue to create a multitude of political, cultural and economic domino effects across the world. We are also seeing positive adaptations in the existing global international power structure and the international banking/financial system. Though many would say that greater and more fundamental modifications are needed in these areas. Simultaneously all nations are coming to more fully realize their global economic interdependence, which is leading to the beginnings of real, valid and significant cooperative efforts between nations. This new attainment of global awareness can be seen in the way countries are choosing to proactively band together to combat both the causes and effects of environmental pollution.

We are not only experiencing social and political turnarounds, we are also experiencing massive social reconciliations and healing efforts such as those that have occurred in South Africa, as it works to heal the emotional scars resulting from the actions of its previous apartheid system of government. Similar progressions toward international and intra-national healing will likely benefit the new political and social systems of the Middle East, if they choose to apply them. This reconciliation is vital since unhealed social emotional wounds tend to continue to fester in some form or another, sometimes for centuries.

Amazingly some of the world's richest people are now banding together and gifting half of their vast personal wealth to various charities. This situation is unprecedented in the history of humanity and can potentially bring about international achievements that entire nations have previously been either unwilling to focus upon or were incapable of funding or managing.

For the first time in human history, we are on the verge of available free high quality education on a global scale via the internet. This educational information, to one degree or another, covers all disciplines and is readily accessible to all levels of society in most countries. We now have the potential to create a fully integrated and comprehensive global educational infrastructure and standardized system of education, covering all educational levels and disciplines, in all major languages. This development could be utilized to leverage the next major positive development in global human consciousness. It could also lead to the development of a completely new written and spoken language of managing change and world transformation. This language would not merely be a "lingua franca" or language of economics and bridging economies. The new language must be a language rooted in peaceful unification and collaboration, shared cross cultural understandings and consciously facilitated global change management and species evolution.

Technological Developments:

We now have the technology necessary to mass produce and distribute food on a scale never before possible. We have also created technology capable of purifying, desalinating and recycling water on a mass scale. A system in Singapore currently recycles a large percentage of the water used by the national population, while another system produces fresh water from the sea via desalination. Many nations will benefit from the development and proliferation of these technologies as potable fresh water becomes increasingly scarce around the world.

Our medical and technological knowledgebase (meaning all we know as human beings regarding these disciplines up until this point in history) is doubling every few years (or sooner). This knowledge is then continually being redistributed out to the world to both professionals and laymen via the internet. This information development, distribution and re-development cycle is leading to amazing and empowering discoveries in both technology and medicine, and it continues to speed up.

A worldwide inter-connective and coordinated technological and knowledge infrastructure is developing that is also supported by the internet. An unintended result of these developments is that doctors and technologists are now often unable to keep up with the speed of new developments in the medical knowledgebase of their field of medicine, thus rendering them unable to fully make ready use of the vast amount of new information being produced. We are now at a point where even experts and specialists cannot know all there is to know in their own fields—that is an impressive development.

We are also developing expert software systems to support decision-making procedures which have the potential to acquire, manage and process more information faster than the people making the decisions. For example, the question-answering software called Watson, the artificially intelligent system designed by IBM for complex analytics, promises to be the foundation for many future expert systems. Watson proved its functionality a few years ago by successfully competing on the game show "Jeopardy" against some of the most intelligent and knowledgeable human players. Watson is now an incredibly powerful player in the diagnosis of cancer and will soon influence many other medical diagnostic processes. Another incredible development is the Deep Mind A.I. project by Google which is demonstrating the cutting edge of artificial intelligence potentials. It is even becoming common for A.I. to be used in a variety of devices such as cell phones and cars and this trend will only continue into many other electronic devices as the "Internet of Things" continues to develop around the world. When mixed with Quantum Computing, a technology which is still in its infancy, A.I. software developments are likely to become far more powerful, useful and transformatively influential in the world.

We are currently developing new types of truly non-polluting energy production technologies which can in the future produce cheap energy in the quantities necessary to meet the world's long-term demand. These technologies include the use of clean burning hydrogen fuel for hydrogen fuel-cell cars and in standalone power supplies. (For examples see new fuel-cell-based car developments by Ford, Daimler, Honda, Toyota and Mercedes Benz). Also included are new synthetic fuels and battery technology, produced via nanotechnology and biotechnology, non-radioactive fusion (not fission) energy technology, and even new forms of free energy. Solar, wind and wave energy production technologies are also being continually refined; still these technologies are not yet evolved to the point where they can successfully and economically produce the quantities of energy necessary to meet current or future public demand.

The Great Spiritual Awakening:

A great spiritual awakening is taking place across all of humanity which promises to profoundly transform the consciousness of the population of the world as a whole for the better. Along with that awakening has come a heightened and growing global awareness of the plight of people around the world that are starving, oppressed, uneducated, diseased and dying. All of this is occurring as we collectively mature into a greater global heart-felt willingness to effectively mobilize to meet the needs of humanity.

We are gradually learning the spiritual value, necessity and contribution of all religions, and there is a shift toward consistent acceptance of and respect for all other's religions. In the past, inconsistent religious tolerance was the best we had achieved; however, we are now realizing that mere tolerance is not enough. In our rapidly arising future we must also respect and trust all religions if we want to harmoniously weave them into the future world social fabric. This is in part true, because as the world is becoming ever more populated and stressed, we are finding that large-scale social or religious conflict can no longer exist if we wish to progress and maintain global stability. The human species must eventually accept and respect everyone's freewill and accept their right to worship God as they choose, without interference, judgment, limitation, condemnation or punishment. (God is defined here as any deity or higher being that is worshiped by any specific religion or spiritual practice as defined by doctrines of that specific religion or spiritual practice). Political, religious and economic systems are all learning from their current conflicted situations and the negative results of their prior choices. This evolutionary learning development will eventually lead social, political and religious organizations to reach a new state of understanding, cooperation and acceptance of one another.

(**Note:** For the remainder of this text please understand that any time I use the word "negative", as in "negative emotions or negative implications", I am <u>not implying</u> either "wrong, bad, unacceptable, imperfect". Nor am I implying any type of judgment of the topics of emotion being discussed at any point in the book. The word negative in this book simply implies "non-optimal or not fully evolved in nature or in current mode of operation". Meaning we all have the capacity as human beings to operate more positively and lovingly than that which is defined or labeled as negative. If we are to evolve and grow as human beings and souls, we must transcend judgmentalness of all kinds.)

There are many ancient forms and systems of spiritual, energetic and physical healing (see chapter nine) which have been developed around the world. Some of these systems even have methods to address issues or conflicts which are believed to have originated in past lives, for those of us who hold those beliefs. All of these diverse systems and techniques are needed, along with Western medicine, to handle the healing of the ongoing occurrence of interpersonal, inter-nation and inter-religion wounding that is occurring, as humanity learns to transcend our prior and lower states of consciousness and ego.

We very much need the timeless wisdom of these healing systems to support all of us in humanity's path of learning to accept and love one another unconditionally. These systems of healing include Catholic and other Christian denominations' practices of laying on of the hands and prayer healing and the rich history of miracles extending back to the time of Christ, which include spiritual exorcisms which could be seen as a form of spiritual healing. Jewish energy healing practices include Kabbalistic symbol-based techniques, prayer healing, aligning oneself with spirit, also include laying on of hands and exorcism. Other healing forms include Shamanic healing, Islamic Energy Healing techniques, Reiki energy healing (begun in 1922), Qi Gong and Tai Chi energy healing, the Ho' Oponopono (a Hawaiian healing technique and one of the most powerful and flexible methods I have found), analytical meditation, transcendental meditation, mindfulness meditation, hypnosis and many others.

This is a special time because for the first time in the history of humanity, everyone, regardless of what they were trained to believe by family, culture or religion, has access to a multitude of other understandings and practices via the internet. These individuals can use this information to create their own customized individual spiritual practice, that then works best for them. This is a wonderful and exciting vehicle for the expression of everyone's personal and spiritual self-sovereignty.

Perhaps the most important of all healing techniques is basic prayer to spirit which is common to most spiritual paths, as well as some specific highly developed systems of prayer and Sanskrit mantras from various religious traditions, including Buddhism, Hinduism and the Sikh religion. Two highly evolved systems of Eastern medicine integrate multiple therapeutic elements such as massage, acupuncture, energy healing and herbal medicine to heal the body and directly affect the human energy system and our emotional systems. These are Chinese medicine and India's Ayurvedic medicine. Both systems include techniques for sophisticated holistic diagnosis.

The Accelerating Power of Individuals:

We are now more fully realizing the power of the individual to affect the world as a whole, for better or worse, and this power can be seen in many diverse situations. Bangladeshi American Salman "Sal" Khan, named by Time Magazine as one of the top 100 influential people in the world, has formed an online academy of free education available to everyone in the world. Khan's system offers good quality information on many different topics, including math, science, business and economics and it will be expanded to cover many other disciplines. This new paradigm in education, though still in its infancy, is proving to be a powerful and effective method of making higher education available to all of humanity for free.

The coming effects on international development, cooperation and competition will likely be profound. In a world of increasing informational and technological complexity, having access to accurate, precise and complete information for quality decision-making becomes ever more critical. Humanity needs to develop and implement more new and socially shared systems and models of cooperative effort, which will support re-conceptualizing and re-understanding our world. We need these new systems of teamwork and refinable evolvable models of social interaction to apply to all the newly available information that technology is producing.

In this way, we are empowered to make optimal use of the information. The advent of the smart phone is one highly refined and integrated and "concrete example" of a system of socially shareable and evolvable models of information management, distribution and real-world consumption and application. As a "front end" to the internet, with all its growing capabilities, the cell-phone is tremendously empowering. These systems can optimally cross-pollinate shared concepts and understandings around the world and facilitate rapid global transformation.

China, one of the most powerful and populous nations in the world, is being directly influenced, on a daily basis, by the statements and actions by a single individual, (i.e. the Dalai Lama). China wants very much to be seen by the rest of the world as a progressive and evolved nation, yet the historic conflicts in Tibet are continually being brought to the fore in global news and the consciousness of humanity by the efforts of the Dalai Lama. The Dalai Lama has repeatedly infuriated the Chinese government, yet none of the government's tactics have been able to significantly affect him. Still the Chinese government has been powerfully influenced by the Dalai Lama to implement positive social evolution. As this situation unfolds, China is simultaneously trying to retain its status quo method of oppressive governance and is at the same time working to modify itself fundamentally in order to meet the expectations of the global community. In today's world of instant global communication, China is continually being placed in the public spotlight and is laboring under the magnifying glass of global conscience and consciousness.

We have seen amazing technological developments occur as a result of the efforts of empowered individuals. These include Bill Gates with Microsoft, Steve Jobs with Apple, Jeffrey Bezos with Amazon, as well as Facebook founder Mark Zuckerberg's amazingly powerful influence on the development and evolution of the computer, the communications industry and society as a whole. Obviously, no one person invented the internet, still it is important to realize that Al Gore, through his legislative, educational and leadership efforts, in his roles as Congressman, Senator and as Vice President has done a great deal from a governmental standpoint to initially fund and support its development. One example of his influence can be seen in an article in "Wired Magazine" April 23rd 2012 by Ryan Singel (See http://www.wired.com/business/2012/04/isoc-hall-of-fame/).

"Al Gore: As a U.S. senator in the 1980s, Gore was the first politician to grasp the potential of the internet. Gore wrote the 'High Performance Computing and Communications Act' that passed in 1991 and which helped spread the internet beyond use by computer science professionals by providing key funding to internet projects, including the groundbreaking Mosaic browser which led to the dot-com boom". According to this article Al Gore was also recently entered into the Internet Hall of Fame in Geneva Switzerland for his internet contributions. Gore has also worked tirelessly to help humanity understand the complexities of global warming, which is now recognized as an unquestionable global threat. All of these technological developments have directly affected all levels of society, economics and political systems—for example, the internet and Facebook have recently been utilized to coordinate Middle Eastern revolutions in the Arab Spring and even to help develop new governments.

Julian Assange, the founder of the WikiLeaks web site, has had global effect on several nations as he acquires and distributes information from whistleblowers around the world, information that many nations would prefer was kept secret. This ongoing global influence by one key figure is directly driving world political shifts and shaking some previously unassailable institutions at their foundations. Wikileaks' and internet whistleblowers' effects such as those of Edward Snowden on international policy are still evolving, yet at the same time global political and military activities are becoming ever more transparent as a result of those actions. While Assange's and Snowden's activities remain controversial, I do see their actions as an attempt to utilize their personal self-sovereign power to bring about what they see to be positive change in the world. At least as far as they are personally able to discern.

Mohamed Bouazizi was an unknown street vendor who purposely set himself on fire (self-immolation) in Tunisia and soon after there was a new government in place in that country. Although this individual's sacrifice may, on the surface, appear very negative and disturbing. His act was the catalyst for a vast transformative political development in Tunisia, which has then led to a domino effect of new developments in several other Middle Eastern nations. This domino effect process is vital to understand if we want to understand how every change by every individual in the world affects all others. Only in this way can we truly understand the rapidly growing power of the individual.

The proof of the power of individual action is becoming increasingly obvious to all populations and governments; this developing process will inevitably in turn lead to more courageous independent actions on the part of individuals. It is an unfortunate and paradoxical truth that human death has in the past been a key method by which human beings achieve understandings and are inspired to take healthy and constructive action. This method of learning of learning from death can clearly be seen in how we create laws, rules, and even engineering and building safety standards after people die in accidents. Until these undesirable circumstances occur, people are often not moved to take decisive action, or even to understand that there was a problem to be solved. Although this method of social change may have great positive effect, I would suggest that we can develop other and more proactive and insightful ways to bring about positive social change.

Currently there are many examples of self-immolation occurring in Tibet and even in Beijing, the capital of China in protest of Chinese occupation of Tibet as well as broader social, political and religious oppression in the country. It is likely that these individual acts of personal power and sacrifice will also ultimately lead to positive social and political developments in the region. Yet other less costly forms of protest might better serve the greater good, for example effectively utilizing social media.

While I have shared with you just a few of the wonderful advancements occurring in the world... what goes up must come down... Therefore, simultaneously, many other situations which would appear to be significantly more problematic, do exist. To start to see the full picture requires that we also look into our detrimental situations as well.

Political and Economic Concerns:

Even with all our technological and cultural advancements, multiple wars are still being waged around the world at great personal, social and economic cost. The threat of terrorism of various kinds by various groups, individuals and even nations is rampant, including the potential for bio-terrorism, nuclear or radiologic terrorism, and cyber-terrorism and cyber-warfare (this new mode of warfare now includes <u>information warfare</u>). There are concerns around the world as multiple countries continue their efforts to develop and proliferate nuclear weapons that can be internationally or globally delivered. (See information on North Korea, Syria, etc.). Those concerns are also related to potential mismanagement and misuse of nuclear fuel, nuclear materials in general and other types of weapons of mass destruction. In addition to these "old style" nuclear weapons we now have sophisticated cyber-weapons and their potential effects on the vitally necessary internet to consider.

Alongside war, the potential exists for global economic downturn, and even global economic depression. These situations are apparently related to previous tendencies of those "in power" toward shortsighted financial gain, inadequate governmental oversight, endemic fiscal mismanagement, the increasing complexity of the economic system itself and corruption at all levels of society and government around the world.

The continued tendency toward nationalist, culture-centric and religion-centric focused values, thinking and decision-making orientations is resulting in a lack of necessary international cooperation. This is occurring in a time when we vitally need teamwork, collaboration and the fundamental commitment to and investment in all human's betterment in facing global challenges. Prioritizing the good of the world above the good of any one nation is a necessity in these efforts, and defining effective and standard for international and intra-national decision-making strategies to support this process of solution development and management is vital.

In many ways the global situation is improving, yet there are many cultures and many nations that are still unwilling to change for the better. For example, some nations are willing to change economically, yet they are totally unwilling to change politically, religiously or socially. It is crucial that nations quickly "learn to learn" how to comprehensively evolve and to cooperate at all levels and in all areas of function, not merely economically.

It is also essential, for the good of the world, that all nations work to learn how to evolve as a unified organized and collaborative whole. If this shift in understanding does not occur then global citizens and nations cannot effectively work together in a timely, well-coordinated and integrated manner to achieve necessary goals and solve shared global problems.

Environmental Challenges:

There exist valid concerns about projected near term and long-term shortages of fossil fuels, which humans are still completely dependent upon, both technologically and economically. The economic effects of fossil fuel shortages are compounded by concerns about the global environmental impact of major oil spills involved in the production and transport of oil. Related to this situation are the recently scientifically validated concerns about human produced climate change created by burning fossil fuels and by other forms of pollution. There are also concerns about corporation's efforts to cover up and produce misinformation for the past 30 or 40 years in regard to how fossil fuels affect global warming.

These concerns emerge at a time when we have no readily available replacement fuel source. Which in turn can lead to more reactive fear. It has been projected by several sources that within a few short years oil will become too expensive to make it cost effective to drill for as existing sources run dry. Oil companies have now resorted to drilling in the Antarctic, one of the most inhospitable regions of the world. (See information available on the internet in regard to "peak oil"). Countries and corporations are already racing to ensure that they get their share of the remaining oil in the future. Where will this unfolding process leave the average global citizen? In the past, there have been riots due to lack of fuel; it is likely that this situation will repeat itself in various areas of the world if a suitable replacement for oil is not identified in the near term.

Burning fossil fuels (including coal) creates pollution. Around the world we see the effects from pollution of all kinds, including long-term effects on human and nonhuman species genetics. (See the study of epigenetics and studies related to the cancer-causing effects of pesticides on multiple generations of offspring, and the effects of pesticides on bee populations). Pollution has become a truly terrible problem in developing and highly populous countries such as China and India leading to literally unbreathable air. This pollution problem could lead to multi-generational and potentially unresolvable genetic issues across multiple species, including humans.

Because of pollution our oceans are becoming warmer, acidified and deoxygenated. Most coral reefs around the world are already significantly damaged by coral bleaching due to warming and pollution. In the United States, it is becoming harder to find <u>any</u> freshwater fish that are safe to eat and free of contaminants such as PCBs and mercury. Among ocean fish the smaller fish, (which tend to hold fewer pollutants), are generally safer to eat on a regular basis than larger species. See EDF (Environmental Defense Fund) web site for detailed fish safety listings.
(http://apps. edf.org/page.cfm?tagID=17694).

Yet even smaller salt-water fish in the oceans are now ingesting small particles of partially broken down plastic which is floating in the oceans. These are of course fish that we humans and other species then consume. At the same time there are concerns related to the advent of newly mutated and ever more virulent diseases (Ebola, Swine flu, Bird flu and now the Zika virus). These illnesses can be spread globally and with great ease by a handful of people flying from country to country. In addition, there is now intentional human scientific development of new and even more dangerous viruses, as an accepted method of ongoing medical research. This potentially dangerous "how to mutate a deadly virus" information has been disseminated broadly to other international research institutions.

Around the world there are melting ice caps and glaciers, rising sea levels, unusual hurricane activity, earthquakes (see the latest research on the effects of "fracking" fuel production methods on earthquakes), tsunamis and other signs of environmental breakdown or disruption. Some or all of these situations are likely either related to global warming or are influencing global warming, with all its potential long-term and broad-based effects, or other as yet undefined earth changes. Everything we change in our eco-system tends to influence everything else in some way and to some degree. It is all

14

connected. The latest science is communicating the potential for massive global climate problems, in the relative near term.

Yet whatever is actually changing in the ecological environment or why, we as individuals are, unlike in the past, being instantly inundated by the news of these events and their effects on local populations on a daily basis. This rapid communications scenario is being further fueled by a news media which significantly feeds upon drama, conflict, disaster, and purposefully inadequate reporting. How information is distributed, to a degree, is driven by special interests, rather than comprehensively and in a more balanced responsible manner reporting the deeper nature and aspects of the world's transformation. Most of the large news outlets are currently owned by very few people, and this situation influences what news information is produced, how, when, where and why. It is crucial that each of us now realize we have the personal power to directly and positively affect these situations for the better, and we need to learn how to decide to use that power wisely and effectively.

In the early days of coal mining there were situations where invisible methane gas would build up in mines and lead to the suffocation of miners. To warn themselves of this potential danger, miners carried canaries in cages down with them into the mines. The canaries would tend to pass out from the gas much sooner than the human miners, and when they did, the miners knew they had to take immediate action or they themselves would die. In like manner, many of our current environmental situations, for example the collapse of some of the main ocean fish populations we depend upon for food, can be seen as the canaries in the coal mine of our world's ecosystem. Swift mindful, powerful and globally coordinated action in addressing our most key environmental challenges is our best solution.

Technological Accountability:

At a time of positive technological revolution, we are simultaneously seeing technology of various kinds run amok. The current system of law and governance for technology is falling far behind the developments of new technologies. Thus as nations and as a world we are having a difficult time regulating what is truly good for humanity in a timely and effective manner. So major problems develop and then our systems of governance, law and regulation try, often inadequately, to play "catch up" in order to influence the problems after the fact. With the world changing as quickly as it is, this simplistic reactive method of managing change and technological development is no longer adequate. Major problems can now develop and effect the world much faster than in the past. **Note:** There are currently few laws governing the use of cyber-weapons in war. We have the Geneva Convention to govern acts of traditional warfare, and we have almost no rules of the road for the use of cyber-weapons. We often don't even have methods to accurately identify who deployed such weapons, so how can laws regarding them be enforced?

It is likely that this gap between technological development and conscious discerning governance will continue to widen faster and faster. This is due to technological developments continuing to accelerate as courts of law become further bogged down by caseloads and at the same time special interests are lobbying to remain unregulated by law. This gap is a literal "danger zone" of ignorance that we must learn to discerningly master, sooner rather than later, since it represents a **zone of non-accountability** for virtually any corporation or country to operate in unregulated territory. Can you see why some groups might want this gap to remain in existence?

Another related problem is that judges and courts cannot fully understand the technological complexity and complete implications of the technological developments they are attempting to regulate. Key to this developing global situation, within the United States, is the conflict between our constitutional rights to privacy and the desire on the part of corporations and even our own governments to know what we are doing, when, where, why and how. There are some experts who feel that privacy as we have previously known it is truly dead, and cannot be recovered.

A part of these developing technological dynamics is that of what are labeled "disruptive technologies" and disruptive business models. Examples would be the advent of cell phones, the internet itself, the Uber car ride system, civilian drone use, etc. In the past disruptive technologies would have been seen in the advent of the printing press, the automobile, electricity, radio and the electric light bulb. Then came later "waves of fundamental change" with the atomic bomb, atomic energy, the computer, the development of orbiting satellites, space travel and antibiotics. Disruptive technologies **are not really disruptive**, still they <u>do bring</u> fundamental, rapid and often global change, that is in some way globally and socially transformative and evolutionary. They also tend to increase the complexity of life and decision-making in some ways, even if it is just because we must choose from more positive options. These developments introduce fundamental shifts and changes in economies, nations, cultures and individuals.

These developments tend to enhance people's and society's options and opportunities, empowerment, quality of functional capability, and quality of life in general. In addition, they often lower costs of goods and services. The key thing to understand is that more disruptive technologies are being developed <u>far more quickly</u> than they used to, and are also being implemented and integrated into society and economies far faster and thus having their effects felt sooner and more broadly than in the past. This "speeding up effect" can cause change shocks of various kinds. The most potentially globally transformative technologies I perceive on the horizon are the blend of artificial intelligence and robotics (which will of course include drone technology and self-driving cars), quantum computing, genetics and epigenetics, and opening space exploration to corporations.

Each day many corporations and governments around the world are collecting, storing and selling massive amounts of information about all of us. They are then utilizing this information to influence our lives and our decisions, and even the practice of governance itself. They are doing so without either effective legal oversight or our legal system being aware of the ongoing situation in an empowering way. Legislation has been passed which allows the U.S. government to access information about its citizens, including internet usage, emails, telephone communications and faxes without the government being required to obtain a warrant or to even include the judicial system in their procedures. There <u>may be</u> plans in place by some government agencies to constantly record <u>all data and communications that occur around the world.</u> If this is so, what are the future implications of this single choice on our world, in regard to how our societies function and on our children's lives are affected?

Taking all the above into account, it could be said that the previous U.S. constitutional and governmental system of checks and balances is being circumvented and undermined, potentially to the detriment of citizens. This intrusive situation is replicated around the world by NSA personnel and their technology every day, probably to a far more extreme degree. With the advent of quantum computing, it is likely that it will not be feasible for any average citizen to keep any personal secret, if it is desired to be known by any powerful government or corporation. This truth is already seen in the massive and methodical state run effort by China to infiltrate many American corporations and government institutions. It is also evident in Russia's recent apparent hacking of the Democratic National Committees email system. Where does the potentially massive detrimental influence of the misuse of information end? It is vital to understand that if the continued competition

17

for information and the desire to control our information continues as it is, that this dynamic could lead to dire circumstances. Meaning it is possible that information misuse on the part of any group or government literally reaches a "critical mass" of detrimental influence, thus triggering a cascade of cyberwarfare dynamics, and this could then trigger a global information management meltdown. In such a case, the global economy would likely quite literally come to a standstill and the resultant problems and human suffering would be globally catastrophic and unimaginable. It might not be feasible to come back, as a global system from such a situation.

Just one of many examples of the profound loss of privacy in the U.S. can be seen in the George W. Bush administration instructed the National Security Agency (NSA) to put in place a system for secretly monitoring citizens' telephone conversations on a mass scale within the United States. Many other intrusive technological efforts by the NSA have been and will continue to be revealed by Edward Snowden. Many other nations are working in collaboration with the United States in creating a massive global information monitoring network.

In an excerpt from an article by Dan Eggen, a Washington Post staff writer, on Friday, December 16, 2005, he writes:

President George W. Bush signed a secret order in 2002 authorizing the National Security Agency to eavesdrop on U.S. citizens and foreign nationals in the United States, despite previous legal prohibitions against such domestic spying, sources with knowledge of the program said last night.

Legislation has also been passed allowing the U.S. government and private organizations to develop and fly unmanned drones within U.S. airspace. Due to sophisticated technological advances these drones can be very small and powerful in their sensing capacity to monitor or potentially to spy on U.S. citizens without their knowledge or informed consent. There is by the way no current governmental mechanism capable of governing the activities of these drones and no comprehensive base of law to govern them. In addition, we are also seeing the application of artificial intelligence to drone development, which is in turn leading to the development of intelligently coordinated "drone swarms", which are of course potentially weaponizable. We are now just at the very beginning of the potential influences of such technology on our lives. How can personal privacy be effectively maintained and managed in such a rapidly technologically advancing and unmanaged world? How much more important will discerning self-sovereignty and self-empowerment become in the future?

18

The development and usage of the internet and the rapidly expanding and increasingly integrated telecommunications networks are driving many new legal and regulatory developments. The internet is certainly providing all of us with timely access to limitless amounts of useful information, improving communications and logistical business coordination and facilitating world and national developments, and yet it is simultaneously opening the door to misuses of power.

Serious examples of this misuse are:

❖ Pedophiles trolling chat rooms in search of unwary children.

❖ Cyber-bullying of teenagers and adults alike.

❖ Illegal internet gambling, distribution of pornography and facilitation of prostitution.

❖ Citizens avoiding paying sales tax by purchasing products over the internet.

❖ Theft of highly classified United States government secrets by unfriendly (and even friendly) governments (including the theft of the plans for all U.S. atomic weapons by China).

❖ The threat of cyber-warfare and cyber terrorism (for example, see internet available information on the "Stuxnet" computer virus and the "Flame" virus used for international sabotage and spying. Stuxnet is believed by many knowledgeable sources to have been developed by the U.S. and Israel and the Flame virus may also have also been produced by the U.S.). Far more dangerous cyber-weapons have most certainly been developed since, and as of this writing hacker groups have claimed to have stolen some cyber-weapons from the NSA. In addition, few if any large corporations have not been hacked and had their information stolen. North Korea's attack on a Sony corporation, and what may be Russia's current hacking of the Democratic National Convention's email servers.

❖ Corporations are both legally and illegally tracking our day-to-day activities on the internet and through all telecommunications channels (for example, monitoring of individuals' internet traffic, smart phone activities, hacking email and voicemail accounts, tracking of citizens' physical locations and daily activities via built-in cell phone GPS chips).

❖ The United States is, according to some sources, currently contemplating the creation of an army of 100,000 cyber-warriors.

19

This development has the potential to escalate cyber-conflicts of all kinds, rather than insuring that they never occur in the first place. This development of a large cyber-warfare team is similar to the system that Israel has created.

In another developing area of technology there are significant concerns over the unfettered potential of genetic research of various kinds. This research includes the development of new highly dangerous viruses in order to learn how viruses mutate and thus how to cure them before they develop naturally out in the world. This research also includes testing of gene modification therapies on humans, a process of which we are just beginning to understand the potential implications of. We are even openly discussing "3D printing" complete human genomes from scratch and thereby "creating designer humans" in labs that never had a mother or a father. Recently mixing human genes with animal genes has also been decided to be "okay" by the U.S. government (see transgenics and eugenics).

These rapidly developing situations are complex and incredibly influential on our lives, whether directly or indirectly, both now and in the future. Yet we rarely have access to all the information necessary for us to achieve comprehensive and thus personally empowering levels of understanding, that would then allow us to effectively influence these situations for our personal, national or global betterment and wellbeing.

Most of us have not been taught the benefit or methods of monitoring these situations, or even fully realize how truly profoundly influential these developments are on our lives. At this time, we have few real time and effective "braking" or management influences on these developments at our disposal. Lastly, it is often not seen as being in the interest of either governments or corporations that individuals gain a clear view and complete understanding of what is really going on or what the implications of these developments truly are. (For example, the usage of spin, propaganda, incomplete information, cloaked activities, blatant lying, declarations of "in the interest of national security", and immersion in endless legal battles. These methods and ongoing misdirection are designed to effectively keep the population from preemptively, proactively and decisively intervening on their own behalf, while denying this fact).

Acquiring complete truth through transparency is becoming ever more essential in a world where power can be wantonly, broadly and rapidly abused, on a vast scale, without complete understanding of the implications of doing so. Even when we perceive some imminent threats we often cannot perceive longer term negative effects of situations. The more complex the world becomes, the more difficult it becomes to put together all the interrelated pieces of any situation. We must learn to put these pieces together correctly in order to precisely, discerningly and effectively apply our personal power. Achievement of a critical mass of functional understanding and actionable intelligence specific to any situation is a requirement of discerning choice and action. Understanding all the domino effects of each of these changes and developments is also challenging. A critical mass of global understanding on the part of many individuals could lead to a shift toward greater discernment in global consciousness.

Religious Friction:

Increasing interfaith religious friction and open conflict are detrimentally affecting the global geopolitical and economic landscape. The complexity and interdependence of international and intra-national social, political, technological, religious and economic systems are increasing very rapidly. So rapidly in fact, that this situation is leading to conflict and unmanaged social diversity well beyond our current capacity to fully understand, wisely manage or positively channel in a transformative way. This is a call to create new, diverse and sophisticated social management systems and methods to resolve and evolve these situations peacefully. Advancement of social and religious tolerance will ultimately occur with the support of internet-based forms of mass cultural education. However, existing governmental, social, economic and religious systems are currently not designed to meet the needs of this changing landscape. It is vital that all groups of human beings learn to change and to manage change in healthy ways. In Chapter Eleven of this book is a method for releasing our conflicted or maladaptive beliefs. This belief release method may help to resolve the "internal belief wars" or conflicted emotional states that many of us are experiencing as we are influenced by rapid world change and unexpected events and situations.

We are also affected by complex changes related to the family unit and moral decay in various cultures. This is in turn leading to various forms of social corruption and a lack of basic and necessary human values we have previously taken for granted. It is not that the world's family models, dynamics or roles have ever been what we would most hope for. The issue today is that we have moved into a more chaotic, pressured, undefined, and subsequently less manageable and less evolvable family situation. Thus, we are, as families, unable to make the most of our transformational climate and resources.

It can be very difficult to evolve rapidly in a loving, conscious and spiritual manner while carrying significant emotional pain or being immersed in social, interpersonal or family conflict. It is true that this pain can be motivating, and thus a spiritual developmental catalyst, yet there are more positive, comfortable and enjoyable ways to become spiritual, conscious and wise. In the face of greater economic and social pressures, it is likely that for a time that this discomfort could escalate.

Social and Cultural Issues:

The impact of the cultural and economic limitations and problems of the country of Greece is a clear example of the potential global problems that can be created with just one country's inability to effectively, and in a nationally comprehensive manner, evolve adaptive cultural values and economic tendencies. The situation in Greece, along with other countries in crisis is educating the world economic system and international cultures on how to better manage themselves as a global economy. What I am saying is that there is a larger dynamic at play here, and there are many nations not much better off than Greece and these nations will all be required to foundationally change and evolve if the world economy is to continue to function and develop. Greece and Spain are just the tip of the iceberg, yet they represent an instructional scenario useful to facilitate an understanding of the larger issues and dynamics. Another example of a nation trying to manage global change is the recent Brexit plan recently adopted by the UK, that was designed to separate themselves from the European Union. Though a key element of Brexit's design was to keep immigration into the U.K. "controlled", it appears that it is now understood to have essentially failed to achieve this goal. How can democratic nations make discerning decisions if they do not fully understand the fundamental implications of those decisions?

The United States political process is in the continual midst of heated conflicts regarding wisely managing its own basic fiscal responsibility. Presently the United States does not have a defined and dependable procedure in place for resolving its internal political, cultural and economic conflicts of interest succinctly and peacefully, yet such a technique can be developed and is needed.

Much of the world is experiencing a sort of mass paranoia which is leading to general distrust, interpersonal distrust, social distrust, distrust of governments and leadership, distrust of religion and distrust of corporations. Many people are even less trusting of themselves and their own decision-making methods, especially when overwhelmed by the mass of new information they have access to via all forms of electronic media. Many people use fear and judgmentalness as their core decision-making criteria and process, rather than discernment, acquisition of quality information and attainment of deep understanding. A key intended message of this book is that unconscious fear driven mistrust is directly disempowering, and that being accurately and comprehensively informed supports conscious discernment, which is empowering.

If fear and judgmentalness are used as the foundational "influencing values" in our decision-making process they tend to create paralysis rather than progress, especially when we become afraid of several different negative possibilities at the same time. These dysfunctional and ineffective decision-making processes are often obscured from our consciousness, meaning we do not realize that this is how we are going about making our decisions, and therefore these influences are not seen for what they are. We often do not want to see our own decision-making processes clearly, due to our "fear of feeling our fear", therefore we do not see their detrimental influence on our lives and relationships. Therefore, we feel unmotivated to fundamentally change these traditional non-optimal decision-making styles. We may even feel that it is our fear that keeps us safe, rather than our conscious wisdom and understanding which could better drive our decisions and actions.

In effect, we become "uncertainty bound" in key areas of our lives and relationships, and this is a main reason people feel unable to profoundly change their lives for the better. Using "certainty" as a decision-making criteria or process is not optimal and is significantly ineffective in navigating complex and rapidly changing relationships and environments. Certainty is an illusion that we tend to chase after endlessly, to our detriment. We want certainty because we fear "something" and often do not realize what it is that we fear. This leads to a habit of reactive, fear driven interpretations of life, and thus reactive decision-making, which is not optimal. It is our tolerance of this fear driven dysfunctionality that keeps us from more efficiently evolving and transforming. This reactive unconscious dynamic is antithetical to conscious creative proactive decision-making and learning from our life experiences.

Fear never kept anyone safe from anything or anyone, and fear undermines being able to focus on making a decisive decision, seeing any situation clearly or taking bold positive action. This is how we get trapped in our comfort zones. Comfort zones are a process of safety strategy decision-making, and an ongoing dynamic in our lives, that are designed to keep us safe, even if we are not truly safe by remaining in them. This situation of widespread social fear reactive paralysis and associated decision-making, and its associated dynamics of judgmentalness has led to political, economic and religious polarization and a general lack of cohesive team-oriented effort, and unwillingness in society and individuals to learn new ways of making decisions and interacting. A new **fearless and loving** style of teamwork is what is necessary to optimally "learn our way through" and accurately navigate our current global issues and transformative developments. We must override our fear with conscious intention, otherwise our reactively fearful subconscious habits will continue to run and damage our lives.

Understanding that we tend to go through these repetitive cycles of dysfunctional fear driven decision-making, without consciously realizing it is occurring, is vital in order to find the courage within ourselves to choose to willfully step out of the old tendency to operate in this status quo supporting way. Until we recognize that this "fear cycle decision-making" is going on in our lives we cannot make this empowered choice. Becoming willing to powerfully make positive choices in our lives for ourselves and those we love is key to attaining happiness and inner peace. Being "busy" maintaining a comfort zone, due to our fear is paralysis, is not progress. There are no "completely safe" decisions in any lifetime, there are only decisions, some of which are more wise or discerning than others. Inability to make powerful decisions creates comfort zone prisons that we then live in, due to engrained habits of dysfunctional decision-making. No one deserves this end or situation.

These reactive fear-based tendencies have existed in humanity for a very long time, yet now they are reaching the point of overt and global maladaptive influence. Rather than just reflecting a "healthy distrust" of government and world powers of various kinds, which would then drive constructive positive change, we are instead experiencing dysfunctional paralyzing paranoia. Humanity is on the verge of learning that there are better ways to bring about social, economic, political and religious change than to allow ourselves to be lost in, and driven by, our fears and judgmental tendencies. Retaining balance in our path of achieving individual discerning and self-sovereign understanding of world events and their implications is crucial. Educated our children, early in life, to function in this conscious manner is also crucial.

- Many people are concerned about the basic quality and safety of industrially and mass produced foods, which commonly include both artificial and natural food additives. (For example, natural does not mean healthy, as in high fructose corn syrup and trans-fats). Genetically modified food ingredients are becoming the norm rather than the exception, often without significant testing or regulation. Although we as consumers are rapidly learning to understand what types of food are good for us, we are simultaneously being presented with purposeful disinformation regarding foods which are rapidly and covertly evolving. This situation creates a scenario in which we as consumers have no comprehensively effective method to preemptively and safely determine food's effects on our bodies.

In fact, if we look at the way sugar, salt and fat are being overtly and unhealthily infused into most foods it becomes clear that some corporations may literally be attempting to create food addictions in consumers. Scientific research on the tremendous biological and instinctive influence of these substances on appetite and food selection decision-making is well known to food producers. If corporate decisions are based upon mere competition in the market and profit as their decision-making criteria, which are very unbalanced and corporation centric intentions, why wouldn't they make these kinds of unhealthy decisions? What are the implications of this dynamic on our children and future generations? How is our healthy discernment undermined by our own body chemistry and visceral motivations? So, "let the buyer beware". (I suggest viewing the movie "Food Inc.")

In many parts of the world there is a lack of necessary basic and advanced education. The United States is currently ranked among the highest in the world regarding its quality of college level education, less so for earlier grades. Still many children are not getting an adequate baseline of quality high school education, nor are they being supported and empowered to attain college degrees. The cost of a college education is now much greater than it has been in previous decades, yet there are no guarantees of jobs being available after this huge investment of time and money. In the age of information this is a great liability; the world needs as many educated people as we can produce now, without understanding there is no chance for widespread discernment to occur. Every moment we wait to educate our citizens, we create more issues that we will be required to solve later.

Is There Hope for Humanity?:

I understand that reviewing the vast positive and negative complexities of the world and its transformation can be quite overwhelming. I know that all that I have covered thus far in the book is important to many people. We could turn our heads and say that we do not have the personal power, knowledge or understanding to make a difference in regard to any of these topics. Still I personally perceive our global challenges, no matter how vast, to be in some way, a bit less important and profound than the need for us to understand and manage the developments that are taking place inside each of us, and in our relationships with other average individuals.

In fact, these large-scale situations all, in one way or another, originally stemmed from the choices of individual human beings. Meaning that some individual or group started them.

Interestingly, it is the heightened and widespread understanding of the large-scale and problematic results from our individual choices that are driving many current positive shifts in individual decision-making, actions and behaviors. (In effect we have created some rather large, complex global challenges. Now mankind, and each of its individual representatives (all of us), are being required by circumstance to learn how to clean them up and how we must modify ourselves as individuals and as nations in order to retain our solvency, safety and stability). We are literally being required by our complex and challenging world situations to deeply understand ourselves for the very first time as global citizens.

The need for this book is driven by the recognition of the basic truth that it was the power of individuals that created these complex global situations. Therefore, we each have the potential to effectively learn to positively manage and then transcend these issues. Anyone and anything can be healed; the same is true of any situation, any group, any nation or the whole world. So yes, there is absolutely reason for hope.

One of the most tremendous influences on the progression of global transformation is the internet and associated forms of electronic computing, media and communications. From these sources of information people are connecting, learning and interacting in new ways at a geometrically escalating rate. The rate at which we access and process information in our individual minds is in turn rapidly evolving the global consciousness and thus the world. The world is shifting as people everywhere consciously realize their individuality, self-sovereignty and personal power in new and different ways, and then in turn affect one another in new and ever more creative ways.

We are just now beginning to enter the *Age of the Individual.* Today an individual can use a smart phone and video record an atrocity in any country in the world, and instantly upload that proof to the rest of the world. This individual usage of personal power can then rapidly lead to vast social and political domino effects and potential accountability. This same application of technology also immediately educates the world's people with a more accurate understanding of many of life's realities. Individuals are now regularly recording police abuses and political abuses, and thus shaking the political power structures with their personal efforts.

A single "Tweeted" sentence from certain people on the internet system called Twitter can directly influence millions of other people in seconds, either to inform them or to misinform them with political propaganda. The jilted lover of a political official or prior recipients of sexual abuse can shift the course of a nation's political history, a religion's credibility or a major corporation's profitability with a single Tweet, and lately has. A single whistle blower can bring down a major corporation or even governmental institutions. A single computer hacker can expose the crimes of a political regime. A single intelligence analyst in a position to manage top secret documents can dump thousands of them onto the internet, and this has been the case with the WikiLeaks.com, Edward Snowden and others. Individuals can now basically directly or indirectly affect the whole of humanity through their technological and informational inter-connectedness. This dynamic is part of our new species evolutionary process and we are only just now learning to manage its powerful effects. This situation will only continue to escalate as time goes by and technology continues to evolve and further connect us, inform us and influence our individual development. These examples precisely describe how individual power can affect worldviews and actions in a manner and scale that has never before been possible. It is useful to understand that the mass of information we are all being introduced to, can, rather than inform and empower us, distract and overwhelm us into a state of mass information processing hypnosis. It can also create within us significant feelings of insecurity or anxiety.

It is simultaneously important to realize that not all distributed information is complete, accurate, clearly communicated or even well intentioned. We currently live in a world where "spin" is often put on much of the information we have access to, whether it is to eliminate political competition, convince us that corporations "care" or even if it is just to get higher ratings for a news station or to sell a product. Due to the empowering characteristics of the global information network, and the current focus on literally and intentionally creating more drama, we are constantly being inundated with hyped sound bites. These sound bites may only show one convenient or distorted vantage point or interpretation of a situation; potentially skewing our interpretations and decisions related to the information we have access to. Our discernment must transcend these evolving situations.

We may assume video does not lie and that it even constitutes unquestionable proof, yet this is not always the case. In today's technologized world of ever more powerful and available audio and video editing software, even amateur video editors can create video which may be difficult to refute in a timely manner, if at all. In a world where large portions of the population have immediate ability to record occurrences on their cell phones, often with minimal background information to support what we are being shown, there is vast potential for reactive or even destructive misinterpretations. Unfortunately, many of us can be quick to react to such distributed information, and not follow up to determine its accuracy or authenticity, prior to discerning whether any particular piece of information constitutes the whole story.

As our personal power increases, so must our power of discernment if we wish to make wise decisions based upon the information available to us. A key element of discernment is patience in our applied method of determining precisely what the whole truth is at every moment of our lives and in every situation and relationship we encounter. It is the precisely accurate understandings we achieve and act upon, and the wisdom with which we do so, that gives us our true power and which then manifests optimal results.

This is the turning point or inflection point in history in which awareness of the true power of the individual is becoming vibrantly clearer to everyone. (Review the following chart to gain clearer understanding).

THE DOMINO CYCLE OF THE INFLECTION POINT

AT LEVEL 11 INFLECTION POINT IS REACHED

SELF-SOVEREIGNTY INCREASES

LEVEL 10	MORE Global Transformation and Evolution
LEVEL 9	MORE Individual and Species Learning from Experience
LEVEL 8	MORE Competition, Confusion, Stress, Conflict and Pollution
LEVEL 7	Resource Usage INCREASES
LEVEL 6	MORE Individual Learning and Decisions Required
LEVEL 5	Life Experience Complexity INCREASES
LEVEL 4	RAPID World Change (Time Speeds Up)
LEVEL 3	Achievement of GREATER Personal Power
LEVEL 2	Education of World Populations INCREASES
LEVEL 1	EASY Access to Technology and Information

CYCLE BEGINS

Oddly enough this realization of the power of the individual is also frightening to some people, and even to whole nations. This is the case in relation to government's fears of "lone wolf" terrorists or destructive acts on the part of those who are mentally ill and who have unfettered access to assault weapons. With the evolution of this understanding of the growing power of the individual come further rapid shifts, sometimes quite dramatically, which will begin to heavily influence every nation, group, corporation, religion and existing power structure—everything can change in a nanosecond. Most importantly in this scenario, we can all learn from each other faster, and hopefully in a gentler way, than ever before.

One seeming difficulty in our unfolding global situation is that there are those who unquestionably believe in and convincingly profess their view of what is going on, or what could go on, now or in the near future. There have been many cases where individuals have claimed that the end of the world was near, with great emotion and conviction. Other people's proclamations have led to unnecessary runs on banks, massive stock selloffs or almost instant drops in the stock market. In these cases, some people listened to these statements and interpreted them to have more meaning and validity than they actually did. Yet our world is still here.

This presents us with a difficulty as we learn and make decisions both as individuals and as groups. How do we know what is really happening, and what will happen and what will or will not affect us? The reason I started off by saying this was a seeming difficulty is because it is just that. It appears to be a difficulty, yet in reality it is a part of our educational path of learning to function in a conscious, non-reactive and discerning manner. In effect those who might attempt to mislead us are sometimes our best teachers and we learn from our every experience, no matter how negative they may appear.

I would suggest that we are each endowed with the capacity to aptly discern and evaluate any information, experience or situation we are presented with. We all now have access to massive amounts of information that we can refer to, which can in turn help us to determine fact from fiction, or fact from simple misinterpretation or misunderstanding. Utilizing these sources tends to reduce our personal ignorance in any area in which we choose to research and learn. I would suggest that it is necessary for each of us to learn to evaluate and research other's communications and statements of fact, prior to emotionally reacting to any information we receive, from this point on in human history.

If we do not learn to do so we may become rapidly reactively emotionally entrained in their agenda to our detriment or distraction. We could look at this process of getting lost in the sometimes inaccurate and often overwhelming flow of information as a sort of "complexity hypnosis and/or complexity paralysis". There are many who would wish us to see the world either as they do, or in a way that would serve their agendas. I am not suggesting adopting a stance of fear-based reaction to any information; this can only lead to a dysfunctional, mild case of paranoia which is itself a form of misinterpretation of reality. I am suggesting conscious, patient, self-guided research and learning, objectively and earnestly looking at many potentially conflicting information sources, rather than just hearing the dramatic voice of the moment. In this way we will learn to live discerning lives and apply our power of freewill most wisely and accurately, at all times, and in this way we also attain the most consistently positive results.

We DO Have The Power:

The message of this book is that we have the power to directly and powerfully modify ourselves and the world for the better. We always have and always will, yet many of us are only just now waking up to this fact. In addition, our power to affect the world at large is increasing and will continue to for the foreseeable future. It is not only important that we realize our power, but also how to wisely and lovingly apply it in every situation. Again, our power and our freewill cannot be taken from us, not by anyone, nor can our accountability for our choices. It is essential that we consciously understand our position of power as individuals and fully accept it, and it is equally important that we exercise it regularly.

We can realize and accept that it is our individual liberty and God given power of freewill that makes all this possible. It is necessary to remember that we have this power and only we can implement it when we see beneficial opportunities to do so in the world, in our relationships and within ourselves. That is how we can make the world a better place; how we can foster and facilitate positive developments, and how we can manifest the lives we want for ourselves and those we love. Many of us fear our own power and thus turn away from the opportunity. In effect, many of us fear making mistakes with our personal power that we will later regret, judge ourselves for, or be judged and/or punished for. I would say that it is only through exercising our personal power that we learn to master it; hiding from it will not solve anything. If we make a choice that we regret, we need only forgive ourselves and move on in a timely manner. Self-judgment and self-blame is a prison, while self-forgiveness is a fundamental key to speeding up our personal learning and evolution, and freeing ourselves from the developmental traps of shame and guilt.

I also perceive that discussion of these world challenges, and many other difficulties that we face, are in no way an expression of fault with any aspect of humanity. I love all of humanity and respect every choice that has ever been made by any human being, as each is only a step on the path of their personal learning and their soul's evolution. Each of these decisions has been a step in the evolution of all of humanity, and nothing more or less. I believe in and support freewill in all its forms, and believe it is perhaps the most necessary, wonderful and creativity supporting component of our evolutionary unfoldment. We cannot learn as individuals, or as a world, without occasionally "stubbing our toes", (i.e. making ignorant or unwise choices and learning from them). Stubbing our toes in the global sense can be seen in our prior acts of war and the learning that has occurred from doing so. We often cannot learn to live in peace and harmony without being taught by someone to do so. Alternatively, we may be able to learn to live in this positive state by experiencing some difficult situations, that then lead us to value more peaceful and harmonious ways of living life.

Pain is a key part of the human learning process, and although hated by many, pain is in fact our "friend". We could not learn and develop physically, mentally, emotionally, socially or spiritually without feeling our pain. Although it is often painful to look directly at our developmental issues and life experiences, it is necessary that we do so in order that we be able to define and accurately work with our challenges. If we are unwilling to do this, then we will be unable to effectively and succinctly solve our problems, and continue to adapt our world for the better.

We must first help ourselves if we want to be able to help those we love. It can be uncomfortable to look at our weaknesses, our ignorance (which all of us have) and our prior unwise choices. However, enduring this discomfort, and courageously facing our ego-based fears, while proceeding through life in a loving and gradually developing manner, allows us to transcend who we have been and to become who we potentially can be. This is, for most of us, a very gradual development that takes place over time. Time itself is a necessary buffer to the ongoing discomfort of our evolutionary incarnate learning process. Meaning that having our life experiences spread out over many years diminishes the potential to be mentally and emotionally overwhelmed by life. If everything happened "all at once" we could not learn as souls, due to the overwhelming influx of information, emotion and experience. Time has other benefits, meaning that it gives us a method of managing, organizing, categorizing, comparing, relating, learning from and sequencing our life experiences. This model of organizing our memory and sense experiences, that we hold and manage in our systems, allows us to gradually learn in more and more complex ways.

Yet time is currently speeding up, meaning that more is happening around the world now faster than ever before. With our increased technological power, we can now create more good, or more destruction, much faster. Accepting this fact and learning to patiently and forgivingly love the gradual developmental nature of human existence is a beneficial perspective to cultivate. We are all worthy of our own patience and tolerance along the way. Willfully holding onto our hope and faith in this developmental situation is also important, as is congratulating ourselves for every positive step we take.

I do not believe in judging, shaming, criticizing or frightening people into changing their ways, and that is not, to any degree, the intention of this writing. I do perceive it is important to understand that if we are unwilling to find the conscious determination necessary to resolve our issues, we will falter as a world and as a species. We can no longer afford to hesitate in taking constructive action due to misunderstanding the nature of our global issues, fear of their negative implications or due to unresolved competing priorities. We can no longer hesitate due to fear. We can no longer assume that mere economic competition or some new technology will solve all our problems. If we do operate on these false assumptions, then our issues will persist.

Competition divides us and is often a self-justifying and self-perpetuating mask for selfishness, corruption and greed, and it is antithetical to teamwork and cooperative efforts. Creativity, innovation, collaboration, teamwork and love unify us. Conscious discerning interpretation of the information we have access to is a key to owning our personal power, and of solving both personal problems and world problems. It is imperative that we be willing to regularly re-interpret our personal experiences of what is actually going on in the world, so that we may learn more.

Chapter Two
The Hidden Benefits of Global Stress:

EXTREMELY BENEFICIAL REASONS EXIST FOR ALL THE challenging occurrences we can see going on around the world today. Can you see that it is possible for the world to receive benefits from all the complexity, challenges, confusion, pain, stress and yes, even death? In fact, all that is happening in the world is due to our having chosen for it to happen, though we did not always consciously realize this truth at the time we made our prior choices. The current global and human scenario of conflict, confusion, intense and rapid shifts, and even ignorance is designed specifically to motivate and help us reach a new plateau of global understanding in how we choose to live, operate and make decisions as human beings and global citizens. The good news is that the global situation of stress and pressure is an invitation to resolve world problems that is nurturing new understandings to help us as individuals, to live in a more conscious, loving, accepting and compassionate manner.

Keys To The Great Breakthrough:

Humanity as a species is on the verge of a great breakthrough. This breakthrough will occur as the result of attaining higher consciousness and higher understanding of more positive ways to live, both personally and socially. All the rapid world changes we are going through now, and all we have ever gone through up until this very point in human history, is inspiring the creation of new developments around the world. These new understandings and technologies will fuel our spiritual unfoldment and advancement. There is a glorious and infinitely complex process of attainment of higher consciousness occurring in our world. All of humanity is learning to more closely resonate with God and to become more consciously aware by doing so. We are on the verge of fulfilling a vast step in humanity's destiny. I believe this new state is something we can and will soon achieve.

This advancement is being fed by the individual efforts of every human being on the planet. All our thoughts, decisions, feelings, desires and actions are feeding this learning process and creating advancement in consciousness. When the consensus consciousness of humanity has crossed a necessary threshold of understanding and complexity, we will all move forward as one. This is the value and contribution that each of us brings to the world. This is our special gift to humanity, as well as our spiritual duty. It is necessary that we see it as such, and offer the world our best contributions, and apply our vast personal power to the attainment of this shift in global consciousness.

Although we are developing amazing new technologies and advancing in many areas, technology alone won't solve our world issues. Nor will technology alone propel us into the new state of social and individual wise consciousness that we require. Technology is merely a stepping-stone to this attainment. What is needed is improved discernment, understanding, love and wisdom in all our decision-making. Truly the power has always existed within each of us to achieve higher states of consciousness. Yet during this rapid evolutionary phase of humanity's development additional learning must occur that technology cannot do this for us. We must as individuals experience these shifts in understanding within ourselves as our future unfolds. Then we can best understand how to add our personal power, gifts or insights to the world's process of development.

If we hope or expect either mere technology, or someone else to learn these lessons for us, we will miss the precious opportunity to contribute to the creation of a new world. We must in effect learn to ride and take advantage of the transformational wave that is affecting our world so profoundly. We are being called into an awakening phase where we can positively revise how we choose to see, think, interpret and feel about ourselves and all other human beings. This rebirth of consciousness is at the core of the transformational situation that is now happening. From this shift in both individual and collective consciousness perspectives, all future decisions, actions and positive results will flow.

The truth is that the interaction and positive intentions of our souls, and our synergistic interaction with the rest of humanity, will lead to the birth of a new state of human consciousness within each of us. This process of evolution and attained empowered self-sovereignty will then lead to vast worldly and spiritual developments.

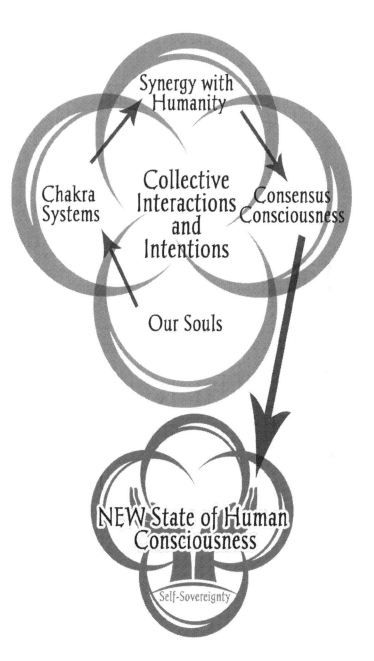

The Consensus Consciousness Impact:

Today a new and developmental step in the empowerment of individuals is occurring; it is a process by which individuals are being powerfully energized by the subtle transformational energies which are now available. These energies arrive to us from the universe, God, the earth itself, and evolved discarnate and incarnate beings. Some of these energies are new, and some have been applied to our individual systems, societies and the world as a whole many times. Their ongoing application and infusion is creating a cumulative evolutionary effect.

Though we are all being influenced by these energies, we can choose to actively focus and draw upon them more effectively in meditation. In this way we can better understand their influence, and harmonize with them, and entrain ourselves in their influence, and thus gain even more from them. These energies are continually and literally bathing the existing consensus consciousness of the entire population of the planet. At the same time the consensus consciousness is trying to remain unchanged due to instinctive fear of change. This resistance to change creates a sort of detrimental consensus conscious inertia, as the consensus consciousness tries to remain on its prior course, which holds back the world's evolution and the evolution of individuals and groups. In effect individuals are, due to the ongoing evolution of the consensus consciousness of humanity, being directly empowered to affect the rest of the world and its people instantly, profoundly and in a development-focused manner.

Our individual attainment of new understandings and informed choices also directly feeds the development of the consensus consciousness. For many people this empowerment is currently a subconscious development. While for others it is a very conscious progression in which they are learning to more effectively and precisely wield their personal power moment-by-moment. We as individuals must take optimal advantage of this opportunity to master individual empowerment. It is also helpful that we learn as much as we can, since education ultimately makes us more powerful, wise, forgiving and compassionate.

After we achieve and integrate our new state of global human consciousness, we will still continue to develop as individuals. As a species, Homo Sapiens can begin a refreshing cycle in which we conduct our actions from a vantage point of loving, efficient, wise and sophisticated consciousness.

As stated previously, a key evolutionary influence in our developing world transformation is the information currently provided to all via the internet. The internet is functioning like a vast sponge and is absorbing incredible amounts of quality information and could be said to comprise a new and more evolvable layer of the global consensus consciousness. It is also becoming more sophisticated in its ability to present and quickly distribute organized and streamlined data that is highly personalized. A big part of this technological advancement is the internet's capacity to store and distribute video in large quantities. This information will, over time, tend to become more accurate, sophisticated, better organized and rapidly understandable to most of the world's population.

As these developments occur, we will again dramatically increase the speed of evolutionary development of humanity as a whole. This development comes not only through brute education, but also through offering people new ways of thinking about their personal experiences and new ways of understanding and constructively working with more readily available information. In effect, newer and better ways to learn are being evolved by us, as we ourselves evolve. Thus humanity will increase its tendency and capacity to act in harmonious and loving concert. This leads to our making better decisions now, and to future actions based upon ever more comprehensive, accurate, precise and timely understanding and information.

In the past we have acted in disharmonious ways, due to the world population's making decisions based upon incomplete or inaccurate information, dividing beliefs, outworn cultural norms, best guesses or in the extreme, simple ignorance or fear. This new, easily available and continually refined flow of information from the internet will be instilled in each of us through our individual learning in increasingly sophisticated and comprehensive ways. Meaning that on a global basis each of us will receive better understandings to work with, and base decisions on, than we would have received from our independent interpretations of our usual day-to-day life experience. Thus the quality of our application of our personal power will improve.

This could happen as a result of the information on the internet being pre-processed into more well-organized, accessible, structured, applicable, personalized and mentally digestible formats. Thus, this cycle of the internet first absorbing expert information, and then releasing it into the population, is creating a new method of well-organized crystallization and distillation of information into the fabric of society and the consensus consciousness of humanity. The internet has already vastly changed how we think… can you imagine how much more it will evolve in just the next decade? With the application of Artificial Intelligence (A.I.) based software to guide how we obtain information? The advent of A.I. will likely result in foundational re-organizations of societies, cultures, organizations and the world through improved global education and consciousness raising activities. In this way, the people of the world will more rapidly evolve, brought together and re-organized—in a similar manner as the internet which is becoming our societal mirror—into ever more sophisticated social structures as we gain access to information, understandings and each other's coordinated support. This will occur in ways we previously could not have dreamed of. This is the process of complexification of humanity, which is a key element of its evolution.

Isn't it exciting that we are all participants and witnesses to the dawn of the next step in human evolution? There could be no better moment in time to be born and live. We must not waste this opportunity.

The Evolution of Desires:

There are many traps in life that are attractive on the surface to human beings. Just a few examples of these traps would be money, drugs, inappropriate or unwise use of power, control seeking, attention, drama and sex. Another less obvious sort of trap is that affects much of the world is relatively low cost (in comparison to other energy sources) availability and usage of fossil fuels. Fossil fuel usage has paradoxically led to a world technological revolution and mass food production capability. It has also resulted in vast pollution, over-population, development of weapons of mass destruction and global dependence upon a rapidly dwindling energy resource.

We can effectively wield our individual power without getting trapped by any of these influences. Yet even if we pursue desires without understanding the implications of doing so, and for their own sake, we will eventually gain valuable experiences in our pursuit. Understandings may come through a slow series of repetitive and painful experiences or very rapidly through very difficult circumstances. Through pursuing our desires, we attain learning and understandings about how to manage ourselves in ways we could not have understood without first having explored our impulses and obsessions. Through this dynamic we gradually evolve our understanding of self and the world to a higher level. We learn what is not in our best interest, and also how to achieve more worthwhile goals without harming ourselves, those we love or our environment in the process. This is a dynamic of trial and error and is part of what makes us human.

In a similar way, the global challenges we face on the current world stage make it a fertile learning environment, designed specifically to help mankind to learn to evolve and to better work together. It is just important that we learn better and faster than we damage our environment. This evolutionary process is happening despite all our past cultural momentum, conflicts, political and economic structures, beliefs, religious institutions, priorities, desires and fears. The pressures of these challenges are developmentally necessary. They exist because they are the best inspiration (though often negative in appearance) that we have thus far found to reexamine and thus overcome our stubborn and limited old ways of functioning.

Many of us are driven more by personal and family survival, economic self-interest, and personal gain of various kinds, than by conscious wisdom. Yet we have all functioned in this limited and limiting way at some point in our lives. At the moment many people in the world are caught in their attachments to fossil fuels, money, luxury, comfort zones, nationalism, ego and the unwise use of power. This is not a new situation of course (aside from the relatively recent usage of fossil fuels); we have been facing these same distractions throughout human history. There are many other aspects of life we can become attached to as we pass through life on this planet, and we are now developing a long list of new ones via the wonders of technology. I suggest evaluating our lives for this type of circumstance and making wise choices based upon the results of our process of self-evaluation.

Historically, it has been difficult for the world to be motivated to make fundamental adjustments to more wise ways of life and decision-making. In effect, we only became motivated when we were fearful. Rather than being motivated by wise understandings. In the past, we have needed a situation undefined enough, big enough and dangerous enough that we, as a world population, would allow ourselves to be herded by our fears (if not by our wisdom or love) to act to change ourselves and our world for the better. In effect, based upon traditional fear driven decision-making strategies we could not become motivated to fundamentally change until and unless one of our fears significantly "trumped" another of our fears.

Today we need all people to function in a collaborative and <u>proactive manner</u>, rather than being driven by reactive fear and other negative emotions. We need to operate from a set of pristine values that consider the value and potential of all of humanity. Is that possible? Could humanity work together for the betterment of all human beings and the world as a unified whole? In this moment of our development as a species we need the challenges we are facing. Without these challenges, we would be unwilling to move and grow in the directions and understandings that are most important for all of us. Those directed efforts will eventually allow us to learn to function peacefully and wisely as a world. Without these motivations, we would be unwilling to prioritize peace, achieving shared goals for the good of all, and international teamwork more highly than personal self-interest, greed, power sought only as a tool of self-interest, nationalism, fear and personal survival.

The reason we are experiencing this rapid change, confusion and apparent barrage of complexities is that humans as a species have an innate spiritual need to continue to become more complex and ultimately enlightened. Like growing plants leaning toward the light via photo-taxis, we are all growing toward the light of God. The challenges that we face and the solutions we create for ourselves are the road we are traveling and the ladder we are climbing. Thus we need to transcend these challenges and attain understanding via facing these challenges.

All these opportunities/perceived problems have been created by us in our earlier and less sophisticated stages of consciousness, existence, development and choice. This was the only way we could find to validate all the effort and sacrifices that will be necessary in the future for cultures, nations, politics, science, technology and economies to flow together, work together, and transform and integrate with one another. It is our grudgingly chosen way to motivate ourselves to arrive at shared understandings, new decision-making models, hybrid social structures and creative leadership models that will be supportive of compassionate global teamwork and collaboration. It is a costly path, yet the one we have all collectively chosen to follow. A model we may use in future to generate such new paradigms of social success can be seen in the EteRNA experiment by Carnegie Mellon and Stanford Universities in which video games allowed thousands of internet game players to work together to solve incredibly complex genetic problems.

The internet can also be utilized to create cyberspace-centric for-profit and not-for-profit organizations. These organizations can in turn create software-supported flexible organizational and operational structures that would in turn support the development of effective coordinated cyber-cultures. These organizations would have the power to accomplish real-world altruistic projects and create collaborative not-for-profit solutions to global problems via entrainment of the energies of the general global population. These organizations could be funded and implemented by like-minded people with aligned intentions and accomplish goals which governments and existing organizational structures and cultures are too inflexible or limited to accomplish. Much of the work they accomplish could be contracted to coordinated groups of existing brick and mortar organizations.

There is also the potential for the future creation of cyberspace-based sovereign governmental entities complete with internationally recognized citizenship status. This concept is currently being discussed for large space based stations, that could function as sovereign nations. These developments would mean that NEW cyberspace governments, which contain all aspects of governmental, political and judicial function, national economy and banking systems and corporations could be created with no geographically defined physical territory to protect or police, and which people could choose to become citizens of. These artificial cyber-entities would potentially evolve much more rapidly, cost effectively and globally competitively than existing "brick and mortar nations". They could even lead the way for evolution of the rest of the world's nations, as these cyber-nations are more rapidly prototypable and testable national models of all key aspects of national entities. These developments could include prototyping of new national economies, political systems and cultures. Eventually they might supplant geographically existing national entities.

For this type of coordinated effort to be consistently and sufficiently motivated and funded we need to define a new set of global goals, meaning a set of goals that outweigh all other day-to-day life considerations and values. These types of goals are currently being generated by the realization of our global problems. Once achieved, these superordinate goals will significantly improve our personal, social and national accountability, conscience and consciousness.

It is no accident that we are facing the global challenges that we are. Our current challenges are a direct reflection of humanity's prior actions, desires, level of consciousness, education and understanding as individuals, nations and as a species. These challenges and problems mirror what we do understand as well as what we do not yet understand. The problems we face today will teach us exactly what we need to know in order to evolve humanity. In truth, our current list of global challenges have been carefully crafted in order to produce a situation where all of humanity will finally be motivated to learn, work and solve problems together. Our challenges will ultimately reduce the common human tendency to fight or argue about the nature of our shared issues or to descend into fear, selfishness, judgment, blame, nationalism and accusation.

This is where the beauty and power of the dynamic of living in an incarnate state in time and space comes in. In that "time itself" is a buffering mechanism designed to support us in having "time" to reflect upon and thereby learn from the results of our prior choices. Material reality gives us a place to see the results of our choices acted out, to see cause-and-effect in action, and then we can fully learn from our choices and ultimately attain conscious wisdom. It is also how we eventually learn to wisely manage our power as individuals, groups and nations.

At this point in humanity's development we have a rapidly shrinking window of opportunity to deal with the challenges we face. The reason the window of opportunity is shrinking is twofold. First, all that is happening in the world each day is "speeding up" while we are simultaneously learning to technologically affect our world so much more rapidly and powerfully, so that we could inadvertently destroy what we call civilization in several ways if we do not quickly become wise and discerning enough not to do so. We are simultaneously running low on resources. Therefore, our "global system reaction time" and management techniques must improve along with our technology, and our application of discernment in this process is key to these improvements. Learning to succinctly manage global transformative stresses of all kinds (i.e. cultural, religious, economic, ecological, etc.) is also imperative. Time is a valuable resource that must be well managed and not be wasted.

It takes time to learn from our choices as well as the intention to do so. Our choices literally manifest our experienced reality. It can often take years for individuals and even for nations to arrive at deep or complex understandings based upon past experiences. The choices we make, and our associated learning process, can create major negative or destructive occurrences. If our choices create negative situations, which unfold too rapidly, or enough smaller problems are created all at once, we may not have the time to truly understand and learn from our experiences. Thus, we may not have the time to solve the problems we have created. If we do not learn optimally from our choices and experiences how can we successfully and safely proceed and navigate as individuals, nations or as a world.

Our growing awareness of the lack of available time itself to deal with our problems will eventually and ever more rapidly require us to work together and to see past our previous tendencies of bias, conflict or judgmentalness. We have needed a set of global challenges that would require the achievement of interdependence and collaboration of all nations in order to solve them. Therefore, the United States and other nations are simultaneously learning that they cannot achieve solutions to global problems alone. We are learning more clearly every day that globally we all sink or swim together. This is a very important step in the growth of global consciousness.

I am not, by the way, making a case for any specific type of future world government by these previous statements. I do believe that at some point this development will occur, simply due to ongoing integration of economies and cultures, technological connectedness, shared international infrastructure requirements, population increase and migration, and the rapid spread of free information. However, if it is achieved, world government itself would not have been the goal, it would only be the natural outcome of fulfilling world needs. (Many people fear this perceived consolidation of global power, the changes it could bring, and its potential misuse or disempowerment of the individual).

The achievement of world government would be the symptom or logical result of our having learned to work together more efficiently and effectively as a global consciousness. In this way, we can, as a world, effectively manage global issues and set global priorities, which will be a requirement for our global survival. Currently we have no efficient, effective and fair method or mechanism to allocate and apply natural resources, money and energy to the solution of international/global challenges. This is due to the fractured nature of our world's nations, economies, cultures, religions and politics; however, this is changing.

In this global evolutionary scenario, many different political and economic models are being "tried out" by different nations, and each is to a degree competing against the others. Although internationally competitive, conflict producing and often not very positive, this act of proselytizing nationalistic economic and political systems is potentially useful. In effect, it gives more grist for the evolutionary mill, ultimately leading to the creation of future world economy and political systems. In effect, it is a necessary step in global learning via tested and proven results. It is also a process which is helpful to determine what specific and tested elements will comprise the essence of the global economic and political system or model that will ultimately be adopted. It is also a situation of each powerful nation trying to, perhaps selfishly, influence the choices made in the development of the arrived at global political and economic system. Ultimately this process will determine the most workable, necessary and appropriate system(s) of governance for the future world. Quality assurance in evolving governance will become ever more important as world complexity increases. The same is true of the need for unshakable integrity in and between governments and the elimination of corruption.

Of course, no existing single model of government or economy will answer all future world needs, therefore it will benefit all nations to learn from one another. The world is watching the political and economic systems of China, the European Union, Russia, the United States and others to see which works best and why. Certainly, each of these entities has its own intentions, agendas, beliefs, values and goals as they proceed forward, and some of them are even destructive to the others. Each is learning and evolving in its own way and at its own speed. That said, in the end we must all set aside limiting, negative and self-centered intentions or face the catastrophic global and national consequences of our shortsightedness.

This may appear to be a stark or even harsh way to view and discuss our reality and a challenging vantage point from which to approach our global situation. If we ignore the world situation while we chase personal gain, survival and desires, or nationalistic agendas, we do so at the peril of all we most love. If we are not motivated in our interactions with others by conscious self-accountable wisdom, love and compassion, we will not make our choices in a socially wise manner. Functioning in this more consciously caring way is becoming more important every day. If we cannot get to this level of globally conscious understanding, it may be difficult for us to be motivated to attain the requisite awareness, discipline, depth of understanding, wisdom, knowledge and technical know-how to resolve the growing world issues.

If we do not accomplish these goals, we may <u>fall backward as a world and as a species.</u> This potential detrimental situation would also profoundly affect the United States, despite all its economic and technological power. This is true because now all nations are completely interdependent, and trying to pretend that this is not true is folly. Yet global economic, ecological or technological collapse need not be a component of global transformation, if we are guided by conscious discernment. Optimal global transformation is the ongoing process of mindful, balanced, managed and coordinated deconstruction of the past and construction of the future. This process, like all other things in life, is based upon the choices and actions of individuals. All of our choices matter and all of us as individuals matter.

The Tug of War Between Conscious and Subconscious:

Our current world situation has developed to the point that we can no longer successfully move backward or undo the major steps that we as nations have taken. We do not have the option of "unmaking" the world economic system we have created, diminishing the world population or of becoming less globally interdependent—the results of doing so would cause tremendous harm to various world populations. However, we have arrived at this point, whatever our prior values, tendencies or governance methods, whether right or wrong, the die is cast; we must make our current developmental direction work or fundamentally adjust its course, as a world.

Certainly, we can and must make constant adjustments all along the way into our future to achieve optimal results. Yet in our current scenario the many factors affecting our lives are here to stay for the foreseeable future. Populations around the world will continue to increase. Natural sources of fossil fuel energy will become less available. The levels of pollution around the world and in the oceans will likely continue to increase, as will global temperatures and sea levels. Our growing dependence upon technology will only increase, and we must all survive our species' technological evolution and growing capacity to accumulate and manage massive amounts of information. Our wisdom and discernment must continually outgrow all our technological capabilities. We all have needs and many of our needs are begging earnestly for resolution.

Accepting our situation and making the best of it is necessary and unavoidable. Judging our prior decisions or path of development is wasted effort, and blaming ourselves or others will change or solve nothing. Still, clear perspectives can create an understanding of how we arrived here as individuals, as nations and as a world. These understandings can increase the wisdom and discernment with which we meet the future. Further, understanding where we are going now and why this is our chosen direction is beneficial. We have no way out and no way back; therefore, our power comes through choosing our next steps wisely and working together to achieve necessary world goals. We now have a prime opportunity to focus our personal power where it will do the most positive and effective good; it is imperative that we do so with newfound wisdom. It is also imperative that we do not act in an unnecessarily destructive or short sighted manner.

All of us have both a conscious mind and a subconscious mind, and this situation serves a useful purpose. For most of us the intentions of our conscious mind bear little resemblance to the intentions of our subconscious. This creates a scenario where we often assume we are making wise conscious decisions and behaving appropriately, and then end up with results which are unwanted and which do not map to our original conscious intentions. Oddly enough our subconscious intentions, and perceived needs, which covertly drive many of our decisions, often are not good for us or others. Yet without consistent self-examination we cannot realize the detrimental influence of our subconscious. Resulting repetitive problems from subconscious motivations eventually lead us to identify their negative influence and can then lead to positive change, if we are paying attention. Therefore, though it seems strange, we often learn the most from getting what we thought we wanted and then afterward realizing that what we thought we wanted, really was not what we wanted, or was not worth wanting or having.

A main difficulty with this indirect learning dynamic is that many of our deepest subconscious patterns and influences may have been (for those who believe in reincarnation) originally created in past lives. Those patterns and the nature of their influences may be so divergent from our current life perspective that we have a difficult time comprehending or validating their existence and influence. We may, for many "seemingly rational real-world reasons", remain in denial of some of our even obvious detrimental subconscious tendencies. We may also remain unaware of how these influences affect the way we interpret relationships and situations, make our life choices and apply our personal power.

In effect, it is difficult for us as individuals to "connect the dots and domino effects" of our experiences to reach deep and comprehensive self-insights. This is one main reason that learning from experience at all levels of our being and awareness, including emotionally learning, rather than merely "intellectually getting it", can take so long. In effect, we must get these understandings at our foundation and in our "gut" for them to do the greatest good. Yet when we do fundamentally learn what we choose to learn from our experiences (for better or for worse), it tends to stick with us until we are forced by life to learn even better. There is an old saying that is applicable here, "You can balance yourself through self-awareness or the universe will balance you". I suggest proactive, constant and conscious re-balancing of oneself.

This dynamic of incongruity of motivation and perspective of the conscious and subconscious is the "human condition" in general. Although it can be rectified with the strong desire to do so, with the conscious awareness of what is actually going on in our lives, and with the application of various available self-help methods. The key understanding here is that when applying our personal power, we can most effectively do so if we are totally internally congruent. Being totally congruent means that our conscious and subconscious intentions are the same or are at least harmonious with one another and are mutually supportive. It is this systemic disparity of perspective, intention, understanding, belief, motivation and goals between

48

the conscious and the subconscious which significantly limits our individual progress in learning from our life experience and then keeps us from learning faster how to make wise decisions. In effect, it makes it more difficult for us to connect the dots of our life experience in a manner that leads to clear understandings and consistently positive actions and results.

This same tug of war that exists inside individuals also exists between the conscious and subconscious cultures of corporations and of nations. Meaning that any group of human beings may believe they consciously know what they want and what they are working toward achieving. Yet due to the subconscious cultural influences of the group on the group's decision-making they may not effectively be empowered to achieve their goals.

All groups of human beings have underlying subconscious motivations which affect their group efforts and the results they achieve. These underlying motivations can have the effect of strong unseen social undercurrents and agendas, which take us off target from our group's conscious or assumed intentions. This situation can be seen in the United States today in the highly conflicted political system, which is being significantly influenced below the surface by the corrupting influence of special interests and wealthy Super PACS. It is also being affected by widely held subconscious social expectations, beliefs, values, goals and intentions.

This same dynamic can also be seen in various nations where the existing cultures are neither designed, equipped, educated nor appropriately oriented to support individual or national fiscal or political accountability, and where distrust and corruption are endemic. These influences create disruptive global social subconscious cross-currents, ripple effects and conflicts of interest. There are many nations experiencing economic issues. The key point to understand here is that whichever nation we are speaking of, it is crucial, for the good of the whole world's economy, that each nation function more consciously and with fiscal integrity and wisdom, and by proactive discerning design, rather than negatively and reactively. Otherwise we will all fail to learn from our ongoing experience and we run the risk of profound detrimental global economic future domino effects.

Another version of this same social tendency can be seen in the conflict between traditional ways of thinking and making decisions and what is often termed "New Age" thinking. All of these are signs of cultural incongruity; simultaneously they bring opportunity for greater shared social understanding. Getting the world to function in a relatively congruent, coordinated and integrated fashion is desirable if we want our nations to be able to work together to resolve world issues, and if we want our personal power to have the positive direct affects we consciously intend. This does not mean forced compliance on anyone's part to any social, religious or political philosophy or agenda. It does require foundational reeducation and attainment of sophisticated collaborative and organized group consciousness and understanding, to consistently succeed and continue to develop as a species.

The hidden benefits of these situations and dynamics are blessings in disguise. Still they become more distinguishable as such, and of greater practical value, when we continually ensure we are aware of them and fully understand their nature and influence on our lives, by practicing intentional discernment.

Chapter Three
Change Shock, Karma and Relationship Dynamics:

A DIFFICULT ASPECT THAT HAS ARISEN IN OUR GLOBAL-evolutionary process is the advent of a tendency toward emotional, mental and information overwhelm. Once we become overwhelmed we may have no more "cognitive bandwidth" with which to manage necessary decision-making processes in our daily life. We may also be unable to acquire or conceptualize the new information necessary to effectively manage change.

Managing our consciousness bandwidth, and what influences it is part of managing Change Shock and its associated stress. When we run out of bandwidth, we become unable to accurately see our current situation clearly, which can be paralyzing, and renders us unable to live in the now, and to function individually in a self-sovereign manner. All of us have a differing tolerance for change, and a differing capacity for constructive and sustainable adaptation to change. A key process of managing change is understanding that whenever we change any element of our world it creates ripple effects of change out into the rest of the world. An example is the massive world changes that have come with the infusion of cellphones. Precise and proactive definition of the most wise, positive and constructive methods and processes of change we choose to effect in every area of our lives, prior to making changes, will reduce change-shock and the detrimental associated ripple effects of change.

This situation of being shocked by rapid change can occur from too much information being thrust upon us too quickly or by our seeing too many things change around us too quickly. Shock also happens when our interpretive and decision-making models, strategies and capabilities do not meet the needs of our changing life circumstances. (In effect, we become lost in a fear reaction to unmanageable change). This can also be the result of being simultaneously assailed by too many intense personal, career, social, religious, emotional or spiritual pressures. Additionally, it can occur when we suddenly find that our traditional or most cherished beliefs, values and priorities are invalid, false or non-applicable to our current life situation. One other way this shock can begin is when we are forced by circumstances or even by our own experiential learning process to let go of cherished beliefs, relationships and ways of seeing ourselves and the world, and are then required to rapidly adopt new and untested ones. It could be said that all new learning requires **unlearning** what we previously thought or believed we knew to be true—this can be a shocking experience if we do not have graceful, seamless and consistent ways to acquire, integrate and apply our new insights.

Clarity is a challenge when we receive too much contradictory information, which leads to confusion related to our own or other's beliefs, motivations or values. In effect, as life becomes more complex, many of us are becoming less able to effectively manage our lives in the midst of rapid and complex changes. The constant inflow of new information now available to human beings is often in conflict with what we have previously recorded in our memories as beliefs, (i.e. old information). This process is occurring in all individuals in the world as we are simultaneously driven by social, economic, technological and environmental developments, circumstances and pressures to make ever more complex and impacting life choices daily. It is useful to understand that human beings tend to base their decision-making on what they "have recorded as beliefs" rather than on information they perceive in the present moment. Again, a belief is just a recording in our memory of what we assume to be true in any given moment. Therefore, our decisions and our decision-making strategies are often made based upon outdated information, (i.e. recorded beliefs).

There is currently no defined teachable standard, complete, precise and refined language and model of change and transformation. Nor is there a defined set of concepts designed to support attaining optimal transformational efficiency in all areas of one's life. Such a language is sorely needed to facilitate transformation. The creation of this transformational language could reduce confusion and conflict, and provide consistent clarity, and thereby enhance cooperation and teamwork in solving complex problems.

One fledgling attempt in this direction was the creation of the new and relatively unused language of Esperanto. This new language, was designed to be used by all of humanity, and to help all peoples communicate in a manner that was not associated with any particular nation or culture. Its intention was to build bridges of shared communication between disparate peoples and cultures. Still Esperanto is not specifically designed to be a language of managed global economic, cultural and technological change nor of facilitation of global transformation.

Adoption of such a developed language of change could enhance global transformation, and entrain the global populations in developing and engaging in a process of optimized global transformation, in all cultural venues. We could also benefit from, and reduce social, organizational and

54

individual stress by developing and teaching a standardized model and language of interpersonal and social situational definition, and interactive logic, and decision-making. These developments can reduce the effects of the "Tower of Babel Syndrome" we are currently experiencing globally, which include rampant miscommunication, misunderstanding and conflict. These effects are often associated with rapid, extreme and widespread social transformation and change, including within organizations. Introducing such new systems of thought may not be easy. (For example see the history of the attempted implementation of the metric system vs. standard measurement conflicts in the United States). Social traditions and ways of thinking and communicating have inertia, and tend to resist transformation and development of new standards and ways of doing things.

There is a reactive dynamic of ongoing stress, associated grief, and change-related loss that many people are experiencing these days. This ongoing feeling of being overwhelmed by change, feeling we are losing our past, and its effects on each of us could be termed aspects of Change Shock. In our present world, we are being driven to make our decisions at an unprecedented rate of speed so that we do not, as individuals, fall behind the demands of our careers, life situations or social responsibilities. Falling behind can be felt to be, and perceived to be, failing socially.

Some examples of this dynamic can be seen when we are unable to take advantage of an opportunity in our career or when we are faced with not having managed a situation in the way that someone or some organization may have expected us to. Change Shock can result in our being rendered incapable of effectively participating in various business or social environments or even in personal relationships. We tend to face more rapid and extreme social or organizational penalties or limitations if we are not able to effectively manage all aspects of our lives.

Participation, Competition and Accountability in a Changing World:

We are experiencing new and increasing levels of sophisticated corporate and business competition. As we become more sophisticated in our methods of technological and organizational development there is ever more that must be known, learned, understood, managed, responded to and dealt with on a daily basis. We are required by the social, economic or business environment to successfully manage all of this, if we wish to be able to continue to effectively participate and compete. I am not suggesting that competition is our best way forward, only practically acknowledging that it is the current process by which we are choosing to evolve our world. I do suggest that we can outgrow this tendency to our overall betterment.

Technology itself is part of this developing issue. The more technology we have and use, the more we tend to believe we need, even if this is not true. We are now finding that we need ever more technology to manage our existing technology. There is an old saying that "when someone learns to use a hammer they start to see everything thing as a nail". Meaning in this case that once they develop technology they then seek to solve all problems via technology, even if this solution is not a "true, good or best fit" for the problem.

An example of this situation is the event that occurred May 6, 2010 in the stock market, on this date when the sophisticated high-speed computer systems which manage the rapid and complex buying and selling of stocks made an instant decision based upon an accidental, inaccurate entry by a stock trader. This in turn caused a mass of unwanted cascading sales. The reason was a simple data entry error by a middle level employee which then created chaos. Simply put, the result was that the system "ran amok" and temporarily rendered the value of the stock of perfectly viable companies to that of junk stock. The system error was caught, yet only after it created a significant issue. The result was that it was then determined that we need an even more sophisticated computer system to manage the already extremely advanced stock market computer systems, to keep us safe from further problems.

With increased communications, faster technology, and more complex coordinated group actions and interactions, we are required to make more decisions, and take more actions, and effect more areas of our lives and our environment faster than ever before. Then either we, or someone else, are required to manage the down-line effects and consequences of our day-to-day choices within the systems we create. Thus, more is happening faster, and this dynamic in turn creates even more domino effects of our actions, which must then be managed to retain interpersonal, organizational, national and global systemic stability.

Increased complexity of organizations, as well as increased size and compartmentalization of organizations, has led to situations where low-level management, or non-management employees, have a less clear and less precise grasp on what is going on in the executive management levels of the larger organization. Strangely enough the opposite is also true, in that executives often do not know many basic details of how their organization's function. Combined with this situation are the developments of newer and more effective techniques organizations use for both covertly motivating and/or manipulating their personnel.

Organizational motivation and manipulation techniques may include:

- ❖ Lack of information, limiting and controlling information, false promises, spin or misinformation and flat out lying.
- ❖ Organizational cultural entrainment of individual employees in regard to corporate perspectives, goals, values and ideals.
- ❖ Firing and discrediting whistle-blowers and/or other forms of intimidation.
- ❖ Application of Neurolinguistic Programming (NLP) to manipulate staff and customers.
- ❖ Managers being trained in increasingly sophisticated interpersonal methods of manipulation and organizational cultural manipulation (in days gone by this would have been called black magic).

Organizations also work to influence global public perceptions of their brand images and products, and these efforts can also influence their staff. This can be accomplished by hiring marketing and public relations firms to create false or misleading public corporate images, which do not in any way reflect the organization's true intentions or executive culture. This manipulative practice is of course utilized by governments too, including some brutal dictatorships.

The process of "Cause Marketing" between not-for-profit and for-profit organizations can be used to manipulate how certain brands are seen and valued by the public. "Co-branding" can be used by multiple organizations to associate the power of certain products and well-known brands with other products and brands, thus creating a magnifying association and subconscious influence in the mind of the public. In these ways corporations, can subtly yet powerfully distort how they are publicly presented, how their products are perceived, and how their communications subconsciously influence our buying decisions.

Organizational transparency and integrity, whether we are speaking of corporations or governments, is becoming ever more important if we as employees or citizens want to truly understand who and what we are supporting through our efforts. Transparency reduces corruption. This transparency is in many organizations rapidly decreasing and is being replaced with the appearance of transparency, whether by clever misinformation or manipulation of perception. Though many organizations may "buy a public image" of positivity and caring through marketing efforts, underneath they can be just the opposite.

In our world, what we feed, either financially or economically tends to grow, so I suggest discernment in deciding which organizations we choose to feed. People should not be punished for telling the truth about organizations, this includes governments. None of us deserves to have our opinions skillfully created "for us" by subconscious manipulation or lack of information. This developing situation must be counterbalanced via highly developed discernment on the part of employees of these organizations. This is occurring to a degree. For example, employees who once prided themselves on their loyalty to organizations have found that this blind loyalty can blind them to the choices and activities of organizations, and this can be true even of soldiers in the military and of government employees. For examples the NSA. Yet our capacity to discern truth from manufactured image and inaccurate information needs to improve.

We are now producing and storing more global information faster than in any previous time in human history and this trend will only continue. With new information, challenges arise when we strive to assimilate a deluge of new concepts, new ideas, new perspectives, arrive at new and potentially more astute decisions, new actions and create new and more complex life management methods and strategies. All of this eventually leads to heightened sophistication of the individual and of organizations, as well as potentially better self-management and organizational management practices. Yet this dynamic also tends to lead to increased stress, anxiety, and unknown or unforeseen and potentially negative situations or results.

Neither technology nor information is inherently negative, nor are the methods we have developed to manage them. Yet if we do not make wise long-term choices in regard to the development and usage of technology in our lives, it can in a way take over our lives. Then instead of making us safer and happier and our lives easier, technology can subtly decrease the quality of our lives through financial cost, emotional stress, confusion, complexity and overwork.

For some, especially those in technological fields, keeping up with world developments and technological developments has become a constant merry-go-round that turns faster and faster. For example, consider an article titled "Top Secret America," written by Pulitzer Prize winning journalist Dana Priest and William M. Arkin. In this article (which took two years to research), the researchers found that America's anti-terrorist response has created a vast and redundant development of multiple intelligence agencies.

58

These agencies are now so large, unwieldy, complex and secret (even from each other) that they are becoming useless as information sources and unmanageable, as each is "too secret" and self-protective to talk to the other. These developments have cost hundreds of billions of dollars and will likely continue to absorb many of America's resources. This is just one example of unwise and fear-based reactive institutional development and decision-making on a large scale. It could be argued that America's knee-jerk reactive fear of terrorists is more economically diminishing and disempowering to America than any actual terrorist attack could be. More world challenges of all kinds create a driving need for more adjustments, actions, decisions, developments and solutions, as well as the development of new systems to navigate and negotiate these situations. It is imperative that we understand this evolving cycle and what influences it. This is necessary to be able to manage it wisely, and not to have the process of developing safety producing systems drive us rather than us directing the process of their development.

Increasing global populations require more maintenance activities and resources to sustain them—more food, more energy, more education, more governance, more health care, and even more entertainment. Every time there is a new innovation or technology developed that people want or need in one area, other groups begin to demand it, which continues to drive the "technology development machine". This process in turn diminishes and damages our natural resources. Our world's population is projected to increase from our current approximately 7.5 billion people to over 9 billion by 2050, and the implications of this escalating increase in resource usage are worthy of contemplation and preparation.

Right now, we have 60 million displaced people in the world and this number is projected to escalate significantly as global political and ecological problems escalate, including global warming and rising sea levels. That said, despite the size and profound nature of this problem, we have no single international organization tasked with managing the needs of these people who are experiencing such plight. Our seeming inability as nations, and **as a species,** to work together to create such organizations is troubling and an even greater problem that we must resolve if we want our species to continue.

Even in this dire situation, with so many lives at risk, fear driven international competition and nationalism is trumping the mass suffering and escalating loss of life. In our current mode of human social existence there is no way to arrive at, and decisively act upon, the requirement of international

59

accountability for these people's wellbeing. We cannot make this decision as a world because from the personal survival focused point of viewpoint of each of our individual psyche's, and nationalistic consensus consciousness's we cannot see that these troubled lives are literally equal in value to our own.

In effect, many of us see the stability of our families, personal wellbeing, and the stability of our own nations, as more important than the lives of 65 million people. At what point does the equation fundamentally shift? How many lives must be sacrificed, and how much suffering must occur for the citizens of <u>every country</u> (not just the leaders of these countries) to fundamentally change their perspectives and take constructive effective compassionate action for the long term? For this shift in consciousness to occur individuals around the world must change their way of looking at life and of valuing other human beings and the world we live in. As populations continue to grow, these questions and issues will become ever more urgent and important to address.

Why Now? The Karmic Connection (Cause & Effect at Play):

We are all blessed to live on this planet at this auspicious time; it is an incredible developmental opportunity for many souls to make a comprehensive leap forward in consciousness. Some spiritual belief systems hold that we have only one life to live and that at the time of our deaths we will either go to heaven or hell. Those of this spiritual perspective can likely see beneficial reasons to take powerful positive spiritual steps for the good of all humanity at this opportune time. Since per these beliefs, once our life is over, we have no more time to benefit either ourselves or those we love.

Many people in the United States and around the world believe in life after death. Still others feel that it is possible that we reincarnate or even return to this world multiple times, for whatever purpose or by whatever process. Others simply feel they do not know why we live or what happens when we die. Still, whatever our chosen beliefs and faith, as we all become more empowered by world changes and developing technology, we gain the capacity to help and heal (or damage) more of the world, faster, than ever before. One need not believe in reincarnation, past lives or an afterlife or be a participant in any religion, to benefit from an understanding of the fundamental **cause-and-effect dynamics of life,** which are referred to here simply as "karma". Clear understanding of cause-and-effect dynamics is a key element of the process of discerning personal empowerment, learning from experience and of self-sovereignty. It is necessary to understand cause-and-effect processes in life, and in the world, in order to make wise decisions in all areas of one's life.

There are spiritual theologies that believe that we, as souls or spirits, have lived before at other times in history, and that our prior incarnations have in effect been our best efforts to "set the stage" for humanity's next great evolutionary step. From this spiritual perspective, the current challenges, concerns and shake-ups that we have discussed so far in this book could be seen as the backdrops or props that are setting the stage for further transformation of humanity.

According to some spiritual paths, it is also believed that it has been necessary for many of us to have evolved through all of our prior incarnations in order to prepare us appropriately to be able to participate and to fulfill our current roles in this new and more complex global situation. From this spiritual viewpoint, others who have either not previously incarnated or are not as spiritually mature or experienced are therefore able to "ride on the coattails" of other's efforts and contributions. Still in this model of spirituality EVERYONE is serving a necessary and valid purpose in the world's transformational dynamic.

I personally see all religions as valid, as they are the chosen spiritual developmental mechanisms that our individual souls are spiritually resonating to at this time. I perceive the presence of God in all people and in all institutions. Whatever spiritual perspective you choose to view life from, I would say that at this time there are many people working very hard spiritually, emotionally and physically for the betterment of humanity. Whatever your chosen spiritual path, you have a part to play at this momentous time in humanity's development.

In the karmic model of understanding life and relationships, the more decisions we make in a day, and the more actions we take, the more positive or negative "karma" or effects we produce. This would be true whether we are speaking of individuals, corporations, nations or as a world population. All groups produce their own karma or cause-and-effect dynamics as do all individual human beings. The more karma we produce faster and faster, the more "karmic echoes or domino effects," whether positive or negative, come back to us, faster and faster. Therefore, as the world speeds up through application of new technology, our current global situation of rapid development and transformation begins to take on the visage of a mass worldwide "instant karma". This type of environmental result feedback loop from our choices creates a reflective learning dynamic (karmic in nature or not). Meaning that we learn from the results of the choices we make. This process is a key and necessary element of our global developmental and transformational process.

It is useful to realize that prior tendencies of decision-making by groups and individuals around the world has created a sort of inertia, momentum or tendency to replicate the old and sometimes dysfunctional decision-making dynamics and results. This habitual set of social and personal decision-making strategies (traditions) tends to create the same results in the world and the ecological environment over and over, no matter how destructive the results. In effect this means that if we do not understand this process we are in effect prisoners of our fear of change and the unknown. This process continues as long as we do not fully recognize the problematic cause-and-effect dynamics and results of our choices and then consciously choose to change them. Therefore, habitual (and therefore subconscious) decision-making dynamics and their associated inertia distracts us from making conscious, willful and discerning decisions, and from learning from our experiences.

My brief working definitions of the terms self-sovereignty, discernment, belief, karma, incarnation, consensus consciousness, simulacra, tribalism, "control", and fear are presented below. These definitions can facilitate better understanding of the topics in this book:

Self-sovereignty: is briefly defined here as the conscious realization and consistent willful expression of our own individual being as the central authority in our own life. Self-sovereignty is most effectively based upon complete impeccability, self-awareness, discernment and honesty with oneself in all areas of life. Self-sovereignty is a state of self-reliant independence from the influence of others on our decision-making, our emotional processes and our moment-by-moment state of consciousness. It is also a complete realization of our total freewill and personal power and influence, in every area of our life and relationships. Attainment of Self-sovereignty is a fundamental requirement of attainment of enlightenment, inner peace and equanimity and of attaining the highest levels of conscious wisdom and empowerment.

Discernment: is defined as the capacity to consciously, precisely and deeply understand the nature of cause-and-effect dynamics and relationship dynamics in our lives and relationships. We can, with discernment, more accurately understand and project the implications and meaning of our choices and actions in life, interpersonal relationships, the world and all of nature. Thus, discernment leads to better quality, more wise and more "intelligent" decisions.

Beliefs: are recordings we have made in our memories of <u>interpretations of experiences</u> and conclusions we have drawn from these interpreted experiences, that we acquire during our lives. Examples would be stored recordings such as "I cannot trust myself or others", "I will never have what I want", or "I am only safe if I am in control of my life". No belief is either completely true, right or correct in all situations or relationships. All beliefs have a "shelf life" of usefulness in our lives and ultimately most are proven to be untrue in some way. When this occurs, we drop them and collect new ones that appear to work better for us.

All beliefs create projections onto life and thus limitations of learning and understanding from life experiences. We tend to see in our lives that which agrees with our beliefs as true and that which does not agree with them as false or wrong. The process of projection is just a way of revalidating our recorded interpretations of our prior experiences (beliefs) and the conclusions we have drawn from these experiences in the past. Basically, we try to "cookie cut" our present reality to fit our previously arrived at beliefs about ourselves, life and relationships.

Beliefs can "generate reactive fears" when any experience in our present life, which goes against the beliefs we hold, is presented to our perception. Conversely fears often <u>generate beliefs</u> that we then record as being true, and which we then re-project in the future. We tend to base our ego-identities, our self-image and our social-image(s) on these beliefs. We then develop our life decision-making strategies from these beliefs and the motivations of our ego-identities. Seeing this belief creation cycle, (i.e. fears generate beliefs and existing beliefs generate fear, over and over) is vital to understanding their influence in our lives. All beliefs are limitations on our process of <u>accurately learning</u> anything new, still they are human's current way of recording and referencing life experiences.

Karma: is the law and dynamic of soul learning and evolution via experiencing "cause-and-effect". Through understanding cause-and-effect, based upon the results of our freewill choices, we attain personal power, wisdom, discernment, understanding and ultimately enlightenment. Karma has nothing to do with punishment for past choices, misdeeds or failures. Karma is the spirit-managed path of our soul's evolution and development, which is achieved via each of our incarnate experience-based learning opportunities. Although it would not be accurately said that the soul itself "learns" through this interaction with physically incarnate existence, it could be said that it is fundamentally "changed" via the result of our incarnate learning experiences.

To say that the soul itself directly acquires experiences would be too simple and inaccurate a statement though, it could be said that the soul does attain understandings as a result of our life experience. It could also be said that karma is the road to our ultimate personal empowerment. Of course, karma is far more complex than simple cause-and-effect interactions and relationships. Still, at its foundation, these cause-and-effect relationships between billions of people constantly acting and making choices have created the world we live in.

Incarnation: is the choice the soul makes, and the step the soul takes, of connecting with and temporarily infusing its energy and a portion of its consciousness into a physical body, within our material world. In effect the choice of ensoulment animates what would otherwise be lifeless material (flesh) and gives the soul a way to experience physicality, and to practically and powerfully function within the physical realm. This process of incarnation opens the door to a vast array of spiritual educational achievements via diverse experiences, and the application of our personal power, within the world. This process is supported by the act of procreation by already incarnate humans, "who help to bring others through into this world", and by the parental act of educating and conditioning each of us while we are children.

Consensus Consciousness: is the "recorded group mind" of all of humanity that has developed throughout the history of humanity and which is constantly influencing all of us. This usually occurs at subconscious levels of our systems without our realizing it. The consensus consciousness surrounds us and operates between and within us. Every group of people has its own "sub-consensus consciousness" or energetic cultural group mind, that these groups of people constantly refer to in their day-to-day decision-making. Each corporation has its own consensus consciousness; each nation has its own and every religion has its own. Each consensus consciousness holds whatever group beliefs, values, decision-making strategies and emotional dynamics that have been recorded by its participants throughout the history of the group's existence.

The recordings in each level of the consensus consciousness are never "right" or better than any other group's beliefs and values or mores. At the same time, for that group, they feel "more right" and better. You could call this process of one group feeling itself better or more right than another as simply a process of "group ego dynamics". These group ego dynamics are always driven at their foundation by fear, and not by actually being more right or better than any other group or individual. If there was no fear in "group minds" then no group would feel the need to subjugate, destroy, undermine, put down or control any other group of human beings. It is a sort of "group think" insecurity complex that creates many of the world's problems. If you question the reality of this dynamic simply ask yourself how many organizations (and even nations) fear public embarrassment, looking weak or vulnerable, or fear being found to be "wrong". It is also useful to see how many nations feel the need to prove their power (and thus feel safer) by "flexing their muscles" militarily.

It is useful to understand that there is actually a consensus consciousness for the male gender and also for the female gender. These two consensus consciousness's are constantly in a state of conflict and control seeking as well as a desire to make peace and to find love with one another.

Simulacra: according to Merriam-Webster's Dictionary simulacra are defined as: (http://www.merriam-webster.com/)

"An image, representation or an insubstantial form or semblance of something." Simulacrum is the singular reference, and simulacra is the plural form of this word.

Simulacra are defined here, for the purposes of this writing as: The holographic recordings we each make in our memories of what we believe or assume to be true about life, relationships, the world, our personal identity and other's identities from moment-to-moment. Simulacra recordings include aspects of memory that are related to each of our senses, including auditory, tactile, visual, taste, kinesthetic, emotions. We also record relational and even spiritual perceptions, interpretations and understandings. Simulacra also include the recorded and referenced conclusions we draw from each of our interpreted experiences and the connections we make with other simulacra and the assumed relationships between these memories/simulacra (whether accurate or not). Meaning these simulacra include beliefs of all kinds, and these recordings drive and support the development and function of our life strategies, relationship strategies and day-to-day decision-making strategies.

Simulacra are the lenses through which we view and interpret all of our current life experiences, how we "make sense" of our current life experiences, and therefore the reason we react emotionally to these experiences. Each Simulacrum tends to have a sense of "self" associated with it, that we then later identify with and relate to, as if simulacra are part of us. Though no simulacrum is a part of our true spiritual identity or reality, they can feel very "real and important". Simulacra are only the building blocks of our mental processes, our emotional systems, our decision-making strategies and our self-perceived ego-identities or personalities. Our ego-identities or social-identities can be built upon identification with any belief system, philosophy, political ideology, religion or spiritual practice, culture, tradition, career, nation or group of human beings.

A detrimental aspect of the process of simulacra is that they become the interpretive lenses through which we learn from our present experiences. Meaning we look at the present through the lenses of our recorded simulacra memories of the past. Another issue is that simulacra hold and contain beliefs and these beliefs can be triggered by life events and also these beliefs project onto our lives and relationships. Once triggered, these recorded beliefs can blind us to even the most obvious truths that are right in front of our eyes. Once triggered they can even lead to reactive violence, bias, bigotry and prejudice.

A term that is commonly used in psychology today is that of a "schema". When I speak of simulacra or a specific simulacrum I am not referring to a schema. Nor am I speaking of what might be termed a "part", which is a facet of the "Family Constellation Therapy Modality" or parts as defined by NLP methods. I do perceive that both schemas and parts can be made from groups or networks of simulacra.

A brief definition of a schema per Merriam-Webster's Dictionary, which can be found at:
http://www.merriam-webster.com/ is:
"A mental codification of experience that includes a particular organized way of perceiving cognitively and responding to a complex situation or set of stimuli."

For example, if we speak of a specific single recorded simulacrum that produces the internal dialog of "I will never have the life that I want to have" (again, this is not merely a belief about life). A simulacrum such as this is a recorded interpretation of life experiences that obviously will not ultimately serve the attainment of our future or present happiness. Certainly, a simulacrum is in part a belief, still there is far more to its operation in our mental and emotional systems than simply holding the belief. There are also more affects in and on our mental and emotional systems of holding this example belief than simply cognitive. Meaning there are also emotional and behavioral aspects and even energetic effects that are associated with past,

66

present and future. While constituting a fundamental building block of larger mental, emotional and energetic constructs and strategies, simulacra are relatively simple in structure.

There is a vast long term influence on our lives of holding maladaptive simulacra. These simulacra tend to influence our decision-making subconsciously and profoundly and detrimentally. They could therefore literally be said to be key determinants of what we could refer to as practical intelligence. Practical intelligence here defined as our individual capacity to accurately and fearlessly interpret, understand and process what is occurring in our environment and in our relationships, and then to function effectively in making wise-decisions and taking wise actions in all areas of our lives. When triggered by life situations or relationship dynamics, these long-buried simulacra immediately color our interpretations of what is going on in the moment. If not actively triggered, they have less effect on our outlook on life, still they do have consistent influence at subconscious levels of our systems.

All simulacra are recorded in our systems, at various levels of our physical systems as energy holograms, therefore they are not merely synaptic recordings made in our physical brains. These recordings are in part cellular memory; they also represent information stored in our energy system of "chakras", some of which are internal to our bodies and some of which reside outside our physical systems. The function and influence of chakras will be discussed later in the book.

As stated earlier, simulacra tend to include information from each of our senses, such as visual, tactile, emotional and auditory information. These simulacra recordings are, for the most part, compartmentalized from each other in the way they are recorded in various levels of our systems. Therefore, we can have a simulacrum in our system that generates ongoing grief, and another that creates ongoing feelings of hatred or guilt, and an additional separate part of our emotional system that generates fear, and they all each operate rather independently of one another. This compartmentalization or lack of integration of simulacra creates profound problems in humanity. Meaning for example, that we can love our families and hate our enemies, due to this compartmentalization process. Or we can unconsciously operate from prejudice, rather than compassion, depending upon the situation or who we are interacting with. When simulacra are recorded, they are recorded while looking through the lenses of other recorded simulacra, therefore our past distorts our recording of our memories in the present.

Paradoxically, groups of simulacra operating in concert simultaneously create what we could call our moment-by-moment moods or perspective and "lens of situational interpretation" from which we view and experience life. These grouped simulacra also literally create our basic personality and ego-identity(s), behavioral tendencies, our general perspectives on life and relationships. Simulacra can be seen as the foundational building blocks of our safety strategies, and also our competition and control strategies. (These and other types of life management and decision-making strategies will be described more fully later in the book).

The totality of all our recorded simulacra constitute our personal **internalized map of our external reality** (whether conscious or subconscious) as well as our perceived self-image within the outer social world. We acquire these recordings gradually, as we age, and they are added to, layer by layer, year after year. The process of acquiring and recording simulacra is similar to that of the way the rings of trees develop. Each year a new ring is added to the tree's circumference. The layers of simulacra are, for most people, transparent to their consciousness, and most of us usually prefer to keep them this way. There is a system of therapy called the "Internal Family Systems Model". In this model of therapy, they speak of "parts" of people and the operation of these parts within our systems, and within our family dynamics, such as "protector parts" that try to protect us socially and interpersonally. In this writing, when I refer to simulacra I am <u>not</u> referring to the parts this system of therapy describes and utilizes, though some similarities and overlap may be perceived.

Each of these simulacra have a corollary or reflection in some aspect of the global human consensus consciousness. Meaning that it is through these shared simulacra that we associate with, communicate with, interact with, and resonate with the larger consensus consciousness of all groups, families, and ultimately humanity as a whole. Still, it is only the ego-identities and ego-dynamics of various levels and aspects of the consensus consciousness that we are interacting and resonating with. The consensus consciousness of humanity is itself is like one giant "***ego***-system". Many elements of which are driven by simple fear and ignorance, meaning fundamental recordings of misunderstandings of our life experiences. So, trying to become "one with the consensus consciousness" is not suggested, as doing so can create many problems and is quite limiting in regard to its effect on our quality of consciousness. Being one with the consensus consciousness is not at all the same as oneness with either God or the universe.

In Chapter 11 we will discuss a system for dis-identifying from maladaptive simulacra, and for breaking down any other non-optimal aspects of ego-identity dynamics.

A **single simulacrum,** that has been recorded in our systems, is a composite of many elements, and these elements operate constantly in our systems. Therefore, although the original recordings of experience in our systems tend not to change much over time, though they are neither completely frozen or inactive.

Each recorded simulacrum is made up of the following basic components:

1. The basic or original belief we recorded in the specific simulacrum, based upon our initial interpretation of the experience we had, (no matter how unrealistic, inaccurate or untrue the belief we record might be). Again, the belief is basically just the conclusion or fundamental meaning we drew from the event, experience or situation about self, life and relationships that we are interpreting.
   With all beliefs we record, we also tend to acquire "things we associate with those beliefs". Meaning for example, that if we were robbed while buying an ice cream at an ice cream store, we then may then associate going to the ice cream store with danger or potential fear, death or loss. Via this process of recorded association, we create simplistic thought and decision tendencies. For example, we could have recorded "if I go to the ice cream store, then I could be killed". This is a simple belief based, "if this then that" form of thought and decision-making. Each belief with its associations then leads to projections of expectation onto life and relationships. Meaning we may actually expect (consciously or subconscious) to be robbed if we go to the ice cream store. Can you see the profound implications of acquiring such limited and simple beliefs on our life decisions day after day and from moment-to-moment?
   We could look at all of the languages that we use around the world and which we have recorded in our systems as simulacra, since we each have a personal unique recorded definition of every word we use. So, for example, each of us has a specific and often subconscious definition of the word "love, hate, good, bad, joy, right, wrong, etc.". Even if these words are defined in a dictionary that does not mean that we all use the same dictionary definition in our day to day lives. It is these unique and often changing simulacra that we reference when we "think" and when we generate internal dialog, or make decisions. No one's definition of any word is exactly like anyone else's. Understanding that recordings of words and language profoundly affect how we process our moment-by-moment

69

reality is very important. This is one reason humans argue, since no one has the same recorded frame of reference as anyone else.

2. The basic emotions we reactively record when we first arrive at the belief or conclusion we have drawn about the life experience. These emotions can include any recorded emotion, though they are often associated with negative emotions, (i.e. fear, anger, hatred, jealously, anxiety, trauma, insecurity, etc.). Still these recorded emotions can also be very positive, (i.e. love, joy or a feeling of security). This emotional recording process also includes a "process of genderzing" the original experiential simulacra recording. We actually tend to apply a male or female gender reference or point of view or lens through which we are looking at the situation we are experiencing when we record each simulacrum. Meaning we record many memories from the point of view of our perceiving ourselves to either be a man or a woman, male or female. We can also record simulacra from an asexual or non-genderized point of view.

Examples of this genderization process <u>could be</u> the recording of a masculine oriented simulacrum holding the perspective of itself as being male, powerful, dominating, assertive, strong and it could perceive femininity as subordinate or "less than" in importance, value, power, etc. Masculine simulacra can also include identifying masculinity with violence, aggression, anger and the willingness to kill or harm others, even if it is justified as necessary to protect self or others. A recorded genderization of feminine orientation to a simulacrum <u>could include</u> wanting to be perceived as loving, beautiful, emotionally supportive, responsible for their relationships, motherly, "nice", approval seeking, non-aggressive, self-doubting, perfectionist oriented or self-critical.

<u>Obviously</u> these attributions of specific traits to the genders that we have just listed are not always the case, (i.e. there are more emotionally open men now than in the past, and there are many gentle and respectful of men in this world). There are also far more powerful and assertive women than in the past around our world. Still, whatever the individual person resonates with, in terms of <u>their personal definition</u> of gender traits, will influence what is recorded in the simulacra. Then these gender orientation memories/simulacra will later be referenced in our decision-making.

<u>This</u> process of genderizing our recorded simulacra tends to keep the simulacra we record polarized along gender lines and thereby capable of operating within socially defined roles. Doing this

helps us feel that we "fit" in with the orientation and expectations of the larger male and/or female global consensus consciousness. This process of genderization is supportive of the function (or dysfunction) of most existing cultures. It also supports the process of family creation and of procreation. Still it limits and channels the human species decisions, energies and evolution, as a whole. It does this by creating "expected genderized channels" of behavior and decision-making. It also maintains and brings along with all the "historical baggage" we have recorded in the human consensus consciousness in regard to the genders, and how they are "supposed to" act, behave or feel. Thereby is created the global script we are each handed in our youths that we feel compelled to live by.

This genderizing influence in regard to what we record within our simulacra occurs constantly and subconsciously. Once these recordings have been made in enough individuals, they then re-influence and hold in place the masculine and feminine aspects, structures and orientations of societies, families and relationships. This is a process of organizing the mental and emotional energies of our entire species in relatively simplistic male/female ways, that are then supportive of the continuation of the traditions of prior generations of human being's. This process drives our evolution into the future. This process is neither good nor bad, it is a profound and subconscious influence on how we function and make decisions as individuals and as groups.

3. The secondary reactive emotional feeling(s) we hold and experience, when we contemplate the **implications of holding the belief** that we have recorded. These are the emotions we would tend to project onto our lives and relationships. (For example: fear, anger, loneliness, sadness, resentment and grief can all be reactively associated with the recorded belief that "I will never have the life that I want" or "no one loves me"). In this example case, these beliefs are somewhat global conclusions we have drawn about life in general, often based upon a single unhappy experience. The negative emotion we experience is the reaction to our own imaginary projection onto our life experience that we choose to make, when we hold such beliefs. We can be sad or fearful about an imagined and projected future that has not yet happened and which may not happen at all, simply because a recorded simulacrum believes it will happen. Yes, I am saying that there is really no such thing as an ego-identity, or a "true self". Since all ego-identities are simply conglomerates or networks

of recorded simulacra we have chosen to identify with and call "me or you". Without our choosing to add a sense of "I, self or personality" to our processing of incoming moment-by-moment sensory information we would not have assumed the identities we hold onto. Doing so, (i.e. creating ego-identities and then holding onto them) has become a species level social addiction.

It is <u>common</u> for the parts of our systems tasked with primal physical survival to "maximally generalize" the recorded conclusions we draw from each of our experiences. This tendency is based upon the erroneous primal assumption that generalizing in this manner will ultimately be "safer". Examples of dysfunctionally generalized beliefs would be "I cannot trust anyone", "Men are all bad", "I will never feel safe" or "I will never have what I want in life". This fundamental tendency to dysfunctionally generalize the beliefs we record creates tremendous limitation on our capacity to think, feel and make quality decisions later in life and in relationships. Meaning any thoughts, emotions or decisions that go against the original overly generalized recorded belief are preemptively limited or blocked from our consciousness, usually without our realizing it is occurring.

4. The internal dialog, "mental chatter", thoughts and visual pictures that the simulacra produce in our minds from moment-to-moment, over and over, during the course of our lives. This process goes on and on until we fully resolve and invalidate the original inaccurate recordings and their associated emotions. Therefore, Simulacra produce what we perceive as "thoughts or internal dialog", which are just generated words in our minds, with associated feelings. The meaning of these words, as we process them in our minds, is derived from both their basic meanings to ourselves, which we have recorded, and the context of other simulacra we have recorded within our systems. They therefore have a significant and unrealized influence on our decision-making processes. This influence occurs because the operation of the simulacra in our systems appear to "seamlessly integrate" their perspectives into our day-to-day process of consciousness and thought. This is what happens when we project our fears onto the future or the present, when there is really nothing to fear.

It could be said that the "mind" as we know it, is just an ongoing process of interactive and triggered simulacra. These triggered recordings are constantly bombarding our consciousness with imaginary projections of what we have previously recorded and believe, sort of like living in an echo chamber of our own internal dialog. Sage Yogis have, throughout history, learned to transcend these mental and emotional dynamics and the internal turbulence they tend to create. Thought itself, in its usual form could be seen as a block to and a distraction from true consciousness. Simulacra are a type of holographic memory, still they are more than simple memory recordings of events, in that they fundamentally change and **form our systems of thought and belief,** emotion and decision-making strategies.

Each simulacrum is a lens that can be mentally and emotionally "looked through" at any time. This means that we can look through one simulacral lens at a time, or we can look through several related simulacra at the same time. This could be said to be what occurs when we "connect the dots" of disparate previous experience, to arrive at a new and more complete understanding of our past. It is also what happens when we are operating and making decisions based upon a strongly held political or religious agenda.

This dynamic of looking through multiple "memory lenses" is, in part, why it appears that our memories seem to change over time. Meaning that our memory of past events appears to shift, depending upon which recorded simulacra we are viewing the memory through in the present moment. Then our memory is, to a degree, colored or changed by doing so, and then it is "re-recorded". This process occurs throughout our day to day life, over and over.

It is <u>crucial to recognize</u> that when our simulacra are triggered our focus on them can "overwrite" any incoming information from our environment, in the present moment, with "replays" of what we have previously recorded at some point in our lives. This is what happens when people are unable to see how others feel or see life. For example, this **"simulacra blindness"** occurs when we are holding a polarized political agenda or set of political beliefs that have a strong emotional and energetic charge. (See item 5 below regarding simulacra energy.) In these situations, we literally cannot openly see or hear what others are saying or why they feel or think what they do. In these situations, invariably, fear and judgmentalness are the blinding emotions we are focused on, to the exclusion of external information sources.

Another example would be seen when those who have been indoctrinated into cults are so totally focused on their internal simulacra generated messages, that any external message appears to be "dangerous or unacceptable". Another example is when anyone has "stubbornly made up their mind" on any topic, to the exclusion of new information or other's points of view. In these situations, the beliefs contained in the simulacra prevent new understanding from being feasible, and thus no new learning can occur. People who have "strong beliefs" about <u>any aspect</u> of life or the world thus have an unrecognized learning disability. Lastly this is what happens when husbands and wives cannot see each other's points of view, because they are already too focused on their own simulacra (desires, beliefs, feelings, fears, etc. and thus imagine to be true), to the exclusion of what their spouse is communicating. This dynamic occurs even when we truly love the other person.

5. The "energetic charge" we retain in our emotional system related to the core belief and the original experience. Often these energetic charges can be quite powerful, as in the emotional energy we may continue to hold related to an early life trauma, or the emotional trauma associated with a divorce, or PTSD acquired after participating in war or from a personal physical assault. This energy charge in the simulacrum drives its process of sending out repetitive messages (belief misinformation that it holds, often in the form of internal dialog). The simulacrum transmits this misinformation to the rest of the mental and emotional systems. Thus, this information is constantly influencing how we think, feel and behave at all levels of our systems. All simulacrum are information <u>processing</u> and interpretive lenses, that are also then <u>information creating and transmission mechanisms</u>.

6. A tendency to be subconsciously literally blocked from acquiring and understanding any new information that does not support or agree with the original interpretation that is recorded in the simulacrum. The reason for this tendency to block our new learning, especially in new situations that involve change in our lives, is that we become identified with the simulacrum as if it is a part of us, and therefore "who we are". Therefore, we feel safer identifying with the simulacra than changing our fundamental recorded belief. This is because the simulacra recordings and memories were originally created by viewing our prior life experiences through the lens of who we perceived ourselves to be at the moment we recorded them.

We therefore tend to primally fear changing the original recorded simulacrum because doing so would feel like we are losing a part of ourselves that we assume is somehow benefiting us, or is somehow producing safety or security. This self-protective resistance to change of each simulacrum creates a developmental self-blinding and self-binding momentum or inertia in regard to how we choose to evolve as individuals and how we make our day-to-day choices. Therefore, these simulacra even resist accepting unconditional love from others and the healing and evolutionary transformational efforts of others. The simulacrum's motivation for this resistance is simple fear. In effect, it is trying to hold onto an illusionary perceived state of safety via, "not changing, learning, growing or facing their own ignorance and limited understanding and perspectives".

Each simulacrum holds within it a sense of "self", that we then identity with, often to the point that we feel that the simulacra are literally "who we are" or a fundamental aspect of our personality. This separate sense of self that each simulacrum holds means that it can have its own specific fear reactions to perceived threats to it or of its own dissolution. It is this tendency to identify with the simulacra that makes it difficult to release them and transcend their debilitating influence. This sense of "I" within each of the simulacra is created at the moment of the experience, therefore it is only as sophisticated as our consciousness was at that time. So, for example this would be why we feel parts of ourselves to be "child selves" and other parts to be older or more mature or sophisticated. In the end, no simulacrum is really useful, it is only a "book mark" on a page of our recorded lives.

7. The mechanism of projection onto life, relationships, ourselves and the world that the simulacrum **lens of belief and interpretation** creates. (i.e. We tend to project what we believe and feel to be true onto the world, and others, and see them as we believe them to be, even if it is not true at all). This simultaneous process of projection onto life occurs along with the distortion of the information we take in from moment-to-moment and therefore skews our process of life navigation. It is the influence of these recorded simulacra that create attitudes of bias, prejudice, and insensitivity to the suffering of others that we believe to be different or less than us, etc.

8. The energetic information transmission we subconsciously send to other people, often through our body language, from these subconscious parts of ourselves. This transmitted information is usually about what or who we believe ourselves to be, and who we believe others to be, or what we believe the social situation to be. Other people feel these subconscious projections from these simulacra as expectations we place onto them, and then these people

often subconsciously try to fulfill our projected expectations. An example of this dynamic would be seen when a person believes the world is a dangerous place, and they then tend to draw to themselves dangerous or problematic interactions with others. In its most overt form this projective process can lead to paranoia.

9. Each simulacrum tends to be "triggered or triggerable" into operation by events or social situations, (i.e. we begin to feel the way the recorded simulacrum felt when it was first created, it also begins creating internal dialog in our minds. For example, a simulacrum could say "I am not safe" or "they are going to hurt me" or "I hate myself" in reaction to a perceived situation. It is this reactive triggered emotional dynamic that we call anxiety, stress, worry, etc. The more simulacra are triggered, the more of these emotions we tend to experience, often without realizing what is behind our emotional experience.

10. In addition, each simulacrum can be triggered into self-protective sub-strategies, by any conflict based interpersonal or social interaction. Each simulacrum can have multiple triggers for these self-defense strategies. Meaning we can be drawn into subconscious negative, controlling and judgmental reactions by any triggered simulacrum, without our consciously realizing it is occurring.

An example of this process in action would be seen when we try to avoid social embarrassment by being reactively critical toward others that we feel are socially attacking or threatening us.

Another example would be an avoidance strategy. Meaning that we are triggered to preemptively affect others via some behavior or communication in order to protect ourselves. This is seen when we try to avoid other's potentially saying negative things about us or thinking negative thoughts about us, or having negative opinions of us.

Another example would be seen when a person is continually seeking to achieve higher and more positive social status to pre-emptively avoid future negative social situations, such as feeling less than others or feeling controlled by others. It is important to realize that the motivating simulacrum that is recorded is not equal to the actual strategy we might employ to achieve higher social status. The simulacrum is the core energetic and emotional driver and point of reference for when, where, how and why such a strategy is supposedly required. It is also the motivating energy for creating and maintaining such social strategies.

Therefore, simulacra are the key support elements for all of our more complex and sophisticated life strategies and decision-making processes. If the simulacra are "healed or cleared" then the often-detrimental strategic tendencies they have previously driven fall apart, because there is no longer any motivation for the strategy to exist or to operate. Therefore, if you clear **all** your simulacra, especially those that produce fear, your ego-identity ceases to "be" or to operate. When this process of releasing all simulacra from your system is achieved you could then be said to be "far more conscious".

11. Each simulacrum can work as an element of a network of all the other simulacra in our systems. In this way, the composite or "mosaic" map of reality we hold in our systems, or **larger network of simulacra**, act in complex and strategic ways to influence our view of reality. In addition, these internal networks of simulacra also interface with, or communicate with, and try to remain resonant with, the larger consensus consciousness of humanity around us, as well as remaining resonant with any group we are part of. Remaining resonant with group's ways of thinking, believing, feeling and operating is generally deemed "safe or safer" than not doing so, and is also perceived to be a way to remain part of the "herd". This is also paradoxically how cohesive, efficient teams of people coordinate their activities so effectively.

This interactive process of simulacra communication, (much of which is subconscious for most people), is how we remain constantly entrained and in step with the consensus consciousness of humanity, and thus remain limited by it. This communications process is supported via "subtle energy fields" we could call our auras. Each of us has an aura, and our aura forms the basis of our subconscious interpersonal communications system. We will discuss these human energy system concepts in greater depth later in the book, along with their profound influence on our lives and the world.

12. The defense system that holds the structure of the simulacrum and its associated core belief(s) and emotional processes in place. This defense system must be circumvented in order to release the simulacrum's core belief(s) and process out the totality of the elements of the simulacrum permanently. When we do resolve the old inaccurate recording that we hold in memory, we are then empowered to transcend its influence with better informed and more accurate modes of consciousness. Then we are no longer limited by the recorded historical misperception and its associated influences on

our emotional systems, our thoughts or our decisions. It is useful to realize that any recorded misperception becomes a learning disability if we hold it to be true and make decisions based upon it, without question.

Element number 12, the last element of simulacra listed above, (i.e. the defense system of the simulacrum), is a very important aspect to understand. In that, whenever we have a strongly held belief, we then invariably assume that changing the belief is an unsafe or wrong thing to do. We may also feel that doing so will invalidate our previous view of reality, that it may disrupt our relationships, or we may primally or instinctively assume that doing so could be potentially pain or loss producing. In other words, no one's ego-identity ever wants to feel they have been "wrong, stupid or out of control" in their beliefs about self, life, relationship or reality. Many of us would rather fight and even die than change some of our recorded simulacra, though this truth is usually obscured from our consciousness. Since we are so identified with our memories/simulacra, changing them feels like a sort of "death" to that part of our systems.

It does not matter how dysfunctional or maladaptive the belief contained in the simulacrum is, as in the dysfunctional beliefs "I will never be happy" or "no one will ever truly love me" or "men are not trustworthy". The simulacra's self-defense systems are self-camouflaging, and consistently hide the falsity of their basic premise from the person who holds them. Just because we believe that no one will ever love us does not mean that we feel safe releasing this inaccurate and non-optimal belief. In fact, part of us feels safer continuing to hold it in our system. The reason is we do not feel safe changing is that if we choose to believe the statement is true, then we supposedly can never be loved (this is the supposedly "known reality" that we have already accepted and can deal with). If we somehow were to be loved, then we might be required to risk losing the newly achieved state of love and happiness or have to risk being abandoned. Therefore, by continuing to hold onto the maladaptive belief and view of life we can supposedly never be painfully disappointed by life, even while we live in a state of ongoing unhappiness.

Of course, it is not true that holding onto these beliefs saves us from potential disappointment. The beliefs simply act as emotional shock absorbers, filters or buffers when we don't get what we want or what we expect. As in when a relationship breaks up we may think, "I was right all along, no one will ever love me". In these cases, we assume that the belief has been proven to be true and we feel a sort of dysfunctional security in this belief. Therefore, we constantly try not to disprove our cherished beliefs. Consequently, these networks of inaccurate simulacra can, for many people, constitute "prisons of the mind", that we live in to our detriment and without realizing we are imprisoned.

We refer to these simulacra that we have become consistently highly identified with as we go through our day-to-day lives, as key supports to our decision-making processes. In their entirety, they constitute the building blocks of our sense of self and our ego-identity(s). Therefore, we may feel or perceive some of these recordings to be parts of our perceived self or ego-identity. Therefore, we find it difficult to dis-identify from the simulacra and thus transcend their influence. In the most extreme situations, this would be a process of transcending recordings of traumas we experienced in childhood. Dis-identification is especially difficult if we feel that holding onto the simulacra will help to insure our emotional, mental or physical safety, stability, control, personal power and certainty of outcomes in life.

It is helpful to realize that the effects of holding various simulacra create our habits of behavior and decision-making in our day to day lives and relationships. This creates repetitive unconscious behavior and often unresolved dysfunctional social and interpersonal dynamics. This process could be seen to having its own sort of inertia or social situation creating momentum. This process can also be seen as a cause-and-effect dynamic, which could be looked at as the process of karma in action.

Groups of these recorded simulacrum become our internal map of reality and thus our default method of navigating our way through life, situations and relationships. They also form the basis of many of our most fundamental decision-making strategies. Including safety strategies, survival strategies, control strategies, competitive strategies and anti-abandonment strategies (see the definition of control later in this chapter). These types of life strategies will be discussed later on in this book along with their source motivations. It is useful to understand that all decision-making strategies in some way empower us, and at the same time create limitations on how we see the world and make decisions. Thus, our various simulacra based life strategies do help us to create our lives and reality, and at the same time they also limit our capacity to understand the world outside the viewpoint of our recorded memories and reactive strategies. This process can create situations where we are literally imprisoned in the web of our limiting life strategies.

Simulacra also support the creation of other mental concepts and constructs, and our emotional and behavioral dynamics. Similar to how many grains of sand combine to build a sand castle, we build from our recorded simulacra complex views of life, reality and relationship. Some of these constructs are:

- ❖ Concepts (how we define concepts and relate them in our systems)
- ❖ Thoughts and internal dialog (an ongoing process in most people)
- ❖ Processes of decision-making and strategizing of all kinds
- ❖ All of the recordings of what we call "knowledge and useful information"
- ❖ Habits, behaviors and tendencies of all kinds
- ❖ Mindsets (tendencies to apply certain life philosophies, habits of interpreting life in general, styles of logic, belief systems etc. to our process of decision-making)
- ❖ Our Self-Image(s) & Social Image(s)
- ❖ Our basic life motivations, desires and intentions
- ❖ Metrics and standards by which we evaluate our decisions and behaviors and evaluate the quality of our lives and relationships
- ❖ Classification and categorization strategies, we apply to our day-to-day choices and experiences of life
- ❖ Assumptions we hold
- ❖ Projections we make onto life and relationships
- ❖ Expectations we hold of ourselves, others, our workplaces and societies
- ❖ Our Life Roles, Life Rules, Values, Codes of Conduct, Agendas and Priorities that we live by
  - ▪ Mental, Emotional and Relationship models and systems of relationships we build and reference within our minds and within our cultures that operate at various levels of our societies. These models lead to relationship dynamics of all kinds. One key example of such models that have had powerful influence in our world is a mental model (i.e. the technology cultivating Scientific Model, along with the process of developing and testing theories). Some results of the application of this model of thought are the development of computers, another is the system of mass production we call the assembly line, another is the theory of Darwinism and its application to genetics.

Some other models of human interaction and social development, that have functioned in various societies and political environments, with varying degrees of influence and success, are:

- ❖ Systems of belief of all kinds
- ❖ Belief in the importance and value of free-speech
- ❖ Marriage agreements (non-arranged and family arranged)
- ❖ All cultural traditions and systems of religion

80

❖ Various legal systems found around the world
❖ Various hierarchical bureaucratic systems and corporate systems
❖ Capitalism, free-market economies and economics of all kinds
❖ Political systems such as democracy in its various forms, socialism, communism, fascism, monarchies, oligarchies and dictatorships
❖ Languages of all kinds are based upon this process of first recording and then referencing over and over the definitions of the meanings of words that we have recorded
❖ The foundations of basic logic, and also inductive and deductive forms of reasoning

The influence of simulacrum remains subconscious and profoundly limiting as well as supportive of day to day life for most people. The consciousness of nations and all groups also record simulacra in their group consciousnesses and reference them as values, traditions, national identities, reasons for laws, etc. Which then support the nation's policy development processes and national decision-making strategies, and thus how nations interact with other nations.

Although beliefs and simulacra are distinctly different concepts, they are at the same time highly related concepts. Meaning that every recorded simulacrum will contain a belief of some sort. For the remainder of this book I will, for the most part, use the term "belief" interchangeably with simulacra, in order to simplify the discussion. Please note that if I do refer to the concept of "subconscious parts" later in this text, I am also referring to recorded simulacra or groups of simulacra.

In Chapter 8 we will introduce and fully discuss the "Belief-Based Reality Creation Process". This is a process which stems from our personal simulacra recordings, each of which holds at least one belief. This belief process is the mechanism by which we each subconsciously manifest and create all aspects of our lives and relationships dynamics. In Chapter 8, we describe how our individual beliefs create our personal experience of reality. In this belief based manifestation process we will be referring to the effects on our lives of our holding the beliefs that are contained in our simulacra recordings.

Tribalism: is defined here as the fear based tendency to group together with other people for the purposes of survival, safety, control over our lives and other's lives. We also gather in a tribal fashion to achieve self-empowerment, goal achievement, self-worth and have access to resources through social exchange. Tribalism was originally an adaptive process of survival, which was an outgrowth of the herd tendency of many kinds of animals.

I am not suggesting that congregating together as humans is not a good thing, in that obviously there are many benefits to be derived from it, in addition to the problems it creates. For example, all forms of inter-group conflict and competition. Of course, there are significant positive emotional dynamics, that are not driven by fear, that can be gained by such congregations. It is these positive emotional experiences that make human group endeavors worthwhile.

In fact, it is the experience of wholesome and positive community interaction, and being valued by others, that many people are so desperately seeking these days. For many of us, it is the fundamental feeling of separateness from community and other people, and the lack of perceived social value, that creates many feelings of loneliness, emptiness, great pain and suffering. In reality, that which we are all truly seeking is to transcend the misperception that many of us hold of there being any separateness from ourselves and God. Though we are all not fully conscious of this feeling of being disconnected, or separate from God, as being the source of our pain, conflict and confusion.

A main difficulty the world faces now is that most of us have not been taught to optimally function in healthy, constructive and emotionally positive ways within the groups we are a part of. Though many of us try very hard to achieve this, it is not something that we are usually able to consistently effect. This situation of dysfunctional ego-identity dynamics then constantly leads to interpersonal conflict of one form or another and a great deal of unnecessary drama and controversy. If we transcend these ego-identity dynamics, we can ultimately blissfully realize and feel secure in our oneness with God and all of humanity.

With all the above said. At our current point of human evolution, we are facing limitations of global resources, several global, rather than merely national, environmental problems, and developing technological complexity. In this increasingly challenging situation tribalism itself has become a problematic and limiting dynamic. Tribalism is driven by and managed by the primitive and primal survival oriented part of our individual brains and nervous systems. Each "tribal group", no matter what size, has a shared sense of primal survival instinct that functions in a similar manner to the individual human system's primal survival tendency. Meaning that the tribe, as a collective consciousness, is focused on continued group safety, security, competition and survival. This survival motivation of individual groups can be blinding, and can keep us from seeing what is truly for the global greater good.

82

Tribalism does not support conscious individual sovereignty or true individual empowerment. Since to be part of, or to participate in any "tribe", (meaning any group of people), we tend to unconsciously give up much of our free-will. Many groups even expect this loss of individual power as proof of loyalty to the group. If we choose to be part of a corporation, a religion, a nation or a culture we will be required to give up some of our free-will. Tribalism is the root cause of all the ultimately detrimental and subconscious interpersonal life strategies that many people participate in. We will discuss these strategies in depth, later in the book.

Tribalism creates social, political and religious traditions that then drive many of our individual decisions, often at subconscious levels. Meaning we fear being abandoned or punished by the tribal group, or of not meeting the groups expectations, and therefore we adhere to the traditions and mores of the group.

As individuals, we literally fear trying to bring about fundamental change to our nation's or group's traditions, due to our instinctive fear of death via abandonment by the group, by going against their ways. This fear is often subconscious. We then rationalize this fear driven survival strategy as a supposedly positive quality, (i.e. loyalty to our group). This dynamic usually occurs without our even consciously realizing it is happening. What tribalism creates is an unwillingness on the part of individuals in the group to powerfully change and evolve the group or nation, even in **fundamentally beneficial ways.** The only influences by the individual that are "allowed" by the collective consciousnesses of many groups are those changes that are seen to directly support the prior beliefs, goals, mores, values and traditions of the nation or group.

Tribalism is the source of nationalism, populism and of another detrimental tribal loyalty dynamic, which is often seen as positive, called patriotism. These dynamics are often used to rationalize war and violence. Neither patriotism nor nationalism are "bad", they are only sub-optimal because they both often lead to an "us vs. them" destructive international competition (rather than collaboration). I am not judging these dynamics, only trying to clearly illustrate their limiting influences. I am also not disparaging the efforts of the American military, or any other military. I am doing my best to facilitate understanding of underlying and often subconscious emotional dynamics that affect fundamental behavior and decision-making in groups of human beings.

Tribal dynamics are in many ways driven by simplistic interactive and consciousness subverting dynamics and cycles of attachment and aversion.

83

Both attachment and aversion are the results of judging social, cultural, national and international situations, values, relationships and goals and either trying to hold onto them, or to use them as rationales for conflict. Tribal dynamics are also driven by consensus consciousness dynamics of the expectations that these groups want met, and goals that the groups want achieved. So, this is a process of managing group dynamics of satisfaction and dissatisfaction. Often through means of social control or threat of force or violence. This use of violence is often rationalized as the use of authority and as necessary for the common good.

Tribalism has a limiting and detrimental social inertial quality which is difficult to transcend. This is true because most tribes, nations or groups want to survive just as they are, rather than being willing to fundamentally change, learn and evolve. Even if this change or evolution is for the good of the nation or of the world. This fear of change can lead to sanctioning or even killing nation's citizens if they are not deemed adequately loyal, even if they are simply trying to bring about fundamental positive loving change. Therefore, although tribalism does create groups of complex and organized human beings, which can then achieve great things as a group, it still has its limitations. Meaning that tribalism then invariably creates a "glass ceiling" on the learning, evolution and attainment of higher consciousness and sophisticated operation of those same groups.

Control: is an illusionary concept that has been created by humans and applied endlessly throughout history. A brief definition of it is the unrealistic belief in anyone's capacity to <u>completely influence</u> any situation, person or group, to the point of completely overcoming the freewill decision-making capability of that situation, person or group. In essence to have the power to take away others freewill. Trying to control ourselves, others and various valued worldly resources, and the fear of not being able to, is the single source of all violence in the world. These valued resources can be money, power, status or social position, sex, time, love, technology, and of course the capacity to keep oneself safe via controlling or even destroying another (this definition includes the activities of nation states).

Since freewill can never truly be taken away, the "wished for" capacity to control others, or even the ability to control ourselves and our day-to-day choices and behaviors will always fail. We choose to believe in this spurious concept because doing leads us to feel a false sense of safety and empowerment in life. Dictators want populations to believe that the population is controlled, so that the population will not be able to gain enough confidence and awareness to rebel or to force change. Although no one has ever had complete control of any aspect of life, (not even through any technology), we have all had personal power and influence. If we recognize this truth then we can never feel or be victimized and will always be able to apply our personal power in the most loving, effective, efficient and constructive manner. Those in positions of power may feel it is to their benefit for us to believe in the possibility of control. Because simply holding this belief (simulacra) keeps us in a "more controllable state" through our ignorance of our own power. Meaning if we have been conditioned, taught or influenced, even by tradition, to believe that we are weak, powerless or ineffective then we will make decisions as if this were true.

The Cycle of Fear: influences all parts of our lives and yet it is rooted in an amazingly simple dynamic. When we feel fear, we are either remembering or subconsciously referring to some past experience of pain, loss or trauma we have previously recorded in our memories or felt. Essentially we are referring to a recorded simulacrum of some sort, often that we do not want to consciously address and resolve. We may also be referring to a story we have been told in the past of some potentially painful situation that we could experience in the future. We can also "learn to react in fear" by copying our parent's fear reactive tendencies and fear projection tendencies or those of our society. We then imagine and project onto our mind's eye a picture or a movie of some similar experience or some version of that old painful experience we remember, that we then assume could occur in our future, (either to us or to someone we care about). We then see this projected picture or movie in our mind's eye as if it were an **external physical reality** and react to it with fear. This whole process often occurs subconsciously; still we feel the reactive feeling of fear, anxiety or stress when it is triggered. Therefore, fear is a repetitive cycle, that is constantly being retriggered and reinforced by life experience.

In situations where our fears are completely subconscious, they can affect our behavior and decision-making without our realizing it is occurring, and thereby keep our lives constrained, busy and limited in the process of fear avoidance. In this type of situation our conscious mind remains unaware of our fear, and we may even tell ourselves that we feel no fear at all, while our actual behavior changes to avoid what we fear and imagine. This situation can be seen when we are consistently worrying, or feeling stressed or anxious, and we do not recognize these as manifestations of unresolved fear. It can also occur when we are stuck in a supposed comfort zone.

85

Comfort zones are often a state of being imprisoned by our projected fears of potential problems related to changing our lives for the better. When we feel fear we generally tend to either deny it, suppress it, avoid it or rationalize it, we do anything other than dealing with fear effectively and transcending it.

When we feel fearful, anxious or stressed these feelings are often associated with situations of perceived uncertainty. Whether it is uncertainty about what we "should do" or what the right thing to do is in any given situation, or the uncertainty about what is likely to happen in our lives in the future or in the world. Therefore, we can feel fear regarding change of all kinds (even positive change), new or unknown situations, and any undefined situation we are faced with. Oddly enough we can also feel fear when we have a high degree of <u>certainty</u> that something that we don't want to happen is going to happen, such as the likely life changes that a divorce that we are in the process of completing will bring. So, attaining certainty in our lives in general is not always a solution or antidote to fear or stress.

When we fear, we imagine potential negative futures. We are creating within our mind a vision or "holographic projection" of a future that we fear could happen and question our capacity to deal with. When we look at the visions which we have created in our mind's eye, our body reacts with fear, because our subconscious literally does not know that the vision it is looking at is not an <u>external reality</u>. Therefore, our bodies go into biological fight or flight mode and we physically stress or feel anxious over what we imagine. Our subconscious does not realize that what we are projecting is not actually happening, and that it is not a physical real world reality in our outside world. Many of us spend our lives reactively imagining things to fear (many people call this process of worry thinking), and then we work diligently to avoid that which we fear, when there is no reality to it at all. Some people see this non-optimal way of processing our lives as an expression of wisdom or intelligence.

This process of fear projection onto our lives is the cause of our physical stress reactions when we are afraid in any social or family situation, even if we do not understand exactly what it is that we are fearing in the moment. Because we physically feel something chemically happening inside our body we subconsciously believe that something "real and potentially threatening" must be happening <u>outside</u> of ourselves. Our subconscious <u>actually believes</u> that what we fearfully project in our mind's eye could happen or in a way "is happening", because it is seeing it happen in our minds. This projection process, and our emotional and biological reaction to it, tend to go on and on unnecessarily, and endlessly. Still it can all be transcended with enough effort and self-awareness.

It is also useful to realize that all of our negative emotions (anger, hatred, guilt, jealousy, etc.) originally stem from fear, and that they are just surface manifestations of deeper un-faced and unresolved fears. This fear reaction process and its associated negative emotions are fully transcendable via various methods, one of which is shown in Chapter 11 of this book and which is continued in **Appendix 1**. These fear reactions are the driving forces for all the safety, control and competitive strategies that we apply to our lives and relationships, which we will discuss later in more detail.

All our fears are reactions to interpretations of situations. They are all reactive fears that stem from recorded simulacra, therefore none of them are reactions to a clear perception of the present moment. We have all recorded thousands of simulacra in our systems. Several of these simulacra can be triggered simultaneously, without our realizing it, leading to confusion, anxiety, stress and fear. None of these simulacra serve us optimally, thus clearing them from our systems is required if we want to transcend fear and all its associated dynamics.

Fears keep us focused on our projections of non-optimal negative potential futures, rather than supporting us in focusing on creating and producing positive optimal futures. Therefore, fears are all detrimental distractions from progress of all kinds. In our current time of rapid change, many unknowns and significant uncertainty, many of us have multiple simulacra being constantly triggered into states of fear stress. Part of this is due to the beliefs contained in the simulacra being challenged as to their truth or usefulness. Just the increase in complexity of life itself also triggers many simulacra. This fear stress is a <u>necessary result</u> of the current process of rapid evolution, learning and increasing complexity of the humanity species.

Note: All fear is driven <u>only by imagination rather than accurate understanding</u>, as is demonstrated in the following scenario. If you were being chased by a tiger through the woods and it was ten seconds behind you, you would not be afraid of the tiger at all, you would only be afraid of what you imagine the tiger <u>might do</u> if it caught you ten seconds in the future. It might turn out to be a tame tiger that just wants to play with you, or a hunter might suddenly shoot it, you cannot know for sure what the future will hold. That said, your fear may not allow you to find out the truth of the situation if you act only upon it blindly. Fear detrimentally distorts all interpretations of our experiences and takes over our consciousness, our capacity for compassion and our decision-making when it is triggered. We cannot arrive at wise decisions based upon the information created from or colored by fear. All forms of prejudice, bias, nationalism, exclusionary decision-making, hatred and distrust stem from fear. Only if we rise above fear do we become able to operate from love.

Time: The definition of, and the experience of time is different for every person. Time is not merely the turning of a clock and it is also not something that is fully shared in concept by most people. I want to offer here a definition of time that is related to the previous definition in this section of Simulacra. I would suggest this definition is another way of looking at time that can be useful in many ways. Time is defined here as: "The process of recording in our individual memory of our personal mental, emotional and social interpretations of our life experiences and sensory information. This recording process is then followed by our process of referring to those recordings and projecting them in imagined scenarios and we emotionally react to our projections. What we call "the future" is actually an imaginary projection of these recordings in our minds and emotional systems". This internal recording and projection dynamic that each of us experiences could be seen as our experience of the "process of time".

Certainly, within each of us, we do have this process of recording and projecting recorded interpreted experience, which we call the experience of time. In addition, our species also has a capability of recording our experience as a "collective or consensus consciousness". Meaning we record our experience of time within individuals and also within the "energetic bubble" of the consensus consciousness of all of the groups that make up all of humanity as a species. One manifestation of this process is the evolution of the culture of a corporation, as it experiences, learns, grows and changes.

Therefore, we experience time both as individuals, as groups, as nations and as a world, simultaneously. We could argue that none of this recorded information is "real", since every recording made within every human's system is unique and different than every other human's recordings. If this is so, whose recording is "true", accurate, right or real? This situation of different recordings is one of several reasons that human beings argue about what is true, right, proper and valuable, and what is not. As groups of humans record experiences, they develop roles, rules, beliefs, traditions and laws. None are true or right, they are, at least to a degree agreed upon within the group. These recorded information constructs are different in every group and every nation.

The Misinterpretation of Karma:

Karma has previously been misunderstood by many, in that it has been misinterpreted to be a mechanism of punishment for past misdeeds, or a process of constantly being tested as we spiritually evolve, thus it has not been seen in the positive light it deserves. (Of course karma is neither punishment nor merely a process of being tested). For these and other reasons we may look at karma with either trepidation, in a negative light or even with a type of fear or resentment. Some of us might tend to unknowingly and inaccurately project our early life's personal negative educational experiences of "learning lessons and being tested" from our traditional worldly educational institutions onto our understanding of karma.

We might also remember and project negative interactions with unnecessarily authoritative, insensitive, controlling or egocentric teachers from our traditional institutional educational process. These may be the only organized systems of learning most of us have been exposed to, and thus have available to refer to, in our understanding and interpretation of the mechanism of karma. Thus, this projected misinterpretation onto the actually loving, ultimately positively empowering and facilitative karmic mechanism would then tend to engender fears and feelings of "pass/fail" or punishing results for our life choices. These reactions are the result of a type of fear of abandonment via being judged by others or by God. That is, of course not what karma is about or how it works and I hope that someday the term karma will be understood to be the beautiful, empowering, life enhancing, guiding and grace giving instrument that it truly is.

The misunderstandings of karma recorded in the world's consensus consciousness have been repeatedly applied to many people's lives. Doing so has served to distort our vision of, and our interpretations of, the true meaning of our sometimes-difficult life experiences. These recorded interpretations, that have contributed to the global consciousness, create a global developmental social inertia, due to its influence on each new generation. Therefore, its influence on us can be detrimental in various ways if we hold recordings of inaccurate concept definitions, maladaptive beliefs and detrimental fear driven decision-making models (e.g. Using war, killing or torture to solve social, political or economic problems). In this manner, the concept of karma itself has attained a negative reputation and an association with pain and suffering. Due to this misunderstanding our attainment of deeper understanding of the true meaning of life events, via a more accurate understanding of karma, has been undermined.

Yet our previous and ongoing application of the inaccurate definition of the term karma to our lives can also be helpful in a way. In that clearly understanding how and why we have applied this inaccurate definition to our lives in the past can help us realize how distortions in the consensus consciousness can directly affect our spiritual developmental process. This means that when we eventually and fully comprehend the detrimental effects and costs of applying any consensus consciousness misinformation to our interpretations of our life experiences, and to our decisions, we will cease to accept them.

There are many other types of misinformation stored in the consensus consciousness, and it is necessary that we clean them up and bring the world's consciousness into a state of accuracy and clarity and pure discernment for the good of all. All the misinformation stored in the consensus consciousness tends to distort and undermine our species' thinking, discernment, emotional processes and decision-making to some extent. In this way, it can undermine our species process of evolution. We are each currently in the process of learning as individuals to discerningly filter out the previously accumulated detrimental elements from our own connections to limiting mass consciousness.

Mass consciousness inaccuracies undermine our species' attainment of wise discernment, and thus directly undermine the optimal conscious application of our personal power. We will eventually grow and learn from all our prior states of misunderstanding, just as we attain understandings from all our life experiences. Without this developing filtration process of conscious discernment these types of recorded misperceptions in the collective consciousness tend to hold people back from more rapidly and painlessly acquiring states of transcendent understanding.

Certainly, pain is involved in every person's life and it is also part of the process of karma. Yet this experienced pain is necessary information and "feedback" from our life experience to humanity's developmental dynamic, it is not punishment. Much of our pain is literally unknowingly self-created due to our life choices, and due to our interpretations of our life experience. **It is only how we interpret what we experience, and what we come to understand from our experiences, that truly matters.** We need not equate pain with learning or the experience of change. I would suggest that karma does not compel you to live life in any certain manner; in fact, it is more accurate to say that it impels you to become all you can become.

Through living incarnate lives we come to understand more and become more discerning about love and what is good, wise, true, worthwhile and

90

harmonious with spirit. This occurs as we live with what we choose to manifest through our choices, actions and intentions. In the past, as a result of experiential learning, most of us have gradually achieved some wisdom and enlightenment one step at a time. In fact, many of us tend to achieve various levels of enlightenment over time or enlightenments in one specific area of life or level of consciousness at a time rather than in all areas.

In effect, karmic evolution is not a situation of being "controlled" by any outer force or system, it is only the process of continuing to be influenced by the results of our own prior choices. Whether we consciously recognize it or not, we have all agreed to live under the effect of karma prior to incarnating in this world as humans. We have also all agreed to fulfill specific spiritual contracts while we are incarnate, and to help others and to allow ourselves to be helped by them—none of us are truly alone in this life. We do in fact, by our choices, create events and situations that cause us to further change and evolve, which is a method of developing ourselves via our choices, actions and the application of our personal power.

There are other ways to evolve than karma, and we may as a species soon choose to adapt to one of these. In fact, it is my understanding that humanity as a whole is considering doing just that, yet at the moment karma is the name of the game. That said, we can achieve our personal and spiritual developmental goals more directly through the grace of spirit, bypassing many otherwise necessary karmic steps, and some of us do so, though it is currently not the norm. In addition, those of us who are already highly evolved are able to draw others into consistently higher states of consciousness through positive energetic and spiritual entrainment in our "spiritual wake", if they choose to participate. In this way, we can effectively transcend many lifetimes of otherwise necessary, though uncomfortable, incarnate karmic growth experiences.

On our planet, at this point in time, we are in the process of entraining many souls into a vast spiritual leap forward, this is occurring as part of our massive world evolutionary transformation. This is in part due to the accumulation and availability of vast spiritual understanding on the internet, while simultaneously there are also other forms of less beneficial or non-constructive entrainment occurring. These detrimental forms of entrainment can be seen in those who are influenced to become part of cults and terrorist groups. (For useful information on cults see the documentary film, "Holy Hell). In these situations, at the physical survival oriented level of our beings, people can begin to gradually resonate with the influencing negative group energy and intentions. This dynamic influences us so much so that a form of

"Stockholm Syndrome" occurs. Stockholm Syndrome is a situation in which hostages begin to express empathy and sympathy with their captors, potentially even uniting with them in their destructive actions and beliefs.

In these threatening situations, people come to feel, and then believe, that their personal or spiritual survival depends upon accepting the detrimental beliefs and attitudes of the group. In doing so their higher mental and emotional functions are shut down and/or co-opted by the highly unified energy pattern, influence and intentions of the group consciousness. Human beings want to feel and be safe and to survive, so much so that they will accept any belief or situation to be true if they assume doing so will keep them safe. This is how people are indoctrinated into cults). This dynamic also happens interpersonally in marriages, for example in "battered wife syndrome" where women feel unable to leave a relationship, and may even defend an abusive spouse. (Men too can be battered spouses by the way, whether physically or emotionally). This influential dynamic creates perceived "prisons" within which our decision-making processes attempt to operate and navigate, but from which we feel we cannot safely escape.

Oddly enough, parenting of children itself can also be seen as a form of Stockholm Syndrome. Meaning that children inherently feel totally dependent upon parents for their physical and emotional survival and feel compelled to accept and model even very abusive or dysfunctional behavior their parents portray. This is especially true in the situation of a child trying to safely make sense of sexually abusive behavior in regard to their perceived identity, personal boundaries, and the nature of both family and intimate relationships at subconscious levels. This dynamic is one of the most distortive and debilitating influences of child abuse, the effects of which tend to be lifelong.

I believe it is obvious that in the past individual and consensus spiritual development has been neither rapid, simple, nor easy from our worldly incarnate viewpoint. Some believe all aspects of our development are guided by God, others believe we have free will, others believe that specific deities and ascended masters manage our developmental paths in a more "hands on" manner. Still ours is not a situation of our being controlled or forced to learn or develop by anyone. What I can say is that unconscious fate can be effectively changed into self-sovereign destiny in an instant, we need only willfully choose for this to be so. When we see with open and discerning eyes, we can realize that all that is occurring in the world—the good or bad, just or unjust, harmful or helpful—is simply fueling the fire of our individual and collective transformation.

The dynamic of karma involves our being required to see, experience, live with and learn from the results of our past choices, either immediately, later in our current life, or as some believe, in another incarnate lifetime. Through karma we gradually, lifetime after-lifetime attain higher states of spiritual consciousness, perspective, intention, understanding and love. Karma is based upon cause-and-effect, meaning that our choices and actions (the cause) create effects, outcomes or results in the world which we then experience and learn from. Each of our choices tends to create some positive and some negative karma in the form of karmic energy patterns. A concrete and common example of karma at work would be the negative emotional retribution we could receive, year after year, from a spouse we have emotionally hurt. Another would be the lifetime of negative emotional fallout of a parent abusing their child.

Karmic patterns are complex subconscious energy patterns which are stored in our individual physical bodies and emotional systems, and they function as lenses for our incarnate life force to be projected through and to view life through—a process which then creates the elements and experience of our perceived reality. These patterns are complex, multidimensional and multifaceted. We may be required to understand and integrate many subtle and seemingly disparate understandings of self, life and relationships in order to fully transcend any particular karmic pattern. Karmic patterns could be seen as simulacra.

No one ever said that attainment of enlightened self-mastery, self-sovereignty, limitless power, creative wisdom and transcendent understanding would be easy, though in fact many of us unknowingly make it much more difficult than it has to be. There are somewhat easier routes to attaining each step on the road to God consciousness, yet without the involvement of divine grace I have not seen it done without long-term effort. If someone appears to easily attain it in this lifetime that does not mean they did not have to work for a hundred lifetimes prior to this one in order to reach their current tipping point of spiritual attainment.

Negative karma could be looked at simply as karma which will involve some form of discomfort or challenge in order to eventually reach a point of new understanding. Depending upon how evolved we are personally, the choices we make will create either more or less positive and negative karmic circumstances for us to learn from. All of us, no matter how we choose to make our life choices, feed the evolution of humanity.

Paradoxically, there are even some of us who choose to play the karmic role of dictator or destroyer and through our actions directly and indirectly we still facilitate the evolution of humanity. This type of choice does not mean that the souls who take on these roles are immature or inexperienced souls, nor does it mean that these people are "evil". That said, it is true that some highly evolved souls do facilitate our development via the creation of what most would perceive as negative or wrong events or circumstances. All of our choices create circumstances from which many souls learn, therefore some good karma is created. That said, even in cases where one helps others, they can still incur some negative karma for having done so because they have, through their well-intended choices, chosen to participate in the other's negative karmic process. If you reach into the mud to pull someone out of a ditch you tend to get a little dirty in the process.

When recorded past-life patterns of perspective, belief and interpretation meet up with our current lifetime experience, this can cause misunderstood conflicts in our lives. It also creates a scenario where our current choices are affected by the old subconscious pattern. We later wonder why we chose what we did, even though in hindsight our choice did not make what we would call "logical sense". However, once we have found our way past the limiting perspectives we acquired in past lives we are far better off, and will, through our efforts, create a new plateau of conscious understanding from which to operate. The fact that most of us do not consciously remember our past lives is not a dynamic of disempowerment. In fact, not remembering past lives is very helpful, in that if we could remember all our past lives we would be totally distracted from being able to live our current lives in a well-focused and grounded manner. Past lives and their unresolved emotions and traumas can be distracting. These unresolved emotions can often lead to seeking redemption in our present lifetimes (see redemption strategies later in this book).

All that we have learned in our past lives is accessible to us at subconscious levels via our intuition—we do not lose the wisdom we have gathered across many lifetimes. This can clearly be seen in the depth of spirit of many children being born now, which could be referred to as "old souls" or indigo children. Owning our power in this world means becoming as self-aware as we can, and then applying that awareness positively, constructively and with discernment. Young soul or old, we can all do this; there is indeed a method to what may appear to be the world's madness.

The system of karma involves our being placed in specific circumstances, environments, relationships and regions of the world from lifetime to lifetime. It could be said that we are all born into the right place and the right time in order to live the lives we were meant to live, and to serve humanity to our utmost. In this way we gradually attain wisdom by constructively putting together and integrating the often seemingly conflicting pieces of information we attain from various aspects of our life experiences. Some would view this system simply and in a non-judgmental way as learning lessons; however, there is more to attaining deep life wisdom than individual lessons. In effect, it is the broader process of "connecting all the dots of our experiences and attained profound insights" that leads to pure wisdom.

Still, karma only sets the stage; we all constantly utilize the creative and unlimited power of our conscious freewill in regard to how we work with and utilize the karmic props. It is true that we "must" eventually achieve the attainment of understandings from our life experiences. Otherwise portions of our energy consciousness which have become enamored with or addicted to illusionary elements of dense reality existence will continue to remain influencing our choices (or depending upon your interpretation "we remain stuck") in lower states and frequencies of consciousness. This can go on lifetime after lifetime until we resolve the prior life misunderstanding.

If we do not attain necessary understandings that raise our consciousness then we must return to an incarnate state in order to retrieve, "heal", raise the consciousness of and integrate the elements of our energy consciousness that we have "left behind". It is true from a karmic dynamic vantage point that if we work hard and serve humanity we are in turn treated well and served by humanity. In effect, we all have vast power to directly affect our own development and that of others. In this way, we can attain great power to benefit humanity through the achievement of understandings which can vastly reduce the suffering of our species. However, if we use our power unwisely and we cause harm we may experience harm, at some point, but yet again never as a punishment.

A main reason we experience negative realities is so that we can personally understand how our previous choices felt to another person, or better understand what we caused another to experience through our choices. This is neither a situation of punishment or disempowerment. These lives represent a few brief, yet influential steps on the path of our immortal souls in their attainment of understanding of the implications of our creative power and choices from the vantage points of others, so that we can become more wise, discerning and loving.

Without these developmental experiences, we would have no reference point in understanding the true effects of our choices and thus could not learn how to love and act from love in a more evolved manner. We must learn to wisely and self-accountably use our power in a universe full of other souls who operate from free-will. Karma is also not a dynamic of systemically supported vengeance. (It is not a situation of "I hurt you now and later you get to hurt me back"). That said, many people do try to seek vengeance across lifetimes due to perceived wrongs done to them that they subconsciously remember. However, these individuals are lost in judgments of others and misperceptions of victimhood, which are only illusionary states.

Whenever we blame anyone else for anything, we unknowingly disempower ourselves by giving our power to them. Still we all have free-will at all times and can, if we choose to, try to harm others if that is our inclination. Yet if we do so we will then be required to experience lives which will lead us to understand that this type of choice is not in our or anyone else's best interest.

There are many things we can only come to understand through personal experience; karma facilitates this fundamental human learning requirement. One of the most difficult situations people can physically face is that of being born with or acquiring a handicap or disability. It is common for people with these situations to feel that life has in some way been unfair to them or that they are somehow less than they were or less than others they may see as "whole". Others may believe that their situation is the result of some prior life's negative karmic decision. I would say that each of us to a lesser or greater extent has impairments, whether mental, physical, emotional, spiritual or energetic. I would say that everyone in the world, due to their living in some degree of ignorance or constrained states of consciousness, could be said to be impaired in regard to the function of their consciousness, though most of us do not realize it. These impairments serve our soul's development and growth; none of them are punishments of any kind. We learn much from states of limitation.

The system of karma only sets up situations in which we are most optimally situated to attain our most foundational spiritual understandings, and to serve God and humanity from that vantage point. This is a very powerful process and at every step of our journey we become more empowered by it. I would suggest that any judgment of anyone else's life situation (or even of our own life) is both inaccurate and unwarranted. In any of these lives we live, the rich can suddenly become a beggar, the healthy can suddenly become lame or disfigured. These are not signs of spiritual wrongness, being less than others or not having done something right. They are only a sign that this is now our form of service to spirit, and we are challenged to make the most of it and give our best in every moment of our lives.

96

If we learn to accept all aspects of life with gracious humility and equanimity, then we can gain the most from any lifetime and situation we live within. This does not mean to say that we should passively face the challenges of life, as we are meant to apply our power, and to create and to grow from doing so. All of us are equal, all of us are worthy, all of us deserve unconditional divine love and acceptance and even spiritual reverence, at all times and in all situations. All of us are powerful, all the time; if you ever doubt this look around at the amazing world we have created. Life is a series of challenges and there is no challenge we cannot meet and transcend with enough understanding, love and willpower.

False Chaos:

Another aspect effecting global development is the proliferation of a false appearance of chaos, which some may interpret our current situations to exhibit. This means that with increased speed, variety, complexity, scope and frequency of shifts in the environment, we as individuals become less able to accurately discern patterns and order within the apparent tumult. Thus, many people may see the current climate of world development as erratic, overwhelming, fear inducing and in many ways potentially unstable.

This point is arguable; however, I do not personally see the world in this way. What I believe is missing in some people's perspectives is the information which would show the relationships and linkages between many of the events that are currently seen in the news and in daily life. If we had access to the whole picture, and from multiple vantage points, we could more accurately see how interwoven everything is, (i.e. life is actually unfolding, evolving and shifting in a purposeful manner). Life would therefore be less stressful, and more easily accepted and worked with in a positive and constructive manner, rather than being reacted to in a subconscious knee-jerk fashion. This global dynamic can be seen as the unfoldment of the often-unseen karmic process, guiding humanity's and each individual's development.

The unhelpful information that we are often privy to through the daily news on television is not complete and is therefore not accurate or optimally useful for decision-making. This is especially true if the information triggers fear or negative emotions in our systems, and many news sources purposely try to trigger these emotions, in order to motivate viewers to keep watching. The subconscious assumption we make is that we will only be "safe" if we remain informed about the most recent drama and controversial topics. Typically, we are not shown all the pieces of the puzzle simultaneously, nor do they clearly show how the pieces fit together. Dramatic and disassociated sound bites created by the media tend to non-productively cause anxiety, create confusion and raise anger levels (perhaps purposely, in order to gain viewership), rather than to simply inform. Humans do tend to react to, and tune in to, the mass production and distribution of judgmental drama and controversy, rather than constructive fact. Drama, like war, is neither a constructive nor functional model for attaining understanding or dealing with world issues or transformation.

Belief Acquisition:

A difficult byproduct of mass produced drama is its tendency to, in a way, hypnotize the viewer. This occurs when people viewing various life dramas become "overly distracted" and even overwhelmed by their emotional focus on and reactions to the presented drama. In this way drama itself can become a drug we are addicted to. At the same time this mass-produced source of misinformation or distorted information triggers many changes in people that are not beneficial.

We as humans tend to create beliefs about life and relationships from what we experience, including what we experience via mass media (television, radio, internet, movies, video games, etc.). Children used to learn from fairy tales that had some morals or virtues embedded in the story, but now our children are currently learning to base their future reality on what they are seeing online and on television, for better or worse. Once beliefs are secured in place within our systems, they tend to become subconscious, and from that point on are taken for granted to be true and accurate. Once this resulting belief acquisition occurs, we tend to identify with and thus become the belief, we then make decisions as if what we believe to be true is actually true. Thus, rather than us managing our beliefs, our beliefs manage us. We often operate this way without further refinement or questioning of the sources of our core life beliefs or understanding their implications in our lives or the lives of others we interact with.

Beliefs can literally limit what thoughts we are capable of thinking or considering, and thus limit our quality of consciousness, our flexibility, our decision-making processes and perceived options, in a time when we need to make more intelligent decisions. Simultaneously beliefs can create thoughts, emotions and behaviors which can be very destructive, as seen in situations of terrorism and relationship abuse. I would suggest that the acquisition of static, narrow and unquestioned beliefs can undermine the attainment of

98

broader and deeper understandings of ourselves, life and spirit, and are ultimately disempowering and thereby subvert the attainment of wisdom.

The domino effects of this dynamic of belief acquisition across the population of the world can be massive.

It is important to understand two things:

1. Those who produce the information we absorb are often interested in producing a specific effect in the world or in empowering their particular agenda. They are focused on this goal rather than our individual good or our attainment of personal power via our personal conscious discernment and understanding.

2. Now more of these information sources are using Neurolinguistic Programming or NLP. NLP technology is used to directly reach into the subconscious of the viewing audience. Then, via this NLP mechanism attempt to directly affect what we believe, think and feel without our consciously realizing it. In this way our thoughts, experiences, interpretations and decision-making processes are potentially fundamentally affected. This can be accomplished in regard to any specific agenda driving the process, whether it be political, religious, economic, social or business oriented.

A simple example of this capability to influence any of us, based upon currently available computer technology and NLP technology is listed below. This hypothetical example is focused on business marketing, although it could just as easily be utilized to influence your perspective on any other aspect of life:

1. You walk into a shopping mall that is equipped with security cameras and facial recognition software (this step of the process is already occurring in stores **today** by the way), thus you are immediately "identified".

2. Next a database of all of your past purchases is accessed through the credit card companies you do business with and a profile of your purchasing tendencies is referenced or is created in a real-time manner. Then data on your history of internet searches is accessed and utilized to further build and refine your profile as a shopper in real time. This information is then used to discern your personal tastes, tendencies, values, _fears_ and perceived needs.

3. A specific set of previously developed suggestion-laden NLP command infused advertisements are then displayed on video monitors in different stores as you pass by them on your way through the mall. These messages register with your subconscious mind even if you do not consciously recognize or discern their

existence or purpose. In this manner the devised system influences how you think, what you are focused upon, and triggers and creates within you a reactive emotional state and motivation of the moment, and ultimately influences your decision-making process. This process need not be able to motivate you to buy a specific item; it need only get you into the "buying mood". This can occur by triggering feelings of need that you then feel motivated to satisfy via a purchase, or by triggering feelings of personal insecurity or low self-esteem, that can supposedly be temporarily alleviated via making purchases.

4. THE RESULT IS THAT YOU BUY when and what you are influenced to buy, and that you even "feel good" about your "wise" decision. You then rationalize after the fact the benefit and necessity of the purchase.

This method and potential of manipulation of people's mental and emotional processes is true, even though it may sound like a conspiracy theory. By the way, the same technology of NLP can also act as a powerful healing agent and method of developing one's cognitive function in a rapid manner. Therefore, it represents a double-edged sword, similar to all technologies in use today. A cell phone can be used to call for help if you have a car accident, or it can be used to coordinate terrorist activities or it can be used to spy on the conversations of anyone who uses it. Still, like any sophisticated and powerful tool, NLP can either be inadvertently or purposely misused. Defining the limitations and laws in regard to how, when and where NLP can be used in communications of all kinds is incredibly complex, and difficult to do. Understandably, for many reasons this regulation is not desired by practitioners of NLP.

Due to the subtlety of NLP's method and influence, effectively policing such regulations is likely impossible. Therefore, our development of discernment regarding potential communications influences of all kinds on our lives becomes our most powerful mode of retaining self-sovereignty. If you think about how competition (competition here defined as: The desire to negate, conquer or destroy those we are in competition with), drives corporations to constantly and more intentionally try to trump each other's financial growth strategies. Does it make sense that they would use any tool, such as NLP, to gain competitive market advantage? If this is the case, is this type of subconscious influence in your best interest?

Unfortunately, once the penetrating subconscious influences of the sort that NLP can bring to bear on individuals have their influence on the world's consensus consciousness, they can be difficult to eradicate. Especially since

100

the consensus consciousness, to some degree, then affects everyone else subconsciously. This is because misguided application of this technology tends to directly undermine conscious discernment and sovereignty, and thus wise application of our personal power. This situation occurs when NLP is used to create subconscious disempowering states we are consciously unaware of.

This process can, in spiritually unsophisticated hands, be used as a weapon in the process of affecting national, political, social or corporate agendas. The technology used to move these influences directly into our lives is rapidly outstripping the degree of personal self-awareness necessary to resist or manage them. Thus we are potentially becoming less able to remain conscious and discerning, due to this broadening gap between technology and our awareness of its influence to remain sovereign, free-thinking and independently acting individuals. In this way, our freewill can be reduced and distorted. Still, it can never actually be completely taken from us.

If you look at how negative political attack ads significantly affect our views on candidates in the political process, you can see the beginnings of this influence on our lives. (These influences can even be distributed via Twitter messages). You can also see how they can influence (or determine?) which leaders we choose to lead us, and thereby affect the long-term direction of nations and ultimately our global situation. What I am alluding to is that the current mass media machine, if not wisely managed, has the potential to change humanity fundamentally without our even realizing it has occurred or how. So it is not merely the introduction of propaganda we need watch out for, it is the method of introduction of the propaganda which can be even more important.

In the past, a charismatic leader, for better or worse, could potentially motivate whole national populations to follow their directions. Today it is not so obvious a process, nor is it as easily counteracted as it might have been in the past. It is not being widely openly talked about, yet it is having its influence. I would suggest viewing all information you receive from this point on in your lives with a discerning eye, though not necessarily a skeptical or mistrustful eye. As skepticism and mistrust are only fear based dynamics, and not ultimately enlightening.

Not all the information that is being produced is necessarily intended to serve our personal good. As stated above, NLP has many positive uses which can effectively be healing, and I am certainly not suggesting that it be vilified or outlawed, since it is just a new technology, like any other; it is all in how it is managed and used. In like manner, the splitting of the atom was

101

accomplished with good intentions, and one result of the process evolved into the atomic bomb. In similar fashion NLP was originally developed and taught with good intentions, and is so powerful that it is also being used in a destructive manner.

The Transformation of Health Care:

Health care is one of the most socially and technologically transformational issues of our time. There are medical miracles and breakthroughs being announced regularly relating to creation of cures for some cancers, engineered and 3D printed human organs and body parts, and DNA targeted medicines capable of extending our life span. Simultaneously there are bacterial and viral epidemics of various kinds around the world.

National health care models around the world for delivering health care have major differences, and not all that is being learned in each is being optimally and collaboratively cross-pollinated and implemented in the others. Most industrialized nations have something close to universal health care systems, which are publicly funded as an economically and logistically practical solution to citizen's needs. Of the 191 nations, the World Healthcare Organization (WHO) ranks, the United States ranked 37 out of the 191 in quality of healthcare. According to the WHO, "France was determined to provide the best overall health care followed among major countries by Italy, Spain, Oman, Austria and Japan".

The tumultuous dynamics of the American health care system are making personal health care decisions complex and costly. In America, evolution and optimization of the health care system are now understood necessities, as its previous cost trajectory was literally projected to bankrupt the U.S. in the near future. Even with these intense motivations, change has been slow, incomplete and not satisfying to all, often hampered by polarized existing unquestioned social and political beliefs, agendas and expectations. The situation is still not resolved, yet one step toward a solution and in the direction of an Americanized version of universal health care is the still hotly debated Patient Protection and Affordable Care Act (PPACA) otherwise known as ObamaCare.

America's health care system has many fine qualities and many competing influences affecting its transformation and development as well as key demographic and cultural trends. These include economic issues, social values, special interests, issues created by a capitalist-focused and fueled health care system model, hidden profit agendas and misunderstood operational and logistical dynamics.

Social Issues:

❖ An epidemic of obesity (approximately one-third of the U.S. national population and on the rise) leading to a host of other medical issues such as heart disease and diabetes, even in the very young.

❖ A significantly increased potential for hospitalized patients to acquire highly antibiotic resistant bacterial infections (such as MSRA).

❖ Some feel that America's national food production system is becoming fundamentally unhealthy, and is being rapidly infiltrated by basically unregulated genetically modified ingredients, and is almost unregulated in terms of fat, salt and sugar.

❖ A significant lack of necessary newly trained medical professionals and doctors, in a time of rapidly increasing need for them.

Perceptions/Beliefs/Politics:

❖ A majority, though not complete cultural and political perspective that all citizens should somehow be able to receive health care in some manner. Due to the complexity of healthcare delivery our citizenry remains somewhat ignorant of the overall workings of the entire system.

❖ An initial minor shift by the medical community toward valuing preventative care as a method of reducing overall health care costs, though this approach is as yet not a keystone of the American medical model.

❖ A culture of medicine which is still not completely comfortable with, or supportive of, partnering with patients in the patient's health care decisions, or of supporting the patient's acting as their own health care advocate.

❖ A rapidly aging and politically powerful voting segment of society requiring more medical care in general, with the overall population tending to live longer and requiring more years of increasingly costly health care later in life.

Ethical Issues:

❖ A cultural and systemic tendency to spend vast amounts on medical treatments just prior to death, and to try to extend life and forestall death even at the expense of quality of life.

❖ An existing American cultural perspective that there should be no limit to the quality, duration, cost or technological extremity of medical support applied, on a per person basis.

❖ Costly "over-testing" of patients and other systemic waste and inefficiency in the health care system.

❖ A reduction in the general effectiveness of antibiotics, along with the advent of new antibiotic resistant strains of bacteria, due to over-prescription of antibiotics, incorrect usage and unnecessary mass ingestion of antibiotics via people's consumption of meat and poultry. So much so that the U.S. ecosystem's water table is now inundated with these and other medicines.

❖ An unreasoning yet powerful human fear of death and dying, which is subconsciously driving many health care decisions.

❖ The American health care system is currently not designed to effectively deal with a potential global viral pandemic, including those with a potentially high mortality rate (such as the Avian flu, Ebola, etc.). Some form of global pandemic is believed by many experts to only be a matter of time.

❖ New health care options are becoming available, such as the proliferation of medical marijuana. Another is the testing being done on the potential health benefits of the previously vilified drug heroine. Another is the now more acceptable option to take one's life, rather than living in unresolvable physical pain.

Economic Issues:

❖ Skyrocketing insurance costs.

❖ 50% of America's massive health care costs are associated with only 5% of its population.

❖ Ongoing investment in new, costly and rapidly evolving medical technology, research and acquisition of new knowledge. Many of the costs are being passed onto the patient and the citizens of the nation in various ways.

❖ The current health care system model and culture is not designed to change in an increasingly cost effective manner over time.

❖ Doctors are being required to minimize "face time" with patients to a few minutes in order to meet volume metrics necessary to pay their operating costs, which can reduce health care quality.

❖ The costly process of producing new drugs by pharmaceutical companies leads to high drug costs for consumers and massive profits for the producing industry. Yet this industry has an unwillingness to produce certain new and vital medicines or to continue producing necessary, yet non-profitable medicines.

❖ Capitalistic competition between various elements of the health care system for patient dollars, sometimes leading to:

▪ A focus on treating illness in a more expensive manner rather than preventing illness in an economical manner.

▪ "Creative" behind-the-scenes agreements among various health system elements to increase revenues in a manner that may not serve the patient.

▪ Various forms of systemic corruption, including bribery of doctors by some pharmaceutical companies to motivate doctors to "push" their products. This situation has even led to purposeful mis-prescription of drugs for illnesses they were not certified with the FDA to treat.

▪ FDA certification of some medicines that turn out to be without efficacious benefit, to have side effects worse than the illnesses they are designed to treat, or which are even hazardous to consume.

The health care industry is changing ever faster as medical knowledge and technology evolve, which makes it more difficult for citizens to be their own health care advocates, and simultaneously its design is undermining the quality of health care. There are now massive amounts of medical knowledge available on the internet to all consumers which can help people be their own health care advocates. Yet this situation can be a double-edged sword in that this information can be both empowering and potentially misleading if misinterpreted. Therefore, we consumers may assume we know more than we actually do about our physical situation based upon this information, and make unilateral decisions, without ever consulting health care professionals.

There are now many health issues for which health care professionals do not have clear and complete answers or guidance. Examples are whether breast cancer x-ray screenings really do help and at what age to have them, as well as how, when, or if it is useful to treat symptoms of menopause, and whether it is really helpful to treat many situations of diagnosed prostate cancers at all. Genetics research is promising, yet it is becoming clear that genetics is a far more complex subject than it was previously thought to be, pushing genetically based cures further into the future. (See the Internet for the latest research on epigenetics).

Medical science knows much more today than ever before, yet there are still a vast number of incomplete areas of understanding that, as of yet, have no assured answers. The aging American population will significantly affect many aspects of how medicine evolves and is administered. Medical care for the aged is, and will continue to create, massive expenditures in the midst of a currently limited economic environment. Extending life is not equal to extending quality of life, yet our discernment may become clouded when we are near death for many reasons, and every moment of even a very limited life can appear precious. Quality of life is not something that we tend to focus on in a balanced way when we are focused on our fear of death, (fear is a very consciousness obscuring emotion and influence).

As a culture, America has not yet arrived at a positive, balanced and constructive view or consensus view of death and dying. This conflicted situation is deeply and directly related to humanity's consensus consciousness fear of death and abandonment. In all of these situations we must do our best to be optimally and preemptively informed from all sources, in order to be our own best health care advocates. Our growing power of discernment is, and will continue to be, a key determinant of our experienced results.

Ripples from The Evolution of Relationship Dynamics:

We are finding that fundamental underpinnings of our lives, for example our historic roles of man, woman, husband, wife, parent and child, employer and employee no longer fit our relationship needs or working situations. Rather than merely following the life script we were handed in our early youth, as we might have done in generations past, we are being required to more often "make it up as we go". We are required to study more, make more decisions, and experience more unknowns, more confusion, more stress, and go through more trial-and-error learning. This leads to massive modifications in the basic nature of relationships, and in family structure and dynamics, which in turn affect many aspects of life and future relationships.

These relationship difficulties also drive the usage of prescription drugs to cope with our maladies and increases in various illnesses due to stress, overeating and unhealthy eating, lack of finances for adequate health care and lack of proper education, which would support healthy living. Yet this situation can also be seen as an opportunity, in that if we choose to, we can learn and develop ourselves in new ways, which will then reduce stress, redefine relationships in new and more positive ways, and learn to manage our work lives in more empowered ways. **Understand that complexity itself is a key component of stress.** If we choose to simplify our lives significantly our stress tends to be significantly reduced. It is we who have power over the degree of complexity of our lives, no one else, not the government and not the environment. It is simply our life choices, our

106

chosen beliefs, values and our understanding of the implications of our choices which create either simplicity or complexity. So, we might ask ourselves, could we simplify our lives in order to more positively and effectively manage stress?

It is useful to note that it is often the subconscious drives, emotions and goals of both genders that affect our decisions, which then create further complexity without our realizing it. These influences can even be seen in how we choose the cars we drive, the houses we own, the work we do, the clothes we wear and the technology we use. Becoming aware of what motivates us and determining whether it is worth the price we pay in terms of stress and life complexity is helpful in making wise decisions. If we approach the reduction of our life's complexity in a methodical and planned way, this streamlining process can result in life simplification which can work wonders.

We are the co-creators of our own social, business and relationship environments and therefore potentially our own stress. The world developments that are occurring and their associated stresses are not truly problems; they are merely symptoms of the results of our own previous choices, (i.e. the process of evolution of humanity), that unfold year after year, day by day. We can however, learn to improve our choices. To do this we must decide to become more conscious of when, where, how and why we make our choices. It is therefore our individual power of choice that has the potential to be our salvation, downfall or something in between. We can each choose to shift the speed and direction of human global development for the better, as individuals, at any moment. We need only realize and accept that we can have this influence, and decide what we want to create. It is simply a question of wisely and consciously choosing our priorities, values, methods, goals and actions, and also of understanding the implications of each.

We all experience many types of relationships in our lives, not the least of which is the relationship with all the various aspects of ourselves, including our mind, body, emotions and spirit. The wise understanding and management of all relationships is a key to life fulfillment and our ability to maintain our health and a positive view of life. It helps to approach any relationship we are involved in from a vantage point of love, service, discernment, sincerity, respect, gratitude, and humility (rather than fear driven egocentricity). Understanding and appreciation can only enhance our relationships.

All our relationships are constantly changing, and will continue to change, as we transform as individuals and as a species. These relationship changes also include our broader relationship with the world. This includes our relationship with our nation, the totality of humanity, our relationship to all forms of life on the planet and even our relationship to the planet itself. We are gradually learning to manage these relationships more wisely and consciously, and to appreciate them, rather than taking them for granted or as an entitlement. Learning to see ourselves as relevant and valued parts of humanity, and understanding what this shift in perspective means from a self-transformational standpoint is important. Arriving at an understanding of ourselves as part of the larger and developing system of this planet (inclusive of all life and all species on the planet), rather than as the owners or rulers of this planet, is also a necessary shift in understanding. In fact, this change in perspective is a key element of the transformation of global consciousness that is occurring.

We Are The Influencers:

For humanity, there is more at stake now than ever before, particularly in terms of the either positive or negative potential global outcomes of our choices. In fact, it is this growing awareness that is driving each of us to show ourselves and each other just how powerful we are. We are learning that we as individuals have both the power and the influence to affect large-scale situations and outcomes. Our wills, knowledge and intentions are being manifested in physical reality much more rapidly and powerfully today than ever before, and in ways we could not have foreseen just a few years ago.

Usually we do our best to be wise in our process of creating and manifesting. Yet we sometimes blindly apply our power, without ever asking if doing so is truly for the common good of the society or the planet. This newly developing global capability of consciously and wisely managing what we manifest is something we must all eventually master. For most of us it requires a great deal of hard work, will power and determined intention to achieve this. It can happen almost instantly, however in these cases, the state of heightened understanding and awareness we achieve either may not last or may be intermittent. Meaning the person described still periodically functions from a state of fear and judgment or can still become entrained in other's dramas and agendas.

Some of the initial steps in the attainment of this state of personal mastery are to transcend:

1. All our primal states of consciousness and negative emotion, including safety, survival and control strategies.
2. Societal, cultural and family conditioning.

3. Negative reactive tendencies, fear projections and simulacra projection driven misinterpretations.

4. Tendencies to project our personal beliefs and patterns and family karmic patterns onto our lives and relationships.

5. All tendencies to create and hold onto beliefs, and to use them in our decision-making strategies, rather than remaining constantly conscious in the present moment

6. All aspects of Victim/Perpetrator/Rescuer dynamics and tendencies to be judgmental.

7. Dualistic interpretative tendencies, (i.e. to see life through the limiting and simplistic and polarizing lenses of good/bad, always/never, right/wrong, us vs. them, safe and unsafe.

This attainment requires one to become optimally self-aware and to work through their personal illusions about life, self and relationships. Otherwise these influences will at some point cause us to be reactively pulled back down into lower states of consciousness, possibly without our realizing it. I suggest patience with oneself in these developments, they are achievable in the long run, still they take time and consistent diligent effort; they are worth the struggle.

The attainment of self-mastery could be described variously as a process of CONSISTENTLY (depending upon which aspect we may be looking at):

❖ Opening, clearing and developing our higher consciousness.

❖ Operating from a state of unconditional love and equanimity.

❖ Attaining wise discernment along with consistent balance in all aspects of our being and our external life.

❖ Disengaging from the influence and misperceptions of the global consciousness, and national or family consciousness's energy dynamics.

❖ Obtaining consistent, impeccable spiritual support in maintaining our spiritual consciousness. (i.e. support from God, Christ, Buddha, Angels, or other highly evolved spiritual beings, etc.)

❖ Developing various intuitive or psychic abilities which are directly supportive of discernment, which give us the capacity to understand and consistently maintain evolved states of consciousness and to access new levels of spiritual information.

❖ Attaining practical and functional conscious self-sovereignty and self-authorizing empowerment.

❖ Transcending all primal and illusionary states of consciousness.

❖ Completely healing and learning our way through our soul's karmic evolutionary and developmental path.

❖ Healing all of what we perceive to be the wounds of our soul.

❖ Integrating the totality of our being into a conscious whole.

❖ Self-educating all aspects of our being to function congruently, harmoniously and in a sophisticated and conscious manner.

❖ Harmonizing with all aspects of self and the universe and resolving all internal and external conflicts.

❖ Shifting to a spiritually transcendent state of consciousness in order to permanently become one with God, all of humanity and the universe.

❖ Becoming more multidimensional in our awareness, yet in an integrated way.

If we continue to interpret life experiences, make decisions, act on or be motivated by fear, anger, guilt, hatred or greed we will literally be unable to function in a consistently consciously discerning manner. In order for humans, as a total species, to get to this state of intentional and willful transcendence, we must first make an informed decision to do so. Being able to make this decision in a committed manner from which we will not later fall back does require us to foundationally accept that it is not beneficial for us or those we love to function in negative emotion-driven ways.

Most of us have been evolving through experienced-based, yet unconscious trial and error methods, for many lifetimes. One of our goals has been to consciously realize the problems of functioning in this way. Another is to develop the methods for attaining and maintaining sage discernment within a social context. This positive attainment is not one which we want to exhibit only periodically, it is important to achieve it in an unwavering, consistent manner. Many people fall back into negative states for long periods of time after having gotten a brief view of this positive state of consciousness.

Attainment of conscious discernment is not precisely achieved via a specific "learned method". Accomplishing it requires us to be very consistently self-aware, which shifts us into a mode of constantly acquiring information about how our system is functioning emotionally, mentally, spiritually and energetically. Ultimately mastery of this maintainable state is highly beneficial, in order to help us constructively and positively keep up with the speed of world change. With great power comes great responsibility, as well as potentially great joy or great sorrow. Time is truly of the essence in this uniquely individual development.

We could envision life and relationships on this planet as a vast construct of dominos. In this game of life, each of us is constantly falling this way and that as we make decisions. In so doing we affect many other's lives, sometimes at great distances, and over remarkably long periods of time. The awareness of our influence upon one another, our complete interdependence, and the need for creative teamwork in this ongoing dynamic bring with it some of the most important understandings we can attain. Learning to manage our new found power constructively and discerningly is of ever greater importance. It is indeed a vast and wonderful opportunity that we all can and will share in.

We Fear Our Own Power:

Many of us do not feel safe, right or validated in the independent application of our freewill choice and personal power in the world and in our relationships. Many of us often harshly judge ourselves for our usage of our personal power, after we have applied it, especially if we have applied our power in anger or seen negative results. If we do judge ourselves we may feel guilt, shame or may even feel anger toward ourselves. This process of self-judgment and self-criticism of our usage of our personal power then tends to motivate us to repress our power and not to trust our own decision-making. This is especially true in relationships that do not work out. Unfortunately, this suppression of our power tends to occur in a generalized manner, rather than just in regard to specific situations. Therefore, we limit ourselves far more than is warranted by the results of our prior usage of our power. We also apply this self-suppression of our power, rather than trying to find a way to apply our power in positive ways. This self-suppression is often subconscious, rather than consciously accomplished.

Many of us also tend to try to repress our negative emotions, because we have a part of ourselves that feels it is not right or appropriate to feel negative emotions in general. Many of us have been conditioned to judge any negative emotion as wrong or bad. This dynamic tension between our desire to apply our power, and our judgments of how we apply our power then keeps our reactive negative emotions bottled up and unresolved. Simultaneously this internal process of conflict between different parts of ourselves deprives us of our capacity to be consciously *self-authorizing* in our usage of our power.

We may feel that others do constantly apply their power toward us or our lives, and we may, in reaction, feel fearful and resentful. This fearful emotional reaction can be especially intensely felt if we have chosen not to allow ourselves to express our personal power. So, we then feel vulnerable and unable to defend ourselves. The problem is that we inaccurately determine, that we cannot safely and harmoniously apply our personal power to the world around us, or to those we interact with. If we learn to forgive ourselves and process out our negative emotions rapidly, and forgive how others apply their power in our lives, then our power is immediately and always consciously available to us. We become able to peacefully and constructively apply our power in all areas of our lives. This ongoing dynamic is the process via which we learn to discerningly and consciously and successfully apply our power, over time, and through the process of relationship.

In every nation and culture there are literally thousands of social and interpersonal rules and norms affecting individual's choices of how we apply our power from moment-to-moment. They also affect how we feel about using our power. Social rules do not directly foster independent conscious thought and awareness, yet in the name of social control we inhibit our usage of our personal power. Most of us have learned through our early life experience to fear social or interpersonal sanction, judgment, punishment or abandonment as a potential result of the application of our power.

We have not often been taught, especially not by our society, how to creatively, constructively and consistently apply our personal power to its maximum potential. We often lack confidence in the free and creative application of our personal power on a daily basis, and may fear being considered different or even radical in our views. In effect, many of us have been "taught" to fear and distrust our own power.

It is true that when we are children that these social rules can be helpful guidelines. These guidelines are our society's social educational device for training and maintaining the society in a mode of operation that is hopefully both productive and peaceful. Unfortunately, these rules can then turn into an unseen prison of fear and judgmentalness from which many of us never escape. These rules and norms should be looked at as more of a set of "training wheels", designed to support us as we learn our way into a state of independent, sovereign and conscious wisdom and effective use of our personal power. Once we learn to manage our own style of conscious sovereign decision-making in alignment with spirit, we become freely and independently empowered. Then we no longer need the support of this social educational system and we can thus dispense with the training wheels.

In the long run these subconscious rules are no substitute for conscious understanding as our guiding decision-making principle. Looking to any simplistic set of rules as the source mechanism for making our life choices is not only severely limiting, it is also detrimental to our active process of learning from our experiences. Nor does it support the dynamic of world transformation that is now occurring. How many social, group or family rules are you affected by in any given day? How much do these rules affect your interpretations, decisions, actions, emotions and stress levels? Do these rules directly support you in achieving your life goals? I suggest meditation upon this situation and being willing, at least in some cases, to wisely define your own set of life rules which do better support your needs and goals. I am not, by this recommendation advocating mindless or harmful choices, nor am I advocating lawlessness. I am speaking in unshakable faith in the potential that all human beings can become more loving, wise and compassionate beings. This attainment requires optimal freedom from the preexisting and prescribed limitation of social rules and norms, and openness to our own God-given creative understanding of our lives. If we want our children to learn to be powerful in their own lives, we must first teach ourselves to be powerful in our own.

There are many hidden benefits to the global stresses we are currently experiencing, and in effect these stresses are forming, reforming and evolving us, and our society, in the crucible of the worldly results of our own intentions. This act of rapidly perceiving and understanding the results of our choices is effectively requiring us to become more discerning. This achieved discernment is the key to wisely utilizing our personal power to successfully resolve all the issues we face as individuals in our world today.

Chapter Four
Self-Sovereignty in the Age of the Individual:

ATTAINMENT OF SELF-SOVEREIGNTY IS OF GREAT IMPORTANCE. Self-sovereignty is a method of conscious overall life and relationship management; it is also a fundamental requirement for our spiritual attainments. It is the process of becoming who you most want and need to be, and of living the life experiences you choose and of being the most authentic you. For certain emotional, energetic and spiritual developments to occur within us we must be able to independently and willfully think and decide for ourselves at every moment of our lives, and at every level of our being, exactly what is most right or good for us. To attain self-sovereignty, we must function in a non-conflicted and internally unified manner, completely independent of the influences of our families, culture, laws and other facets of life. We must also be fully accountable for managing all aspects of our moment-by-moment emotional process. In this way, we can live in a maintainable state of constant inner peace and serenity.

External influences serve a purpose in daily practical life, yet they may directly impede or distract us from attaining complete spiritual focus and life fulfillment. The often-lifelong effort of attaining conscious sovereignty goes against most cultural and family influences, as well as the very natural herd instinct of humanity to group together and conform to the culture's beliefs and expectations. Self-sovereignty is not self-centeredness; it is being totally centered within oneself and making all decisions from this balanced and self-aware point. The main reasons for our tendency to group together in non-sovereign ways are the influences of the two underlying primal fears that everyone has, which arise from the influence of what is called the root chakra in the human energy system of chakras.

(See chapter nine for a more in-depth description of chakras and their influence).

Our two main fears are:

1. The fear of death, in all its forms and all its implications. This fear includes the fear of associated physical suffering and debilitation that we project or assume could occur on the way to dying. This fear includes the fear of the pain of loss and lack we assume we may feel if someone else we care about dies. It is vital to understand that it is this fear that is the core emotional dynamic that validates killing in all of its forms.

2. The fear of abandonment in all its forms. Including abandonment by those we love and depend upon, by parental or authority figures, or even abandonment by society in general. This fear includes the fear of the associated pain and loss we assume we will feel in situations of perceived abandonment. We can also fear that abandonment can bring about the loss of social or personal safety, security, control, power or status via the death of someone else, such as our parent or our spouse. Many of us have fears of not being good enough, of being less than others, of not being lovable or acceptable. All of these fears are simply reflections of the root fear of abandonment. We can even fear abandoning ourselves through self-judgment, self-blame or shame, guilt and self-hatred.

All other fears we experience stem from or are reflections of these two basic primal fear states. If we understand this, and face these two fears, then all other perceived fear states lose their power over us. I would suggest that the influence of these two fears be neither underestimated nor overlooked on one's path of spiritual development, as well as in one's basic way of living life and making decisions. These fears will affect everyone at some point in their lives and it is best to be well prepared beforehand.

The sooner we constructively face and work through these fears, the sooner we will be freer to live, create what we want in our lives, develop spiritually and enjoy life. These fears cannot be successfully extricated from our lives by either suppression, denial, by simply being "courageous" or by sheer will power. If we attempt to apply these less than functional methods to fear management then our fears will continue to influence our interpretations of our experience and our decision-making at some level, often subconsciously. Most of the time we won't realize it has happened, but the results of our decisions will, in general, be of lower quality and less fulfilling than we consciously hoped if we make choices in fear. We might even inaccurately attribute our lack of positive results in our lives to external social or relationship conditions or we may feel victimized by life because our interpretations of life are distorted by fear. This is the profound power of our primal subconscious or more accurately (from an energetic standpoint) the potentially dysfunctional influence of our root chakra, which is the part of our systems tasked with survival and safety management.

Chakras are centers of subtle energy within and around our bodies, and from our chakras emanate the layers of our auras or subtle bio-energy fields. Chakras are also centers of consciousness, awareness, information processing and decision-making, and they store recorded patterns, interpretations of experiences, information and beliefs that we acquire throughout our lifetime.

116

Our major chakras are located along our spine and the beliefs and patterns they absorb define and even distort the information that reaches our brains and our minds from moment-to-moment.

The root chakra is the simplest major "in body" chakra and it functions in very simple ways. The root chakra sees all of life in "black and white" polarities. For example, root chakra function sees life only from the vantage points of true/false, right/wrong, good/bad, safe/unsafe, life/death, perfect/imperfect, accepted/abandoned, in control/out of control, always/never. This obscuring process has profound influences on our learning and our interpretation of our life experience from moment-to-moment. Meaning that life is far more complex than any polarized view can conceptualize. Therefore, the influence of the root chakra is tremendously limiting and distorting, while supposedly being the mechanism that keeps us safe and empowered in life.

It is the root chakra that motivates fundamental distrust between all people's. Our human tendencies to buy into fear based worst scenario thinking as well as conspiracy theories of all kinds, do damage to the collective of all societies. We do need positive change in this world, NOW, still fear is not the optimal driver for this progressive change, nor is it a constructive method of solving problems, nor is the violence fear often engenders and blindly motivates a solution.

The root chakra is also the "root driving mechanism" of all judgmentalness and fear. From the root chakra standpoint, if we do not have safety, recognition, approval, attention and social/relationship status then **we will die or be abandoned, or both**. (It is not a situation of I may die. It literally imaginarily projects that the situation of being out of control, and the lack of control, will invariably result in danger and ultimately our death). It is these simplistic subconscious dynamics that rationalize and lead to killing in all its forms. It is a simple form of subconscious "if this then that" dysfunctional logic. (i.e. If I am not in control of my life I could die or be abandoned OR If I do not have social status then I am worthless OR If I do have social status then I can have money, power, safety, etc.) It is dysfunctional logic because life is never this simple. It is then our attempt to escape these projected feared results that keeps us chasing after safety, control, fame, etc. If we are lost in this dynamic, there can be no trust of others, ourselves or God, no matter what we do. These subconscious primal patterns and thought processes cannot conceptualize the oneness of all humanity. As long as we are in the reactive emotional space of trying to

117

protect ourselves or anyone or anything, we cannot become fully conscious, because we are living in fear, because fear cannot be conscious.

Due to the influence of our previously acquired beliefs, acting within our chakras, the function of our chakras tends to preemptively literally define what we will think (and what we <u>can</u> think), feel, experience, interpret or come to understand consciously. Therefore, keeping our chakras clear and balanced is vitally important if we want to have a clear mind, clear emotions, make wise decisions and have a clear energy system. Our chakras fundamentally influence what we experience and how we interpret and understand all aspects of our life experience and how we choose to act or react. Practically speaking chakras are the energetic vehicle of our soul's evolution via their influence on our process of learning from moment-by-moment life experience.

The root chakra emanates from our tailbone and governs our fight-or-flight decision-making, as well as our perceptions of our status in all of our relationships, families and community. It is the driving mechanism of our wanting to feel or be superior, better than others, or above them. Therefore, its fundamental and often unrecognized insecurity is the emotional source and motivation for all types of social and business elitism. The root chakra also manages our perceptions of our personal safety from moment-to-moment, which then drives our desire to control all aspects of our lives and relationships due to unresolved fears and insecurities we hold.

Although it is a simple chakra, the root is tasked with maintaining our physical and social survival, thus it can totally and <u>literally override</u> our upper level chakra thinking, interpretive processes and decision-making (i.e. our capacity to love and understand) via the fear energy it produces (meaning the 4th, 5th, 6th, and 7th chakras). This is evidenced whenever we reactively and mindlessly run from perceived danger or blindly and unwisely strike out at others when we feel threatened. This situation can also be seen when our fears override our compassion and sensitivity toward others, or when we are unwilling to be open to others because we project our fears onto them (i.e. distrust them). The root chakra's influence can therefore override all "higher thoughts" and states of consciousness, positive philosophies, loving spiritual values, or socially positive behavior.

Below is a diagram of the seven major chakras:

The Seven Major Chakras

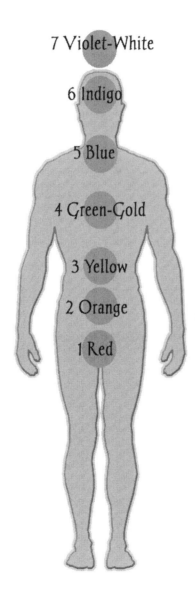

7 Violet-White

6 Indigo

5 Blue

4 Green-Gold

3 Yellow

2 Orange

1 Red

The root chakra can directly and fundamentally influence what we believe and perceive to be true in our moment-by-moment experience of life. If a root chakra belief or fear pattern (a simulacrum) is triggered by an environmental or relationship situation, it instantly projects onto that situation whatever the root chakra believes to be true or fears could be true. Thus, we see what we believe to be true, rather than what truly is occurring, and then make erroneous decisions based upon this false data. This can occur even if our subconscious projections are totally inaccurate, significantly maladaptive or harmful to ourselves or others. This root mechanism is the source of all violence in humanity.

The root chakra is also the portion of our system which is triggered by fear-based political rhetoric and social dramas and any type of social or interpersonal controversy. The root chakra is extremely powerful and at the same time subtle in its effects on our consciousness and our emotions. The short-sighted and primal root chakra is the least sophisticated of our seven main "in body" chakras. We need not allow our root chakra's, fear and safety seeking motivations to highjack our minds, our lives, our emotions and our relationship decision-making. However, if we do not consciously intervene in the root chakra's instinctive style of reaction, we can be sure that at some point it will intervene in our lives. Our self-sovereignty is literally dependent upon the discerning use of our conscious mind's capacity to govern our primal emotional reactions and influence on our decisions. Conscious discernment is dependent upon accurate interpretation of experience, relationships, facts, emotions and information, as well as our capacity to subtract all negative emotions from our decision-making. If our root chakra distorts or even shuts down this precious capability, then we instantly lose much of our sovereignty.

In the past, the concept of sovereignty has usually been applied to governments, and those persons in positions of power that run them. It could be said that the United States is a "sovereign nation". So, within its borders, the United States makes its own rules, laws and decisions. Therefore, for the most part, other nations are not allowed to interfere in American's way of life or to define these internal processes for Americans. This is not to say that other nations, groups and individuals do not diligently work to affect or influence America's internal national systemic function. I am only stating that as a sovereign nation America is free and even duty bound to do its best to stop them from doing so, if Americans wish to retain their way of life, national sovereignty and cultural identity. This same statement is true of all other nations. I would however also say that each individual American has the same right and the same duty to themselves to manage and retain their self-sovereignty.

Self-sovereignty requires discernment, self-awareness and self-accountability and is a consciously willful process. It is not a license to unilaterally do whatever we choose in life. It is factual to say that our God given right to freewill allows us to literally make any social or personal choice we want, still there will always be consequences for doing so. It is simply true that when we function in a discerningly self-aware and sovereign fashion that there is less need for laws and rules of social conduct, since we tend to operate in wise and respectful ways by self-aware choice.

Consensus Consciousness Responses:

Every human being has a root chakra. Interestingly every nation, organization, religion and corporation also has a root chakra energy center. This means that as a collective consciousness they each have an ego, an ego-identity and a primal survival reaction to perceived threat or attack and a desire to protect and control their environment. All nations and all groups of people with a shared consciousness or "consensus consciousness" can fear for their survival and therefore make decisions out of ignorant blind fear. We could look at this as a simple fight or flight reaction which fundamentally colors and distorts the nation's decisions.

We can see how the United States' consensus consciousness root chakra reacted in fear and anger to the 9/11 attack on the New York World Trade Centers. Its response was both swift and deadly in its method of rationalizing and then waging war with Iraq, although like most root chakra decisions it was not as wise a response as might have been hoped for. Yet once the root chakra is triggered its reactions tend to fully run their course, before our conscious minds are once again feel safe enough to become engaged. In this situation America's citizens in a way gave up some of their self-sovereignty and some of their previous freedoms in order to "fight" the perceived enemy, possibly to their future detriment.

Some of the initially unforeseen or even purposely overlooked initial costs of the Iraq war are: (These numbers do not include costs since the war of battling ISIS or other terrorist factions).

- ❖ Over 1 trillion dollars (spent both abroad and at home to support the original war effort).
- ❖ In addition to the deaths on 9/11 in the United States, 4,000 American soldiers' lives lost.

121

❖ Over 32,000 soldiers physically wounded.

❖ Approximately 100,000 civilian Iraqi deaths (I would ask if the reader sees these civilian deaths as equal in value to American deaths).

❖ Continued conflict in the region that has since spread to multiple other nations, including Libya and Syria of late.

Whether one supported the war with Iraq or not, this discussion is not a judgment either for or against the results or the people involved in the conflict. This is simply a quick review of the role of the root chakra and the energetic and emotional dynamics the chakra creates in international politics and decisions related to war and other forms of violence. It is just as accurate to say that terrorists, in their own way are motivated by the root chakra's influence.

It is useful to realize that the negative root chakra reaction of those who were predisposed to terrorism has since created the various terror networks. The newer terrorist factions are becoming far more virulent. You could look at this as a form of reactive evolution of terrorist networks. In that various nations, and we as individuals, are inadvertently spawning more intensely negative terrorists, due to our own escalating destructive actions and hatred of the terrorists. There are of course far more costs that have been incurred, including social, human and financial, in the fighting that has occurred since the Iraq war. It may be that the most powerful way to keep terrorist networks from growing is simply to contain them, without trying to engage or destroy them. Oddly enough such a sage reaction to terrorist activities goes directly against our root chakra wish to control and destroy them, and so may not "sell well" politically to various nation's citizens. Of course, it is understandable that all people simply want to feel and remain safe and accomplishing this goal is becoming more complex.

In this section I have described the dynamics of root chakra function in individuals and in nations, and worked to illustrate how they lead to real-world events and costs. It is beneficial for us to understand this series of reactive steps if we are to ultimately transcend fear-based decision-making and action and thus outgrow war and violence as a method of managing human affairs. It is also necessary for us to transcend our fears if we wish to function as conscious sovereign individuals and to enjoy our lives fully. The landscape of the world is currently troubled. This global situation represents the **seeds of our karma** which have been previously sown to inspire us to act from a mindful, advanced and discerning perspective. This type of perspective is not possible from the limited and thus limiting vantage point of the root chakra. Still, the root chakra perspective can be transcended and ultimately will be by all.

All individual human beings, regardless of the circumstances we were born into, have been given freewill by our creator and subsequently are sovereign beings. That divinely given right cannot be taken away by any earthly authority, nor can it be overcome by any application of power, influence, manipulation or force applied to an individual. Yet many people alive today are unaware of their unchangeable sovereign status and its importance in their spiritual development and evolution. In fact, many may unknowingly choose to reduce their self-sovereignty in exchange for a variety of compensations which they erroneously believe are somehow more important.

One example of this tendency would be in the case where one person marries another for financial or physical security rather than love. I would not describe this as a situation of "emotionally selling out" as much as prioritizing root chakra values and focus over the emotion of love or even spiritual values and intentions. It is useful to realize that marrying for love is a relatively new invention of Western society. There are many areas of the world where marriages are still arranged by families. It is the root chakra's fear reaction tendencies that lead to what are called "honor killings" in these areas, when a family's children disobey the tradition.

This same root chakra influence also occurs in political circles, when some politicians choose to allow the function of their offices to be overtly influenced by lobbyists of corporations or representatives of special interests that are funding them. In effect, they may have chosen to prioritize their financial gain or support for reelection above higher principles, social need and love for the people of their country. Some would look at this "choice of focus" as corruption or even treason, yet I suggest that judging these people or the practice will not stop the practice, nor make the world a better place. I would suggest looking at this behavior as an indicator of these politicians not having developed their spiritual consciousness to the point where they can clearly see the comprehensive drawbacks and consequences of their choices. Whether in regard to the nation or to their own karmic progress.

I would also suggest asking ourselves as citizens the following question. What can we do in our governmental management efforts to ensure that such activities do not occur in the future? I would also ask why do we tolerate such rampant disruptive activities and unwise decision-making in the process of national governance? The answers to these questions will, in part, require that our politicians literally be trained in a standardized educational environment prior to holding office. This is a far superior process to our current, somewhat arbitrary system, of choosing from a pool of political candidates that have simply chosen to be our leaders, without standardized education or mentored experience in a certified environment.

Another example can be seen on a national scale in how Americans make decisions related to their personal safety and security. It is probably obvious, especially in these times of global fear of terrorism, that most individuals are willing to give up some personal freedoms, such as privacy, if they believe that in return they will remain safe or at least be safer than if they had not given them up. With discernment, it is also obvious that no one in our world is or ever will be completely truly safe in the absolute sense of the word. Any one of us could die at any time for a limitless number of reasons. However, we do constantly make many of our personal decisions in the ultimately vain attempt to retain at least the semblance or feeling of safety and security. In this pursuit, individuals weigh, often in an inaccurate fashion, what they see as the value of a continued state of safe living for themselves and their loved ones against the loss of certain freedoms. This fear driven process can, over time, erode our fundamental freedoms.

I believe it useful to note that the true odds of any individual American citizen actually dying in a terror related situation on U.S. soil are remote and not just because of America's diligent anti-terrorism efforts. However, when individual Americans work through the steps of making their decisions about what freedoms they are willing to give up, they often fail to accurately weigh the true probability of negative occurrence affecting them and those they love. Because Americans are used to looking at themselves through the lens of their national consensus consciousness, they may also mis-interpret, assume or imagine that attacks on any part of their nation are in some way potential threats to them personally. In effect, they "emotionally project themselves" outwardly onto the population of the nation via the consensus consciousness.

This type of reactive and projected fear-based reaction can cause even people who live in rural undeveloped areas of the U.S., where the probability of a terrorist attack is close to zero, to live in constant fear and to see negative possibilities and threats all around them. This can be seen in the development of unofficial United States state militias, which are generally not of value (or are "of no value"). Yet some people do believe that they will be more secure if the such militias exist.

Certainly, there are places in the world, such as certain areas of Latin America, where rurally located people are under constant threat from gangs

124

or criminals associated with drug lords, and their efforts to work together to protect themselves are literally crucial if they are to survive. I would distinguish these situations by looking at actual physical results that can be readily seen, factually supported or statistically evaluated (rural Americans do not generally see the bodies of their neighbors piling up daily or ongoing direct acts of torture or coercion). This comparison illustrates the difference between projected imagination and survival-oriented fact. It is useful to realize that this fear can also push some people to become "super patriots" and to judge and negatively admonish anyone they do not see doing or believing the same things they do.

One caveat to this situation is that there are corporate forces in the United States which I feel are "on the attack" in regard to the rural farmer, in that they are developing genetically modified seeds they have patented, and which they are then strategically requiring farmers to buy and use in specific highly controlled ways. Farmers who do not purchase new batches of genetically modified and disease resistant seed each year from the corporations are not allowed to save and replant any harvested seed grown from the prior year's crop, as farmers have been doing for thousands of years. This monopolistic situation may lead to the end of small independent farms and their more assuredly healthy non-genetically modified crop yields.

This same dynamic may also affect farmers around the world as the use of genetically modified seed spreads. It may be that we are approaching a more significant problem than just whether or not to genetically modify foods. It may be that we are fast approaching a level of technology-based competition and control in the world which can lead to detrimental product monopolies, limitation on future product development and destruction of what we have previously called day-to-day life for many. If someone creates and patents a new technology that then manifests many detrimental ripples in the economy and thereby destroys other elements of society in the process of its proliferation, is that a good thing? (e.g. Some people feel that pesticides are detrimentally and widely affecting bee populations). Question: Is there any adequate law on the books that can manage this situation of insecticides affecting bee populations?

How do we balance the current good of humanity in relation to the potential good that new technology brings? How do we manage ownership of genetic patterns, when allowing ownership can have such limiting consequences? Patenting genetics is becoming common at this time (even patenting human genes). Yet there may be unforeseen consequences of this legally supported process which go far beyond mere profit and ownership

125

issues. If the legal system and government regulation are far behind in understanding corporate and individual technological development, who will govern the creation of our futures, and how will they accomplish this, and how can we as individuals retain empowering understanding and influence in this developing process? The science of "extrapolating the implications" of any of our choices or actions onto our world's future is growing rapidly more complex. Discernment is a skill that is vital in this process if we want quality results and to avoid problems.

There is currently inadequate information on the potentially detrimental effects of genetically modified foods on our physical health necessary to determine what the long-term influence of this situation could be. The same is true of the potential for mass laboratory produced meat which is now on the horizon. This situation of unmanaged technological development could be seen, in a way, as "bodies piling up" in the process of new technology influences on world transformation.

Again we as individuals may in certain situations imagine a highly unlikely negative possibility, outside of its true probability or context, and then base our personal power, decision-making and resources on that imagined potential to our detriment. In this tendency toward fear-based projection onto reality we may be "helped" by fear inducing political rhetoric, detrimental social influences, detrimental corporate public relations and mass media hype. Deep discernment, based upon complete information in everyday life is imperative if we want to effectively navigate and adapt to a rapidly changing, complex and conflicted world.

These scenarios illustrate just how many detrimental, distortive and nebulous influences we can meet up with which can potentially undermine our discernment. In these situations, people of significantly divergent backgrounds, beliefs (whether conscious and subconscious), feelings, perspectives, agendas, motivations and intentions meet in ongoing conflict. In this way they compete for agendas, goals, priorities, power, territory, money and their individual definitions of what it means to be spiritual and to live in freedom. The same situation can be seen to be replicated in many areas around the world, and all of these situations need to be optimally navigated if we want optimal global results.

As previously stated, the messages we receive via the news media these days are often designed more to make money, create destructive drama, punish someone, take or hold territory or the moral "high ground" or to support political agendas rather than to inform, support or protect us. Often social dysfunction-creating political communications have been carefully designed and scripted to optimally trigger our fears and imaginations and drive us like a herd of spooked cattle. These "fear projectors" would rather spook us than consciously unite us in a constructive loving vision of who we can become as nations and as a world.

The primary reason for this dynamic of distorted information transfer by the media is their conscious or subconscious intention to affect our decision-making processes in such a way as to get us to willingly support their agendas (without in depth questioning). In this way, they hope to motivate us to passively agree to the loss of valuable freedoms or to put our consciousness and personal power on a shelf to collect dust. We are being intentionally triggered and even conditioned over time to function only from the low level of our personal root chakras and to discard our own higher level spiritual perspective and astute discernment.

This triggering of our root chakra creates a sort of fear-based tunnel vision on what others in positions of influence want us to focus on, similar to the way magicians distract their audience in order to allow them to fool us without being observed. Due to our tunnel vision, which is subsequently fixed upon the imagined negative future, we lose emotional balance and accurate mental perspective in terms of fully realizing the broader and longer term negative implications of the loss of our personal freedoms. In effect, we give up some of our sovereignty without recognizing it has happened. Yet we may not choose to deeply explore these decisions and their implications in the heat of the moment. With today's life and economic pressures, information overload and complexity, we may simply feel too overwhelmed to do so. Then we may later rationalize that we had no other choice in the matter and move on in life without fully realizing what happened or effectively addressing the past detrimental situation. Thus, we do not learn from the experience.

The Illusion of Safety:

This willingness to give up sovereign rights and freewill is replicated in a variety of ways across the globe in all nations, not just the democratic ones, and it is often insidiously gradual, with rationalizations provided for the losses at each step of the way. The reason for this is that even in dictatorships many people would rather live with limited freedoms and significant governmental controls than to be made to feel, or believe themselves to be unsafe by their own government. So, in effect, the decision on the part of the individual is the same in both situations. In both governmental situations, we are trading the illusion of safety from what we have been trained to fear for

127

an actual loss of freedom. The only difference is that the decision is being made within a different or more extreme governmental context. The perceived threat which drives the fear based decision may actually be internal to the nation and government, rather than originating from external sources. (i.e. See the current situations in many nations that are raising the fear of external threats to their citizens in order to retain the current political regime).

I believe it is important to note here that the descriptions of sovereignty and issues affecting our self-sovereignty listed above are indeed more complex than can be fully described in this text. However, my intention is to present their relevance and influence on the process of maintaining human freedoms and of consciously attaining spiritual and worldly goals.

If we wish to better perceive the broader picture of what is happening in the world regarding our sovereignty, we could start by entertaining the following concepts:

❖ That any external or internal influence on our daily decision-making which renders us unable to freely and consciously choose at any moment what we want to do, is, in some way, taking away a portion of our sovereignty. This includes all influences that trigger fear in us.

❖ Any person, relationship, situation, belief, philosophy, religion, marketing campaign, corporation, institution or government which tries to make decisions for us, or to influence our decision-making without our consent or understanding is directly undermining our sovereignty and our freewill.

This process of influencing or even actively undermining our personal decisions via manipulation of our emotional triggers goes on constantly from a wide variety of sources. These include marketing, political and social propaganda, misinformation and interpersonal manipulations. I would simply suggest we insure that we are fully aware of what we are actually incorporating into our beliefs and thoughts as "true" each day, and how and why it affects our choices, lives, freedoms and personal power.

Managing Our Self-Sovereignty:

Many of us have either become numbed to life's influences or simply haven't deeply considered them or their implications in the past. However today, in the age of the individual, individual power is scaling up rapidly. Understanding the nature, preciousness and vulnerability of our self-sovereignty is growing more important. It is just as crucial to understand how to consciously develop and maintain our self-sovereignty, since to one degree or another we are the ones accountable for all our choices, and how they work to manifest our future life. This does not mean that we may in some way draw any future punishment to ourselves for our choices via karma. It only means that we do literally create our future reality through our choices and actions, whether it be five minutes in the future or five lifetimes.

This is the price of the vast creative power to manifest reality we all possess and wield daily and why it is necessary to make our choices with discernment, patience, love and wisdom. None of us are victims of anyone or anything. Other people do influence us, our choices and our development, sometimes destructively. Yet we are all still powerful sovereign beings and accountable to ourselves for our actions from lifetime to lifetime, which determine our paths of spiritual evolution. Accepting this is a key to truly being empowered and spiritually mature, since when we accept that we are the creators of our futures, we learn to create wisely and accountably and in ways that truly do please and serve us. In these actions of creating ourselves, our experiences and our world self-judgment or judgment of others has no purpose or validity.

The steps to attaining self-sovereignty are complex and subtle, yet none of them are beyond our individual ability. Self-sovereignty must be managed at all levels of our being, including our minds, emotions, bodies, energy systems and our souls. If we overlook any of these key areas or leave them to chance or on subconscious automatic, we may unknowingly be placing ourselves in circumstances where our freewill and our life choices are reduced. Then we will be required to live with the results of our unconscious choices. Even to choose not to choose is a choice. I personally want all of us to live happy lives; I know from personal experience that we are more likely to be happy if we choose our personal paths in life. If someone else chooses our life path for us, we may not feel comfortable with it, nor be willing to accountably take ownership of it or the power that produced it.

At its core self-sovereignty could be seen as conscious, discerning personal freedom, in harmony with God, along with the application of our personal power, in action; a person actively and successfully expressing their personal freedom would be seen as sovereign. This way of life does not include imposing our will or beliefs on anyone else; it simply means that we are committed to living life by and through our own conscious power of choice.

Conscious sovereignty is a requirement in the attainment of more complete, integrated and complex degrees of collective spiritual evolution for humanity. I would also say that it is also necessary to attain what could be called "God consciousness" on an individual level. Because technically speaking it is through the opening of our "upper chakras" 4th chakra through 10th and above to the spiritual realms, which are only accessible through these chakras, that the most astute spiritual understandings are accessed. Conversely there are aspects of spirit that function at all chakra levels and consciously mastering these levels of our systems is necessary in our process of collective spiritual evolution.

In this way, we become able to "ground" into this dense energy reality we live in, the most evolved, astute and high-frequency spiritual energies. It is my personal intention to facilitate this process of grounding the energy of spirit into this world and all aspects and levels of all peoples. It is my hope and perception that all will benefit by this process.

I personally perceive that it is more beneficial to facilitate bringing God's love, light and energy to all aspects of humanity and human existence. Rather than to try to help others escape the difficulties of this world into some more positive after death state, as some spiritual paths might suggest. If we simply escape to heaven or some higher realm, then what have we created or done for everyone else with whom we share this world, and who have not escaped?

The spiritual development path requires one to be willing to disconnect from any limiting or non-optimal beliefs, attitudes, habits, roles, values, reactive emotional patterns, karmic patterns and relationships that no longer serve or support our spiritual development. On my personal path, I have benefitted by seeing beliefs only as temporary training wheels that are useful in the preparation of attaining and functioning on more astute levels of understanding and conscious awareness. Therefore, I do not see any beliefs or even quality values as long-term ends in themselves. Though they may point toward the higher states of consciousness we most benefit by attaining.

Still, it is important to note a simple fact. If we choose to fundamentally change our internal and social mode of function, due to positive spiritual intention, we are likely to encounter some degree of social friction. Meaning that not everyone we interact with, or are in relationship with, is ready to make major shifts in spiritual consciousness in sequence with us. This friction can be uncomfortable and raise fears of loss of prior relationships. However, I believe the benefits of choosing spiritual focus above all other goals and relationships to be immense, and well worth the associated discomfort.

I am not suggesting becoming a monk, nor a social outcast, nor living an impractical life, nor walking away from our relationships, nor judging others

130

who do not agree with our spiritual perspectives or pursuits. I am suggesting heightened awareness of the often-detrimental influence of our conditioned social decision-making tendencies and habits on every situation in life and every relationship we choose to engage in. In this way we can more wisely manage our influences on the world at all levels of our being. By making this choice we can optimally support our own spiritual development, (whatever spiritual path we are on), while simultaneously insuring that we do not inadvertently incur social or relationship conflict or limitation.

When we have achieved the ability to manage our interpersonal interactions consciously and harmoniously we become optimally empowered to consistently and freely choose that which is spiritually, physical, mentally and emotionally in our highest and best good at every moment of our lives. Thus we attain and maintain the state of conscious positive mental and emotional self-management and sovereignty without the influence of disharmonious or detrimental personal relationships and their associated negative emotional energies. We can attain this state without conflict of any kind, or by giving up our existing relationships. With this spiritual development, we retain sovereign mind, emotion and will, in all conditions and situations. This state of sovereignty is the true, lasting and dependable source of authentic and discerning personal power and positive support to our spiritual development.

The Power of Limitations:

There are many influences in the world that may either enhance individual spiritual development or limit or detrimentally effect this development. The existence of these environmental, social, political or familial influences does not mean that we do not all have personal power. It only means that everyone else has power too, and that other people's power continually and reciprocally affects us, though we can significantly mitigate this influence if we choose.

We all exist in a perceived state of limitation of some sort, including limited life options, resources, knowledge, cognitive capacity, time, money, power, etc. (Even the very wealthy have some of these limitations). This ongoing state of limitation is a necessary and fundamental aspect of our personal evolutionary process. At the same time we all have unique gifts and capabilities which we are given to us in order that we may learn from using these specific forms of "personal power". Therefore, although sometimes uncomfortable, limitations are in fact good things, as every limitation we have will in some way help us attain fundamental spiritual understandings. So,

131

from a soul evolutionary standpoint, states of limitation are in effect equal in benefit to states of perceived power or capability. This is because all states of empowerment, whether lesser or greater in expression are potentially educational experiences.

A simple example of this type of limitation-based learning and development would be the following: If a person was right handed and we wanted to teach them to learn to use their left hand very well in their day-to-day life, we could tie their right hand behind their back. If they wanted to live, work and eat they would quickly become adept at using their left hand. This is a very basic example of how limitation in life motivates and teaches us and thereby ultimately empowers us, via limitation, in the midst of the pressure of life's necessities.

Other, more profound examples of limitation based learning can occur when our soul chooses to:

❖ Understand how to be very disciplined, in which case we might be presented with many life challenges and dramas which require us to learn all aspects of discipline in order to successfully traverse our life path. These life experiences could require us to become well grounded, focused, detail oriented, patient, conscious, determined, organized, introspective, mature and optimally emotionally self-managing. All of which are key facets of advanced states of functional, conscious discipline.

❖ Learn to feel deeply and to understand love and emotion, in which case we might be presented with many painful losses of people we love. We could also live with no experience of feeling related to by others, or of feeing understood or loved at all. Most of us would not wish this circumstance or path of spiritual attainment. Still it can lead very directly to our learning to love ourselves and others divinely and unconditionally and to appreciate the importance and value of love as the foundation of spirituality and of life.

❖ Learn to understand courage, in which case we might be placed in dire circumstances of war, poverty or familial abuse. Thus, in order to survive and transcend our soul-chosen life situation we would be required to develop courage.

❖ Become more spiritual, thus we might be placed in circumstances which limit our other options in life. We might be born poor and into a family or culture which both reveres and expects spiritual attainment or we could be abandoned by others so much so that our relationship to God is understood to be our only solace and support.

❖ Attain deep wisdom, thus we would likely have access to higher education of various types, including spiritual developmental information. We would also likely experience many relationships and situations which required us to achieve deep understanding and insight into ourselves, others and the world.

Our learning from the circumstance of being faced with personal limitations in a gradual and building way is similar to a traditional structuring of an advanced educational regimen, in which we take certain classes in a sequenced manner. The sum total of these classes will eventually build up to the "attainment of a degree" or from the perspective of the soul the attainment of wisdom, insight and consciousness. We are, in effect, required by these imposed limitations to focus on certain aspects of life, at certain points in our lives, in order to directly facilitate our attaining key understandings. This karmic evolutionary support mechanism is a method of facilitated management of our learning via management of our personal, emotional and energetic focus. Without the guiding support of the karmic process we would be unlikely to understand ourselves, or life, comprehensively enough or deeply enough to then empower us to make the disciplined decisions necessary to place ourselves in such uncomfortable and yet fruitful learning circumstances.

Our Personal Spectrum of Influences:

Although it could technically be said that all of us have the same amount of potential power, it could also be said that some of us have more "practically applicable power" in our day-to-day lives than others. Our potential power is dependent upon the spectrum of influence that we are capable of functioning within, based upon how adept we personally become in managing our current incarnate state and what karmic circumstances and limitations we are born into. So it is true for example that some of us are more educated than others. Some of us have more emotional intelligence, empathy and insight than others. Some of us are conditioned by family to seek higher education, wisdom, wealth or power. Some of us have higher social status or more money. All of these states are in effect developmental "double-edged swords". This is because they require us, through our experience of the paradoxical combination of capability and limitation to focus on attaining certain soul-chosen states of understanding, knowledge or consciousness.

Whatever external influences we experience in life, whether positive or negative, we can be assured that they will, at least for the short-term future, be influenced by our personal, family or national karma. Although I believe humanity is on the verge of transcending karma as our chosen educational process (i.e. cause-and-effect learning), it is currently still in effect as our evolutionary governing mechanism at this time. Our karma therefore "initially sets the stage" of our personal functionality and potential as individuals, as well as guides our ongoing development. We can transcend our karma, yet we must first know how and why it is influencing us if we are to work and understand our way past it.

These karmic life influences can create distortions in understanding, and even undermine how consciously, wisely, effectively and broadly we use our personal power, and thus directly affect our choices, life results and future karma. For example, if we are born into a state of wealth and power we may not be motivated to develop and display discipline, wisdom and a strong work ethic in our life choices and/or we may harm others with our power without empathetic concern for their wellbeing.

Some key influences on the development of our personal power and how we use it include:

❖ Loving, stable relationships.

❖ Good-quality models of personal development (for example, parental models, relationship models, spiritual models, social models, mentors). We all learn via both models and examples.

❖ The religious, cultural and political context in which we grew up.

❖ The social strata into which we were born.

❖ Our key early life experiences (for example, did we receive loving family support vs. mental and emotional trauma or abandonment).

❖ Financial resources.

❖ Healthy food, clean water and a safe and healthy living environment.

❖ Availability of advanced education and access to good information (i.e. internet access and higher education).

❖ Quality work or career opportunities.

❖ Each of our personal karmic impairments and gifts necessary to support our soul's learning path.

❖ The experience level of our soul, including how many human incarnations we have lived.

Limitations and capabilities affect the quality and power of individual decision-making worldwide, and at every level of society. Therefore, they directly affect the quality of the global results we create and experience as cultures and as a species. If our societies eventually develop higher functioning individuals (not just better educated, I am speaking here of full spectrum functionality, including mental, emotional, spiritual, physical, social and energetic), then we can basically be assured of more optimal global results and a more auspicious path for humanity's evolution.

Some people exhibit greater personal power than others, meaning they either have more or better resources, education, social status, social connections, etc. This, however, is not a situation of the haves and have not's, meaning anyone who has wealth, power and knowledge have them for useful spiritual developmental reasons. That said, if humanity wants to take itself off of the karmic autopilot mode of evolution and create overall social and economic equality among all of its citizens, we will then be required to transcend the usefulness and effectiveness of the current karmic developmental mechanism and replace it with something new. This new situation is being achieved, in that around the world we are developing more people to higher levels of mental and spiritual understanding than ever before. The higher each of us raises our individual consciousness, the higher we raise the frequency of the consensus consciousness of the whole world. Ultimately we will reach the point as individuals and as a world where we will become free of our self-chosen and limiting karmic learning method. There will be something truly new under the sun.

Beyond Current Leadership Models:

The past choices of individuals throughout history, have created our current global and intra-national situations, both positive and negative. We as individuals have also created our own personal limitations and capabilities through our prior choices. In the evolutionary process of humanity, we have depended heavily on our spiritual leaders as guides and examples of who we can become. We also use them as points of reference in shaping the quality of our decisions (for example, Christ, Buddha, Muhammad, Mother Teresa, Gandhi, various incarnations of the Dalai Lama, etc.). These people and their teachings have had tremendous positive influence on the development of humanity to date.

Leadership in all its forms is important in that it provides a mechanism by which large groups of people can function together harmoniously and constructively, according to a clearly professed positive and functional vision.

Simultaneously this same mechanism run amok can in some ways be terribly damaging to human evolution. For example, in situations where charismatic dictators have in effect mis-led whole nations. This has occurred in situations where leadership has been based on erroneous interpretations of religious doctrines, and also where invalid and questionable political, economic or cultural ideologies were used to influence and detrimentally motivate national populations. In these cases, the citizens of nations are effectively entrained into negatively resonating together and thus following and supporting destructive and dominating paths, for example, Adolph Hitler and others.

I would say that in all its forms, healthy and pure leadership, whether we are speaking of spiritual leadership, corporate leadership, social leadership or political leadership is always guided by spirit, and benefitted by the egoless humble willingness to submit to its guidance. Leadership in its highest form is true and selfless surrendered service to humanity and God.

There are many who have previously governed in our world who by the above optimal definition would not precisely be called leaders. Holding the position of an elected official, an executive, a king or president does not make one a quality leader. Yet whether these offices are held by people of vision or not, the people occupying them have still had significant influence on the development and history of our world. These are historical contexts and dynamics we reference today to support our social and political understandings, interpretations and decisions. There are many aspects of competency in leadership; some of these are spiritual in nature, some are technical, some administrative, and some are related to emotional or social intelligence. Still others are related to the leader's charismatic capacity to bring others together in peaceful collaboration to achieve envisioned goals.

There is far more to high quality leadership than mere governance, dominance, management, productivity or giving orders. Leadership is about the heart-felt capacity to formulate and hold a positive vision and then to communicate this vision in a way that not only motivates and achieves goals but also guides other's complete development in a positive and multidimensionally healthful way. Leadership is also about the capacity to integrate the human, the creative, the practical, the spiritual and the intuitive into all aspects of guidance and governance.

People who have served in positions of governance in the past have affected every area and level of societies, and have, in effect, been the architects of our governments, political systems, legal systems and educational systems. In these ways, they have fundamentally affected our developing national cultures and our potential as a world and a species. The

136

quality of these individuals' personal wisdom, understanding, agendas, experience and education were direct determinants of what they created for their societies. Their efforts have not only influenced our current political, governmental and educational systems, they have also directly affected their present-day citizen's expectations of what makes a good leader. Ignorant expectations, though to a degree socially formative in their influence, can be tremendously limiting.

Previous leader's influences, across history, have thereby had significant effect on present day citizens' expectations of how contemporary institutions can and should function, and what they can and should become and achieve in the future. These socially recorded beliefs and expectations from past developments have social, political and cultural inertia, and can become direct limitations on what we create and build now, and how we are willing to transform as individuals, nations and as a world.

Today various sources and levels of management education teach individual courses, which include education on "leadership styles", that managers of people and those who govern can apply to various organizational, social, cultural or political contexts and situations. In most cases these are not true leadership strategies as much as management strategies. In contemporary political and organizational circles, leadership is not seen as a complete role in and of itself, it is seen more as an adjunct to what are deemed "more important" or basic management skills and functions. Leadership development is sometimes seen as only adding "soft skills, good interpersonal skills or acquiring a modicum of emotional intelligence".

The much-needed leader of tomorrow is in effect just starting to awaken to their own potential and self-sovereignty. This is an awesome learning and developmental opportunity. I believe that leadership can and must be taught in such a way that other organizational functions and management skills are seen to stem from it, rather than leadership being seen as just another method of more effectively achieving a preexisting goal or agenda. Leadership is fundamentally different than mere management.

In this suggested educational paradigm, creative leadership becomes the cornerstone for the other governance disciplines. Rather than a low-priority, and an only periodically included ingredient in governance. **Leadership is a traditional key** mechanism **by which the world is transformed and evolved in a** *proactive* **and conscious manner. However, now all individuals are also becoming empowered to bring about foundational global change.** Mere managerial reaction to world problems cannot be our

137

motivating global developmental mechanism. The sophistication of our global and corporate leadership must get ahead and stay ahead of the change and complexity curves the world is experiencing. If we want to continue to successfully develop globally and individually.

As stated above, past choices of all who have previously governed in our world have influenced and to a degree defined our individual expectations of the quality, nature and results of what most of us would term "quality leadership". Our individual expectations, though often unconscious, are still direct expressions of our personal power and influence our application of our power of choice. They determine many of the choices we make as individuals, therefore they are a key determinant of the quality of leader we allow <u>and require</u> to guide and govern us. In effect if we as individuals, nations or a world want quality leaders, we are accountable for achieving this result. In effect we must choose to begin creating leaders, rather than merely hoping they will create themselves and then serve us.

Many people today may feel that leaders should be "strong, confident, competitive, intelligent, commanding, experienced, smart, tough, charismatic and always have all the answers". These are root chakra-influenced safety-oriented perspectives, and many would likely prefer this type of person to run their countries. In effect, they are looking for a powerful and safety producing father or mother figure to lead them, and to give up their personal power and self-sovereignty to.

Oddly enough, even in many developed countries, valuable personal qualities such as those listed below are not appropriately prioritized:

- ❖ Authentic integrated self-awareness and intuitive ability.
- ❖ Personal authenticity, integrity and honesty.
- ❖ Discipline and wisdom.
- ❖ A kind and loving nature.
- ❖ Patient, methodical, discerning and fearless decision-making. (Fearless does not mean bold, arrogant, unwise or "leaping before you look", it means the absence of fear. We only get to this point when have first faced and resolved our fears before we choose to make decisions.)
- ❖ Emotional intelligence and sensitivity.
- ❖ Innovative and creative thinking.
- ❖ Systems analysis skills.
- ❖ Technical and scientific understanding, education or knowledge.
- ❖ The ability to generate and clearly articulate their visions.

138

❖ Fluidity and flexibility, rather than being stuck in any limiting belief system or mindset.

❖ Visionary ability to foresee ripple effects of decisions at all levels of society.

❖ Authentic personal spiritual values that are openly tolerant of all other spiritual and religious paths.

These characteristics are often deemed to be less important than some other qualities. Traditionally leadership training has not been commonly taught as part of a basic core educational curriculum. Therefore, leadership tendencies are often neither understood, valued, required, fostered, evolved or enhanced by the current educational system. Oddly enough, many corporations shy away from independent-minded, truly leadership-oriented people in their hiring process and tend to actively weed them out in the hiring phase. Choosing instead those who will manage the organization to the status quo or their existing cultural agenda. This is simply the expression of the organization's cultural inertia and root chakra fear process in action. Yet what is needed is the conceptualization, development and implementation of culturally transformative organizational and corporate leadership strategies. This cannot be achieved by mere management or followers.

I would suggest that there are a significant number of leadership oriented capacities related to developing, facilitating, guiding and mentoring other's understanding and decision-making, as well as facilitating organizational cultural evolution which can be taught. I see true leadership as a process of guiding cultural evolution on the scale of the individual, the corporation, the nation and on the global scale. We need sufficiently sophisticated and comprehensive leadership classes available to the masses focused on managing the evolution of national cultures, how else can democratic constituencies make truly wise decisions when they vote?

Though there have been some experimental and basic attempts in this regard, they are not yet comprehensive, sophisticated or complete in their understanding of leadership or its application. It is necessary that each nation quickly learn how to educate and optimally develop its culture since cultural limitations of various kinds are some of the most profound barriers to national and world transformation. If all nations are to learn to work together harmoniously in the future, they must learn to effectively and rapidly modify their own cultural norms and social dynamics, and thus someone must teach and guide them. I am of course not speaking here of mere "change management". I am speaking of designing and implementing entirely new kinds of leadership and associated social transformational dynamics.

One of these future capacities is facilitated belief modification and management, which is a foundational way to facilitate other's developmental transitions. (Beliefs and their influence in our lives are discussed in some depth later in this book in chapter nine). I perceive many as yet unplumbed depths to leadership which can be broadly taught in future educational curriculums. These enhanced leadership capabilities can be mentored, modeled, and taught in a standardized way and made prerequisites to political governance and organizational management. If we as individuals want to optimally exercise the power of our self-sovereignty, then we must insure that those who govern us also support us in doing so. Otherwise when they make decisions on our behalf they may intentionally or unintentionally undermine our best interests. Competition alone will not take us where we need to get to as nations or as a species, since its very essence is the destruction of collaboration and teamwork.

At this time, it is not likely that one could easily obtain a master's degree or Ph.D. specifically in leadership skills, because the need for or benefit of doing so is likely not well understood and thus not valued. Still I would suggest it is a worthwhile discipline to develop. We need a transcendent personal, social and cultural developmental process which goes beyond the apex of our current conscious understanding and motivations. This process can be utilized by the leaders of tomorrow.

The simple fact is that we need a new breed of leader to deal with our increasingly complex world. We can continually evolve the quality of our governmental leadership, if we are willing to invest in and require teaching ever more sophisticated and comprehensive university level leadership skills to those who serve in government, before they choose to serve us.

One of the more sophisticated sources of leadership training available today is the military. I would say they teach many beneficial elements of leadership, including selfless service, leadership by example, empathy, fairness and respect, rather than merely using threat of force to motivate their staff. That said, I perceive military leadership styles, although of high quality in some ways, to have been originally developed within a highly-structured culture of potentially forced compliance, and top-down hierarchical command and control, all of which have built-in limitations.

Simplistic command and control styles of leadership no longer adequately meet complex world needs. I am not saying that this leadership style is not positive, only saying that as refined as it is for the purpose it was developed, it

140

still does not include the necessarily sophisticated and subtle leadership elements I envision. Thus, I perceive it to still not be optimally evolved enough to meet our incredibly complex social, political, environmental and economic needs in the present or the future. Thus, I feel it is not ready for transplantation into social, corporate or political venues. Leadership must be rooted in love and consciousness if we want to survive as a species.

An additional evolutionary root of military leadership is that it is based upon the achievement of a very specific and limiting set of overall organizational goals. Meaning that currently, the focus of military leadership is on the expeditious conquering, control or destruction of a perceived enemy. This type of goal, (although it is not often realized to be so) is, at its core, fundamentally driven by judgment and blame (see the Judgment Cycle later in this book). It is also specifically designed to support violence, and to combat violence with violence, rather than to directly focus on achieving peaceful resolution to conflict.

I do not see leadership as a process of managed battles, although I am sure that there are people who do. Our world issues cannot be resolved by violence, threat of violence, or control strategies of any kind. At this time, there are some corporations attempting to employ those schooled in this leadership style, (i.e. military trained leaders). Some of these corporations even literally have their own staff of mercenaries on salary to deal with various difficult world environments and situations. I do by the way support the hiring of all war veterans and believe they have gone above and beyond in their service to their countries; I simply do not suggest transplanting military culture or leadership styles into corporations, when there are other educable leadership styles we can develop that will achieve better results. Therefore, I would thus question the wisdom of a military style approach.

My question to corporate executives around the world is this. Is executive management of corporations attempting to attain greater control over the individuals in their organizations via a command-and-control style leadership style? If so, is that process truly empowering to the individual in the organization, at a time when the development of our individual power and self-awareness of it is crucial to humanity's evolution? If corporations are attempting to compete with other organizations in an ever more ruthless and regimented manner, is this healthy for the organizations' culture and for the world? What part of our humanity are we giving up in the name of efficiency, control, profit and goal attainment? I would suggest that simply "upping the ante" in competition cannot lead to world peace.

The United States is currently experiencing what I perceive to be a crisis in leadership—and like all human situations it has a silver lining. In America's current political system there is extreme polarization and conflict. Simultaneously, it is true that America does have many skilled leaders in its government: however, it is those same leaders who have brought their nation to this precipice, often by allowing themselves to be influenced by special interest groups and lobbyists.

Those in positions of governance are currently effectively paralyzed and have been rendered so by their own conflicting choices, fears, priorities, beliefs, tendencies, judgments and agendas. Therefore, they are unable to effectively lead and to accomplish necessary goals in a timely manner. Certainly, there is polarization among America's citizenry, yet the political party leaders do not appear to be working to resolve this dynamic—some of America's leaders actually appear to be feeding it. I am not criticizing anyone by saying this; I am only working to accurately describe the situation and the dilemma. I perceive that all the world's leaders will learn from this situation and eventually utilize what they learn to improve governance as a whole.

It is fair to say that this situation is also in part due to the built-in limitations of the United States' two-party system, which engenders an "us vs. them" dynamic of democratic government and politics. This is a system which Americans have designed and chosen, yet which can still be adjusted and evolved for the better with insight, collaborative effort, willingness to change and compromise.

There are some existing dysfunctional rules of governance that were put in place by America's political leadership that require constructive adjustment. This situation is in part due to the overt influence of special interest groups and the ruthlessly corrupting influence of lobbyists with the capability of effectively co-opting the functions and decisions of congressional offices. (See the 60 Minutes show titled: "Jack Abramoff: The Lobbyist's Playbook" on the effects of lobbyists on American governmental function). It is useful to realize that many lobbyists probably do not tend to see their work as an expression of political corruption; many may see it as a "service" they are providing or just as a job.

According to Jack Abramoff this situation of spreading lobbying corruption is achieved via forms of subtle bribery and buying off of key support staff in these offices through promises of future lucrative jobs. It is an unfortunate operational truth that a congressperson's office support staff can be co-opted via bribery without the congressional representative fully realizing it has happened.

142

Another potentially corrupting element in American politics has been created by the Supreme Court's 2010 ruling in the case of Citizens United vs. The Federal Election Commission, which stated that laws prohibiting corporate and union political expenditure were unconstitutional. This decision by the Supreme Court has led to the creation of what are called Super PACS, or organizations and consortiums of wealthy individuals which are now free to spend virtually unlimited amounts of money to sway elections to whatever their agenda may be. These Super PACS can spend hundreds of millions of dollars to convince voters of their point of view on a candidate. This is potentially a recipe for the corruption of the democratic decision-making process in its entirety. Once candidates are beholden to these "investors" they may find it difficult to operate in personal integrity. These Super PACS may even try to affect selection of all political offices at all levels of government from behind the scenes, if allowed. Is this a process of government by the wealthy? (By the way I feel many involved in these Super PACS firmly believe they are helping their nation by their efforts, still these are not cross-party collaborative efforts).

I would perceive this situation as potentially a method of co-opting the voting process to serve powerful corporations and the wealthiest of American citizens, without the guarantee that the Super PACS' intentions match the will or perspective of the nation's citizens. In effect, they can, through this mechanism of mass propaganda creation, at least to a degree, manufacture and shape the consensus political perspective of the citizenry and pepper the national consensus consciousness with misinformation that can have long-term detrimental effect. On the surface this scenario appears to undermine or distort the influence of individual citizen's personal power by overtly influencing who will be chosen to lead and govern America. It also appears to be a recipe for further corruption in the political system itself, as massive amounts of loosely regulated and previously unavailable money are infused into the political arena. That said, the United States will achieve understandings from this situation as individuals and as a nation and balance will ultimately be restored.

These powerful influences are affecting America's political system at its foundation and appear likely to escalate rather than to slow down. I would suggest that within this rapidly evolving political environment that getting the legislative process accomplished can only become more difficult, hierarchical, conflicted and complex, and so be less directly driven by the power and needs of the sovereign individual citizen. If citizens' political wills are hijacked by the political system itself, where does that leave democracy and

143

the nation's citizenry? That said, I do still see potential positive evolutionary aspects to this developing situation.

If individuals need to learn not to relinquish their sovereignty to corporations and the wealthy…how better to learn this lesson than to be faced with a situation in which they could potentially lose sovereign power and feel the pain of it by their own ignorance or inaction?

If America citizens feel their leaders have in some way failed to meet their expectations, they may eventually be motivated to require the development of a modified political system, whereby they can assure governmental leaders' integrity, skill sets and to some degree positively shape their leader's intentions, knowledge and skills prior to electing them.

1. If America's citizens are harmed enough economically they will eventually require greater balance, transparency, oversight and safeguards in the economy from their leaders.

2. Each of the above listed situations is not a problem, it is an opportunity; it is simply part of the path of our learning to apply our personal power wisely on our own behalf.

3. In the act of growing beyond our polarized and limiting perspectives and traditional tendencies, we will learn compromise and collaboration, and also learn why they are necessities.

Better educated people improve their countries and the world as a whole. Certainly, institutionalized education has significant limitations in its current form, and is therefore not the whole answer, unless it were to be fundamentally overhauled. Still if we want to be led by people of loving and wise integrity, we must in effect choose to develop them and require that they meet the necessary standard of quality leadership. I see the current state of humanity's leadership development in a way in its infancy. In a similar fashion, we individuals are just now experimenting with ways to wisely manage our newly acquired personal power. It is better to discerningly build competent leaders by conscious intention than to select who leads us from a potentially random group of people who desire to run whatever nation they are a part of via their own personal agendas.

There are many social, political and economic mechanisms which limit the availability of support for each individual's personal development in our world. This means that there are significant influences and systems in the world's societies which work to either undermine the development of the individual or which are not specifically designed to fully support that development. For example, America's current business school educational system is significantly influenced by corporations who contribute financially

144

to it in order to create a "certain type" of business graduate. The goal as I understand it is to create a graduate who will fulfill a specific set of business requirements that corporations believe they want and need. This is a very closed, non-creative and constraining system, and one main reason that pure entrepreneurial business skills are not widely taught in universities.

The main interest of those contributing financially to schools is not in the individual achieving a goal that they want to achieve in life or empowerment of the individual. The interest is in the individual becoming part of the existing "business machine and model" in order to support already existing businesses and the systemic economic status quo. We might see this as in effect a cloning process rather than an educational process.

There are also now systems in place that are literally melding the higher educational system and its educators and students with the real-time corporate product research and development cycle. Meaning that corporations are insinuating their agendas directly into the educational process and influencing how we teach and what we teach. This integration of education and corporate product development can, while being "good for research", undermine the purity of the intentions of the educational system. This can potentially further limit freedom of self-expression and development in order for corporations to be "more competitive". Still, when organizations' cultures and consensus consciousness grow more sophisticated, they will seek higher goals and thus require more self-empowered people.

I am not faulting our systems of education, business and economics for producing the types of people they believe they need. I am simply suggesting that the type of people the system is "designing" are not the types of people who are prepared and educated to solve our current and future world problems, or to find and implement solutions appropriate to the level of complexity of those problems. If we want solutions to more sophisticated problems, we must develop more sophisticated and creative people, and we must teach them to function and to lead in an optimal manner. This situation will change because it must if we want to have the world continue to develop and not fall back into a state of overly complex dysfunction, conflict, corruption or chaos.

I would simply suggest we can be proactive and do much more than we are, sooner, faster and better. If we make a conscious commitment **now,** to achieve this new situation of comprehensive support to the development of the future individual, we will then all prosper. In entering the Age of the Individual, the individual has the power to more directly and broadly affect

145

the world…we are not powerless to change education, society or government and we do not have to start a war to achieve this… times have changed. The power has shifted and it will continue to shift in the favor of all individuals.

We all have vast potential when we function as consciously sovereign empowered beings; there are many steps to attaining and maintaining this state, yet all are within our ability to achieve and all are worthwhile. Letting go of the past, letting go of fear and focusing on our creative potential is key. To achieve this essentially free and empowered state we must be willing to work with and ultimately understand and master (not control, ignore, invalidate or suppress) our emotional influences on our decision-making. Once this has been accomplished we are freed to live lives of consistently, willfully chosen joy and peace and to benefit the lives of all whom we interact with and love.

Chapter Five
Leaving Disempowering Negative Emotions (Illusions) Behind:

WHAT EMOTIONS DID YOU EXPERIENCE WHILE READING the previous section? Did you feel empowered, excited and ready to go? It is necessary to understand that our emotions are a double-edged sword, meaning they can empower us and motivate us or disempower us and undermine our conscious intentions. Disempowering negative emotions (often fear, anger, jealousy and hatred) are a part of everyone's life and have been present throughout human history. Our feelings, whether positive or negative, create perspectives from which we look at life and make our decisions. In the past these emotions may have been allowed to drive and influence many of our decision-making steps and our behaviors in relationships to one degree or another. We are now facing the detrimental global results of these negative individual emotional influences on the development of our personal styles of decision-making.

Yet we are still trying to face the global situation with the same types of cultural conditioning, negative judgmental emotional states and reactive behavioral styles that produced the difficulties in the first place! This is neither a recipe for good-quality global outcome, nor conscious discerning individual or group decision-making in our current information rich world. What are commonly termed "negative emotions" are neither wrong nor bad, and judging them or ourselves for having them will not make them go away or improve the situation. These emotions are simply not the most optimal path forward for us as individuals or as a world. They can be effectively transmuted and transcended; and we all have the power we need to accomplish this. We need only apply intelligent methods.

We always have a choice about what and how we feel and also how we act upon what we feel. We have the power to positively and consciously change our personal emotional tendencies and to make the world and our relationships better by doing so. If we change our emotions, then we literally and immediately change our experience of life and thus how we make our life choices—the effects are that potent. It could be said that all disempowering emotions are in effect illusions, in that they are not exactly "real" or accurately reflective of what is happening in our lives.

In most of us, emotions are the reactive result of the projection of our subconscious beliefs, assumptions and expectations onto our lives and relationships. We human beings literally want to continue to believe what we believe, even in the face of evidence to the contrary, and even if our individual beliefs are directly detrimental to our own personal happiness. In effect, we build our feelings of personal security around our chosen beliefs, often beliefs we acquired before we were five years old. An example of this would process in action be the case where a person has the conscious or subconscious belief that "nobody loves me". In this situation, for this belief to remain true (and yes, we all want even our most dysfunctional beliefs to be true) we feel motivated to insure through our life choices, that no one treats us in a loving manner.

If someone begins to show us love, and yet we want to hold onto our fundamental belief that we are not loved, then we must either:

❖ Deny their love.
❖ Mistrust their stated feelings.
❖ Actively and subconsciously sabotage the relationship.
❖ Remove ourselves from the relationship in order that our cherished belief not be proven false.

After the relationship has ended we then feel sad that we were again proven "right" that nobody loves us. So, beliefs often become self-fulfilling prophecies and directly manifest our reality. The sadness we feel after the belief is supposedly again "proven true" is self-created and thus this sadness is itself in effect illusionary. In fact, the belief itself is illusionary, in that virtually everyone on the planet is loved by someone. Yet we may often feel as if we personally are not loved and may hold such a general belief about all of life without fully realizing we hold it or the implications of doing so. Some of us even feel God does not love us, though this is never true.

Observing Our Core Emotionally Driven Belief Patterns:

If any of our core beliefs are proven false in our day-to-day life, we tend to become frightened and insecure. In effect our world would suddenly seem very different than we previously and firmly believed it to be. Thus, in order to avoid these insecure and fearful feelings, we continue to believe beliefs that manifest life limitations, misery or unhappiness. In effect, it is a case of "trusting the devil you believe you know, rather than the devil you don't". The situation I have briefly described here is a main reason for human suffering.

Most of us have been taught to accept a core belief of the validity and importance of our emotions, whether these emotions are empowering (positive) or disempowering or destructive (negative). We have even been trained to believe that if we feel it, then it must be true or real. Though what we feel is often only our subconscious emotional reaction to either our misinterpretations of events or relationships or a reaction to one of our own subconscious projections onto reality.

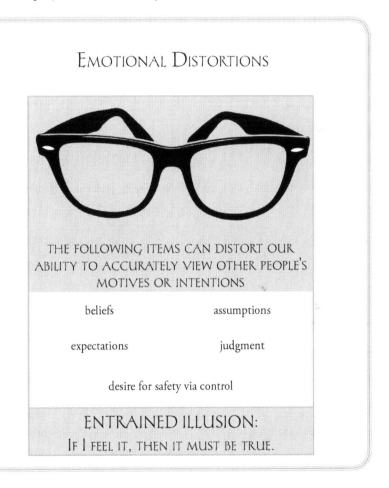

EMOTIONAL DISTORTIONS

THE FOLLOWING ITEMS CAN DISTORT OUR ABILITY TO ACCURATELY VIEW OTHER PEOPLE'S MOTIVES OR INTENTIONS

beliefs	assumptions
expectations	judgment

desire for safety via control

ENTRAINED ILLUSION:
IF I FEEL IT, THEN IT MUST BE TRUE.

In the case of negative emotions, many people have been trained to interpret that whenever they feel negative emotions as a result of interacting with other people that they have in some subtle or gross way been victimized or "disrespected". Victimization is an illusion; we all have power and always have. Many of us have bought into the Victim, Perpetrator, Rescuer model of looking at life, yet all aspects of this model are false, misleading and disempowering. By interpreting our emotions and relationships in this way, we abdicate accountability for our own emotional process and also remain unaware of what actually triggered our emotional states. We also become unable to formulate the intention to positively change our lives. We project that our emotions and emotional interpretations and decisions are somehow under someone else's control or are the results of other's actions. This can be seen in the statements, "Don't make me angry!" OR "Why are you making me feel bad?" OR "Why are you trying to hurt me".

No one can make us feel anything; it is always our choice to feel whatever we feel, though we often do not realize it or choose to be consciously accountable for it. If we choose to believe others can make us feel what we feel, then we give away our personal power and so cannot own and effectively wield it.

Some of the key disempowering emotional states that many of us take for granted as being necessary, real, unavoidable, justified or true, are:

❖ Fear, anxiety, worry, insecurity, depression, stress, shame, guilt and self-blame.

❖ Anger, hatred, blame, rage and the desire for revenge or punitive "justice," which is just another name for institutionalized revenge.

❖ Greed, lust, desire for power, desire to be in control of self or others and other unfettered desire states.

❖ Jealousy, envy and covetous materialism.

❖ Arrogance, pride and wanting to feel and be seen as being better, smarter, more right, perfect or more powerful or more knowledgeable than others.

❖ Feeling we are not good enough or are somehow less than others.

❖ Possessive conditional love (yes, believe it or not, possessive conditional love, codependency, etc., are not optimally positive states and do not facilitate quality management of life change, relationships, emotional happiness or self-empowerment).

❖ Negative emotions and repressed emotions that are acted out in addictive states of all kinds. (Addiction is here defined as: anything we cannot consciously choose not to do at any moment. This can include addictions to (i.e. Feeling that we cannot choose not to) over work, eat chocolate, drink alcohol, take drugs, engage in drama, start relationship arguments or feeling sad or depressed). We can just as easily be addicted to not doing something, (i.e. working so hard to avoid that which we fear, that we create decision-making paralysis). All addiction is driven at its roots by unresolved fear at some level of our systems, whether we are conscious of it or not. We are often influenced by multiple fears simultaneously, to our disempowered detriment. If we resolve our personal fears, at their cores, then all emotional motivation for the addictions they are driving dissolves.

When we feel these emotions, we often deny that we are either feeling them or acting upon them, even if we are currently punishing ourselves or someone else, due to our emotional motivation. We might attempt to suppress our emotions, or we may judge ourselves and punish ourselves for having them in the first place. The truth is that whenever we suppress or repress any negative emotion we feel, whether it is out of fear, guilt, judgment of our own emotions or willful refusal to feel them, we create conflict within ourselves. Emotions are meant to be expressed, to flow, and to be processed completely through our systems, whether these emotions are positive or negative.

If negative emotions are not allowed to flow in some manner, their negative energy stagnates and becomes stuck in various parts of our systems. I am not suggesting acting upon negative emotions; I am suggesting fully understanding and fully processing them out of our systems in order to be freed. If we suppress our emotions they tend to show up in other ways we are unaware of, as in passive-aggressive behaviors, addictions, OCD (Obsession Compulsive Disorder) or PTSD (Post Traumatic Stress Disorder). In the long run emotional conflict and emotional suppression can damage the areas of our energy systems they are stuck in, thus causing physical or mental illness. Negative emotions can also limit healthy energy flow overall, causing a domino effect of other disempowering emotional states such as fear, depression or anxiety. In this way negative emotions and their associated detrimental energy and bodily chemical byproducts get stuck and fester unnecessarily.

Rationalization of why we are somehow correct to feel and remain in negative emotions is a trap that breeds more negative, disempowering emotional states and decisions. We tell ourselves why we are not accountable for our negative feelings, why someone else is, or may even feel self-righteous about our **decision** to feel dysfunctional emotions. As in "this is the way anyone who really cared would react to this situation".

We can easily slip into a perspective of victimhood. This occurs when we deny that feeling negative emotions in regard to life situations is actually a result of decisions we chose to make (whether consciously or subconsciously). To many of us maladaptive emotions are perceived as something that happened to us or as something that we simply could not manage (for example, "They made me feel this way," OR "Look at how you make me feel"). This choice of rationalization is of course part of the basis for the disempowering emotion-based victim mentality. It creates a tendency to refuse to learn from life experiences.

Rationalization may create more illusions, and illusions can create suffering. Rationalization is also a driving portion of the process of believing in judicially judging and punishing others. We could look at some punitive aspects of the judicial system as a somewhat short-sighted, reactive and non-adaptive system of institutionalized revenge seeking, rather than as a proactive, realistic and long term solution to social issues. The highest achievement of justice need not involve punishment; it can be seen from a perspective of sagacity as a process that is better aimed at achieving peace, understanding and harmony within and between ourselves, nations and the world. Punishments do not achieve this higher goal; however love, mutual understanding, healing and education do.

I can honestly say that many of us can spend a lifetime judging ourselves for having felt negative feelings and that all this effort of self-judgment and its consort of shame will not make a single negative emotion go away. There are however a wide variety of methods of working with maladaptive emotions that actually do work. This is only true if we are willing to first acknowledge our negative feelings and then love and forgive ourselves and others enough to find and apply these methods diligently and consistently. It is important to also realize that all negative emotional states are driven at their roots by one or both of the fears we discussed previously. If our fears are released, then all our negative emotions related to them cease immediately.

One thing I hope will be taken away from reading this book is that ALL experienced negative mental and emotional states are merely stepping stones to more positive states and understandings. It is on the path of learning to work our way out of these negative emotional states that we are empowered to transcend them permanently. This is achieved by valuing, validating and fully embracing loving positive states toward self and others. Detrimental emotional states can eventually lead to positive personal developments. So if we judge, curse or punish them we simply hold ourselves back from effectively and rapidly working through them, learning from them and transcending them.

154

A difficult aspect of detrimental emotions is that we are often taught that it is correct and even socially expected that we feel them. The lesson states that if we choose to be willing to feel them that doing so makes us right, better or more powerful than others in some way. This is only a process of playing into drama dynamics.

A common way this happens is when someone in authority, such as a parent, communicates (directly or indirectly) something akin to the following non-adaptive statements during our formative years:

* ❖ "Now don't you feel badly about what you did?"
* ❖ "What you did was wrong / bad."
* ❖ "Why did you let them do that to you?"
* ❖ "You should be angry about what they did to you."
* ❖ "You are an innocent victim in this situation."
* ❖ "You deserve justice for what they did to you."

In addition, we may feel more powerful or safer if we speak angrily to others as in "I am the boss, and if you do not obey without question you will be fired". The same is true of threats of physical violence or emotional abandonment in relationships.

Can you see how many of our emotional states can disempower us and keep us from maintaining our personal power and still finding happiness? Another important relationship is that of dysfunctional emotions and how they are affected by the expectations that we hold about life and relationships. For example, if a person (whether male or female) has the expectation that their marriage partner should love them always and forever, there is a high probability that their expectation will not be met. This is not because their partner cannot choose to love them for a lifetime, it is simply becoming common these days for people to fall out of love or to change fundamentally after getting married and then to get divorced. In addition, during the course of a long relationship it is highly likely that their partner will temporarily feel many other emotions toward them, which are not love based at all (for example, anger, jealousy, hatred, fear, resentment, frustration, etc.). Despite these realities, we often try to "enforce" our emotional expectations and relationship beliefs onto our spouses.

Of course, having these detrimental emotional states does not mean that our partner does not love us. It simply means that they are human and that some of these non-peaceful emotional reactions are conditioned into us early in life, so that they become a part of and undermine almost every relationship. These detrimental emotions can also be assumed to be key

155

components of our current form of individual spiritual and emotional evolutionary process, and to a degree in our current process of evolution they are, yet they need not be.

Other examples of erroneous relationship assumptions which create less than optimal relationship dynamics and negative emotional illusions could be the following thoughts/beliefs:

❖ "If I just have a relationship then I will be happy."
❖ "If I have what I want or get my way then I will be happy."
❖ "If I just get married I will be safe and secure."
❖ "If I am in a relationship then I will have self-worth and be somebody."
❖ "If I give and give in a relationship then I will be loved in return."
❖ "If my spouse does not love me or is unkind to me then there must be something wrong with me or I must not have done what I was supposed to do in the relationship."
❖ "I do not deserve to be loved."
❖ "I am not good enough and therefore I must continually try to make up for not being good enough by over-giving or sacrificing what I want in relationships."
❖ "Men are all bad."
❖ "Women are all bad."
❖ "Children are all bad."
❖ "I am beyond redemption."
❖ "I have to be perfect all the time."

We can all choose to transcend these belief states; the keys to doing so are first recognizing them for the illusions they are, and then making the conscious choice to work through them constructively, and thus to reach a point of transcendent understanding by doing so.

Assumptions in Relationships Create Opposition:

There are a vast number of possible erroneous assumptions about life and ourselves that we can consciously or subconsciously hold, based upon what are called our "core beliefs". Assumptions are just the projections of the beliefs that we hold to be true. A belief is only a recording in our memory of an interpretation of the meaning or implication of a prior life experience. Our individual system of beliefs are an internalized map we hold in our memory of our understandings of the world and our relationships, and are a model of how we "believe" life works. Each time we have a significant life experience

156

we form new beliefs or change old beliefs about ourselves, others, life and the world. This whole process is usually automatic and unconscious for most people.

We reference our internal belief maps constantly as we move through life, work and relationships in order to make our best decisions and choices. These beliefs are the reason for and form the foundation of our personal values, motivations and priorities. It is the process of making decisions via these beliefs that creates and manifests our life results and experiences. These beliefs form the foundation of our ongoing relationship dynamics and results.

We often hold a significant emotional charge associated with our beliefs, especially if the beliefs were formed as a result of a traumatic or emotionally wounding experience. These emotional charges tend to strongly "hold our beliefs in place". The emotional charge we have recorded with the belief can be fear, anger, love, shame or guilt or any other emotion. The problem with this process is that most of us tend to assume our beliefs are true, often without questioning them, especially if we formed these beliefs when we were very young. This makes it difficult to learn anything new that might be in conflict with our existing beliefs. Recording beliefs is part of our process of learning about life as well as learning from our life experiences. It can also become a learning disability if we fail to understand how the process works.

We tend to record beliefs without realizing we have even done so, and they can then continue to paint our interpretations of our experienced reality for a lifetime. We may even assume our beliefs are more true than any external source of information we have access to or are experiencing in the present moment. This means that our beliefs project onto our reality from moment-to-moment without our realizing it.

For example, if we break up with someone we deeply love and are heartbroken we could interpret the meaning of this experience to be "no one really loves me" OR we could record "no one will ever love me". From that moment on we would tend to project this dysfunctional belief onto our future relationships and by doing so create exactly what we most fear. It is vital that we learn to understand what beliefs we hold, how they affect our thinking and decisions, and how to change dysfunctional or limiting beliefs. If we believe we are weak we can learn to see ourselves as strong, if we believe we are alone we can learn to feel our oneness with God and all of humanity.

Most of our behavior stems from the results of our referencing our map of beliefs. We choose, whether we realize it or not, to believe the beliefs that we have recorded, and to accept them as "true or factual". A core belief is an interpreted meaning that tends to affect many aspects of our lives and relationships profoundly. Assumptions about life and relationships stem from and are projections derived from beliefs which we have previously acquired. These projected assumptions lead to expectations.

Expectations of others and of ourselves (though often seen as necessary and beneficial) are, in reality, a method of attempting to enforce behavioral compliance via control. Any of these inaccurate assumptions can therefore lead to unfulfilled expectations. These unfulfilled expectations tend to then lead to disappointment, judgment, blame, anger and jealousy, feelings of abandonment or betrayal.

Assumptions and the expectations they lead to are in effect a method of projecting a false reality into our own consciousness and then onto the world, which we then, often unsuccessfully, try to depend upon in the real world. Rarely do we realize that the seeds of our dysfunctional reactive emotions were planted when we originally chose to create and hold our beliefs and assumptions in the first place. (Regardless of where, when or by whom the seed was planted, the results can be seen as ultimately disempowering). The seeds then come to fruition when we choose to apply this inaccurate information to our lives and relationships. This is how assumptions undermine accurate discernment and disable us in our quest for the freedom of sovereign personal power.

Choosing to live via beliefs, projected assumptions and expectations results in our consistently living in a state of unrealized illusion. Hindus and Buddhists might refer to this process as living in the worldly illusion of "Maya". I would call it living in resonance with the consensus consciousness of humanity. This is an extremely subconscious tendency which creates much of the emotional pain and resentment we feel toward ourselves, others and our relationships. A very constructive thing to realize about all assumptions and expectations is that they have nothing to do with love or loving in relationships. They have everything to do with trying to be in control of our lives and relationships, and trying to manage our subconscious fears of loss, abandonment, being devalued or of being hurt in relationships. Thus, they are simply life's dysfunctional emotional coping mechanisms. In fact, functioning from the standpoint of assumptions and expectations in relationships is the opposite of loving and allowing ourselves to receive real love in the present moment. Many of us just do not realize it.

If we are willing to accept that we often base key relationship decisions on inaccurate projected assumptions, then we can consciously choose not to do so. We can realize that much of our pain and feelings of victimization have been the result of these unquestioned assumptions and their associated

158

expectations not being met. We can cease functioning from the standpoint of assumptions and expectations of what we want and expect "should be" in our lives and thus cease falling into the trap of our own unfulfilled expectations. When we release our assumptions and expectations and we directly improve our self-accountability and self-reliance, cease feeling victimized and free ourselves to truly love and be loved.

This type of choice does require us to first acknowledge our erroneous assumptions, then to face our fears and be willing to give up our illusions about relationships. We can then to take effective actions on our own behalf in order to positively shift our consciousness. I understand that this is not easy, especially if we have become unhealthily immersed in our non-optimal emotions, unhealthy relationships, feelings of being victimized, wishful thinking, denial, etc. However, if we do not choose to change we can fully expect that our negative emotional states and painful relationship dynamics will continue. If you write out all of your key beliefs, assumptions and expectations about your relationships, and then evaluate them, I think you will see what I mean. They can all be released and transcended via various methods that are available today.

We may also become so immersed in our non-positive emotions that we try to use them (rather than love) as our main motivation to achieve goals in life. We may even try to validate the application and feeling of detrimental emotions as actually being a positive or necessary part of life. This can be seen when we use anger, fear, shame and self-judgment as our driving motivations in order to take effective action or to achieve relationship goals or career goals. For example, anger may temporarily make us feel stronger, focused and more right about getting what we want.

Anger is also often used to hide our fears and insecurities from ourselves or others, thus anger is only an ego self-defense mechanism. This dynamic is very prevalent in males by the way, though women are catching on. However, when we choose to do this we unknowingly taint the quality of our decisions and actions, and thus the quality of our results, and damage our relationships. We also end up blinding our consciousness with the very narrow emotional perspective of expectation-based interpretation (or misinterpretation) we have chosen to apply or project onto the situation. By making this choice we also breed distrust and anger in our relationships and thus diminish the quality of our interpersonal communication and collaborative effectiveness.

These cultural, family and individually based patterns of negative emotional reaction and interaction are taken for granted, as if they were unquestionably the correct way to feel and act. We may even feel guilty or somehow wrong if we do not feel as negatively as we are "supposed to feel" according to other's expectations. Nothing could be further from the truth; we need not live at the mercy of conditioned family emotional dynamics or habits.

Patterns of belief, assumption, expectation and reactive emotional tendencies are passed down from generation to generation. It is important to realize that these negative emotional patterns are absorbed by our children and then cyclically re-enacted in relationship after relationship later in their lives. In this way the existence of the detrimental emotional family dynamics is continually rationalized and erroneously revalidated. This negative hereditary learning process need not occur if we are all sufficiently motivated to divinely love ourselves and our families without condition or judgment. These patterns and emotional dynamics could be called family karma.

Negative emotional dynamics often function at subconscious levels; they then drive us and/or hold us back in various situations and relationships. We are rarely fully aware of the implications of the influence of our emotions on any aspect of our lives. Our subconscious ego self-defense mechanisms tend to motivate us to keep us operating unconsciously. Anyone who really wants to change their life for the better will at some point realize that their conscious intention is often directly at odds with many of their subconscious desires or emotional motivations.

Positive foundational self-change requires willful decision-making, increased self-awareness and effective methods of managing, dis-identifying and deconstructing the subconscious parts of ourselves which have covertly been making our decisions for us. It also requires us to face our fears of the changes we want to bring about. We must construct new and conscious decision-making models and tendencies which do work well and do support our conscious intentions. Therefore, fear must be consciously extracted from our new decision-making models.

Though it is true that we all have what are usually labeled as negative emotions, this does not mean that these emotions serve no beneficial purpose in our lives. In fact, negative emotions once expressed (whether verbally or physically acted out) are one of our most powerful self-development and self-healing tools. Meaning we are often on automatic in our daily lives. Yet when we feel a negative emotion, whether it be anger, hatred, sadness, fear, etc., and if we choose to notice it is occurring, we are being given the first breadcrumb on the trail to self-awareness of an imbalance somewhere in our lives.

Whenever we feel any non-positive emotion we are being given a clear signal that we do not adequately understand some aspect of a life situation or relationship. I would also say that the existence of this often-unwanted emotion means that it is part of our spiritual learning path. Often, we must first experience negative realities and emotions in order to come to a point of transcendent understanding from which we can finally choose to feel more positive, compassionate, forgiving and loving. If we had never felt negative emotion and been required to grow past it, we would not know what to avoid in our interactions with others and in our relationships with ourselves. Yet no negative emotion directly or ultimately supports divine love.

Judgmental thoughts toward any of our own emotions (whether negative or positive) only holds back our potential to learn from them. Whatever we choose to focus on in life or within ourselves determines our emotional reactions, decisions and behavioral options. Therefore, learning and applying conscious focus management translates to improved discernment. Ultimately when we have fully given up on trying to live life and make decisions based upon negative emotion, we are freed to focus on developing loving, astute spiritual perspectives and tendencies. With enough understanding and effort in this regard we eventually achieve enlightenment. Great understanding leads to great wisdom, and great wisdom ultimately leads to enlightenment. Therefore, I suggest we forgive ourselves and others for all apparently negative emotional states and actions.

A significant challenge as we evolve into the **Age of the Individual** is that everyone's emotions are being triggered, meaning that our negative emotional tendencies and habits and our associated stress reactions are on double duty at this time. This is an uncomfortable situation for most of us and yet it is also good. If these emotions were not expressed in our relationships, we would have no mirror through which to see aspects of ourselves and our emotional choices that can benefit from improvement. Relationships are therefore a vehicle for our spiritual evolutionary process. Without them we literally could not learn a better way to live and interact. The circular path of experiencing the results of our emotion-based choices within relationships is the key to our emotional learning.

We need new positive role models or teachers who have worked through these emotional issues to such a degree as to empower them to be able to consistently guide others in this often-complex pursuit of self and relationship understanding. We have had some role models who answered this need in the past (for example Jesus Christ and his apostles, Buddha, Muhammad, various saints throughout history, ascended masters, etc.). More

161

recently we do have many shining examples that can be looked to and who teach peace, love and forgiveness and through their efforts raise our spiritual consciousness (for example, Mother Teresa, Gandhi, Nelson Mandela, Archbishop Desmond Tutu, Martin Luther King Jr., the Dalai Lama, etc.). Still, these wonderful people are unfortunately not directly and personally available to most of us to learn from. There are many subtle steps in spiritual evolution which can only be facilitated by subtle mentoring or direct contact with someone more spiritually adept than ourselves.

Feminine and Masculine Energy Dynamics:

Women, femininity and feminine energy have gotten a "bad rap" over the centuries. Women and the female consensus consciousness have been conditioned, and in effect socially taught, through male domination and threat of male violence, in most societies, religions and institutions. Some of the lessons were that women were in some fundamental way weak, fragile, not rational, flawed, dependent, emotionally inconsistent, powerless, incapable, wrong, bad, unacceptable or not as good as men and masculine energy. Please understand that nothing written here is designed to "bash" either men or women, nor any of their tendencies that have been exhibited throughout history. I am trying to illustrate some important issues that require resolution, if we want to have happy, loving relationships that do not end in divorce.

Masculine energy (and the masculine consensus consciousness) has wanted to see itself, and to be seen by women as "whole", complete and unquestioned in its own rightness, all knowingness, and as the answer to all situations and problems. (i.e. The bringer of safety, financial prosperity and empowerment to the world and to women). The male consensus ego-identity has been "selling itself", and trying to prove itself, for a very long time as better and superior to women and femininity. This is by the way simply a mass male consensus consciousness safety strategy in global action. Meaning that men's underlying insecurities, fear of abandonment, and fear driven desire for control and power are the main drivers for these illusionary perspectives. In these ways, female energy was literally conditioned to see itself as less-than, turn against itself in self-judgment, self-devaluation, shame, guilt, self-doubt, mistrust and fundamental self-non-acceptance, in order to support the fears and insecurities of men. These are historical male and female consensus consciousness dynamics, and they are changing in many areas of the world for the better rapidly. Still we have a long way to go.

162

In addition, many men (**not all men**) have abdicated their capacity to learn anything of significance via the feminine aspects of their own emotional being. In fact, aside from the conditioning they receive from their mothers, almost no men in today's societies have access to any comprehensive method of opening to and developing their own emotions. Therefore, the decision-making of many men has a fundamental emotional learning disability built into it, in regard to conceptualizing life and relationships and of solving global problems. Thus, in order to solve problems in their lives and in the world, these men have done everything they can to subtract the feminine in all of its forms from participation and power in the problem-solving process, so that men can retain their position of supposed dominance. For example, men control a disproportionate amount of financial wealth in the world at this time, and this has been the case for a very long time. Men have even used violence and killing to hold their social position and as proof of their "superior perspective on life". Of course women can be violent too, men are simply more effective in their application of violence. It is useful to understand that violence in all its forms is driven by fear, not strength, courage or wisdom. Due to shutting down their feminine sides many men live in their minds, and not their emotions or hearts, and rationalize that this is a superior and necessary mode of function. This choice is constantly re-rationalized and socially revalidated. A big part of the problem is that many men feel they are not allowed to openly admit their fears, and often do not admit them to themselves. If one cannot live in one's fears, they cannot have access to the rest of their emotional potential. This situation is occurring because in the consensus consciousness, admission of fear of any sort, is seen as weakness and thus is not respected. It would do us all a lot of good to admit our fears, for if we do not consciously recognize them and their detrimental influence then we cannot transcend them.

Yes, times are changing, still the world has far to go, and this is especially true in countries where women are treated as second or even third class citizens. In many areas of the world, at the foundation of the male consensus consciousness, women and femininity are seen as little more than a natural resource, to be directed and used as men see fit, rather than seeing women as totally equal and valued human beings. Often this masculine perspective sees women only as sexual objects and as projected stereotypes. As long as masculinity remains in "dominance mode", and in "better than women mode", and in seeing itself as the solution to all things, the masculine consensus consciousness, and many individual males, cannot become fully conscious or fully emotionally empowered. This subconscious fear driven

163

tendency for men to be "stuck in intellectualizing life" is part of why men are not more motivated to change and to more fully integrate emotionality into their life process. In essence, since these strategies have appeared to work in the past for men, they have become a societal habit that is hard to break. Feminine energy is good and it is powerful and to be respected!

These destructive and unnecessary historical social gender conditioning tendencies and invalidation of women have led to a subconscious feeling of distrust of the feminine and of feminine energy, and feminine decision-making and power in the general human consensus consciousness. This situation has in turn led to feelings on the part of many women of fear, victimization, vulnerability, powerlessness and anger toward masculine energy, and males' often myopic, domineering, dismissive, judgmental tendencies toward the feminine gender. This conditioning has even led to situations of some women mistrusting other women.

In its own defense, feminine energy has evolved to function in somewhat covert, egoless, and by necessity, even manipulative ways for the sake of its own literal safety and survival. This unbalanced power dynamic has in turn led to reciprocal and understandable judgment and blame on the part of women toward men and masculine energy. (I am not painting women as victims. All women have power; I am only describing energy dynamics that have been in play throughout human history). This previous trend has created a resulting negative and conflicted emotional and energetic set of dynamics between the genders. The process of painstaking reconciliation of this imbalance has led to significant conflict, and as a consequence, an unbalanced and maladaptive restructuring of today's family dynamics. It has also led to massively high divorce rates and problematic maladaptive conditioning of children. It has also resulted in unresolved and massive inter-gender resentment, hatred, misunderstanding and confusion. All of this is occurring without a clear path of consciously moving forward by men and women, in harmonious, loving, respectful, intimate and trusting intention.

A powerful undercurrent exists that may not be clearly visible and which causes more conflict and confusion—meaning that both genders have both male and female energy and tendencies in their systems. This is simply the nature of the humanity, souls and the universe. So, whenever a man hates a woman, he in effect hates his own feminine energy and nature. Whenever a woman hates a man, she in effect unknowingly hates her own male energy, nature and aspects of her own being. I am only being fair and accurate when I say that both men and women have the capacity to hate, to function in ruthlessly mercenary ways, to act destructively or even violently or viciously.

Neither gender is immune to these tendencies. It is true that both men and women tend to use different methods in regard to their application of their destructive tendencies. It is important not to "genderize" violence or destructiveness, and not to assume that only men want control, power or can cause conflict. If we do so then we may fail to fully recognize and fully root out these tendencies from all of humanity, in all its various forms. All of this said, it is still true that men have had a far greater tendency to act with physical violence to achieve their goals than women have.

Speaking candidly, at many levels of their system's men often fear women, feminine energy, emotions and power, at least as much or more than women fear men and their negative tendencies and misuse of power. Both genders have the capacity to deeply emotionally or even physically wound the other. That said, many men are just afraid to admit the situation of their fear of being emotionally hurt by women's negatively applied power, even if they are self-aware enough of their emotions to feel this fear consciously. In the long run we must blend male and female mental and emotional tendencies, if we want a healthy peaceful world. If we cannot transcend our fears we cannot be emotionally intimate with each other or truly love one another.

All of us are connected to the consensus consciousness, which is where these gender battles are constantly being fought out, and we are all the recipients of this gender-related negative energy in our daily lives. It is the ultimate battle of polarities and humanity is evolving due to the pressure of the conflict caused by the imbalance, the positive desire for loving relationships and the negative and confused process of ongoing misunderstanding. Still our personal emotional problems, negative emotional states and reactions cannot be solved by requiring or forcing anyone else to change themselves, or by expecting them to solve our emotional issues for us. We all feel how and what we choose to feel, it is always our option to choose love.

We only change for the better by our own freewill choice. Paradoxically if we love someone and really want to help our relationships improve we must be willing to "meet" and clearly understand our partner's deepest fears, needs and pain. We can be mirrors for each other, yet we cannot be responsible for another's emotional process. Still we are all one; all human beings are part of the larger human energy system, so if we harm each other we harm ourselves, and we harm the world as a whole. In our current dynamic of working to balance the energy and power of the genders, the tendency on both sides to invalidate the values, perspectives and emotional processes, decision-making methods or goals of the other undermines our success at reaching global and individual peace and harmony. We cannot get to peaceful relationships through either judgmentalness or victimization.

The as of yet unreconciled historically oppressive treatment of women has led to fear, distrust and shame in regard to the direct and open application of feminine power in society, business and in relationships. This can be true even if feminine power was submissively or adroitly expressed. This situation of unwillingness of men to hear, learn from and positively respond to the valid, beneficial and empowered communications of women is directly harmful to the evolution and development of quality relationships and the world as a whole.

Feminine energy and power are just, good, valuable, necessary and wise in intuitive and emotionally intelligent ways. The time has come to establish harmonious, balanced and comprehensive appreciation for, and application of, feminine energy in all areas of the world, all levels of society, institutions and in all relationships. Neither gender can ever "win" this battle, because the result of winning only creates unbalanced limitation and/or subjugation of the other gender, or having a winner or loser in the process, which just creates more problems. Therefore, we can only hope to create balance, mutual respect and peace as a result of all our efforts.

A fundamental shift in masculine energy is beginning to occur. Understanding and attitudes toward feminine energy, including a completely nonjudgmental acceptance and appreciation of the feminine and its value are beginning to take hold in the male consensus consciousness. Although this shift is currently in "seed" form, the choices we are now making globally will determine how quickly this attitude transforms the world. The main reason relationships do not work, and end up in divorce at this time, is that our old relationship paradigms must first be fundamentally demolished and invalidated. This is necessary in order to make room for and to validate the creation of new, balanced and more functional relationship models. The foundation of relationships of the future needs to include the truest forms of mutual respect, acceptance, trust, open fearless communication and thus potential for pure conscious integrous emotional intimacy and commitment.

We can either go about creating these new models peacefully or we can fight our way to them. Either way, necessary relationship developments will occur because they must. Yet the cost to both men and women, and to our children, could be very high if we choose the road of control, opposite gender invalidation, conflict, condemnation or punishment.

Another necessary shift occurring in the feminine energy dynamic relates to women transcending the prior conditioning of mistrusting their own feminine energy and power, and not feeling confident in feminine power. Working toward global feminine empowerment is fundamental to our transcendence of this prior tendency. I am pleased to see that much of this is going on in a well-organized manner which is reaching many women. Yet men, in mass, require assistance and <u>literal mentoring</u> to develop the necessary mental and emotional skills, self-awareness and self-acceptance to evolve their own understandings of the positive nature of femininity and feminine emotional styles. Currently there is little comprehensive or sophisticated societal support for men in this developmental effort or acceptance by male society of this effort. Until this system of support and social/interpersonal education is active, and new ways of female/male interaction are created and broadly taught, there will continue to be conflict.

This society and gender dynamic shift will have a positive effect, leading to greater emotional trust between the genders and ultimately to the creation of a new, sustainable and more optimally functional styles of male/female relationships, as well as a more functional society. Balance and harmony between masculine and feminine energies at all levels of society, in all relationships and in all social, cultural and religious contexts is a primary ingredient for the healthy creation of all future generations and for all cultural and relationship modeling developments.

It is only through attainment of conscious self-awareness that we can transcend all of the negative emotional states and dynamics which affect our relationships. It is only through the acknowledgment of the ultimate goodness of all aspects of our own being, including both our masculine and feminine energies, that we become willing to love ourselves enough to fully transcend all of life's obstacles. We all have the option, power and potential to accomplish this, we are all on the same path in this regard. Accepting this truth can help us find greater compassion for ourselves and all of those we are traveling through life with. In the long term, becoming fully internally healed, balanced, self-aware, unified and congruent can result in transcendent understanding and wise, consistent, discerning ownership of our personal power within our relationships.

Letting Go of Shiny Things...:

Years ago, I heard a story about a tribe in a far-off country that hunt baboons as a source of food. According to the story, the tribe's way of hunting is to go to a spot near a group of baboons, a species that can be quite dangerous, and which are also very curious. The baboons would cautiously watch as the tribesmen carved a hole in the side of tree. The tribesmen would make the inner volume of the hole they dug out larger than the opening into the space they had created in the tree. They would then hold up a shiny object for the baboons to see. Then they would toss the shiny object into the hole in the tree. At this point the tribesmen walk away and simply watch the tree from a distance.

Since baboons are curious creatures, one of them will eventually go to the tree and reach its hand into the hole in the tree in order to obtain the shiny object. However, when the baboon clinched its hand around the object, its fist became too large to fit back out through the small outer hole. The baboon is then unwilling to open its hand and free itself from its self-created trap because it is so focused on holding onto the object. At this point the tribesmen can walk up and safely hit the baboon over the head with a club, while the baboon remains imprisoned by their own choices and intentions.

In human beings, as in baboons, this degree of focus on achieving goals or attachment to any specific desire can tend to shut down the higher levels of intelligent mental function and decision-making. These types of situations can be seen in human cultures and in the lives of individual humans every day, as people and even nations attempt to attain and retain that which they desire without adequate understanding or forethought as to the implications of their choices. What we desire is not always good for us, and once we start down the road to achieving it we often become, in an odd way, imprisoned by the process. Often the more we put into the process of attaining a desire, the less willing we are to let go of the desire, even when it becomes obvious that it is beneficial to do so. Individuals and societies can become so entrained in the goals, beliefs and values of their economic systems, political systems, general societies or their religions that they lose focus and discernment of the implications of doing so. Despite the pain and conflict the process produces.

Learning to become more consciously discerning, and thus to be empowered to choose to detach consciously and gracefully from our prior and less optimal desires, motivations, beliefs and values as we learn and evolve, is vital to our progress as individuals and as a world.

We can see that in the long run these types of attachment dynamics create individual, national, international and thus global stress. This stress is simultaneously requiring us and motivating us (through pain) to learn to let go of what is not beneficial and to discerningly focus on what is truly worth doing or keeping. Thus, it is part of our species evolutionary process and an ongoing process of "filtration of reality and our choices", by being willing to change our ways, that leads to attainment of conscious wisdom.

168

This is true whether we are speaking of:

- ❖ Social definitions of right and wrong
- ❖ All our definitions of success
- ❖ Cultural beliefs and traditions
- ❖ Selfish tendencies
- ❖ Religious dogma
- ❖ Egoic tendencies
- ❖ Comfort zones
- ❖ Addictions of all kinds
- ❖ Personal or social habits
- ❖ Decision-making styles
- ❖ Expectations of ourselves and others
- ❖ Greed of all kinds
- ❖ Corrupting influences
- ❖ Negative emotions such as hatred
- ❖ Our own ignorance

The process of blindly holding onto anything in life is not beneficial. The list of things I would suggest letting go of also includes all interpretations we have made of our past experiences as to what is supposedly true or right, (i.e. our recorded simulacra and associated beliefs). We often value the recorded interpretations we hold in our memory more than we do our conscious awareness of this present moment. Doing so only creates internal conflict and disharmony. Projecting the past onto the present colors our experience of the present, and by doing so unnecessarily and detrimentally limits our options in the present. This tendency is worth meditating upon.

The Social Dynamics of Ants:

Ants are amazing and socially intelligent creatures that have lived and survived many of the world's most destructive natural and human made disasters. Ants have evolved an interesting strategy of working together that is very supportive of their survival. When a group of ants is threatened by a dire situation, such as needing to escape a fire, they have found a way to cross bodies of water that block their paths. In order to cross flowing streams the worker ants will grasp onto one another and make a bridge of their bodies that spans the stream. Even when those ants that have created the bridge drown, they remain locked in a tight connection. Then the rest of the ants climb over the bodies of those who have given their lives to create the bridge to get to the other side of the stream.

169

Another similar example of this behavior is seen when ants create a literal miniature floating island of the bodies of their group. The ants on the bottom tend to drown, while those on top of the island live. Eventually the "ant island" floats to a safe place for those ants that are still alive to disembark, and continue the ant's hive in new safe territory. Another tendency that is seen in ants is the willingness to "wage war" in an organized fashion against other species, so that their group continues to live.

Humans have shown similar tendencies of species survival, in that in many aspects of human development we have been willing to sacrifice ourselves and other humans in many different ways in order to achieve what appear to be necessary goals. This willingness to sacrifice humans for progress has been seen in the building of many large structures around the world, such as the construction of several large dams, the Great Wall of China and the Suez Canal. In human wars, we willingly sacrifice our young and often least prepared citizens to achieve what are perceived to be necessary goals. In so doing we tend to rationalize the necessity, and to refrain from significant questioning of the supposed necessity. We do this while continuing to be unwilling to find more sophisticated and peaceful methods of preemptively dealing with social, economic and political problems.

Of course, humans are not ants, and we have vastly greater capacity to make conscious, wise, loving and self-sovereign decisions. Still, we as a species have shown the repetitive destructive propensity throughout human history and have not yet chosen to proactively learn our way beyond it to live in peace. Indeed, there are those who have consistently profited from war and unresolved conflict. One telling example would be the Military Industrial Complex of the United States, which has vast capacity to influence U.S. governmental policy and laws, via lobbying congress. Another example would be any corporation that knowingly supported product sales that created global warming, without regard for the potential loss of life and destruction to the ecosystem that would be incurred globally. Humanity's self-centered tendencies tend to become magnified in any situation of perceived lack of necessary resources, especially if we have previously grown used to having access bounty. They also become magnified in situations of perceived profit. In fact, there are many corporations right now looking at ways to monetize climate change. Not to solve the problems, but to profit from them.

What I am hoping to communicate in this section is that we are not ants, we have other understandings, options and technology. We can change as a species; we can learn not to use or sacrifice other humans for the attainment

170

of any materialistic goal. These sacrifices, although often painted as such, are neither necessary nor noble. It is simply a choice that all of us can consciously make at any moment to raise our consciousness. I suggest it is in our best interest, for all of us as a world, to make this decision, as quickly as we can. As "time speeds up", our window of opportunity to fundamentally change from our past primitive, unloving and destructive tendencies is rapidly shrinking. The costs of holding onto these prior dysfunctional methods of dealing with problems and achieving goals are becoming greater and more obvious in all areas of the world, as time goes by. There is no need or benefit to tolerating these prior behaviors or ignorant decision-making, we need not hold onto unwanted species habits.

Chapter Six
Transformational Toxicity in Times of Rapid Change:

DURING TIMES OF RAPID CHANGE AND TRANSFORMATION of any kind, whether in a personal relationship, a corporation, a nation or a world, there is the potential for the buildup of toxic energies and emotions within individuals and groups. This toxic energy is often released in unmanageable ways and the release often occurs most intensely when we reach a boiling point. This dynamic is dangerous because the energy is then unconsciously expelled as a primal destructive reactive process.

Examples of this would be the layering on of one unmanaged or unresolved stress after another, one change shock after another, or one negative emotional reaction after another. In an individual human body, the impacts of those changes and the related stresses tend to accumulate over time in our energy and our body chemistry. This means that without the application of ongoing methods of detoxification and rehabilitation, the stresses can lead to eventual breakdowns of various kinds. Mindfulness meditation is one of these methods.

These toxins can be seen in accumulations of resentment, fear and anxiety, being judgmental, deep anger or hatred, depression, negative outlooks on life, decrease of trust in self and/or others we depend upon (including friends, family, corporations or governments). Their effect can also be seen in physical illnesses that result from unreconciled internal conflicts and emotions. These toxic effects can be, and need to be, continually cleared; day-by-day in any situation, environment or relationship. These detrimental effects can be cleared with the application of various available methods. Whether we are speaking of a toxified individual, a marriage, a family, a corporation or a nation, achieving this healthy state requires astute awareness of the existence and costs of these toxins. It also requires a disciplined consistent willingness to highly prioritize our investment in resolving these effects.

The worst-case scenarios of this kind of accumulated toxic stress on individuals can lead to significant mental, physical, emotional or spiritual damage.

These situations can be seen in people:

❖ In the military who served as soldiers fighting wars and suffering for years from post-traumatic stress syndrome (PTSD).

❖ Who live in conflict zones (for example drug or gang infected areas or regions subject to extreme poverty and/or war).

❖ Working in corporations that are subject to layoffs and who are just waiting for the day they or people they care about lose their jobs.

❖ Who lose their jobs and cannot find work year after year, (especially those with families to support).

❖ Who care for the terminally ill or the mentally ill.

❖ With long term debilitating and/or painful illnesses.

❖ With families impacted by multiple divorces, deaths or illnesses.

❖ Who have experienced spousal abuse or child abuse of all kinds.

❖ With long term depression and/or various forms of mental illness.

❖ From families with a history of ongoing generational addiction.

❖ With any combination of the above conditions.

The people who make up organizations and governments and their associated cultures and group consciousnesses experience a dynamic of ongoing toxic backlash as these groups are subjected to stresses. This dynamic creates organizational and interpersonal relationship strain and damage at various levels of the organization due to the pressures of rapid change and/or resource scarcity. In these situations, organization's cultures can become distrustful, depressed, fearful, fatigued or angry.

Within organizations certain key departments or key individuals in these areas can be massively stressed in their attempt to meet organizational needs and requirements or customer/market demand. This can lead to what could be termed energy blocks and distortions in the organization, which then in turn lead to reduced productivity and negative domino effects flowing out from these departments or individuals. These dynamics can then have tremendous detrimental influence on the overall function of the organization.

In organizations, these situations also lead to breakdowns in:

❖ Communication between individuals or between any level or segment of the organization.

❖ The organization's capacity to intelligently change and adapt, and its capacity to navigate the changes in the world around it.

❖ Interpersonal and intra-organizational trust.

❖ Teamwork, collaboration, organizational operation and creative efforts.

❖ Focus on defining and effectively working toward organizational goals, mission and shared vision.

❖ The integrity of the organization's culture, values, beliefs and rules.
❖ Organizational viability.

This process of organizational dysfunction can readily be seen in tough economic times where organizations are continually trying to be more productive with less people. There is a fundamental need to create support systems to decrease the change stress the world is experiencing as well as ways to "flush out" the built up negative emotions and energies that tend to accumulate. Organizational and cultural emotional maintenance and revitalization is rarely looked at as a serious issue in most corporations. In many organizations, people are seen by management as interchangeable parts that are simply replaced when they are worn out or become less than optimally productive or functional. This attitude leads organization's management cultures to emotionlessly close ranks and move on when they go through difficult times or lose personnel. Instead organizations could choose to heal, revitalize, nurture, forgive, forge closer interpersonal ties, develop, retrain, and learn from their experience and in turn continually evolve.

A very public example of the dynamic of group toxins can be seen at this time in the United States in the form of the toxic and rapidly degrading relationship between the Republican and Democratic parties. The ongoing and intensifying battles over topics such as health care and the cost of military efforts, along with the constant attacks of one party on the other, and the ongoing dynamic of jockeying for power and votes have created a highly toxic and unproductive political environment. This is one obvious and exhausting example, yet this scenario is being played out over and over around the world, and just as this dynamic in the United States is intensifying so it is in other nations. In effect the ongoing conflict is a call to action so that we can explore new models for culture, government and politics.

In these stressed times the concept of revitalization and nurturance of governmental cultural systems, national cultures and of corporate cultures is for the most part being put on a shelf, and with it the welfare of the individual human being. In many areas, the focus on organizational survival and defeating the competition has taken the place of vision, creativity, teamwork, emotional intelligence and collaboration. This has led to division and fracturing of global endeavors rather than unified conscious transcendent intention and accomplishment. These are not utopian ideals; they are global survival requirements.

175

We must methodically and comprehensively increase the consciousness, compassion and quality of decision-making of all nations, cultures, religions and corporations. As self-sovereign individuals, we must prioritize transcendent values, goals and principles above our personal comfort and security. This realized intention of purposefully instilling sage consciousness into institutions and organizational cultures is the only thing that will save humanity from our own baser instincts and associated subconscious and often negative group dynamics. Technological inventions alone will not change human nature or our basic global situation. Certainly, we are learning as we go, as individuals, corporations and nations, yet at some point we must choose to mature, mentally, spiritually and emotionally. In this way, we can apply the discerning wisdom necessary to solve our issues. It is this positive energy, intention and perspective that will hold us together through the difficult times.

This is a social developmental necessity that we can no longer do without. Due to our current toxic situations in all areas of life, we are being called to revise and live by new standards which are the key to the literal survival of humanity. Because we all have freewill we can choose to move in this more positive direction.

Information Rich and Information Poor:
(Another Situation of the Haves and the Have-Nots)

Many of life's problems are aggravated by a lack of complete, accurate and timely information, or enough refined and organized information, which we might call astute knowledge. Information is a necessary resource, the same as shelter, food and water and it leads to understanding and personal empowerment. Many people are experiencing mental, emotional or social issues due to the acquisition of information that is inaccurate, incomplete, conflicting or misinterpreted. This is especially true if the information was acquired at key developmental points in their lives. Once we acquire this misinformation, whether from family or society, it becomes what we believe to be fact and it is often not questioned in regard to its validity or applicability. We can see this process at work in its most gross forms as social and political conditioning and indoctrination efforts in North Korea, China and Russia and other nationalist nations. It is useful to say that all nations tend to condition their citizens to some extent, even democratic nations.

This acquired information becomes our "truth" and what we then base our current and future life decisions upon, for better or for worse. This is what happens when we acquire non-adaptive and dysfunction inducing

176

information in early childhood, at a time when we are not mentally or emotionally developed enough to question its essential nature, authenticity or usefulness. Later, we may judge ourselves and others and create expectations based upon this misinformation or lack of information. In these situations, we are functioning and deciding key life issues from a state of simple ignorance or misunderstanding. We may feel safer seeing life situations simplistically and as black and white, right or wrong, win or lose, true or false, or good and bad rather than the subtle, complex, interdependent and interwoven truth of reality. Thus, we tend to judge ourselves and others based upon intentionally simplified viewpoints, distorted interpretations and inaccurate decision-making models.

Lack of balance and comprehensive understanding in our decision-making perspectives and interpretive methods literally creates emotional indifference and lack of compassion. It also creates internal emotional conflict and toxicity, interpersonal and relationship toxicity and social conflict and toxicity. Therefore, amazingly, just the introduction of astute accurate information can be profoundly healing either in relationships, social situations or within oneself. Once this healing occurs at foundational levels its associated emotional toxicity tends to dissipate naturally. A more effective method of preemptively reducing toxicity is to educate everyone in regard to proactive and discerning acquisition and usage of quality information.

Discerning usage of information that is available to us has nothing to do with judgment or blaming anyone for anything, in fact judgmentalness is not part of quality decision-making at all. (Judgment here described as a process of judging ourselves or others in a critical manner and often as a prelude to anger, disappointment, and/or punishment of some sort for not meeting our expectations or agreeing with us. Meaning with an underlying desire to control ourselves or someone else through negative means). Discernment is about clear complete situational and relationship understanding and thus it directly supports wise decision-making and actions. There has never been a value or need for any of us to see ourselves as above, better or more righteous than anyone else, nor is there any validity to our seeing ourselves as less than anyone else. This is true because we are all totally equal in the eyes of God, all are lovable, all are completely forgivable for anything and everything we have ever done. Living in loving and compassionate humility is optimally supportive of discernment. We cannot be discerning if we are blinded by ego or ego dynamics. (Humility here is defined as a way of seeing ourselves as fundamentally good, acceptable and worthwhile in all ways and situations, yet still not in any way better than anyone else. Humility is a positive state of loving spiritual peace and grace, and with it comes an openness to receiving new understandings that ego states are not open to and cannot understand).

Due to the advent of the internet and related computer technology, the world is now awash in information. Of course, not all of it useful, comprehensive or accurate, yet it is for the most part much better than not having access to information. The introduction of this vast source of information around the world is driving various kinds of change, new perspectives, new decisions and thus unexpected results and events. It is not merely connectedness that the internet brings, it is the information that it carries that has value, power and creates the profound effect in our lives and changes our decisions moment-by-moment. Many people have not been taught to wisely and efficiently manage the mass of information they have access to in a mature manner. Nor have they been taught to interpret, integrate, synthesize and apply their information resources in an optimal and effective manner. Achieving discernment in regard to the information we take in to our minds is an ongoing and evolving process that is currently spreading across the world.

An interesting flip side to this situation is that of information and knowledge hoarding. Which is in effect power hoarding. Governments acquire and hide vast amounts of intelligence and technical data which they then only grudgingly share or trade with other nations or even more grudgingly their own citizens. Not only do governments withhold information, they refuse to even acknowledge that they have it to begin with. Corporations, in the name of competition, profits and in avoidance of legal actions against them, tend to hide technical and operational information or may even create misinformation in order to mislead competitors, their own employees, customers or sometimes their own stock holders. Right now, Exxon and other energy companies are being investigated to determine whether they concealed scientific knowledge that their products were directly contributing to global warming since the 1970's. It is also being determined whether they concealed facts and data that would keep citizens from realizing that man-made global warming was going to occur, long before its impacts were felt.

The attainment of conscious and wise discernment regarding how we acquire, manage, interpret, distribute and apply information at the level of the individual and at all levels of organizations and governments will become more crucial as time goes by. It does not appear that this information management capability is a well understood requirement at all levels of our educational systems. Nor is it understood in social systems, such as governments, who are supposed to be managing and facilitating positive world change. It is a fact that most of today's scientific research and papers are not available to everyday people and that this important information can only be had by paying a significant price. This lack of open distribution of information that could help the world is a crucial issue and limitation regarding solving world problems. As of this writing President Barak Obama has taken steps to release some of this information to everyday people.

Various Costs of Corruption:

Corruption costs everyone in many ways and inhibits and undermines the development of wise and evolved individuals, cultures, societies, corporations and governments. It strikes at every level of every society. Short term self-centered material valuations of life's pleasures and security can be highly seductive and reduce our regard for higher insights, values, wisdom, spiritual perspective, philosophies or even the implications of our personal choices. This influence can be countered by access to comprehensive ethical and spiritual understanding and guidance which supports discernment and decision-making. If we ignore the direct corrupting negative impact of our choices and actions on others we may, without realizing it, enter a state of non-compassion and this can lead good souls into corruption. Putting love and compassion above personal goals and pleasures helps keep corruption at bay.

The state of non-compassion toward those we have either purposely or inadvertently hurt through our actions can in some cases be directly tied to chakra system limitations (of the individual or the group) and the dysfunctional energy patterns they contain. Corruption is an inherently destructive disintegration of personal integrity, which often grows beyond the individual to the point of becoming socially and politically institutionalized or sanctioned. Once socially institutionalized, it becomes even more difficult to effectively resolve since there are usually entrenched interests keeping the corrupt status quo. Corruption is also expressed and based in a fundamental devaluation and distrust of others. Corruption is neither based in honesty nor integrity and the worldwide cost of its existence, which goes far beyond the monetary, affects generation after generation. This is especially true when we are discussing its distortive impact on the developing power of the individual in the world today. Corruption is always driven by ego-identity motivations, fear, insecurity and blind self-interest, many of which are subconscious.

179

Paradoxically corruption can be a useful part of our human process of ultimately attaining wisdom, discipline, discernment and full spiritual resonance with God. In essence, we learn what not to do, from first having done that which is not good for us. Our world's corrupt aspects provide an environment in which we can learn from clearly seeing the problems with, and costs of corruption, and of not living in integrity. Corruption therefore has a minimal type of value to humanity's evolutionary process.

Today corrupt individuals can have vastly more detrimental impact on the global situation than was previously the case, whether this impact is intended consciously or is just an indirect byproduct of corrupt activities. This is in part due to the interwoven and interdependent system of technologies that make up our current world. It is also due to the rapid advances in technology that make it more difficult to police illegal activities and for the legal system to keep up with technological developments. In many ways, the current process of developing new technologies is literally invisible and immune to governmental and judicial influence. Governments all over the world are making corrupt use of the information that new technologies are making available to them. This corruption includes using this information to overtly influence their citizens in ways that serve the current political agenda, and also serve the economic self-interest's of the governments themselves. As of now, privacy is non-existent.

It is necessary to understand that in this new and vastly more complex world merely policing corrupt individuals, groups or nations is no longer a workable or effective option. This is because the cost, difficulty, complexity and societal disruption of catching people we define as criminals and punishing them is rapidly increasing. The problem is growing and mutating at an alarming rate, without the average person fully understanding how and why it is occurring or its implications on their lives or their future. What is needed is preemptive facilitated attainment of self-awareness in human beings so that they never get to the point of acting in this destructive manner in the first place. No amount of "militarization" of the process of policing any society, via the application of more technology or military weaponry in police forces, will solve this problem.

Corruption of individuals usually occurs in a gradual and escalating manner, meaning that it is a "learned" way of life, thinking, feeling, interpreting life situations and relationships and of making decisions. In this downward spiraling process, we see a habitual tendency toward making decisions based upon primal and self-centered motivations. Learning to shift our focus to higher principles, as a species, is vital in order to transcend this influence.

Examples of these primal / self-centered motivations include:

- ❖ Fear and the desire for safety and security
- ❖ Greed and desire for power or control over others
- ❖ Attention seeking, glamour or fame
- ❖ Sense gratifications of various kinds including sex and various addictions

These motivations can be driving distortive influences on consciousness and life results if not counterbalanced with discipline, integrity, discernment and wise understanding of the implications of our decisions and actions. Without this counterbalancing effect, corruption can begin to gain a foothold in our lives. These influences also produce chakra levels of incongruity of consciousness, which can be very difficult to fully recognize, understand and effectively reconcile. Once this situation of corruption occurs our fear of its being discovered by others becomes another corrupting influence. In a way, a highly competitive environment itself can sow the seeds for corruption, as can a focus on material and social attainment to the exclusion of love and compassion.

If we develop in a vacuum of adequate decision-making information, quality role modeling and education then we tend to fall back into simple and reactive ego self-defense patterns and erroneous subconscious beliefs as our decision-making criteria. This non-optimal tendency can develop gradually without our realizing it. In this way, we may demonstrate and then rationalize detrimental "moral flexibility" in our interpretations, decisions and relationships. If we have not been taught to function in a discerning manner, and if we do not have the tools of basic information and understandings necessary to support quality decision-making, then we will tend to make unwise or destructive decisions. In addition, due to subconscious ego influences we may exhibit a short-sighted focus on personal "ego survival".

There are many forms of intelligence and some have been studied and theorized by scientists and though intelligence is a good thing it does not equal discernment, spirituality or wisdom. Dr. Howard Gardner the author of "Frames of Mind" theorizes that there are multiple forms of intelligence, and has defined nine different types of intelligence, including: Linguistic, logical-mathematical, musical, spatial, bodily-kinesthetic, interpersonal, intrapersonal, naturalistic and existential. While these are all practically useful descriptions of aspects of intelligence, there are aspects of intelligence and consciousness which I feel are neither describable nor quantifiable. Labeling aspects of intelligence does not equate to either understanding them or their discerning application in our lives. (Highly intelligent and educated people can exhibit very negative emotions and make very unwise choices). In the future it may be that humans will naturally or artificially create new types of human intelligence from which to learn and evolve. That does not mean that new forms of intelligence will all lead to goodness or love.

Still all forms of intelligence to one degree or another can, if applied wisely support the process of attained discernment which is the antithesis of corruption. Yet high intelligence of any kind is not an absolute prerequisite or determinant in how discerningly we weigh our life choices. For example, if we apply patience, focus and methodical discipline to our choices we then act discerningly. I would also say that God-aligned creativity and intuition are not precisely processes of intelligence, yet impeccably expressing them in our lives can be the cornerstone of sovereign astute self-mastery.

None of us are comprehensively highly intelligent, completely knowledgeable and simultaneously self-aware; we are all a mixture of various types and degrees of intelligence, awareness and understanding. Nevertheless, most of us have the potential to make better decisions in a manner which accurately and comprehensively considers the long-term implications of our choices. We are challenged to learn through our experiences how to best leverage our particular mixture of intelligence, creativity, intuition, personal spiritual nature, emotional intelligence, situational and relationship understanding and conscious self-awareness with integrity. Then we can augment our unique personal capabilities with supporting knowledge, training and information from external sources in order to achieve optimal decisions and results. Yet all of us still have karmic patterns, subconscious conditioning, consensus consciousness influences and limiting beliefs which distort or even negate our discernment in some area of our lives.

Criminal behavior is not merely a function of lack of the intelligence necessary to make integrous decisions, yet other factors are. It is useful to understand that the current judicial system is designed to blindly and dysfunctionally treat everyone as if we all have the same capacity to make discerning decisions. It is also designed to use a simple method, (i.e. punishment) to address these social and psychological problems. <u>Neither punishment nor the threat of punishment will stop corruption.</u> This is blind, "one size fits all approach" is why there are a large number of incarcerated people with undiagnosed or untreated mental and emotional illness. (Neuroscience is just now beginning to profoundly affect the law in this regard to help the legal system learn to make more discerning decisions regarding the mentally ill). Additionally, there are many differences between each of us in terms of basic brain function and brain chemistry which affect our decision-making and thus our degree of practical wisdom. Lastly, whatever maladaptive simulacra recordings each of us has made in our past, and which we use to determine our decisions in the present moment are key to understanding crime and corruption, as well as how to solve it. As our understanding of the complexity of our world and reality evolves we may get to a point where we understand that a simple rule based judicial system is no longer adequate to meet our needs.

High intelligence of any kind is not a defining characteristic of personal integrity. There are many highly educated or charismatic individuals and politicians who are fundamentally impaired in their decision-making processes, base motivations and personal integrity. The often-subconscious dynamics of denial, greed and rationalization, as well as the habit of subconsciously projecting our own corrupt perspectives and tendencies onto the world around us can occur regardless of education or intelligence, and thus impair our ability to accurately gauge the detrimental implications of our choices.

There is much wisdom in the quote by Lord Acton, a British historian of the late sixteenth and seventeenth centuries, who said, "Power tends to corrupt, and absolute power corrupts absolutely. Great men are almost always bad men". What does this statement mean in terms of the technological power that governments and individuals can now wield? Yet, there exists no absolute necessity for this to be our future. Part of the problem is that when we have great power, we tend to ignore or lose focus on the implications of its use on others, because we do not understand enough to be personally concerned about the consequences of unwise power usage. The dynamic of karma ultimately motivates us to spiritually purify and in essence "de-corrupt" any corrupting tendencies we acquire on our evolutionary path.

A great spiritual teacher, Jiddu Krishnamurti, (not to be confused with UG Krishnamurti, also a spiritual adept), refused to have an organization created around him and dissolved the worldwide organization called "The Order of the Star" that wanted him as its leader. Later some of his followers did create organized schools to transmit his teachings, though Krishnamurti stated that he had found no one he felt capable of teaching his understandings. It is my personal perception that he felt that no organization could lead anyone to true spiritual understanding and that organizations

183

inherently dilute, distract from or corrupt the expression of even the highest of spiritual intentions. I would agree with this viewpoint in principle. That said, we live in a world where billions of people are still developing spiritually, socially, emotionally and technologically. Thus, we are not ready as nations or as a species to function without the support of organizations and bureaucracy in some form. So far in our evolution maintaining our physical existence requires organized mechanisms and institutions of physical support. Therefore, I suggest it is useful for all of us to support the achievement of sage understandings in all of the world populations, and within all existing and future institutions.

THE DOWNWARD SPIRAL OF LIMITATIONS

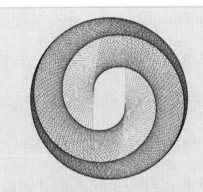

EROSION OF OUR PERSONAL POWER, SELF-
SOVEREIGNTY AND DISTORTED VIEWS
OCCUR, CREATING LIMITATIONS WHEN

we are seduced by negative or illusionary beliefs experiencing the effects from our own or other peoples' corruption	we are infected by environmental /social toxins negative or illusionary beliefs and/or unconscious karmic patterns are active

we lack necessary and/or accurate information resources

SOLUTION? SITUATIONAL DISCERNMENT.
CONSCIOUSLY AND WILLFULLY CHOOSE TO
CEASE TO BE ENSLAVED OR ENTRAINED BY
THESE DOWNWARD SPIRALING EROSION
DYNAMICS.

Once we enter the state of complete self-sovereignty and enlightenment, even the idea of organizations and bureaucracy become obsolete and antiquated for us as individuals. Yet until the world fundamentally and comprehensively makes a transcendent shift in this regard we, as individuals, may still be required to interact with organizations to some degree.

The key to understanding and resolving organizational corruption is accepting that all organizations have a root chakra, which inherently and subconsciously focuses only on the survival, security, growth and continuance of the organization. The root chakra mechanisms of organizations have no capacity for compassion, sympathy, love or altruism. Thus, the root chakra's influence fundamentally and constantly undermines the quality of the organizational culture and it's decision-making. It also drives almost all organizations to try to grow larger and larger, since size is seen by the root chakra as power, safety, security and competitive advantage. Therefore, integrity in operation for many organizations is subconsciously usually deemed to be a low priority.

It is true that there are organizations that are altruistic and that are guided by higher principles, yet these organizations almost always start out with these goals and focus. Meaning that these types of organizations principle reason for existence is altruistic and they were therefore designed to fulfill these altruistic intentions. Therefore, their cultures are designed to be driven by more evolved values than mere profit motive, economic dynamics, shareholder equity, or "the financial bottom line". An example of this type of organization would be charitable organizations, such as The Red Cross. Still even charitable organizations are not immune to corruption. This situation can be seen in "charitable" organizations that spend eighty percent of the monies they collect as donations on marketing, to then produce more contributions, rather than applying the money they collect to those in need.

Another key to understanding corruption is that all organizations are mixtures of people who are on very different life paths, have different values, and are functioning at different levels of spiritual maturity, wisdom, discernment. Thus, they influence the organization with different degrees of potential personal corruption. Therefore, we get inconsistent, mixed, diluted and conflicted organizational results, sometimes simply based on who is hired by the organization. This is why, practically speaking, the hiring process could be seen as the most important function of any organization. Therefore, I suggest willfully developing ourselves as independent spiritual and discerning individuals, since doing so can only benefit whatever organizations we participate in. On this path, we can intentionally and proactively work to "de-corrupt" and constantly develop and refine all aspects of our own being and of the world.

If we focus only on personal gratification we lose focus on the detrimental effects of our choices on others, and the needs of the rest of the world are literally not part of our decision-making process. If we feel we have been victimized in our past, we may then feel that our personal unresolved pain is valid reason for functioning in unbalanced or even corrupt ways. We can for this reason lose perspective, and with this loss we then lose the capacity to fully and emotionally understand our influence on those we are in relationship with and on the broader world.

In our relationships, emotional corruption can gradually "creep up" on us. This occurs when we come to feel that our relationship roles don't work or when we are under constant life stresses, relationship conflict or economic pressures. It can also occur if we misinterpret our karmic emotional pain and confusion as our being emotionally "victimized" in our relationships, then our personal integrity can "crack". In these cases, we may lose focus on love, and make self-centered and rationalized choices which do not meet our needs or those of our most precious relationships. In the worst cases, we can strike out in hatred. Clearly understanding the implications of our interpretations of what is happening to us and around us is a key element of discerning decision-making.

Personal corruption is the result of misunderstanding and ignorance of our wise and loving relationship to self, God and humanity. Therefore, I suggest that judging or punishing corruption will not resolve it. Judgment and punishment do not lead directly to understanding.

Solutions to the potentially relationship corrupting influences of the world's developmental and transformational process (which we are not the victims of because we are each creating it) include constant willful, diligent and positively intentioned:

- ❖ Understanding of the profound and sometimes disrupting influences the world's transformational process has on each of us.

- ❖ Attaining greater emotional self-awareness and deeper understanding of ourselves and those we are in relationship with.

- ❖ Working to gain confidence in our management of our emotions in order to support our feeling "safer" as we learn to develop greater foundational trust in our interpersonal relationships.

- ❖ Realization that our relationship communications are affected by a naturally occurring mirroring effect in which we project our own tendencies onto others, and they project theirs onto us. This mirroring dynamic is designed to assist each of us to develop and attain wisdom and understanding. The mirror shows us both pleasant and unpleasant aspects of ourselves, yet these achieved understandings facilitate our learning and development.

- ❖ Being willing to redefine or discard old dysfunctional relationship roles. And to be tolerant and flexible in this practice of letting go of that which no longer serves us.

❖ Developing shared relationship goals based upon increased discernment while expressing divine love.

❖ Tolerating and appreciating our spouses "imperfections" and our own.

❖ Healing our emotional wounds and our relationship issues. We can choose to forgive no matter what the situation and choose to discard victimhood.

❖ Expressing and building trust and safe communication in our relationships.

❖ Gaining confidence in our own ability to be discerning in relationships and so develop self-trust.

❖ Releasing expectations of our mates as they tend to set us up for disappointment.

❖ Managing and gracefully integrating ongoing changes in belief and understanding throughout our lives.

To attain mutually acceptable results and an ongoing state of peace in our relationships requires non-judgmental acceptance of all aspects of ourselves and our spouses. The constant willingness to negotiate and re-negotiate any aspect of our relationships is critical. I am not suggesting that anyone remain in abusive, dysfunctional or codependent relationships. In all relationships discernment is needed to determine whether a relationship truly serves the best good of all of the people involved.

Eventually the development of divine love of self and others will transform the world for the better. Soul love or divine love does not mean having no boundaries, nor does it mean continuing to interact with those who act in destructive ways. Constant forgiveness and love does not equal passivity in the face of interpersonal problems such as drug abuse, physical abuse or sexual abuse; it simply means that we handle these situations without hatred, anger, punishing tendencies, etc. It means we manage our lives constructively rather than destructively. If we cannot get effective help for those we love in these kinds of situations, then we can become willing to manage them out of our lives until they heal or develop beyond their destructive tendencies.

Excluding someone from our lives in order to remain safe does not mean we cannot still have compassion and love for them in their impaired or negative state. For example, we can still pray daily for a child hooked on methamphetamines, though if we were to interact with them physically they might try to steal from us or even harm us to feed their habit. We need not allow our feelings of soul love to create unwarranted vulnerability or risk.

Doing so will not truly help those we love who are in destructive states of mind or emotion.

We can heal and transmute the seeds that could grow into corruption in our family units and closest relationships. From there, we can extend outward, with great clarity and intention to reduce the corruption of governments, cultures, corporations and other individuals. When all parties are brought to levels of consciousness, where they can accept and willfully support the need for education regarding personal and organizational integrity, the results will be quite exquisite.

The development of emotional intelligence, and what I would term "cultural intelligence", is a key part of the solution. (Cultural intelligence is here roughly defined as the capacity of individuals and cultural groups to develop and function in a self-aware and consciously self-evolving and self-educating manner). We need to learn to trust that the process of creating and maintaining a more optimally functional society is not merely the responsibility of religious institutions and that this goal cannot be accomplished solely by them. Nor can this achievement be the responsibility of the judicial system, since its purpose is to function in a reactive and punitive manner rather than a developmental and educational manner. Coordinated development of ethics, principles, the various intelligences, compassion and discernment in all groups and cultures is required.

We can deal with corruption in a preemptive, proactive and constructive manner, via the development of educational infrastructure and support systems designed to resolve social issues, before they have the chance to develop. If individuals are not schooled early in life as to the positive and negative implications of the application of their new-found power of individual choice on the world, they will continue to act in ways that are increasingly and powerfully detrimental to the world. As the world increases in complexity and precious resources become ever more scarce and polluted, some people will choose to undermine the quality of life for everyone else, as long as they themselves are physically, emotionally and/or financially benefitted. By saying this, I am not judging any element of humanity; I am simply observing that many of us may continue to function in corrupt ways simply because we do not know any better. In the long run this dynamic cannot end well for anyone, not even for those who have been made wealthy, famous and powerful by following this well-trod path of blind and blinding self-interest.

Chapter Seven
The Challenges of Social Identity Management:

Every person on the planet has either a self-defined, relationship defined or a socially assigned identity. We may each have multiple perceived social identities, whether we are speaking of the identity we assume at work, at home or when out with our friends. These identities are ever changing and in some ways evolving, although many of us might assume ours to be fixed or immutable. These identities are directly associated with our process of managing our self-image and our social-images and thus all of our relationships.

Our various identities are all egoic in nature and are parts of the larger construct of our ego-personality. Here, when we speak of our ego-personality, we are not referring to an online social identity or a consciously constructed social self-image; we are instead looking at all of our self-perceived identities as a "composite whole" made up of many parts. Our ego-personality is often reflected back to us by our social or interpersonal interactions. These ego-identities grow with us as we age, from birth to death. On the next page is a diagram which lists and describes the relationship between the various aspects of our composite ego-personality, our various ego-identities, our various life strategies, and the foundation of simulacra and beliefs that they all stem from. Each of the elements of the diagram will be described along the way in the book.

Basic Levels of Consciousness & Ego

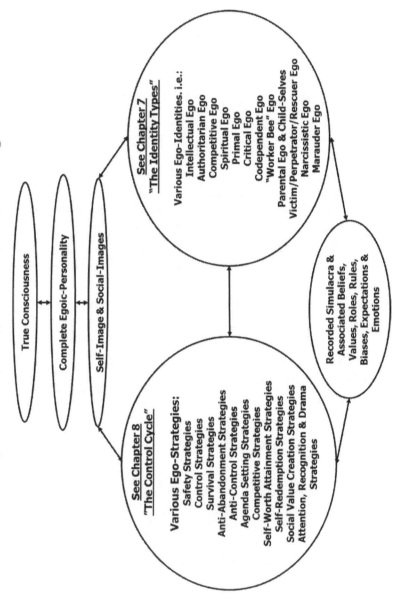

True Consciousness

Complete Egoic-Personality

Self-Image & Social-Images

See Chapter 7
"The Identity Types"

Various Ego-Identities. i.e.:
Intellectual Ego
Authoritarian Ego
Competitive Ego
Spiritual Ego
Primal Ego
Critical Ego
Codependent Ego
"Worker Bee" Ego
Parental Ego & Child-Selves
Victim/Perpetrator/Rescuer Ego
Narcissistic Ego
Marauder Ego

See Chapter 8
"The Control Cycle"

Various Ego-Strategies:
Safety Strategies
Control Strategies
Survival Strategies
Anti-Abandonment Strategies
Anti-Control Strategies
Agenda Setting Strategies
Competitive Strategies
Self-Worth Attainment Strategies
Self-Redemption Strategies
Social Value Creation Strategies
Attention, Recognition & Drama
Strategies

Recorded Simulacra &
Associated Beliefs,
Values, Roles, Rules,
Biases, Expectations &
Emotions

We learn and record the elements of our ego-identities as we grow. It is from the vantage point of these perceived ego-identities that we make decisions and wield our personal power in an infinite number of ways. It is also from the various aspects of our identities that we interpret our life experiences and their meaning and implications. Thus, the constructs of our identities are both the mechanism and the filter through which we learn and develop ourselves. Paradoxically our identities promote and facilitate our learning and simultaneously they represent a significant and pervasive limitation on our attainment of understanding and capacity to learn and change. Meaning we often try to hold onto elements of our self-perceived identities, even to our detriment.

If we clearly and comprehensively understand how the dynamic of our identity development works, then we can take advantage of it and ultimately transcend its limitations. Our identity is a good and useful thing, yet it is like a set of training wheels on a bicycle that can be discarded once we no longer need them to learn to ride through life safely. This means that once we learn to function without the support of a defined ego-personality, or any personal or social identity, then we become far more flexible and capable of many more personal and spiritual developments, and so do not miss the identities we previously depended upon.

Our identities and their associated strategies are a powerful and limited social vehicle and a ticket for social participation. Some benefits of having an identity are that our identity:

- Supports and orients our making day-to-day decisions and orients us socially and interpersonally.
- Is used as a personal developmental measuring stick in regard to success, self-worth and social status.
- Gives us a way to see and work with ourselves and organize our lives that is relatively functional, prior to attaining full spiritual consciousness.
- Is often used as a measure of our social acceptability.
- Creates a frame of reference for evaluating our interactions with others, based upon the comparison of our identities to their identities (for example how we relate to "the boss" at work or to a police officer on the street, or how we as a child relate to our parents).
- Allows us to function within groups, bureaucracies and organizations in a defined and organized way.
- Functions as a social buffer to keep emotional distance between ourselves and others until we are ready to get emotionally closer.
- Functions as a relationship management buffer regarding managing our exchange and transaction based personal emotional relationships.

193

❖ Gives society a way to measure, monitor and manage our social value, behaviors, decisions, potential or status.

❖ Gives us a way to relate to and feel ourselves to be a part of society and social groups via shared culture, group identification and tradition.

❖ Can be a mechanism for developing our self-esteem and confidence.

Many of us define and measure our personal and social worth based upon our chosen or developed identities. Therefore, we may feel very good about ourselves when our life situations and relationships are good, or badly if our life or social situation is not as good. Yet most of us unknowingly and unconsciously live at the mercy of that which influences our perceived personal and social identity. This can be seen in cases of identity theft or in cases of destructive gossip or misinformation being spread about us. The same is true when we experience the pain of not feeling understood by others from the vantage point of the identity we perceive ourselves to be. These situations show the fragility and vulnerability of an identity. Still most of us do not yet understand how we could live without a social identity, and most of us do assume we will derive many positive emotional experiences from our identities.

Most human identities are, to a significant degree an outgrowth and manifestation of the ego which is largely fed in its development by cultural and familial conditioning, as well as by positive and negative past-life karmic experiences and patterns. Each individual human identity is also influenced by and reflects the world's consensus consciousness, the consciousness of our surrounding society, our family's group consciousness and the group consciousness we participate in at our workplace(s). Our identity is also a reflection of, and a reaction to, all our memories of our close relationship interactions. Our perceived identity is a lens through which we view ourselves and others. In this way, our identity is profoundly, yet temporarily, useful in supporting our social interactions and relationships, while simultaneously it is also a source of interpersonal conflicts.

We also see life vicariously and empathetically through the lens of other's identities and make decisions based upon this assumed information when we interact with them. In relationships of all kinds it is often practically beneficial to submit to the ego-identity elements and interpersonal styles of others (for example in marriage, if only to "keep the peace"). Unyielding or inflexible attachment to any element of our ego-identity leads to conflict.

Most of us tend to see ourselves in rather polarizing terms as man or woman, straight or gay, father or mother, carpenter or plumber, strong or weak, smart or stupid, businessman or statesman, American or Italian, Christian or Hindu.

These defined and chosen identity characteristics, as well as other subtler aspects of our identities, make up the totality of our "identity composite elements".

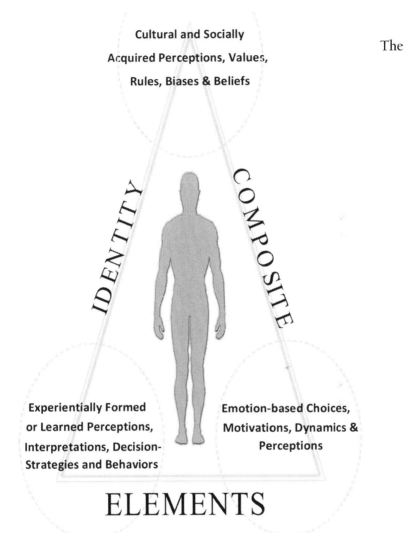

The

Cultural and Socially Acquired Perceptions, Values, Rules, Biases & Beliefs

Experientially Formed or Learned Perceptions, Interpretations, Decision-Strategies and Behaviors

Emotion-based Choices, Motivations, Dynamics & Perceptions

ELEMENTS

Identity Types and Their Composite Elements:

ELEMENT 1:

Experientially Formed or Learned Perceptions, Interpretations, Decision-Strategies and Behaviors:

❖ All our past recorded experiential interpreted memories.

❖ All we have learned or recorded including via standard education, the location of our birth, our family, our culture and our nationality.

❖ Our life themes and stories we tell ourselves about our lives, including who we and others are in our life stories, which we then live by.

❖ Chosen lifestyle and activities, self-developmental strategies, life management strategies and methods.

❖ The definition of our life mission, goals, values, motivations, desires, preferences and priorities, life rules or codes of conduct.

❖ Our patterned and habitual emotional reactions and dynamics (fear, shame, anger, guilt, love, compassion, kindness, generosity, etc.).

❖ Our individual beliefs, assumptions, expectations and projections onto life.

ELEMENT 2:

Emotion-Based Choices, Motivations, Dynamics, and Perceptions:

❖ Our social and career reputation, and the type of work or career we choose

❖ Our self-image and how we feel about ourselves (meaning we all have an ongoing relationship with our perceived selves).

❖ Our physical characteristics, perceived attractiveness and perceived physical, social, financial, mental and "sexual" power.

❖ Our chosen or socially defined and/or assigned roles.

❖ Our personally defined or chosen social and interpersonal boundaries and our sense of ownership of whatever we assume we own.

❖ Our personal emotional and relationship dynamics and styles of interaction.

❖ Our conceptualization of ourselves as mental, emotional, sexual, physical, racial, cultural, religious or spiritual beings.

❖ Our perception of ourselves from a gender assignment vantage point.

❖ Who we dynamically choose to present ourselves to be socially and at work, including in person, in writing, on Facebook and/or Internet dating services.

ELEMENT 3:

Culturally and Socially Acquired Perceptions, Traditions, Values and Beliefs:

* ❖ The collective history (positive or negative) of our nationality, culture, gender, race and religion.
* ❖ Influences from family history, values, beliefs, habits, dynamics and conditioning.
* ❖ Our ongoing perceived history, experiences and interpretations of past personal and social relationships and our associated degree of self-trust.
* ❖ Religious, political party system or philosophical beliefs and values we live by.
* ❖ Habitual tendencies to identify with either empowered or disempowered states of consciousness and how powerful we perceive ourselves and others to be in the world.
* ❖ The economic system(s) we participate in and our beliefs, rules, motivations, dynamics and values which relate to them.
* ❖ Our perceived social and economic status and reputation.

The composite elements of our ego-identities and their dynamics are always based upon subconscious understandings and agreed upon social and cultural patterns, norms, beliefs, traditions and protocols which often go unquestioned and are accepted to be right, true, just, necessary or unavoidable. Our chosen, conditioned and perceived ego-identities are not very malleable, change oriented, conscious or personal transformation supportive. The value we put on our identity and how powerful or safe it makes us feel are key determinants of whether we are willing to change it.

Our ego-identity is a mosaic of chosen elements that culminate in the picture of ourselves we see and the social-image others see. We use each element as a point of conscious orientation and subsequently as a lens to look through for interpreting our experience of life and relationships and for making our decisions. Any element of our identity can either directly undermine or directly support our discernment, consciousness, sovereignty and wisdom. Eventually we must shed all aspects of our identities in order to attain true conscious enlightenment, which is a state beyond any individuated sense of ego-self.

It is important to realize that for most of us our perceived identity is seen to be our life. If we "lose our ego-identity" or any key part of it because of some life situation or choice, we are often devastated and may be thrust into

197

feelings of deep guilt, shame, loss, grief or failure. This is the case in divorce, when we lose a job, and in major shifts in our financial status (whether significantly increased or decreased), or if we become physically or mentally impaired. In effect, we fear the death of our perceived identity or any part of it, often just as strongly as we fear physical death or interpersonal abandonment. We can literally grieve any perceived change in our identity, even if it is a positive identity shift, as if part of us that seemed to exist before has now somehow died. This is one reason people so often fear both change and the unknown, and this tendency does not support graceful proactive personal transformation, learning, attainment of sovereignty or of personal power.

Our ego-identity has the assumption that if we were to physically die that it would die with us and that we would simply be "gone", since our ego-identity does not understand or perceive our immortal spiritual existence. Any fundamental social invalidation of the existence, value, safety, "rightness" or accuracy of our ego-identity's perceptions and decisions can be frightening.

There are many different types of ego-identities that we can hold, and that we utilize as the basis of our life management strategies, and our day-to-day decision-making. These ego-identity strategies are often utilized to rationalize our individual style of interaction with others. No ego-strategy is either right or wrong, it is simply the best "recipe" for life management our subconscious has arrived at up until this moment. All of these strategies are simply coping mechanisms for our fears, and for how negatively we feel about ourselves at subconscious levels, and they operate quite foundationally in our personalities.

These ego strategy elements of our selves can fear and even hate feeling judged socially, or fear the feeling of abandonment or the loss of social or relationship status. Another fear that they often have in common is the fear of not existing as an identity or person, and they can also fear being "nothing" or of no worth to others. All ego-identities are at their foundation wanting interpersonal or public attention, validation and approval, which is often seen as equal to power, safety and control, and as being "understood" by other people.

All ego-identities are also ultimately looking for self-worth outside of oneself rather than within oneself. All ego-identity strategies are designed in some way to attempt to attain higher social status, and thus "becoming or proving oneself better" than other people or ultimately "the best". They are all driven by comparing ourselves to others and finding ourselves lacking,

198

which is a constantly repetitive cycle. They are also processes of projection of our desires and our fears via imagination, created so that the ego can have what it wants and avoid what it does not want. What it wants is of course only to feel secure, in control and safe via some strategy.

The process of interpersonal and social comparison and competition, leads to placing a value measurement upon ourselves as either less than or more than others. Without this comparative dynamic ego-identities themselves could not exist. The ego fundamentally believes that it is possible to be better or to be less than other people, and uses this misunderstanding to feed its process of managing of its perceived social safety from abandonment. Ego-identities also want **raw power** (whether it be social, interpersonal, financial, political or personal power), and they want it in order to attain safety, control, security and status.

Realization of the true and equal oneness of all human beings ultimately leads to dissolution of these ego-identity constructs and their dynamics. No one has any more value than anyone else. No ego-identity can ever be at fully at rest, or at peace, because they are all constantly driven by fear, insecurity and misunderstanding of our experiences and of ourselves, God, others and life. All ego-identities are also mechanisms of camouflage and buffers for our primal fear based and destructive subconscious tendencies, as well as a rationalization mechanism for continuing to act via these underlying tendencies. All ego-identities tend to compartmentalize aspects of themselves subconsciously, so that they are not required to consciously face their own mode of operation. None of us needs to be improved, fixed or made better. We do benefit from understanding and fully accepting ourselves and others as spiritual beings, each on our own path to God.

Some of the most common ego-identity strategies (i.e. social-image and self-image management mechanisms), which all of us have functioning within our systems, to one degree or another, are:

Intellectual Ego:

Operates via being or appearing smarter or knowing more than others (often via higher education). This can include the intellectual-ego of technically knowledgeable people, including scientists and computer knowledgeable people. High intellect is not equal to high wisdom, understanding or discernment, nor any degree of emotional intelligence. Still the intellectual ego's focus is often on valuing itself and seeking to be valued for its apparent cognitive superiority. Oddly enough the intellectual egos of some people in today's world are trying to supplant or replace spirituality as the highest valued mode of mental, emotional and conscious function. Knowledge and the supposed power it seems to offer is being valued by some people as being more important than love in the core of humanity. This can be a very cold, self-blinding and self-rationalizing way of living and making decisions. In effect, the intellectual ego, in some people can want to "undermine spirituality in its many religious forms". This occurs because the deep essence and processes of spirituality cannot be comprehended by the limited, and ego driven processes of the intellectual mind and thus this ego-identity cannot compete in that arena. Obviously not all intellectual ego dynamics are geared in this direction.

People who function in this ego-identity mode may even assume there is some form of "mind-only oriented enlightenment" that they are working toward, have achieved or may achieve. Still this ego-identity is usually only on a mission of attaining a state of felt superiority toward other people and of finding some sort of emotional safety, paradoxically by disconnecting from their emotions. Their ego-identity defensive process is to appear to have more knowledge, perceived understanding or intellectual capability than others.

Note: Of course, not all intelligent people operate as a result of the Intellectual Ego, and the choice to do so is usually made at the level of the subconscious. We live in a traditionally competitive world, and many people assume that it is good or necessary to be intellectually competitive in order to prosper, be safe and to survive. This competitive environment is therefore a ripe breeding ground for self-defensive (or even offensive) intellectual-ego development and dynamics.

Authoritarian Ego:

This ego operates via acquiring or having more power or being more "right" than others, and feeling the need to constantly prove it. It also means having the social or institutional power to enforce one's will on others, sometimes punitively. The authoritarian ego is unable to understand the detrimental and undermining influence it has on other's self-esteem or emotional processes. It rationalizes its operation as necessary "for the good of all", "because I know best" or "for national security", etc.

Competitive Ego:

This ego-identity operates via achieving most goals in life through competition with others, i.e. devaluing others, proving oneself better than others, manipulating others, distrustfully undermining others, etc. This requires the person operating with this ego-identity to shut down any feelings of love or compassion toward others while they are competing with them, in order to make it easier for them to emotionally rationalize a ruthless mode of exchange or transaction based style of interacting with other human beings.

The person(s) operating with this ego-identity is not usually aware of this emotional dysfunction. This ego-identity is constantly comparing itself to others and is dependent upon continued success in achieving its goals for any feelings of self-worth or well-being, which is never satisfied because there is always someone "better or more powerful". The competitive ego can never be truly happy, at peace or fulfilled, and cannot perceive the equality of all human beings. This ego-identity operates within individual people and in all group consciousnesses of human beings, including corporations and nations.

This competitive ego-identity is the foundation of all conflict and division between human beings, including religions, cultures, nations, etc. As long as competition reigns as a common or lauded social dynamic peace on earth is unattainable. This ego-identity process is fear and distrust driven, and the ego desires to achieve control and power through competition. It is therefore antithetical to teamwork, truly collaborative efforts of all kinds (i.e. non-competition oriented) and is thus antithetical to world peace). For example, a corporation driven by internal competition between its members can never work together optimally.

Various venues of competition are:

- ❖ Money (having or making more than others, including having all money can buy)
- ❖ Power and authority (political, economic, social, religious and even applying personal power within monogamous relationships)
- ❖ Knowledge or access or control of information (or disinformation)
- ❖ Social status, organizational status and personal relationship status
- ❖ Control
- ❖ Sex
- ❖ Influence
- ❖ Attention seeking (see the current social media competition for attention, evidenced by many people who financially "live by the number Twitter followers they have, and then attempt to monetize or make money from this social media dynamic". This situation has degraded to the point where people are even being paid to produce literally false news stories. False information of all kinds is often

utilized in various kinds of competition, even internationally, and the trend is increasing.

❖ Safety and survival (many of our competitive dynamics are driven by these two influences)
❖ Simply to appear to be more "right" than others
❖ To appear more politically correct than others
❖ To be more perfect than others
❖ To appear more spiritual or Godly than others

Spiritual Ego:

This ego involves supposedly being comparatively more righteous, religious, spiritually attained or evolved, attuned to God or knowledgeable of spirituality, or more spiritually pure or closer to God than others. This is usually a highly manipulative coping mechanism for deep subconscious feelings of unworthiness, intense self-judgment and desire to redeem oneself. Until these deeper issues are resolved we cannot feel safe and good intentionally fully surrendering to God.

This ego-identity tends to present itself to other people as sincere, credible and righteous, extremely well educated in religious dogmas of various kinds, and at the same time as being fundamentally spiritually superior to others, all the while holding the "appearance of humility". Therefore, it is a process of false humility.

Holding this type of ego-identity has nothing to do with directly resonating with or surrendering fully to God at all levels of our being or of consciously serving God. Only through true surrendered humility (i.e. understanding we are all equal in the eyes of God and being in a state of surrender and full spiritual, mental and emotional submission to God), can we hope to be most fully resonant with God. Holding any tendency to resonate with spiritual ego is driven by subconscious fear of God. Fear of God, in some cases can even lead to subconscious hatred of God, and hatred of surrendering fully to God out of fear of vulnerability to God's power. (See the previously defined full definition of hatred, i.e. feeling vulnerable, powerless, angry, blaming and wanting destroy that which we feel fundamentally threatened by). Spiritual ego is a spiritually self-blinding process of a sort of narcissism, and of attempting to appear to be "perfect" to other people, and thus above other people. Therefore, it calls for the submission of others to its "higher understanding".

In its most extreme or detrimental forms, this ego strategy would be found in some tele-evangelists, some judgmental and destructive religious

202

leaders, cult leaders or some new age spiritualists. This ego-identity wants to arrive at enlightenment, via being spiritually better, superior or higher than other people, and while retaining its mind, its ego and control over its life in some form. Oddly enough, the subconscious belief of this ego-identity is that the only safe way to be closer to God is by proving oneself better than other people, which is of course only a process of ego safety seeking and control via comparison. If caught in this dynamic, we cannot simply fully consistently resonate and surrender to God, because we are busy doing something else (spiritually competing) that is not aligned with surrender to God. In large group dynamics, it is group consensus consciousness spiritual ego that leads to competition, violence and even war. When we are focused on operating within any ego-identity, we become unable to see life, relationships or the world clearly and without bias.

Paradoxically, even some of the most consciously well-meaning and apparently altruistically motivated spiritualists and religiously focused people can fall into this trap, to some degree. (i.e. Because we are all still incarnate humans, and as such incompletely spiritually evolved, this is the result of our lack of complete conscious awareness and spiritual resonance, which is just a simple fact of life). Spiritual-ego often leads to the attempted monetization of religion or spirituality; this is especially true in the United States. Meaning making money, for the sake of making money, via religion or spiritualism, without realizing the underlying motivation. Monetization of spirituality is of course often corrupting and undermining in its influence on the spiritual process. Money is not "evil" or bad, money is only a form of energy, still it can influence us to our detriment. This subconscious motivation and tendency is "baked right into" subconscious capitalistic ego-identity tendencies and competitive tendencies in many people in some countries. It is necessary to understand that no one that is driven by or operating in spiritual-ego, can truly and completely facilitate anyone else's spiritual evolution to the point of full enlightenment. This is so because the spiritual-ego itself creates a sort of "glass ceiling" or barrier of holding onto some aspect of ego, mind, status and desire for control over one's life, that then inhibits profound or complete attainment of spiritual evolution and consciousness. The words "no attachment and no aversion to any aspect of life" helpfully apply here.

The spiritual-ego-identity can also be seen on the global scale in the egoic competition between religions, as an aspect of, and an expression of, mass religious consciousness, or a sub-aspect of the global consensus consciousness. Strangely enough, it is fear driven competition, social status seeking and group safety seeking itself (tribalism dynamics) that lead to the disagreement, hatred, judgment and resentment that occurs between these groups. We could see a very influential expression of the spiritual-ego in the tendency for many religions (like many cultures) to be dominated by males. This is simply an expression of the larger consensus consciousness male spiritual-ego in action within large religious groups. Of course, there also exists a "female spiritual-ego" and it operates in its own non-optimal ways. The feminine spiritual-ego's operation is not as potentially violently domineering as the male spiritual-ego.

I have no judgment of any of these dynamics, as they are all necessary for the ultimate learning and evolution of humanity to thereby attain higher levels of consciousness, through trial and error or cause-and-effect learning dynamics. Documenting these ego-dynamics here is useful in order to ultimately facilitate their transcendence. Men and women are all equal, in all ways, in the eyes of God. Men do not see, relate to, experience or understand God "better" than women. The male ego's often subconscious fear of, and judgment of female power, and desire to control feminine power for the fulfillment of men's purposes (feminine power, in my experience, is vast and generally positive) is at the root of this dominating ego-dynamic.

Primal Ego:

This type of ego utilizes ruthless force or manipulation to dominate others to get what it wants, or feels it needs, or to protect itself and feel safe. This type of ego strategy is often applied more by men than women and far more destructively. This is the ego process that leads to war, killing and abuse of others of various kinds. Primal egos are willing to compete with others, even to the extreme of the destruction of others, (i.e. even killing them). Primal ego is cold, relatively sociopathic or psychopathic in its methods and unable to love or feel other's love.

Strangely, both men and women often want to be in control and to dominate each other in their relationships, in one way or another, and to one degree or another. Both genders have developed many manipulative strategies to try to control each other. Simultaneously both genders want to avoid abandonment by the other and desire to be loved and accepted by the other, without requirement of any kind. While simultaneously not recognizing that these simplistic dynamics are all driven only by fear. So being dominating is only an expression of one's <u>fearfulness</u> of being dominated or controlled, or of being abandoned. The more fearful we are, the more driven we are to exert extreme and potentially destructive control and domination strategies toward others. These strategies also allow us to be far more manipulative of others when they feel either ignorant or vulnerable.

The flip side of this dynamic is the "appearance of ego-submissiveness", which is often used as a strategy to avoid abandonment and to subtly influence without appearing to influence the other. It is very good to truly and consciously submit to the good of those we love, because we truly love and respect the other, not because we fear the loss of the other. There is no true benefit to control or domination, and there is no solution to our deep fears of abandonment, death or of being dominated, by dominating others.

All forms of safety seeking are illusionary, as is the desire to be safe via domination that drives the primal-ego. The primal-ego is fundamentally amoral, sociopathic and literally and unconsciously totally blindly ruthless in its operation, and this is how it can rationalize all destructive acts. Like all egoic parts, the primal ego cannot see that we are all children of God and love others as totally equal to ourselves. This is the part of human systems that can devalue, dehumanize and thereby rationalize destroying or killing others, or rationalize destroying them through blind competition. To the primal ego, interactions with others are seen only as a form of battle that we feel is necessary to attain some perceived feeling or state of safety or something else we desire.

Still this ego-dynamic lives <u>only</u> in a constant process of fear projection of lack. In its constant battling, this ego-identity is endlessly in the process of trying to avoid what it imagines, projects and fears. (i.e. vulnerability, powerlessness, victimization, lack, abandonment, competition and competitors, punishment, criticism, social and interpersonal devaluation, worthlessness, not being perfect and not being good enough). In its conflict producing dynamics, it imagines that it is somehow making itself safe from potential conflict or harm, via participating in conflict.

Critical Ego:

This ego element is the source of our internal dialog that is self-judgmental or judgmental of others in its process. It is the foundational element of our ego-process that is attempting, though self-criticism, to be perceived to be perfect to oneself or to others. It is motivated by fear of abandonment and wants to attain safety and control via judgment and punishment of self and others. Though it does not realize that this state cannot be attained via this mechanism.

This ego-identity is not simply a subconscious "self" or "part". It is actually made up of a network of interactive subconscious-selves. For this one reason it is very difficult to fully transcend, since it is the central voice for so many aspects of our conditioned subconscious being. This ego-identity is constantly trying to drive us, often mercilessly, to be better, and be more right, perfect or acceptable to others. Like all ego-identities it must be fully transcended in order to reach a state of inner peace. Many people live their lives in a constant state of self-punishment, as a result of this ego-identity's critical operation.

Narcissistic Ego:

This type of ego-identity strategy often wants total control over other's lives and resources, and it also wants to have control over all aspects of the narcissist's own life. In its more extreme forms narcissism will do anything, no matter how ruthless, non-integrous, self-serving, destructive or dysfunctional, to achieve this perceived control. A narcissistic ego-identity can rationalize virtually any self-serving interpretation of any situation or relationship. This type of ego-identity has little regard for anyone's boundaries or other's emotional priorities, values or dynamics or their worth as a human being. It is this mindset that those who have chosen to enslave others function from, and it is also exhibited in extremes of possessive "love" and tendency to make use of co-dependently oriented people. Narcissists are all about comparison of themselves to others, while living in superficial states of pride and arrogance.

This ego-identity can actually rationalize "owning or possessing" someone else in a relationship in very practical terms. It also has a tendency to be willing to destroy or use destruction or the threat of harm to obtain whatever it wants. Therefore, narcissism can be seen, in its core, to be driven by unresolved and unrecognized hatred (i.e. subconscious). Hatred being used as a control strategy. (See Chapter 8, "The Control Cycle", for the 5 element definition of hatred, i.e. Hatred is made up of feelings of vulnerability, powerlessness, anger, blame and the desire to destroy that which we feel threatened by). Again, hatred is neither a bad or wrong emotion, although it has been vilified to the point of misunderstanding its core dynamics. Hatred is, in reality, only a maladaptive emotional reaction and defense mechanism which is triggered by a perceived profound threat that we feel vulnerable to and powerless to protect ourselves from. It is a simple and dysfunctional method of protecting ourselves from experiencing the pain we feel others could inflict upon us. It is also blindly narcissistic and self-centered in nature; therefore, it is always unbalanced in its expression. Men are more often seen to exemplify the more extreme forms of this narcissistic dynamic, and to do so more destructively and physically than women. Still women can be just as destructive in other ways, and by using other methods, for example by using emotional or verbal tactics. Narcissism does not want to be held accountable to anyone or anything for its actions, decisions or expressions. Hatred can even be justified by the ego-identity as a competitive necessity.

This ego-identity-strategy of narcissism is driven by, and is a coping or compensation mechanism related to deep, unresolved and often unrecognized subconscious feelings of fear, shame, guilt and inadequacy. Most of these dynamics the narcissistic person is usually consciously unaware of. This strategy is, at its foundation, also a consistent ego-identity self-defense strategy and orientation, designed to keep the narcissist "safe" from being dominated by others, by dominating them first. This ego-strategy gives the person exhibiting it an overblown sense of their own self-importance and value in order to <u>distract themselves</u> from their own deeply buried painful and negative feelings about themselves. Therefore, they are unsuccessfully trying to deal with a deep unhealed emotional wound by operating this way.

Narcissism can <u>appear</u> as significant arrogance, "know it all'ism", always wanting to appear to be right, and is a basically ego-centric view of the world and all relationships. Still narcissism itself is only a coping mechanism for underlying shame and guilt, which is all driven by fear of abandonment and death. Narcissism's mode of operation is literally an attempt by the ego-identity to authoritatively define social or relationship reality for everyone else around it in in a dominating way, in order to resolve its underlying fear of being abandoned by others or of dying. So, narcissism is the underlying energy of dictatorship and authoritarianism of all kinds and it presents a <u>false sense of certainty</u> that could supposedly then lead to an equally false sense of safety for others if they follow the narcissist.

Therefore, narcissism desires to get everyone else to agree with its perspective on life, relationship and reality, and to exclude or dismiss other's perspectives. In other words, to "try to kill" other's ego-identities, perspectives and free-will (not trying to physically kill them of course in most cases) in order to be socially safe from the power of their free-will. Narcissism blinds the narcissist to their own fear, and the implications of their actions, and thus their fears remain unresolved, and the narcissistic dynamics continue cyclically.

Because this ego-identity is only a cover for underlying subconscious feelings of guilt, fear, insecurity and shame, its distracting focus on having what it wants in order to feel better undermines the person's capacity for empathy or compassion. This ego-identity strategy is never satisfied or "safe enough" with any result, or any attainment of power and control. It therefore constantly requires others to submit to its perceived needs in order to feel ever more secure. In addition, the ego-strategy consistently tries to prove its superiority and higher status and to make others less than it, and to claim victimhood in interactions with others, in order to rationalize its unbalanced tendencies. This narcissistic dynamic and aspect of the global human consensus consciousness is a core reason for our stratified societies, gender inequality, ethnic inequality, militarism as a method of problem solving, and the prevalence of hierarchical organizational structures. Narcissism is a close relative of the competitive ego-dynamic previously described, and the combination of these two strategies is destroying our world, while we are simultaneously blinded by their supposed usefulness or necessity.

These narcissistic dynamics can be very complex, subtle and manipulative, and intellectualized and intellectually self-rationalizing, since the narcissist is disconnected from their emotions. They are therefore confusing and undermining of the narcissist themselves realizing their own core nature and motivations, and of their understanding their detrimental influence on others. Again, people who exhibit these tendencies are neither bad nor wrong, they are only lost in their subconscious fear driven reactive ego-identity dynamics. (It could be said that all of us have some of this tendency within us, just waiting to feel safe or validated enough to show itself.) This ego-identity's underlying perspective is "if I have what I want, and get my way, then I will be safe, in control, and will not live in the potential pain and fear of vulnerability". This is of course a totally illusionary perspective, since if we truly love we must be willing to be vulnerable. The strategy also lives in an "if this then that" mode of thought. As in "**if** I do not apply self-centered and dismissive means that involve dominating others, **then** I won't get what I want and so I won't be happy and safe". These are all also basic "root chakra dynamics" (see root chakra information later in the book.)

When its narrow and limited attitude towards others does not work, the narcissist reacts and often moves into a mode of more intense criticality, hatred and even destructiveness. This ego-identity is the most tenacious ego-identity dynamic, and is driven at its core by fear of death and abandonment in order to be safe. Its fear is used as its ongoing justification for these "kill or be killed or eye for an eye" perspectives and behaviors, and this point of view is projected onto all of the person's reality. These destructive narcissistic tendencies are, to a degree, shared by the global <u>male and female</u> consensus consciousnesses, which is one reason there is so much violence of all kinds in the world and conflict in relationships.

This ego-identity could be seen, in its most extreme form, in fascist dictators. These dictators are very fearful people, who are operating under the influence of their own subconscious control and safety strategies, while using sense fulfillment of various kinds to distract themselves from their underlying negative emotions. Their fear motivates them to try to try to dominate and assert control over the larger world around them. Having power over others becomes the coping strategy for their fear and is an addictive process. Although consistently fearful, these people still usually try to appear to be confident and powerful, and their focus on the "drug of power and control" distracts them from their own negative emotions and their effect on others' lives. This ego-identity is a vast process of denial of the surrounding social and interpersonal reality. This dynamic is also represented clearly in all forms of social, political and economic elitism.

This dynamic can be seen in various nations where "powerful" egocentric personalities run amok, and ultimately create great suffering due to the influence of their internal emotional imbalances on their leadership process. Examples would be Germany, with Adolf Hitler, Syria, with Bashar Al Assad, or in Libya with Saddam Hussein, or Kim Jong-un in North Korea. Therefore, I feel it is a useful question to ask: Are fascism, dictatorships or even communism truly modes of national governance, or are they simply an ego-centric fear/control management strategy that has taken root in the process of governance? In this question, I am suggesting the value of each of us having discerningly understanding of the powerful and covert influence of narcissistic ego-identity dynamics, at all levels of society, in all groups of human beings, and in all aspects of human evolution. I would also ask, what fear driven dynamics in populations of human beings tolerate and even feed such ego-identities? If we all realized our personal power would we tolerate poor methods of governance?

The narcissistic ego-identity strategy, like all ego-strategies is driven by fear of abandonment and ego-death. Its ongoing operation results in fear of loss of the ego-identity's safety via loss of social and interpersonal status. Therefore, this ego-identity desires control through ruthless and potentially sociopathic insensitive misuse of personal power. To a narcissistic ego, not constantly feeling "special and better than others", is feared almost as intensely as death. Social rejection and not being "socially important and relevant" is seen, by this ego-strategy, as the most terrible of all possibilities. This strategy's core fear sometimes manifests in the Machiavellian "will to power", that drives some people to be socially hyper-competitive. This ego-identity tends therefore to be dismissive, undermining and even aggressively attacking in the presence of feminine energies of open emotional vulnerability.

In this ego-strategy, power is felt to be equal to safety, and safety is seen to be equal to power. This type of person often seeks relationships with codependent-ego oriented people (see this co-dependent ego description below). The narcissist's ego-identity tends to devalue all others in reference to itself, in order to feel it can control them, and to rationalize doing so. Therefore, narcissists are unwilling to be open to other's views, interpretations, perspectives, beliefs and desires. The ego-identity wants to always "set the agenda" in all social and interpersonal contexts, and to be "in charge" and thereby control others via dominance. Paradoxically, people who live in other forms of fear and insecurity (co-dependents) can actually seek out narcissists, since narcissists can appear to "have it all under control", and thus are supposedly safer to be in relationship with for the co-dependent person. Co-dependents may have previously been dominated in this way in their childhood, and thus see it is familiar, and therefore in a way a "safe" type of relationship to be in, that they understand how to navigate their way through from day-to-day. It is important to realize that no one is a victim of this ego-identity, we all always have the power to say no to such behaviors and dynamics.

An expression of the narcissistic ego-dynamic can be the intense insatiable desire to obtain attention from as many persons as possible, and to compete intensely for this attention, since attention itself is deemed to be a sort of power over other's decision-making processes. This intense attention seeking process is felt to "produce emotional safety and power for the narcissist", yet it can never be fully satiated, because it is always driven by unresolved fear. This dynamic can be seen in today's usage of social media by many people to create mega-ego-identities and then to profit by them. The narcissistic ego is constantly and truly only self-involved and self-focused. Simultaneously it is incapable of recognizing or clearly understanding its own non-optimal way of operating in relation to others, and endlessly rationalizes the damage it does to other's lives and can even be self-congratulatory, as in "it means I am smarter than other people or a better competitor". One other way it rationalizes its destructive behaviors is by playing the victim, by calling others perpetrators or "bad", and by focusing on preemptively judging other's behaviors in order to disempower them socially or interpersonally.

210

This behavior is often seen in personal relationships, when the narcissist blames their mate in order to escape self-accountability.

In narcissists, the fearful narcissistic wounded part of self has completely "circled the wagons" in fear of all other human being's potential rejection and abandonment, which to it represent a dire threat that it wants to control. Like all ego-strategies, this ego-strategy cannot learn anything of significance from life experiences or relationships, unless what it learns supports the ego-identity's safety strategy. It is truly the most fundamental and tenacious learning disability. This is because it is constantly in fear projection mode regarding perceived threats that blinds it to more accurate information available in the present moment. Therefore, it cannot heal itself, and for this reason it continues to consistently operate self-protectively, without resolution for long periods of time. It is useful to understand that narcissism operates on a sliding scale of intensity. Meaning some people are more influenced by it and others less, still many people (not only men by the way) have some of this ego-identity influence in their systems. Obviously not all narcissists are dictators, nor do they all operate with obvious and destructive strategies; indeed some are very covert in their manipulations. Again, narcissists are not "bad people", they are just not yet emotionally healed and conscious, and want only their way.

One additional view of narcissism is that it consistently causes others to reactively reject, judge and emotionally abandon the narcissist, since it creates such unbalanced and even abusive insensitivity in relationships. Therefore, the narcissist experiences ongoing bouts of conflict with others, which leads to their feeling more fear, guilt and shame and desire for control, and the cycle continues. This results in a flip flop dynamic between guilt and shame emotions and unilateral insensitive decision-making in relationships without empathy or sympathy for their partners. Paradoxically, their feelings of guilt and shame hold their self-centered and non-empathetic tendencies in place, rather than resolving or redeeming them.

This situation creates a tendency for the narcissists to blame those who blame them, as a form of denial of self-accountability. Meaning that while narcissists often create relationship problems, they also tend to blame or try to make their partners responsible for these problems. Thus, narcissists can claim themselves to be victims of other's (often very minimal) expectations, or victims of others not giving them what they want. This blame can even lead to rationalized relationship violence. Narcissism is driven by ongoing unresolved and unfaced subconscious fear, guilt and shame, which the narcissist is trying to lessen via the distraction of getting pleasurable experiences of all kinds. These negative emotions are constantly competing with the narcissist's self-centered focus on fulfilling their personal desire to have whatever they want, to the exclusion of other's wellbeing. These dynamics result in an inability to be in true emotional integrity or emotional intimacy in any relationship.

Narcissists are driven by an ongoing process of <u>attachment</u> to what they want, desire or expect to experience in life. At the same time, they are also driven by a deep aversion to not having or getting what they want. Not getting what they want can occur when they are being blamed by the people they are in relationship with, triggering them to feel guilty or ashamed of their extreme relationship positions and dynamics, which can lead to defensive behaviors. In this ego-identity, attachment and aversion are literally two sides of the same dynamic, and they play off of and feed on each other.

Attachment and aversion influencing dynamics keep the narcissists lost in unconscious dynamics that are constantly supported by a stream of internal dialog that is self-rationalizing and self-validating. Narcissism is in effect an unresolved and unrecognized addiction to wanting to have what one wants, *and* of feeling badly about it. This process creates a type of "paralysis of true consciousness", since the person is lost in their subconscious dynamics, without the capacity to recognize that this is what is happening. Narcissism is a dysfunctional prison of fear driven choices and misinterpretations of life experience, and of one's own emotional dynamics, which is tremendously blinding and entrenched and thus difficult to resolve. It is difficult to resolve because the mind of the person (mind which is here defined as only an extension of ego, does not equal their consciousness) cannot arrive at any adequate reason to face and conquer their fears or their addiction. Therefore, they are unwilling to fundamentally change their lives, their ways of making their decisions and their behavior. This is because they are so focused on what they think, feel and want that they cannot value what anyone else thinks, wants or feels. Due to being lost in this dynamic they cannot truly be motivated by unconditional love because their style of love is so fundamentally conditional on first and constantly having what they want. The consensus consciousness of nation's can also be lost in narcissistic perspectives (i.e. nationalism and populism). Some would say that these dynamics have led to the Brexit vote in the United Kingdom, the fallout of which is still occurring. Others would see some of these effects on the process of all levels of the elections in the United States and the current focus on United States nationalism rather than balanced and harmonious globalism.

This discussion is not an indictment of narcissists, it is a necessary description of the fundamental ego-identity of narcissism and its associated dysfunctional dynamics, at all levels of society. This description is necessary so that this ego-identity can be fully understood in order to ultimately transcend it, both in individuals and in groups. (i.e. Individuals, organizations, groups of people, and even whole nations, can be fundamentally influenced in their emotional dynamics and decision-making processes by narcissistic tendencies that are recorded in the consensus consciousness of the group.) Still narcissism is a part of the human species learning process, that is useful to understand, if not to follow. Meaning we often must learn what does not work and why it does not work, before we are willing to cease this addictive and dysfunctional behavior. This ego-strategy is also a mechanism by which individuals and groups attempt to empower themselves at the expense of others, while rationalizing doing so. While it may appear to achieve positive goals in the short term, in the long term the costs are far too great to make it worth continuing.

Some would say that the United States exhibits some of these self-centered tendencies due to an addiction to the various luxuries many of its citizens enjoy and have come to take for granted. (i.e. "The American Dream"). Some would see the United States' consistent tendency to interfere in other country's political systems, in various ways, as narcissistic. Simultaneously they have recently take great umbrage over Russia's apparent attempt to influence U.S. elections. (Throughout history, many nations have operated in this way, and many still do, I am only using the U.S. as one example of a larger world and human dynamic). Some would also say that narcissism is a core aspect of the larger social dynamic and process that drives humanity as a species, (and thus humanity's global consensus consciousness), to assume we have the "right" do whatever destructive things we want to this planet and all its inhabitants, simply to fulfill our personal desires and survival.

Humans have tended to operate this consciousness encumbering manner, until now, with the illusion of impunity, and with the unquestioned value of human survival and financial gain to be a higher priority than the survival of any aspect of our environment. This irrational subconscious dynamic literally cannot take into account the long term rational requirement of a stable environment being a requirement for humanity's survival. So, our conscious wisdom is constantly battling our narcissistic drives and motivations. Climate change is only one of many global situations that are telling us that the assumption of human impunity is fundamentally false. So, in the end narcissism can be seen as a strategy of sometimes predatory prioritization of self or tribe above all other considerations, including love, discernment and wisdom, that we are as a species in the process of learning our way out of.

Co-dependent Ego:

This ego-identity strategy can be seen in people who placate others, are people pleasers and approval seekers, and who deeply fear abandonment and who do not feel self-empowered or intrinsically valuable in their relationships or in the world. This is often a strategy of over giving and trying to be responsible for other's wellbeing, of constantly trying to prove one's value, or of wanting to be "indispensable" in relationships. Therefore, it is, in its own way, a safety strategy, an anti-abandonment strategy, and to a degree a control strategy, that is often utilized in many kinds of relationships. It is common for co-dependent-ego identified people to fall into relationships with narcissistic people, who appear to be "in need and demanding" of lots of support and attention. Oddly enough we could see co-dependency as the other side of the coin of narcissism, or both as different faces of the same core ego-dynamic. Meaning that codependency, though seemingly not as self-centered as narcissism, is just another method of dealing with similar underlying fear and insecurity. On a personal human level co-dependents and narcissists are mirror reflections of each other. On a global scale, nationalism and terrorism cultural ego-dynamics, that are in their way somewhat distorted mirror reflections of each other. Yes, I know this is a controversial statement.

Codependents can be just as control seeking as other ego-identities, albeit in what appears to be a submissive or non-egoic and self-centered manner. At a fundamental level, they assume that if they just keep giving and supporting their partner or those they are in relationship with, that they will then eventually receive what they feel they need. Though they may appear to receive safety and security they do not receive actual love and emotional fulfillment, because the narcissist is fundamentally incapable of truly caring about them. The co-dependents may also naively assume they will in some way be empowered by being in relationship with a narcissist, unfortunately narcissists do not have the capacity to share power in relationships in a balanced way. Therefore, codependency is fundamentally a control and safety strategy, although not dominance or confidence oriented in nature, that cannot achieve its desired results. Lastly co-dependents assume that if they are responsible for other's emotional needs, wants and feelings that they will

214

be appreciated and valued for it, and thus not be emotionally abandoned. This is of course not true.

Codependents can be significantly emotionally punitive in relationships when they feel victimized due to their not achieving the comprehensive results that they have worked so hard to achieve in their relationships. Meaning that when they feel victimized by the lack of results of their relationship choices they can then validate becoming resentful perpetrators. That said, they usually do not have adequate feelings of self-worth or empowerment to make a decisive stand in the face of the domineering tendencies of a narcissist. Codependency and narcissism are, as previously stated, distorted mirror images of each other. One is focused on giving and the other is focused on taking in order to achieve their goals. (Again, all negative emotions that produce these relationship dynamics stem directly or indirectly from underlying fears, which are the byproducts of recorded simulacra). The following dynamics of these ego-identities may be helpful in better understanding them. I do hope this is the case, I also realize they may appear controversial.

Codependency and narcissism are both:

- ❖ Maladaptive relationship strategies and life strategies that cannot really successfully work in any relationship situation because both are unbalanced and unbalancing, and neither has a core capacity to love themselves or value themselves in an unconditional way
- ❖ Control, safety and anti-abandonment strategies
- ❖ Transaction and exchange based relationship dynamics
- ❖ Motivated by fear, safety seeking and seeking to fulfill desires
- ❖ In their own ways, dynamics of abdication of personal accountability for our relationship choices, and denial of the effects of our usage of our personal power
- ❖ Significant influences in dysfunctional relationships that undermine shared communication and understanding
- ❖ Based upon simulacra and beliefs that are dysfunctional
- ❖ Feel they must be wanted and important in other's lives in order to be and to remain safe
- ❖ Undermining of quality thinking, decision-making and accurate processing of emotional information on both partner's parts
- ❖ Diminishing in their influence on one's general quality of consciousness

❖ Are based upon the fundamental emotional premise that "I cannot be happy unless I have what I want and need" (they just have very different strategies for going about getting what they want and feel they need)

❖ Distorting in how they influence each partner's interpretation of day-to-day relationship reality

❖ Supported in their process by the Victim/Perpetrator/Rescuer process, the Judgment Cycle and the dynamics of blaming others for our situations. (See the definitions of these cycles later in the book).

Parental Ego-Identity:

This ego-strategy is also a common "role" many of us play in life. Yet it is far more than just a role. This ego strategy is one we learned from how we were parented, by our own parents. When this identity is applied to our lives we tend to treat other people as children, or as less than ourselves, and often in a dictatorial, controlling, self-righteous or judgmental manner. This ego-identity cannot see and respect the free-will rights of other human beings, because it is too busy "telling" others how they "should be or must be" from its point of self-perceived authority. Often spouses in a relationship take turns "righteously parenting" each other, without realizing it is happening, or understanding the conflict and stress producing implications of the process.

There are of course many **"child ego selves"** in each of us that were formed earlier in our lives. These child-ego identities can have profound influence on our thinking, emotions, behavior and relationship understandings and interpretations. When we feel ourselves being "parented" by someone else, we often tend to subconsciously and reflexively operate from these child ego selves. Full consciousness cannot be attained until these child selves are evolved, matured and thus transcended.

The "Worker Bee" Ego-Identity:

This ego-identity can be seen as a sort of workaholic ego-identity, that is focused only on work and day-to-day task accomplishment and nothing else. When someone is operating in this way they see only the process of "getting things done" in life as being relevant, necessary and safety producing. This ego-identity is not only applied to managing one's time and energy resources, it also tends to be applied to all of our money and spending decisions. This strategy is usually applied in a dictatorial way within the context of our monogamous relationships. It is this mechanism that keeps in place a constant process of second guessing our selves in regard to our day-to-day decisions, in order to meet some preconceived standards and self-expectations of achievement.

This ego-identity is constantly wanting to make sure that it is safe in its process of making decisions and taking decisive action. Therefore, it is a safety strategy, and it also operates as a way of reassuring oneself that we are worthwhile partners in relationships (i.e. unlikely to be abandoned). Lastly this dynamic also tends to project itself onto others we are in relationship with, (i.e. wanting to make sure that our spouses are "pulling their weight" and meeting our safety related expectations in our relationships). A difficulty this ego-identity creates in our lives is that it does not tend to be empathetic in its process, either towards ourselves or those we are in relationship with. Therefore, it does not support emotionally astute and sensitive relationship dynamics and decisions, as we "coldly focus" on results and performance rather than feeling and working with relationship emotions.

Victim, Perpetrator and Rescuer Ego-Identities (V/P/R):

This set of strategies is designed to empower the individual via perceiving themselves as either a victim, a perpetrator or a rescuer of others. Each of these self-perceived ego-identities are in fact ways of managing personal self-worth and social-worth. They are also control and safety strategies. Even to be a victim, brings with it a sort of social power. This power is seen in victim's ability to get others to rescue them, to proclaim themselves as innocent and other's guilty, and in a lessening of other's expectations of them if they are defined as a victim.

Being a perpetrator brings with it a different sort of perceived power, (i.e. via bullying or threatening, etc.). Being a rescuer brings with it a sort of self-worth, self-validation and social validation, and thus acceptability and empowerment. We would say that the V/P/R strategies are interdependent because there could be no victims if there was no perpetrator, and no rescuer if there were no victims, etc. Operating within the V/P/R strategies keeps the detrimental dynamics of the V/P/R model of interaction in place, bought into and believed in. We will discuss these important interdependent dynamics and their influence on life and relationships further on in the book.

Oddly enough, individual human beings can exhibit **multiple ego-identities** at the same time. So, for example, we could have a narcissistic strategy, a spiritual ego strategy and a parenting authoritarian ego strategy all at the same time operating in the same person. We could also have an intellectual-ego operating with a primal-ego, which could lead to a cold, calculated and very destructively intellectualized person that was not in touch with love or compassion. We could even have a co-dependent ego-identity who exhibits some narcissistic tendencies. Whatever ego-identity elements we have can be triggered in any number of ways in today's complex and stressed relationships.

When people have these complex ego-identity situations of multiple ego-complexes it is very challenging for them to transcend these habitual tendencies, and it is even difficult for them to be consistently motivated to do so. Especially when these people feel safer unconsciously holding to their ego-identity dynamics, beliefs and tendencies. Ego-identities and ego-identity dynamics are never really about how good we feel about ourselves. It is vital to understand that all ego-identity strategies are designed to help us feel better about ourselves, when we really don't feel good about ourselves, without being required to directly deal with our emotional issues. Therefore, we don't get to feel better about ourselves as long as we engage in these ego-identity dynamics.

The various ego-identities create habitual and reactive tendencies of decision-making, emotional reaction and behavior that are not personally or socially optimal. It is useful to understand that ultimately transcending all ego-identity tendencies is to our best spiritual and social interest. Most of us swing back and forth between consciousness and subconscious ego-identity dynamics, throughout the course of our day. Ego states are not really dynamics of social or personal power, although they are often felt and perceived to be so. Though they are often felt to be necessary in our day-to-day lives, they are not necessary at all. Our true power is found when we transcend these states. Attainment of authentic conscious humility and resonance with God is far more powerful than any ego state.

Who we truly are is far more than our ego-identities. Therefore, the ongoing dissolution of all the detrimental influences of our ego is foundational to our spiritual advancement. Consciousness cannot reign supreme in our lives until subconscious tendencies are removed or resolved. Through the attainment of conscious grace-filled humility, we come to realize the expression of God's love that we each truly are. We previously described humility as a way of seeing ourselves as completely and unconditionally lovable, acceptable and worthy, and not better than anyone else, therefore only equal in every way to every other human being. The attainment of humility does not require us to experience humiliation, though many of us initially move toward humility via the process of humiliation. Via humiliation we learn to let loose of ego driven motivations, goals and values. So, though painful humiliation serves a beneficial and temporary purpose.

Humility is a wonderful and internally peaceful state and is not in any way associated with punishment or loss of anything that is really of value. What could be better than fully realizing oneself to be a child of God, and by doing so fully understanding that we are completely and only equal to all other children of God? Our true spiritual identity, which is based in God consciousness, is often slowly growing and evolving from what we learn from the ongoing operation of our less evolved ego-identities, yet who we truly are is more than the sum of our ego's, personality or identity parts.

It is helpful to realize that the effect of our fears of death and abandonment have led to the creation of the social and primal process of tribalism. Tribalism is governed via judgment and punishment (the Judgment Cycle and various Control Cycle Strategies) and our tribes or societies have become more complex, defined and <u>somewhat more civilized</u> as humans have evolved. Though this is not the case in all areas of the world. Our ego-identities are formed as we are born, live in and grow within the families we are born into (mini-tribes). We then continue the development of our ego-identities in the social "consensus consciousness soup" of the larger tribe or society we belong to or are born into. Each of our tribes works to condition us (sometimes through domination and intimidation) to conform to its traditions, beliefs, values and ways of life. The process of tribalism invariably leads to the creation of complex social-identities within each of us, we then reference and manage the evolution of these social-identities as we interact in our relationships. Tribalism also leads to, and motivates, the creation of our underlying ego-identities, perceived self-images, and our safety and control strategies. Only through recognition of these social influences and dynamics can we then transcend personal ego, negative social dynamics and attain self-sovereign consciousness.

Marauder Ego-Identity:

This ego-identity uses the world and all its people, without concern for the welfare of anyone else, and therefore has many similarities to the narcissistic ego-identity. It believes that having its own way in all areas of life, and fulfilling its personal desires of all kinds, is the solution to all things. When it does not get its way, it turns to manipulation and other more destructive tactics of goal attainment. This identity could be seen in wealthy or powerful people who have used their status to maintain the capacity to manage their fears of death and abandonment. This ego-identity is predatory and uses its manufacture of an artificial social image to keep itself safe and to attain its goals. If the façade of the ego-identity is somehow lost (oddly enough this can occur when the person learns something new about themselves and their tendencies), then the ego-identity fears loss of control which leads to hatred.

This ego-identity is constantly concerned with evaluating and knowing and controlling what others are thinking and feeling about it, and uses this information to manage its social interactions and status. It could be seen as a sort of psychopathic manipulative dynamic, which coldly looks upon everyone and everything as something to be consumed, controlled, used and everyone else is seen as less important than it. This ego-identity cannot feel empathy or compassion. Like the narcissistic ego-identity, this dynamic is a coping mechanism for avoiding its own deeply buried feelings of shame, guilt and self-judgment. Therefore, remaining in this ego-identity holds the shame, guilt and self-judgment in place and these negative emotions continue to support the perceived need for the ego-identity. Therefore, the ego-identity is a coping mechanism and an addictive attempt to sooth these negative emotions without either facing or resolving them. This ego-identity does not have the capacity for compassion, love or true kindness. Of course both men and women can exhibit this ego-identity, though in my experience, men tend to manifest it more often and more destructively.

Who Am I?:

Some spiritual seekers spend lifetimes diligently working to simply know their "true identity" by focusing and meditating on the single eternal question "Who am I?" This was a teaching of the great spiritual teacher Ramana Maharshi and he produced a book by the same name. These teachers are leading the way in the evolution of humanity's mass consciousness. Still, this path of intense spiritual development is impractical and too demanding for the average person with a job and family to focus on with the same degree of consistency as a full-time spiritual seeker. Still everyone in the world is in some way engaged in this process of self-discovery, since we are all to some degree working to better understand ourselves and our place in the universe. We are just not all going at it in a conscious, consistent, disciplined, discerning, systematic, constructive, spiritual or intentional manner. Yet with enough discipline, love, motivation and intention any of us can make substantial spiritual process in any lifetime. We get out what we put into our spiritual self-developmental efforts.

Any identity we choose to assume in our lives brings with it a great deal of unacknowledged, unmanaged and limiting baggage and conflict which can manifest itself in our day-to-day reality at any time. This baggage could be seen as part of our karma, and it is neither truly positive nor negative, yet its influence will eventually lead to further understanding, consciousness and evolution. Therefore, identity elements, though somewhat limiting, are simultaneously helping us to organize our consciousness and our experience of life, a step which is required for our spiritual development.

We are required in our interactions with other people and their chosen identities to focus our decision-making and the results of our decisions, based upon the limitations and parameters of our perceived identity. This process requires us to become more self-aware and aware of others and thereby facilitates a form of somewhat consistent interaction with the rest of the humanity. Our perceived identity is therefore a fundamental vehicle of our soul's development, since it supports our social participation and learning in each lifetime.

Part of our identity could be our religion, for example various versions of the Christian faith (Roman Catholic, Baptist, Mormon, Presbyterian, Anglican, Methodist, Lutheran, etc.). All religions are in essence good, and as such are helpful steps on our individual spiritual developmental paths and therefore benefit the world.

Still it is useful to understand that if we participate in any religion, we may then be required to meet the religion's rigorous expectations of:

- ❖ Personal conduct and/or submission to church authority.
- ❖ Adherence to doctrine, rules, norms and ways of prioritizing our lives and relationships.
- ❖ Adherence to a particular style of conduct and emotional, personal and interpersonal self-management.
- ❖ Spiritual goals we are expected to work toward or to attain.
- ❖ How we are supposed to relate to God and how we are to conceptualize God.
- ❖ Adoption of specific beliefs about what is right and wrong, good or bad, acceptable or unacceptable.

If we do not conform to these religion-based rules and beliefs, we might find ourselves at odds with or unsupported by other people who identify with that specific religion. We would likely lose the social support, and interpersonal validation, of our particular individual religious social identity, and could even be branded heretics or sinners. We could also, in the case of most religions at some point in history, be judged, punished, cast out or even killed for our non-compliance.

The same result is, to some degree, true of membership in any political party, social organization, race, gender or even of membership in organizations such as corporations and governments. There is a common group tendency, of all groups, to try to control or overtly influence their individual members. This tendency is, as described earlier, a primitive dynamic of "tribalism". Groups also try to influence people outside the group. This tribal tendency (us vs. them) is a key reason for the existence of bigotry, prejudice, racism, social and judicial bias, political hate speech, populism and nationalism.

The flip side, or positive side of this dynamic can be seen when we, as individuals, fully identify with any specific group, and by doing so feel more secure, and thus safe or safer. Due to our group participation, and resonating with the group mentality, we may also feel we are a valued and empowered part of the community, and thereby work together positively with others as a team toward shared goals. This double-edged situation of positive and negative group dynamics is also the case when we look at the motivations of patriotism and nationalism which are often intended to "do good", and have, in some cases, turned into atrocities. The same dynamic can also be seen in regard to groups of police personnel, who are trying to serve the public good, and can, like any group of human beings, become fearfully triggered by perceived threats. Meaning that their fears, their desire for their own safety, and their desire to be able to control situations, can then lead to abuses of power. In these detrimental situations, decisions are always made from fear based negative emotions, rather than conscious loving wisdom. All negative emotional dynamics, and acts of violence, no matter "how they present or are interpreted", are driven at their foundation by fear.

All groups and nations have a perceived identity that they continually try to protect and maintain. Our individual and group identities are constantly striving to manage their degree of social acceptability, value, safety, security and support. This is even true of a nation's identity fearing global public embarrassment, as can be seen when any nation is publicly embarrassed or proven inept. Nations also fear appearing weak or vulnerable. In these situations, when a nation appears to be less powerful, and thus less secure in relation to other nations, it can lead to negative international interactions. One glaring example would be North Korea's tendency to negatively act out, and in their insecurity, making constant threats to other countries.

To add to the complexity, it is important to recognize that everyone's definition of what it is to be a good person, a good American, a good Russian, a good man or a good woman, or a good spiritual person is different and ever-changing. These definitions are changing constantly as our world and its inhabitants continue to evolve, transform, grow and learn. Yet no person's or nation's perspective or set of identity-based values, priorities and beliefs is right, or "more right" than anyone else's. Though many people believe that there is a right way to feel, think, make decisions and live, and that they personally and unquestionably know it. Therefore, when others do not meet their expectations, they become hostile.

In a very practical sense, at least compared to how our world functions now, there is ultimate truth. Yet it is not a truth that can be spoken or interpersonally communicated in the traditional ego-identity interpreted sense. It cannot be verbally expressed; however, we are all working to become wise and conscious enough to truly and completely understand it. At the point of rejoining of our souls to God, when we have reached the end of our personal developmental soul adventures, we will each know this truth completely. Until we reach this point, we are each given only the portions of truth we become capable of understanding. In other words, we are all just doing the best we know how, from moment-to-moment.

None of us are better than any others; we are all, in the eyes of God, equal. No matter what our choices, achievements, level of understanding, race or nationality we will all forever remain equal. In this transcendent truth ego-identity has no applicability. The assumption that any person or identity is better or more valid than any other is a key reason for the state of conflict in the world today. Total humility, filled with grace and unconditional acceptance of our complete and total equality as individuals, religions and nations is the answer to this fundamental world problem. Humility as individuals, groups and nations is a necessary prerequisite to being open to sage understandings and insights. Humility can be achieved by conscious choice and intention to realize our equality, and as previously stated it need not involve humiliation.

Territorial Identity and Security:

Other facets of the concept of identity are those of attempted control of territory, ownership and boundaries. Any identity brings with it an inherent desire for the perceived identity to be safe, secure, stable, competitive and free to be expressed, and from this state to apply its power and to continue to thrive and survive, and also creates the willingness to kill. With any desire for safety and security comes the fear of losing it. This fear creates the subconsciously driven motivation to create a defined safe territory for the identity, with specific social and interpersonal boundaries. This fear driven territorial tendency is just as true for a nation, a religion, a corporation, a family or an individual. This fear also drives the fear of loss of control over anything we assume we own or have control over.

Once we have carved out our identity's territory in our world we then desire to protect our perceived territory, to police its boundaries and to punish perceived transgressors or anyone not supportive of our territorial identity security. When the protection mode of any entity is significantly triggered, whether a person or organization, higher level thought processes disappear, and very primal decision-making styles take over. This dynamic invariably leads to conflict and even to killing. These primal tendencies also drive the ongoing competitiveness of all kinds we perceive in the world which is antithetical to attainment of world peace.

To a greater or lesser extent our consciousness, and with it our wisdom is always lost in the name of control, competition and protectionism if we allow it to occur. With this loss of consciousness goes our capacity for trust, learning, change, negotiation, teamwork, love, compassion, mutual understanding, fairness and a positive view of the process of interpersonal and social transformation. We also lose sight of all truly creative options, since fear-based decision-making is the unwitting antithesis of creativity, free thought and action.

Once we drop to the low energy frequency of root chakra fear and competition we literally lose our humanity, as well as all the more sophisticated elements of our identity that we would otherwise apply to our decisions. We also lose our true spiritual consciousness and nature. In this way, the application of our personal power becomes distorted and limited. It is useful to realize that capitalism itself, without loving altruism at its core, invariably grows in inhumane directions. I am not advocating socialism or any other specific political model, nor any specific economic model or social philosophy; I am suggesting that the humanization of the existing process of capitalism, or whatever economic model the world eventually chooses to function on, is required, if we want to progress as a world.

At this time, in even some of the best run capitalist societies there are many people trapped in economic situations that border on indentured servitude. By this statement, I mean that these people really have no dependable and broadly available path to acquiring a better standard of living in their futures. One example is the extreme limitations that people who are raising families in the U.S. face when they are required to make due on the current U.S. minimum wage, (which truly is minimum). At this time the minimum wage in the U.S. ranges somewhere between $7.25 - $15.00 per hour, depending upon the state you look at and how far in the future you look. Another example of this situation is the rising cost of quality higher education, that has now reached a point of financial inaccessibility by many average people. Even if these people borrow money for their education they have no guarantee of a job when they have completed their education. This situation is truly one of trapped service without resolution or progression to a higher financial state.

In many countries, the systems by which citizens are developed, empowered and educated are either non-optimal or fundamentally broken. As it currently stands, "the U.S. system" is not optimally facilitating the development of its citizens in order to empower them to attain their true potential. This situation translates to nations not achieving their potential. When you add all the nations of the world together, in regard to their various ways of facilitating their citizens, in spite of all of the technology and wealth that exists in the world, you could say that the world of human beings is not optimally being supported in reaching its potential. This situation can be resolved, (fixed) and transcended if we only choose to do so. From this vantage point you can see why U.S. citizens are calling for fundamental change in the way government works. This change cannot be accomplished by merely changing the individuals that are elected to positions of governance.

I am therefore suggesting that a completely new paradigm of international and intra-national socio-economic operation and cooperation is required. By integrating altruism with capitalism, I am not merely speaking of corporations trying to improve their image by giving to charities. I am speaking of a core and fundamental paradigm shift that must occur across the globe and in all societies, if we are to learn to love one another, and not to lose this loving orientation on the altar of a blind and callous capitalistic profit motivation.

Paradoxically, many people in businesses today are out of touch with their own motivational emotions, and so are unable to feel the subconscious fear that often relentlessly drives them and their decisions. A current commonly used "buzz phrase" among CEOs is "you can never be too paranoid". Is this the statement of a confident loving consciousness? Instead they focus on rationalizing the superficial and often short-term benefits of consciousness distorting fear-based decision-making and short term profit. In this way, they idolize cold competitive dynamics as being a potential solution to the world's issues. This is, in effect, a narcissistic and potentially predatory organizational dynamic. Neither maintaining the status quo of the current

Enter the Era of Empowerment

system, nor hiding in our comfort zones will solve our fundamental world issues.

Understanding the various social and individually dysfunctional implications of ego-identity protectionism can make the difference in our attaining and maintaining the conscious willingness to evolve to a higher plane of understanding as individuals, as nations and as a species. If we are part of any group that even periodically functions at this low level of "tribal" fear-based consciousness, we will feel pressured to agree with it, and then compromise and participate in its protectionist perspective and actions—though we may not consciously realize we are doing so. We become energetically, emotionally and unconsciously entrained in the organization's method of making decisions and acting at this low frequency of consciousness.

We may then later rationalize all our negative thoughts, emotions, actions and reactions based upon our fear of losing our place in the organization, or of losing our social identity, our safety, our status and security. In this way we become unconsciously imprisoned in group thought patterns and decision strategies. This dynamic is often played out by participants in groups who are focused on devaluing other human beings who are not part of their group. Those not of the group are often painted to be "against the group", or as not fulfilling the values of or obeying the rules of the group. In its grossest form this dynamic manifests war, religious cults, prejudice, unnecessary policing actions and even genocide. Many nations and some religions have operated in this way at some point in history.

Consciously Refining Our Identities:

The influences of social pressure on what we as individuals are supposed to think, feel and how we are supposed to function and behave socially and interpersonally can be subtle or blatant. These influences create many of the challenges we are facing related to global development and transformation. For example, how does a "good American citizen" function as a truly responsible global citizen in regard to the good of the global ecosystem, and still remain a good American? As soon as we try to do both simultaneously we run into internal or external conflict of some sort. Therein lies the profound limitation of ego-identity and its implications regarding world peace and the process of world development and transformation. America has economic, social and religious interests and goals, which to some degree oppose that which is good for the world. For example, America is the second highest polluter in the world, and still it strongly resists changing its self-

226

centered polluting ways for the long-term good of its citizens, the planet and all of humanity.

The same detrimental dynamic of egocentric identity conflict applies to our personal participation in any group or corporation, in that the values of the group often run counter to the good of the world. This internal emotional conflict can be seen in people who work for large oil production companies, or companies that significantly pollute the world or for those employees who develop technologies of war. Some corporations actually try to influence (through incentives or threats) their employees to vote for specific political groups that appear to serve the corporation's interests. These corporations do not tend to ask their employees what they believe or value, politically or otherwise in these situations.

If we want to evolve either our personal or group consciousness and understanding in any significant or comprehensive manner, we must redefine our ego-identity in a foundational way. For example, consciously choosing to shift to a self-perceived world citizen identity rather than a national citizen identity. Yet if we do choose to do this our nation's ego and consensus consciousness may not like or respect our choice and can even try to control or punish us. It also means that we will be required to accept and manage whatever the change in identity brings with it, whether it is the effect on our personal or family relationships, work situation, financial security or religious affiliations. In some nations making such a choice can even directly affect the choosers safety or the safety of their family.

These feared identity choice repercussions are a key reason that people do not more often evolve as sovereign individuals, independent of the influence of their social surroundings. We always incur significant social and environmental resistance, friction or conflict when we choose to change fundamentally and rapidly as individuals. This occurs when we choose to change in a way that is out of sync with our social environment. The worst of this resistance may be felt in a sense of aloneness, being different or even of abandonment. Yet even these disharmonious states can be healed and transcended with enough conscious awareness of our total oneness with God and humanity. Those with whom we are in relationship want us to remain the same person they used to know. Others want to be able to continue to depend upon elements of our identity for the achievement of their agendas, or even to more comprehensively control us. Still others want us to conform to their social norms or workplace cultures.

These influences, though possibly well intentioned and firmly believed in, must eventually be opened to reevaluation if we are to make the best of this global transformational climate, and to fully realize who we are. If we are unwilling to constantly reevaluate every element of our perceived identity and beliefs, we will then likely be unwilling to change fundamentally as a human identity and a soul. Traditional human roles are changing despite our primal tendency to cling to previously constructed identities, mores, motivations, traditions and ways of maintaining social status. Ever more rapidly we are realizing that old or traditional roles and rules are no longer functional in our current social world. (For example, what used to be workable roles of husband and wife no longer work in this new world we live in; this fact leads to ego-identity and role conflict, confusion, fear, blame, stress, divorce and broken families).

However, this evolution of identity is also bringing about positive changes in how we can see ourselves, in that as we break the old molds we become freed to become something better, more joyful and more functional. It is often the attempt to apply these previously learned and unquestioned roles and associated dynamics to new and changing life situations that cause many of the challenges and conflicts we currently face.

This developmental process creates many negative emotional dynamics. It is not yet fashionable and supported, or even allowed in most cultures, to truly be a sovereign individual who is independent of any group. Nor is it common for people, groups or governments to understand, fully accept and respect such individuals, though these sovereign individuals are likely the source of our long-term salvation. Nor is it considered a positive thing in most cultures to redefine your social or personal identity on a daily basis, yet it is still happening. Hence the evolutionary friction, misunderstanding and life stress. There is no telling how long this process will go on.

As the world continues to change and integrate, the task of ego-identity management will also become more complex, subtle, conflicted and difficult. Population increases, population relocations (i.e. Syrian, Libyan and Bangladeshi refugees, and soon to be more), technological developments and scarcity of resources and their associated issues will also profoundly affect this ongoing identity transformation effort. Population driven stresses, pressures, conflicts and negative emotions will likely escalate unless effective preemptive mass educational action is taken to help individuals learn to consciously direct their personnel ego-identity management and transformative process. Only this educational process can stem the tide of ongoing confusion and conflict. This positive educational process might then help stem the world's rising tide of terrorism.

Unmanaged and subconscious dynamics of ego-identity change tend to feed drama, disagreement, miscommunication, misunderstandings and interpersonal conflict. These dynamics can lead to a "Tower of Babel" type of miscommunication in our interpersonal and intergovernmental interactions. So we need global support for global development, collaborative efforts, attainment of shared understandings, teamwork, transformation, harmony and peace. Organizing the collective intelligence of the world's people to solve these problems in a well-coordinated manner can now be supported via the internet. Though so far no group or government has taken the lead in creating this type of software supported infrastructure or laid the foundation of this collaborative effort for world self-preservation.

All chosen ego-identities are in a way inherently good. Meaning they are the result of the freewill choice of the individual, and freewill is a wonderful and blessed thing. Difficulties arise with the fear-driven inflexibilities and primal motivations of the ego-identity that stem from the root chakra. Other reasons for these difficulties are that we are often taught that there is a right way and a wrong way to be and live, and that our chosen identity is, or must be right. Therefore, other's chosen ways of living and their associated identities are presumed to be either wrong or just not as right as ours. This is a situation of dualistic and polarized interpretation, thinking, decision-making and emotion, which limits our lives, understandings, relationships and decisions. For these reasons our ego-identity can create fundamental limitations on our capacity to experience consistent compassion, caring and even emotional intimacy.

These polarizing perceptual tendencies cannot lead to comprehensive and congruent acceptance of all aspects of ourselves and others as sovereign individuals. Nor can they lead to us, as individuals, unconditionally accepting any other group, nation, religion, set of beliefs or culture as good and valid, if there is a perceived breach of security or fundamental conflict of interest. In some societies, free-will and individuality can neither be fully accepted nor supported, whether the nation is democratic in nature or not. An identity-based "glass ceiling" exists on the current developmental methods and dynamics of the consciousness of the individuals in most nations and in most groups. A glass ceiling which we are running into repeatedly without clearly identifying the cause or the nature of the limiting issues, nor their implications. Attainment of conscious personal sovereignty is the universe's "grass roots" method of transforming and transcending existing cultural and societal identity limitations and thereby evolving the species.

A main reason for these reactive territorial and judgmental patterns and their associated negative effects is that we have been taught that there is a single right, safe and necessary way to live. Our response to this situation is to deeply fear being found socially "wrong," and then being judged or potentially abandoned by others of our group or society if we step out of expectational bounds. Our personal and group fears can create unnecessary and problematic self-limitations. Therefore, we usually either choose to create a set of rules of safe social operation or we are socially conditioned by a set of rules that are designed by our family or society specifically to harness our potentially non-conforming behaviors and decision-making tendencies. This is true whether the group we belong to is a family, a nation or a corporation. This style of social conditioning is not a recipe for free thinking, independent interpretation, transformation, positive change or healthy creativity. This suppression of the individual, during our current highly transformational global process can lead to negative and even highly destructive actions and behaviors.

Human beings are herd creatures. We connect in groups, identify with those groups, and find our self-worth, value, life meaning, guidance and security in those groups. We also experience a primal fear if our position or status is lost within those groups. When faced with what might be perceived as a threat to the security of our chosen groups or the loss of our status or membership in the group we respond with fear, anger, judgment, blame, hatred and the willingness to destructively defend our group and our position within the group. We can act destructively when we perceive change of any kind if we do not understand the influence of the change in a positive way.

These reactive destructive dynamics are seen in acts of war and in cases of severe intergroup competition, especially in national, religious or corporate competition, and in the most intense form of social competition, (i.e. terrorism). This whole destructive mechanism, with all its complex dynamics is driven by simple primal fear and ignorance and is neither wrong nor bad; it is just an unnecessary leftover element of our species' early development. Yet when these dynamics arise, we as individuals then tend to rationalize the need for them, and our detrimental decisions and actions after the fact. We do our rationalizing at what we assume to be our conscious level, though we are not truly and fully conscious at all. We are operating at a level of thought and emotion where we tell ourselves why it was "unquestionably necessary" to destroy, harm, control, punish, judge, abandon, be prejudiced or undermine our perceived enemy.

We also rationalize why it was necessary to give up what we spiritually and personally value and believe (i.e. love, tolerance and compassion) for the fear reactive values and beliefs of the group. Fear is just one of many emotional states that undermine consciousness and wisdom, still fear is the root emotion for all negative emotions. Hatred, anger, resentment, jealousy, shame and guilt are just domino effects of primal fear. We can cease to be enslaved or entrained by these downward spiraling emotional dynamics if we consciously and willfully choose to do so.

We are all spiritual beings, and we all have a spark of God within us. This divine spark is our guiding light for spiritual development and refinement of our true spiritual identity, until we reach the point of full understanding of our God consciousness. We are all works in progress and are all wonderful when seen as such. With the consistent application of the intention to attain divine spiritual love and compassion, all our prior detrimental tendencies are washed away, revealing our true spiritual identity and essence. We all have this power and we will all get there.

Emotional Availability VS. Self-Sovereignty, Finding the Balance:

Is there a definition of emotional availability that fits every relationship? No, there is not. Certainly, there are many different individual interpretations, expectations, beliefs and preferences in terms of relationship behavior that people would tend to associate with emotional availability. There are also numerous behaviors or relationship dynamics which may be associated with emotional unavailability. These kinds of emotionally non-available behaviors and dynamics can be seen in both men and women. It is not only men who may appear to be emotionally unavailable, although it often assumed to be more the case for men than women. Men and women can both be emotionally unavailable to others, just in very different ways. It is inaccurate and detrimental to blindly assign these dynamics to gender or to look at availability in a polarized or black and white view. Everyone is emotionally available to some degree, in some situation and in some relationship. It is always a matter of degrees.

Some examples of emotional unavailability are:

❖ Not being willing to be open to, or fully listen to, or respond to a spouse's emotional communications or discussion of relationship issues, perspectives, processes, feelings or preferences

❖ Being unwilling to be open to recognize, validate and respect what is emotionally important to those we are in relationship with.

231

❖ Being focused on work, career or life goals to the extent that our time and energies are not there for those we are in relationship with in a balanced way.

❖ An unwillingness to involve oneself consistently in the details of our spouse's day-to-day life and emotional dynamics, thus potentially appearing to be cold, uninvolved or uncaring.

❖ Ongoing open criticism of a spouse's decision-making, behavior, thought processes or emotional processes.

❖ Inability to empathize or sympathize with those we are in relationship with.

❖ Being so involved with our own emotional processes that we have no emotional bandwidth for others. These situations can occur when we feel victimized, abused, wounded, dismissed, disempowered, emotionally hurt, depressed, abandoned or invalidated.

❖ Desiring to be so in control of those we are in relationship with, and of our own lives that we become unable to love them and accept them as they are.

These situations and more could be deemed representative of emotional unavailability, although this is not always the case. In many cases, when our relationship expectations are not met by our spouse we may claim that they are emotionally unavailable. We may hold this opinion, even if we have a very attentive and positively emotional spouse. This is particularly true of people who have previously been or felt abandoned and then inaccurately project that experience onto their current relationship. They expect to experience abandonment, so much so, that they manifest the experience within themselves. Their dissatisfaction can then alienate their spouse into creating the precise situation they have feared and wanted to avoid. It is worthwhile noting that creating emotional drama or conflict, on the part of either spouse does not equal being emotionally available.

Emotional availability requires:

❖ Commitment to the relationship
❖ Consistently open emotional communication
❖ Positive emotional focus on the relationship
❖ Intention and effort in relationship building
❖ Trust and integrity
❖ Willingness to equally share power in the relationship

❖ Tolerance of differences of perspective, expectation and emotional processes

❖ Respect

❖ Consistency and dependability

❖ **Openness to being emotionally vulnerable**

These characteristics must be displayed by both participants. If either spouse is stuck in control strategies, safety strategies, a victim strategy, negative emotional dynamics, judgmentalness or criticism, then they cannot be truly emotionally available. If either spouse feels disempowered, or wants to be dominant in the relationship, then they cannot be authentically emotionally available.

It is important to understand that choosing to be a consciously sovereign, self-empowering and self-authorizing person may mean choosing not meeting other's expectations. This choice may lead to being accused of not being emotionally available to them. It is personally always up to you how you choose to meet other's expectations or not to meet other's expectations. The important message here is that as you become more conscious, others may not understand or validate your personal process. It is always your conscious choice how you choose to interact with others, in any relationship.

I would suggest that for those on a spiritual path it is a fine line that must be walked in order to retain your spiritual developmental sovereignty and still interact with others via consistent love and compassion. Doing so requires us to develop both significant discipline and consciousness. In the end result, self-sovereignty leads to a significantly greater potential for relationship intimacy. It is true that it is confident and authentic emotional and spiritual intimacy that is the ultimate solution to negative emotional dynamics. It is also true that this positive intimacy solves perceived **emotional unavailability**.

The Fear of "Emotional Hurt" That Holds Our Self-Sovereignty Hostage:

When we do not meet other's expectations they can react self-righteously in many negative ways. For many people, having their expectations met equals love. Therefore, they may feel hurt and then try to "hurt us" in reaction if their expectations are not met. They may claim that they are victims of us, and that we are bad, wrong, non-spiritual, non-loving, selfish or even being cruel and insensitive to them. They are claiming that we are "hurting them", by not meeting their expectations. Many people believe that their expectations are equal to "needs", and that if these perceived needs are not met that they cannot be happy or live a full life. Of course, this is not true.

Each of us is responsible for our own emotional process, though many of us do not want to be. Many of us fear hurting those we love. Many of us would also prefer to try to control other people's behaviors, choices and emotions rather than managing and being accountable for our own emotional process. In this way, we try to hold other's hostage to our control strategies, via threats of abandonment, guilt trips or criticism. It is very important if we want to be self-empowered, conscious, self-authorizing and self-sovereign that we intentionally choose not to allow others to influence us in these ways. Their attempts to control us do not mean that they are bad or wrong. It only means they are not yet conscious enough to transcend these tendencies and to see a more optimal way of relating and loving. In the end, it is not worth it to live in a prison of fear or expectation.

Chapter Eight
Beyond Judgment and Control to Discernment:

ACCORDING TO WEBSTER'S DICTIONARY, TO JUDGE MEANS "to discern, to distinguish, to form an opinion, to compare facts or ideas, and perceive their agreement or disagreement, and thus to distinguish truth from falsehood".

Note: No part of this definition states that judgment is an act of seeing ourselves as above or better than anyone else, more right or righteous, blaming anyone for anything, or that judgment is a judicial mechanism by which we control others or ourselves through any type of punishment. Still we often choose to judge, punish and control in these detrimental ways

Transitioning *From* Judgmental Control *To* Discerning Power:

I use the term "Judgment Cycle" to describe a habitual personal and social cyclic pattern which directly undermines our attainment of personal sovereignty by blocking our ability to objectively discern truth. This disruption of our thought processes affects our internal emotional management and potentially all our interpersonal interactions. The Judgment Cycle is a process of negative interpretation and decision-making toward self and other's actions, decisions, beliefs and emotions. This cycle often involves punishment of self or other, in order to redeem self or other for perceived wrong doing, and as a way of managing our feelings of shame and guilt. This process has become ingrained in the mental and emotional systems of most individuals and into various aspects of all human cultures, religions, families and at all levels of all societies. **The Judgment Cycle is not a method used to make good judgments or quality decisions in life**. In fact, I would suggest that making conscious, wise and discerning decisions in life has nothing to do with judging, criticizing or blaming anyone to any degree for anything. Shifting to conscious discernment as the foundation of our interpretive and decision-making strategies creates a state of optimal personal empowerment and maintains consciousness.

In this discussion judgmentalness is synonymous with rendering a verdict regarding someone's choices, emotions, beliefs or behaviors. This tendency often leads first to assigning blame and is usually followed by some form of punishment. The Judgment Cycle is an incredibly subconscious, reactive, detrimentally influential, and pervasive pattern of behavior and decision-making, as well as a widespread social and cultural dynamic. It has infiltrated all levels of society and is the basis for most conflicts and even wars. In effect, judgmental tendencies can become a fundamental and detrimental mindset, motivational principle and foundational decision-making perspective. Yet we cannot solve the tendency to judge ourselves or others by judging our tendency to judge. We can only love ourselves and others into states of love and compassion and ultimately enlightenment.

When in ignorance we attempt to use judgmental formulas as a developmental process, we create a built-in "glass ceiling" of misunderstanding. Meaning that self-judgment is a process of self-imposed limitation and self-suppression, rather than of freedom, gained through loving transcendent understanding.

It is useful to understand that the process of judging and blaming is a process of emotional abandonment, which creates great suffering throughout humanity. It is also helpful to recognize that these judgmental patterns are simply a self-defense mechanism of our ego-identity(s), thus these tendencies can be discarded. By doing so we become empowered to intentionally create a more productive, loving and sovereign identity.

The Judgment Cycle has a definable cyclic and repetitive pattern. Here is an example of how it typically plays out in our lives.

The Judgment Cycle Pattern:

Early Conditioning:

We are often taught from early youth to first fear and distrust ourselves, our decisions and our personal power. Because of this we then tend to judge everything we think, do, say, feel, want and believe. We assume that if we follow this practice that we will somehow become "good" people. We are also taught to judge and criticize everyone else we interact with.

Exercising "Learned Judgmentalness":

In many situations, we find ourselves or another person to be lacking in some perceived way. For example, when we or they do not meet some preconceived standard or expectation which we hold to be true, right or necessary. In these situations, we are taught to be ready to punish ourselves or the other person for being wrong, inaccurate, non-conforming, bad, evil or unacceptable. This is a process of emotional abandonment of either our self or the other person. This dynamic of either abandoning ourselves or others can occur at several levels, including emotionally, mentally, interpersonally,

238

socially and even spiritually. This process of judgmental abandonment creates separation, suffering, insecurity, social uncertainty and isolation issues.

After Judgment We Must Punish Others:

The punishments we inflict upon others can range from public to private:

- ❖ Criticism/derision.
- ❖ Rejection and abandonment.
- ❖ Assignment of blame.
- ❖ Feeling anger or hatred toward another or seeking revenge.
- ❖ Retribution by using social or legal systems against them to control or punish them.
- ❖ Working to undermine another person's efforts or reputation.
- ❖ Social or political demonization of the perceived transgressor.

The punishments we may choose to apply to ourselves can be:

- ❖ Becoming unwilling to apply our personal power on our own behalf.
- ❖ Self-criticism and disapproval.
- ❖ Self-hatred, self-blame, self-distrust.
- ❖ Guilt and shame.
- ❖ Creation of a negative self-image.
- ❖ Seeing oneself as a failure or as unacceptable.
- ❖ Feeling worthless or less than others.
- ❖ Subconsciously sabotaging ourselves or withholding our
- ❖ own happiness.
- ❖ Undermining our own creative passion and feelings of joy and self-love.

Enmeshment in Hatred or Anger:

Once we have begun engaging in the punishment step of the Judgment Cycle, we often forget to limit the duration of our punishments to a specific time frame. Meaning that we either forget to, or choose not to forgive ourselves or others for perceived wrongs. In the case of self-punishment, a person can hate or be angry at themselves for an entire lifetime, even if this occurs at a subconscious level.

In the case of judging and punishing others we can hold a negative opinion of others, or hate them, and even feel motivated to get others to hate them, sometimes for a lifetime. In this way we become prisoners of our own negative decision-making process. Using judgmentalness in any form to support decision-making is detrimental. Judgmentalness is invariably based upon simplistic interpretations of right/wrong, true/false and good/bad. Life is never this simple, and trying to make it this simple in order to make decision-making simple only creates simple and dysfunctional decisions.

The Turning Point:

When we do get to a point in our spiritual maturity that we can forgive ourselves of a **single** perceived transgression, we suddenly become empowered to change that area of ourselves for the better. Until we choose to forgive the offending part of ourselves, that part is in effect frozen in place and becomes difficult to effectively change for the better. As long as we are in judgment of ourselves we are unable to significantly change ourselves, our lives or our relationships for the better.

The reason for this is that at the moment self-judgment occurs we have turned against that part of ourselves. We in effect are saying "this transgressing part of me is not good enough to be part of me, and so I will suppress, punish, destroy or get rid of it". This of course does not work, since whatever we are against is just a part of our self and thus cannot be gotten rid of. In addition, it is usually a part of us that is driven by unknown subconscious motivations, (unknown does not equal negative, and does not make it an enemy). Again, the solution is comprehensive and complete self-love, self-acceptance and self-forgiveness.

Once we choose to forgive ourselves completely, we become free to change all parts of ourselves for the better. After we do so, we tend to like ourselves better, and others may also like us better. Yet if we are not watchful, the next phase of the Judgment Cycle will begin, and we will look for something new to judge ourselves for. This occurs because we assume that continually judging and punishing ourselves will make us a "better person", or that judging ourselves is necessary to motivate us to perform in some socially acceptable and constructive life direction. To judge anything, or anyone, is in essence, to disdain it or them. Therefore, the better solution is not to judge anyone or anything, and in effect to "disdain nothing whatsoever" in any area of our lives. In this way we can find the value and presence of God in all things, persons and in ourselves.

Return The Cycle Or Choose Otherwise:

Some of us judge and punish ourselves dozens or even hundreds of times per day, and often regarding the most trivial issues. Without conscious understanding of the Judgment Cycle, and direct intervention in it, we get

240

sporadic positive results in life. The infrequent application of self-forgiveness most of us tend to employ falls far behind the ongoing negative effects of self-judgment and self-punishment. Is it any wonder so many people suffer from low self-esteem, high stress levels and depression?

This cyclic and repetitive dynamic of judgment is *always* based upon some fundamentally false premise; some of these premises are:

❖ "If I just judge and punish myself and others frequently enough and harshly enough then both I and they will somehow become good or better people, learn from the punishment, and the world will be a better, safer place".

❖ "I may somehow be redeemed as a spiritual being through my guilt, shame, self-rejection, suffering, self-punishment and pain."

❖ "If anything goes wrong or in an unexpected direction in my life, or in the surrounding social environment, then there MUST be someone at fault and thus to blame."

If we do choose to blame and punish someone, then we assume we have somehow made things better, changed them for the better or have resolved the perceived issue. Many believe that by blaming someone that we can make them feel our pain and that this is somehow just, right and necessary for us to feel better, for them to learn, and for us to then let the situation go.

Another inaccurate assumption is:

❖ "I cannot trust either myself and my decision-making or others and their decision-making. Therefore, assuming this to be true, I am expected to judge and punish myself and others as the antidote to distrust."

The Judgment Cycle works to undermine and even destroy self-trust and self-confidence, as well as to destroy trust between individual people and groups. Therefore, the Judgment Cycle does <u>not support</u> open non-fear-based communications, loving kindness, forgiveness, tolerance, acceptance, achievement of shared goals, priorities and understandings, collaboration or teamwork. The Judgment Cycle also teaches us to fundamentally distrust other people, their values, decisions and motivations without first really trying to understand or respect them. The Judgment Cycle is a mode of learned and culturally, economically, religiously and politically institutionalized distrust of self and others. Thus, it represents a mechanism of ongoing destruction of positive social interaction at all levels of society, and holds back the learning and evolution of humanity.

Many of us are taught to utilize the Judgment Cycle to self-monitor and manage our behaviors, thoughts, emotions and choices. (Meaning we have been conditioned socially and interpersonally to prefer to arrive at simplistic black-and-white interpretations, answers or perspectives on any life topic. Because of this we erroneously see the Judgment Cycle as an appropriate and beneficial way of leading us to supposedly wise decisions or of achieving meaningful understanding of situations, self or others).

This process of, and desire for, the over-simplification of life issues and relationships is ultimately detrimental to the goal of achieving deeper and more subtle understandings and wisdom regarding our life issues and relationships. How can we make wise decisions on complex issues if we are constantly trying to see these same situations in black and white, or in over simplified terms? How can anyone arrive at any higher truth through this dysfunctional method?

This desire for simple answers is driven by our root chakra's influence. Some aspects of root chakra dynamics are listed below:

Our Root Chakra's Tend To <u>Fear</u>:

- ❖ Pain
- ❖ Danger
- ❖ Loss
- ❖ Dying
- ❖ Social or interpersonal abandonment, criticism, attack or embarrassment or being alone
- ❖ Loss of social status or power
- ❖ Complexity itself in any area of our lives, (i.e. uncontrollable situations)
- ❖ Not being in control of ourselves or others
- ❖ Being controlled by others
- ❖ Being "wrong" or being perceived to be wrong or bad by others
- ❖ Feeling and fully owning our emotions and recognizing their fundamental influence in our lives (whether we are speaking of men or women)
- ❖ Unknown or "unclear situations" of almost any kind
- ❖ Giving up or losing <u>the option</u> to be able to use hatred, killing or destroying our way out of our problems
- ❖ Vulnerability, powerlessness and surrender of all kinds, in all relationships of all kinds, to the "good of the other", which it equates to being unsafe, (i.e. being unconditionally loving, and

resonating directly with God is seen as fundamentally dangerous and unsafe and a loss of control)

❖ Giving up its fear oriented dynamics that it assumes are keeping it safe

❖ Recognizing consciously that it is living in an ongoing process of fear

Our Root Chakra's intensely <u>want or desire:</u>

❖ Safety and security (or at least the perception of it)

❖ To have the power to control, dominate and manipulate others we are in relationship with, or to have power over the larger world around us

❖ To be "right" in almost any social situation or decision

❖ To feel more important than or have higher status than others (including our siblings and those we work with)

❖ To appear to "be smarter, or know, perceive or understand" more than others

❖ The illusion of certainty in all areas of life (even if this means living in denial about many things)

❖ To "be somebody" within our society

❖ To avoid any situation of perceived vulnerability or powerlessness, especially if we also feel threatened in some way. Basically, the root chakra wants to avoid that which is required for true emotional intimacy, because true intimacy is a process of trusting surrender to the person we love.

❖ Clarity and simplicity, including simple and defined rules, roles and social dynamics

❖ To be taken care of by someone else

❖ To have power over others and to continually have our things our way interpersonally and socially

❖ To have the option to attack, harm, criticize, hate, to kill or to destroy that which we feel threatened by

❖ To have others feel dependent upon us or to feel needed, necessary or relevant in the world

❖ To have others agree with our recorded simulacra interpretations or beliefs

❖ To not be required to be self-accountable

❖ To have the option of devaluing anyone and to take what we want from others

❖ (Often in men), the root charka wants the option to use women and feminine power to achieve male goals, to have women act as adornments and status symbols, and to function as safety strategies

❖ To avoid directly dealing directly with what we fear in life and relationships, (i.e. Any degree of fundamental vulnerability). Thus, root chakras motivate us to act and speak in emotionally violently, destructively, and in cold and selfish ways (violence, destructiveness and domination are seen by the root chakra as safety and control producing)

❖ To feel righteous when claiming victimhood

The Judgment Cycle is therefore a key support mechanism to the various detrimental forms of personal, social and political polarized decision-making we see in the world at this time. One example of this is the ongoing battling between the republican and democratic factions of the American political system. Both sides trying to use simplistic dynamics of judgmentalism and demonization of the other to trigger voter's fears in order to influence voter decision-making, just so that one side can have more control of the political process than the other. Another is the battle between the genders which tends to apply the same detrimental tactics. These are only the "dynamics of fear" being acted out on all levels and in all aspects of our nation's culture.

Judgmentalness itself is falsely seen as a mechanism of avoiding potential pain, guilt, shame or social sanction. Judgmentalness actually disempowers and imprisons us and our perception of available choices in the myopic projected fear of negative results. We assume that if we judge other people, situations or ourselves, and then threaten punishment or some type of social, personal or financial disincentive, that we will then be safe from the potential pain that we have projected (imagined) onto the situation.

An example of this process would be a parent who fears their child will not behave in a desirable manner at a social event. So, they prejudge the child in their own minds, and assume the child will act in a manner which is not acceptable. Then the parent threatens the child with punishment and emotional abandonment in order to avoid their potential undesirable behavior and to preemptively coerce desirable behavior out of them. This is done instead of the parent choosing to model desirable behavior to the child and consistently training and rewarding positive behavior from the child. This dynamic could be termed controlling behavior and conditional love, and of course adults also use it on other adults.

The choice to judge and punish our children can be seen as a way parents avoid:

1. Feared potential negative social results of our child's undesirable behavior.

2. Their own shame, self-judgment and self-punishment for not being an effective parent or not parenting the "right way".

3. The potential shame and guilt of feeling they have failed in their parental role.

4. Feeling guilty for punishing their children for negatively acting out in social situations (meaning that acts of pre-judgment and preemptive threat of punishment are supposedly a "positive parenting process", and will supposedly save the parent from feeling guilty later for punishing the child for bad behavior if it did occur).

Items 1 through 4 above are examples of the non-constructive circular reasoning of the emotional subconscious.

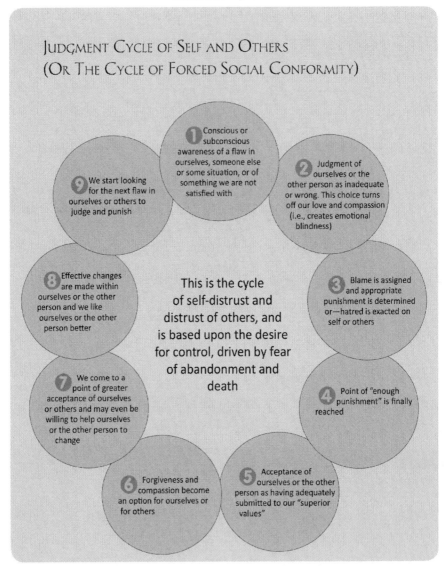

JUDGMENT CYCLE OF SELF AND OTHERS (OR THE CYCLE OF FORCED SOCIAL CONFORMITY)

1 Conscious or subconscious awareness of a flaw in ourselves, someone else or some situation, or of something we are not satisfied with

2 Judgment of ourselves or the other person as inadequate or wrong. This choice turns off our love and compassion (i.e., creates emotional blindness)

3 Blame is assigned and appropriate punishment is determined or—hatred is exacted on self or others

4 Point of "enough punishment" is finally reached

5 Acceptance of ourselves or the other person as having adequately submitted to our "superior values"

6 Forgiveness and compassion become an option for ourselves or for others

7 We come to a point of greater acceptance of ourselves or others and may even be willing to help ourselves or the other person to change

8 Effective changes are made within ourselves or the other person and we like ourselves or the other person better

9 We start looking for the next flaw in ourselves or others to judge and punish

This is the cycle of self-distrust and distrust of others, and is based upon the desire for control, driven by fear of abandonment and death

The Control Cycle:

The Judgment Cycle is driven by an even deeper and more primal cycle I call the Control Cycle. The Control Cycle is energized by people's subconscious fear of abandonment and loss and/or the potential of harm or death (for example, their fears of not being safe, secure and supported by society, family and the environment). In the Control Cycle, we start out by feeling unsafe, or in some way threatened in regard to the uncertainty of the

246

outcomes of our lives, events we experience, our decisions, situations we are involved in, relationships we are involved in, or of others not meeting our perceived needs. Fear and distrust lead to the desire for control. Therefore, we try to control situations and other people through various means in order to attain a feeling of safety, all the while rationalizing the necessity of doing so.

In the Control Cycle, it is not really a specific outcome or situation we are seeking, it is the feeling of safety, security and empowerment we seek; we simply assume that a particular outcome or result will lead to this feeling or perception of our situation. Therefore, it does not matter what our strategy for safety and control is, and it does not matter whether we are truly made safer by attaining control over others or a situation. What matters is that we believe we are going to be "safer or in control" if we affect the particular type of control seeking behavior over other people or the situation.

For example, if I believe that "if others do as I say then I will be safer", then "I will also feel safer" if others do as I say, even if what I have instructed others to do somehow in reality makes me or them less-safe. This cycle drives the tendency many of us have of trying to affect our will over others in relationships or in the business world by intimidating, criticizing, threatening and demeaning people in order to force compliance. This cycle is particularly destructive to interpersonal relationships and to other's personal self-esteem and can lead to depression and/or conflict. At the root, the Control Cycle basically disempowers self and/or others rather than intelligently empowering anyone.

These safety/control strategies can drive us to be so tunnel-visioned on becoming safe, via our specific "safety belief strategy" that we ignore whether we are really safe or not. Meaning the control strategy based on our subconscious beliefs about what will keep us safe is believed and felt to be "more real" to us than the surrounding reality or information input we receive. In these situations, our subconscious projection <u>becomes our reality</u>, often to our detriment and without our realizing it.

Some examples of safety strategy beliefs are: "I am safe if..."

- ❖ I have a committed relationship.
- ❖ I am in control of my spouse.
- ❖ I make more money than my spouse.
- ❖ My spouse or family are dependent upon me.
- ❖ I am stronger than others or am physically intimidating to others.

❖ I know more than others or am better educated or more experienced than they are.

❖ I don't show my emotions or allow myself to be emotionally vulnerable.

❖ I can convince others to believe I know what I am talking about.

❖ I assume I can control other's decisions, behaviors or emotional states.

The Control Cycle is the underlying source of both the Judgment Cycle and of another cycle which could be called The Hatred Cycle. Hatred is a complex blend of emotions that is driven by a profound fear reaction. Although it is often not recognized to be so, hatred is based upon an underlying feeling of, or interpretation of oneself being victimized. Though hatred is vilified socially, politically, religiously and judicially, it is simply our natural most primal reaction to this intense fear. Therefore, although hatred is unwanted and misunderstood, it is normal and natural, and it can be transcended. Therefore, we will now define what the emotion of hatred actually is.

Note: Hatred is not a "bad emotion", it is a fundamentally misunderstood emotion, and a common emotion, and an emotion that we are taught to deny feeling and judge ourselves for feeling. Hatred is a feeling we are taught to feel ashamed or guilty for feeling, and to judge and punish ourselves for feeling. Therefore, when we feel hatred we are often then caught in feelings of guilt and shame for feeling the hatred, which keep us trapped between hatred and guilt, in an unresolvable cycle. The process of hatred is made up of five main elements.

The five elements of the fear driven Cycle of Hatred are:

1. A feeling of being powerlessness to affect a situation or relationship that we feel we need to effect. (i.e. we can hate it when we don't get our way or when we feel controlled by others).

2. A feeling of vulnerability in regard to a situation or relationship. (i.e. we perceive that the situation could result in profound harm or loss to us, even if this is just a projected or imagined outcome).

3. The emotion of anger in regard to the situation or relationship.

4. The specific blame or judgment of someone or some situation, (including ourselves, as in "I hate myself or some part of myself") that we feel threatened by.

5. The primal and often subconscious desire to harm, punish or destroy (and thereby "completely control") the person, group or situation that we feel so threatened by and vulnerable to. We can even want to destroy ourselves if we are in a harsh enough state of self-judgment of our own emotions or some part of ourselves. We can hate our own bodies, our emotions, our thoughts, our behaviors, anything we regret having done in the past, or even who we feel ourselves to be personally, socially, racially, religiously, sexually or culturally. It is vital to understand that this Cycle of Hatred is driven by the underlying **Cycle of Fear,** which was described earlier in this book. The Cycle of Fear drives all control strategies, safety strategies and survival strategies which we will discuss later. The Cycle of Fear also drives the **Judgment Cycle and the "Victim, Perpetrator, Rescuer" Strategies**, which we will also discuss later.

If you feel you personally do not experience hatred, or never have, I would ask you the following questions. Have you ever felt powerless and vulnerable in a relationship interaction with someone you either deeply loved, needed or feared the abandonment or punishment of, (i.e. parent, spouse, friends, boss, authority figures, siblings)? Have you ever then been angry at them and judged or blamed them for the negative and apparently unresolvable aspects of the relationship situation? Have you ever then felt victimized in these situations? Have you ever then been so intensely emotionally triggered that you felt that if they somehow just "did not exist or could in some way be completely controlled" that all your pain and problems related to the situation would not be happening? If so, you very likely have hated the other person, whether you recognized and interpreted the emotions you were feeling as hatred or not at the time. One of the key situations in which we tend to feel hatred is when we fear being abandoned by anyone of importance to us for any reason. One more question about hatred is how can we heal an emotion (hatred) which we are not even willing to feel and acknowledge exists within ourselves? Hatred itself is emotional violence and I would suggest that violence of any kind can never be justified or serve anyone's best interest.

Of course, hatred can be felt in a wide range of degrees and intensities. Hating does not mean that we always act or behave destructively or violently. We all have many other parts of ourselves, which are simultaneously either well intentioned and loving, or that are in conflict with our feelings of hatred, or which actually fear or hate our own feelings of hatred. These "more positive" simulacra simultaneously tend to suppress the hate driven motivation to either harm, kill or destroy. Still we <u>do feel this unwanted motivation to hate</u>, suppressed or not, and we often feel it repeatedly through these currently stress filled days. This is why children can sometimes hate their parents, and parents can sometimes hate their parents, and this emotional reaction can come on quite rapidly and unexpectedly. Whenever we feel pressured to meet someone else's expectations *and* we feel we cannot succeed in doing so, (especially if it is someone we love, need or are dependent upon) we can then turn to hatred. This is especially common if we also fear being emotionally punished, abandoned or attacked by them (i.e. blamed, criticized, punished, dismissed, devalued, misunderstood, disconnected from them) for not meeting their expectations.

Hatred is often expressed as vehemently blaming someone (including ourselves) for our unmanageable feelings of fear, powerlessness and vulnerability for any situation we do not want to be as it is. Therefore, this process of blame becomes the rationalization for wanting or choosing to destroy, kill or harm whoever we blame in order to create a perceived state of personal or emotional safety from them. We feel we will be safe or safer if the other person or their power to hurt us is destroyed. Hatred is a self-validating and self-rationalizing emotion. Although we may sometimes feel "safer" hating, by hating we tend to obscure or hide our own process of hatred and its detrimental implications from our conscious awareness. Thus, we can continue to hate without being motivated to find a way to get out of the emotional state of hating, or even to become fully aware that we are feeling it or acting on it.

Hatred is a maladaptive process of self-protection, so it is not "wrong" to hate, it is simply extremely misguided in its mis-perception and process. When influencing us, hatred does not allow consciousness, compassion, tolerance, reason or accuracy to rule our minds, decisions or interpretations. Hatred, being a fear driven process, like all fear states, is a process of <u>projection</u> onto our present reality of what we fear "could happen", rather than what truly is happening. When we project our hatred, just as when we project any fearful imagining onto any situation, we cannot see what is really occurring right in front of us. All we can see is what we are internally projecting onto the screen of our mind's eye. Therefore, it is primally and blindly assumed that destroying whoever or whatever is mis-perceived to be threatening us is the safest route or choice in the misunderstood moment. The emotion of hatred is what drives and rationalizes the utilization of killing to achieve political or economic goals, and the goal of self-protection.

250

When we hate, we feel strongly desirous of controlling others actions or choices, and at the same time unable to control them through peaceful means, all while feeling very threatened by their power over us. This leads us to feel that we have no other option available to us other than to attack or destroy them, whether verbally, emotionally or physically. Therefore, by hating we are supposedly potentially effecting "total control" over the other person. Meaning we want the perceived feeling of safety of control so much so, that we may become willing to harm, kill or destroy others in order to achieve it. All hatred is, in its basic process, a maladaptive control, safety, protection or survival strategy. Although the survival we may be fighting for may only be that of our ego-identity, our social status, our perceived personal power, a valued relationship, etc. Again, hatred is only a common human emotional reaction.

Hatred is what happens:

❖ In crimes of passion
❖ When someone is vilified on social media
❖ In political competitive "hate speech" of all kinds
❖ In destructive actions that are based upon social bias or prejudice, including in situations of terrorism
❖ Whenever we are operating in, and making decisions from, a mode of narcissistic ego-identity
❖ When we make choices that are self-destructive
❖ One nation goes to war with another
❖ When we feel our culture, beliefs or traditions are being disrespected

Fear driven hatred is the underlying emotion that subconsciously motivates any human being, even well intentioned people to kill, when they feel fundamentally threatened, whether they are truly threatened in reality or not. No amount of preemptive training can suppress these primal feelings when we are triggered by perceived threats. It is the process of fear driven imagination and projection from our recorded simulacra, which leads to instant subconscious hatred, that then makes someone reaching for their cell phone appear to be someone reaching for a gun.

Note: Many things have and will be said in this book in regard to terrorism and radicalism. That said, I make no claims as to being an expert in these areas. My intention in this writing is to bring new and hopefully helpful information and perspectives on this topic. My single intention is to work to reduce the great suffering that is occurring around the world at this time. To any readers who do not accept or feel uncomfortable with anything that is written here, please accept my sincerest apologies. The topic of terrorism is one that is perhaps more contentious and controversial than any other at this time and one that requires everyone's input and focus to solve.

Hatred is driven by our root chakra's reactive fear, vulnerability and powerlessness simultaneous to our feeling threatened. Meaning that choices to harm or kill, whether in policing, military or mob actions are always driven by the same blinding subconscious process of fear, no matter how apparently "necessary, justifiable, righteous, within specified legal or moral guidelines, etc.". (No, I <u>do not</u> mean military or police personnel that kill are "hateful"). It is useful to understand that the process of hatred, although emotionally extreme in nature, is only a simple root chakra driven and completely polarizing control strategy that we reactively apply to life and relationships. No one <u>has to</u> kill anyone, still our inability to consciously understand clearly why we choose to kill keeps us, as individuals and as a species, from learning, changing and choosing to no longer hate and to no longer be willing to kill. At the same time, since hatred is driven by fear, then hatred, just like fear, is also a learning disability. All states of fear tend to blind us to new, more creative and more complete, loving, accurate understandings of self, life, relationships, others and the world.

The emotional dynamic of hatred validates and rationalizes killing and harming others in both war *and* in the mirror of war, i.e. terrorism. Hatred is subconsciously assumed to produce the "feeling or reality of safety" in the person who feels hatred. Hatred of "some other group" of people is always at the root of what are sometimes seen as "positive or safety producing social dynamics", (i.e. patriotism, racism, nationalism, gender inequality, the dynamics of competition, gender bias, religious intolerance, xenophobia, protectionism, elitism, populism, culturalism, prejudice), though again this emotional process is mostly subconscious for most people. Hatred is <u>only</u> a control, protection and safety strategy used by individuals and groups, and is learned social and emotional behavior. It is important to understand that almost every human has at some point hated. By saying this I am suggesting that hatred is a sub-optimal approach to any situation or relationship. Therefore, due to the obscuring nature of focusing on the "seemingly positive" aspects of hatred, the relationship between these tendencies to hate ourselves or to hate others remains obscured and denied and therefore remains unresolved globally. We cannot learn our way out of a situation we are unwilling to admit exists.

Most of us have been taught to so personally and socially vilify the emotion of hatred that we suppress our awareness of it when we ourselves are operating via hatred. To transcend hatred, it is vital to understand its dynamics and nature thoroughly. When we do understand, then our intense fear reactions and projections of others having power that they could use against us go away. Then we can realize that each of us always have our own personal power, that we can choose to apply in a loving conscious manner. Therefore, the feelings of fear, powerlessness and vulnerability that drive hatred are always, illusionary and maladaptive and they are therefore unnecessary and non-optimal emotions. Still we must learn our way out of the habit of hatred. Hatred cannot trust, forgive or love. Paradoxically we can love and hate others simultaneously in different parts of ourselves.

Resonating with hatred is equal to resonating with an inaccurate self-perception of powerlessness, which leads us to feel unable to act in a positive and loving manner in the face of any perceived threat. From the vantage point of **Tribalism**, that was defined and discussed in Chapter Three, hatred of the "enemies of the tribe or of the state" is often seen as proof of loyalty to the tribe or the state, and may even be rewarded. Hatred of "the enemy" is literally even looked at as proof of "love" of the tribe, and as a way of operating safely within the tribe, and of attaining value and status within the tribe or the nation.

Though hatred has no direct relationship to love, we can fear that the tribe, group or nation of people we feel we are part of could turn on us if we do not show allegiance to it. This same dynamic of fear of being turned against by others occurs in corporations, in the military, and can occur in any group of human beings, (i.e. even with our families, loved ones and neighbors). The world is currently experiencing an epidemic of unrealized and powerfully influential hatred dynamics at all levels of all cultures and societies. These dynamics are a result of, and a reaction to, our feelings of being unable to control the rapid change and uncontrollable situations we ourselves are creating. These dynamics are not being recognized as hatred producing by the general population, and thus they are not being constructively focused on in order to be healed and worked with effectively and permanently. Until we become consistently and consciously self-accountable for our reactions of hatred, we cannot transcend them permanently.

Below is a graphic description of the steps of the Control Cycle that can then lead to and trigger the Cycle of Hatred:

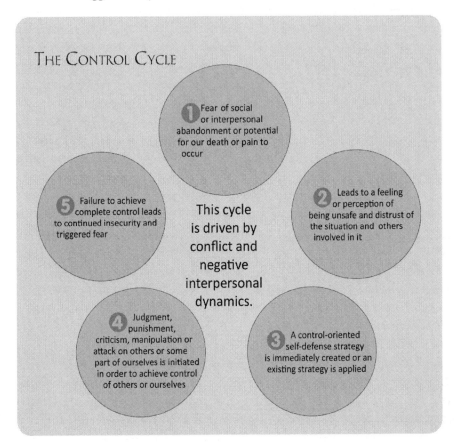

The Control Cycle eats up our energy in the fear that drives the desire for control and thus safety, and in the behaviors and activities that would supposedly produce control, and it does so in a manner which has no truly beneficial outcome. Therefore, the Control Cycle interferes with our social and personal learning process while we are expending untold energy trying to achieve a state of control that is completely unattainable. Can you see these dynamics and their affects leading to, and creating, a global learning disability, and their being a sort of emotional and mental trap for nations and humanity?

A common expression of one form of the Control Cycle is seen in the very common tendency (especially among some women) of perfectionism. A perfectionist mind-set drives a continual and unsuccessful attempt to completely control our lives, and the results of our decisions and actions, by being perfect, whether socially, physically, personally or in our relationships. These attempts in turn create nonconstructive stress and are motivated by the underlying fear driven desire for safety from abandonment via control. Therefore, perfectionism can be seen as an unsuccessful and debilitating method of coping with subconscious fear. Perfectionism is our social defense mechanism against being judged, abandoned, criticized or attacked. Yes, it is true that perfectionism can lead to some good results, as in quality assurance processes. Still judgmental perfectionism is a stressful path to quality.

Humans are herd creatures by nature. The Judgment, Control and Hatred Cycles are unfortunately assumed to be very effective ways to punitively influence ourselves and others in the herd, and to keep us from acting outside of acceptable societal guidelines, traditions or family expectations. Disapproval, guilt, shame, threat and fear are all powerful root chakra motivators. Meaning these emotional reactions tend to make us feel unsafe and socially less than others. Of course, the fundamental emotion that drives us in all of these dynamics is the fear of abandonment, pain of punishment or in the most extreme situations fear of death.

Strangely enough most of us unknowingly live in constant state of dread of our own potential emotional self-judgment, self-punishment (via shame and guilt) and thereby emotional self-abandonment, for not meeting our own self-expectations. Emotional self-abandonment is exactly what occurs whenever we judge ourselves and react with feelings of guilt, shame and self-hatred. Many of us are constantly pressing our own "fear of abandonment buttons" by projecting fearful potentials onto our relationships. We do this because we assume that by doing so we will perform better and thereby avoid abandonment. However, this does not work since we cannot ever completely control how others feel about us or interact with us. Nor can we completely control how we feel about ourselves.

A statement from the Bible (King James Cambridge Edition) by Jesus Christ in Luke 6:37: "Judge not, and ye shall not be judged: condemn not, and ye shall not be condemned: forgive, and ye shall be forgiven." It is a useful and subtle distinction to say, that it is not wrong, bad or evil to judge ourselves or other people. Still it is functionally and practically speaking unwise, as well as personally and socially limiting to judge, and produces untold suffering.

Judgmental behaviors of all kinds are only expressions of dysfunctional and detrimental social self-defense mechanisms and ego self-defense mechanisms. There are several main types of ego-self-defense strategies, all of which stem from fear, and all of which are manifested via judgmentalness and punishing tendencies toward self or others. All these strategies are of course ultimately only strategies for managing our subconscious fears of abandonment, pain and death in all of their imagined forms.

These usually <u>subconscious strategies</u> are:

Survival Strategies:

These decision-making strategies are designed to specifically keep us from physically dying or being significantly physically harmed. These strategies drive and include all social dynamics of self-protection, including individual choices to avoid danger, to be willing to fight, to carry and use guns and other weapons or even to learn karate. These same strategies, on the more global scale, drive police and military activities all around the world, often in the guise of being in the interest of national security). In essence, we try to control ourselves, or others, often through violence or threat of violence, in ways that we feel will keep us physical alive and safe from harm. Survival strategies can of course lead to conflict, violence, battle and even intentional willingness to kill others.

Survival strategies also include ego-identity survival strategies. Meaning that our ego-identity and our social-identity literally fears dying. To understand how these strategies work, it is useful to understand what actually constitutes death or harm to the ego-identity. Paradoxically, ego-identity death or perceived harm can occur for either negative or positive reasons. The negative experience of ego-identity death is exhibited when we:

❖ Fundamentally lose the sense of "who we are", as in the situation of a mid-life crisis. Another form of ego-identity death occurs when we lose a highly identified with social position or lose social status, (i.e. lose a career, we retire, we lose a marriage relationship, or feel ourselves either interpersonally or social condemned in some way).

What we could see as the positive form of ego-identity death, which we still instinctively and unconsciously avoid is experienced when:

❖ We become spiritually conscious and knowledgeable enough of our limiting subconscious ego-dynamics that we wisely choose to cease living life via this ego-identity. Achieving this sagacious state of consciousness requires us to fundamentally transcend our fear of ego-identity death.

256

Safety Strategies:

(These strategies are designed specifically to keep us feeling safe from physical, mental or emotional pain, and all forms of interpersonal and social abandonment and punishment). Of course, feeling safe does not mean we truly are safe, still we all prefer to feel safe, whether we are or are not safe. These are therefore strategies by which we manage fear, stress and anxiety. Hatred is itself one of these safety strategies.

Control Strategies:

There are three main types of control strategies:

1. **The first group of control strategies** are designed to control our own emotions, thoughts, decisions and behaviors, so that we do not act in a socially unacceptable manner, and thus risk social abandonment or the pain of social or interpersonal punishment. We may also try to control our decisions, emotions and behaviors in order to avoid acting in a way that would then create feelings of guilt, shame or self-judgment or self-punishment. Our usual way of trying to control ourselves is, oddly enough, to emotionally threaten ourselves or some part of ourselves with anger, punishment, self-shaming, self-destruction or feeling "bad about ourselves" if we fail to meet our own expectations.

2. **The second group of control strategies** is designed to keep others from hurting us, abandoning us or socially devaluing us through various forms of attack or criticism. (The more detrimental examples of control strategies operate by criticizing others, attacking them or preemptively threatening them with some form of abandonment or punishment).

   These types of control strategies are designed to require ourselves and others to meet our expectations, no matter how dysfunctional, self-centered or illogical those expectations may be. One example of this type of control strategy would be seen when a man or woman threatens to abandon their spouse, if their spouse does not meet their desires or expectations. In effect the threatening spouse is trying to hold the person they are in relationship with emotionally hostage to their expectations. Yet another is the control parents attempt to apply to their children to get them to behave in expected ways, (i.e. conditional love) again the children are being held emotionally hostage to potential emotional abandonment.

3. **The third group of control strategies is that of the ANTI-Control-Control Strategies**. These strategies are strategies that motivate many people, including terrorists and those who engage in

257

war. Meaning that this strategy develops when the person becomes so afraid of being controlled by others that they will do everything they can to control the people they fear being controlled by. Of course, the most extreme method of trying to completely control someone else is to kill them.

In a monogamous relationship, this process translates to a spouse trying to control every decision their partner tries to make. This strategy is reasoned to be necessary to remain emotionally safe via always being in control of the spouse and the relationship. This strategy, in its most extreme forms can lead to using physical or emotional abuse on the part of one fearful spouse who it trying to control the other.

In a terrorist situation, a terrorist can fear being controlled by the nation they deeply perceive the power and threat of. They are often taught to judge that nation or group via an authority figure of some sort, and their judgmentalness is driven by the fear of not being able to control that which they feel threatened by. In these situations, it is determined, believed or assumed by the terrorist that only through killing or destroying their enemy can they achieve a "complete solution" to their fear, (i.e. maximum control over their enemy). So, for terrorists, killing their enemy becomes the only acceptable and optimally functional control strategy that is potentially completely fear resolving.

It is important to realize that if we have strongly held beliefs about any aspect of life, that we feel others around us do not share, that this perceived situation creates its own kind of reactive fear. In these situations, we are acting upon recorded simulacra in our systems, with their associated assumptions as to the meaning of our beliefs supposedly being true. We also have assumptions as to the meaning of others not agreeing with our beliefs, (i.e. they could be interpreted as "not like us", or even as "the enemy" if they disagree with what we believe). For example, if we believe that our beliefs are the "only true or accurate beliefs", then we may assume that anyone who does not share our beliefs is fundamentally untrustworthy or even that they are in some way against us or that they are "bad". This projected perception of fundamental un-trustworthiness creates its own form of reactive fear of those who do not share our beliefs, which can lead to conflict and violence.

As previously stated, killing is the most extreme form of attempted control of another person. Of course, complete control of anyone is not possible. Still many people live in the illusionary belief that killing will somehow achieve or result in this degree of control. This is simply delusional thinking, since it has been repeatedly found, for example, that killing terrorists just motivates more people to become terrorists. As time goes by, we have therefore been "socially breeding" ever more extreme forms of terrorism, through our escalating violent interactions with terrorists. Also through our unwillingness to care more about those who may someday grow up to be terrorists, now and in the past. Love begets love, hate begets hate, emotional indifference begets emotional indifference. Cause-and-effect dynamics come back to us.

When people are consistently emotionally triggered at the level of the root chakra, and are therefore in an ongoing state of fear and insecurity, they tend to seek to control their environment and relationships as a supposed antidote to their uncomfortable feelings. In effect, they lack a conscious and effective strategy or way to constructively maintain a feeling of safety, positive social-worth and self-worth. It is this unresolved subconscious fear and emotional pain that drives people to seek other solutions, (i.e. to become *radicalize-able)*. Narcissistic and competitive ego-identities, as defined earlier in this text can also play a profound role in this dynamic.

In effect these unresolved emotional situations are simply waiting, like a landmine, for a situation or available "empowering life control strategy", such as radicalism, to become available, to then supposedly offer them relief from their emotional distress. This is partly how and why radicalism occurs. Meaning that the person first arrives at a misinterpretation of their life situation. The misinterpretation they hold is that they are under some perceived threat and that following the radical ideology and taking associated destructive actions will solve their fears of not being in control of their lives. They then assume that these types of actions will offer them power, status, self-worth and social-worth.

In such a situation, any degree of destructive extremity can be rationalized, if it appears that it will solve their emotionally difficult state. Especially if they choose to use some form of perceived victimhood of themselves or others they care about, along with a validating demonization of their perpetrators or the enemy, to support dehumanizing those they attack. Once the enemy is dehumanized in the radicalized person's emotional process, they tend to feel little or no guilt, shame, remorse or fear in killing the other person(s). They may even feel "good" about it, and about themselves for doing it. How many hunters "feel good", and in a way empowered, by successfully killing an animal they are hunting?

259

This emotional disassociation is what happens in the mind and emotional process of the radicalized person. It is similar to the mental and emotional process that occurs in any situation of gun violence or other crimes of passion, which have become endemic in American culture and some other cultures. Strangely enough it is also a distorted mirror reflection of the mindset that military personnel are taught to employ in order to feel emotionally "okay" about killing terrorists or perceived enemies of their nation. In essence they are taught that killing or violence is often the only solution to violence, and the social problems that drive it. This is of course not true. I would suggest that all forms of violence only create more violence.

Radicalism is a mixture of mental and emotional dynamics that is quite potent and even addictive. It is a process of choosing to see life in a very black and white and polarized way. Once bought into, it is difficult for the affected person to consciously choose to escape into a more loving and balanced view of life, self and relationship. Meaning once they have recorded the inaccurate simulacra of not being safe in any other way they are then locked into this point of view. In our world of growing empowerment of the individual via technology and knowledge, understanding the dynamics of radicalism and extremism of all kinds is crucial, in that it is vital to channel this growing power of the individual toward positive ends, rather than toward violence. It is also important to ensure that no one who is becoming more technologically powerful and better educated (yet not necessarily feeling more emotionally secure as they do so), is mentally and emotionally hijacked by these dysfunctional radical social and emotional dynamics. By the way, even highly intelligent and educated people can be seduced by their own distorted simulacra and thus radicalized, since these emotions are often a completely subconscious process.

These radical dynamics, as discussed, are not a sign of mental illness, although they obviously can be, and although they can manifest dreadful behavior and actions. They are signs of lack of emotional ability on the part of these people to cope in healthy ways with the world's rapidly increasing "change stress". These dynamics can potentially occur within the mental and emotional processes of any person who experiences enough foundational fear, unresolved loss of self-esteem, perceived loss of control of their lives, or loss of power and social self-worth. This is especially true if the person has no more optimally functional method of consciously understanding, and then successfully managing, their mental and emotional processes. Therefore, what is needed in order to avoid these detrimental radical developments is to help

260

others increase their emotional intelligence, and to help them learn effective methods of conscious emotional self-management.

To the fearful person, radicalism and an extremist ideology can appear to be a simple and complete solution to all of life's problems and conflicts. The extreme viewpoint can appear to save them from any internal conflict, uncertainty or doubt in their moment-by-moment decision-making processes. In this way the ideology may appear to resolve their uncomfortable primal emotional dynamics. The existence of this global situation, of so many people feeling fundamentally insecure, is the reason why it is vital to preemptively teach as many human beings as possible to manage their emotional processes and to unconditionally love each other and themselves. This attainment of understanding is necessary so that these radicalizable people never get to the point of feeling fearful, out of control, powerless, without self-worth, and without positive options or solutions to their problems.

In general, in order for a potential terrorist to become "radicalized" five things are required. These prerequisites are for the radicalized person to:

1. **Perceive** that there is a significant problem or threat in their lives, or the lives of other people that they care about, that then produces significant reactive fear or insecurity in the radicalized person. For example, fearing that the people they are in relationship with (i.e. friends or family) are in danger from a significant external threat of any sort (i.e. military threat, religious threat, social or economic threats, etc.). In some cases, these days, terrorists fear various westernized countries, including the United States, and they may also fear some powerful religious factions. These entities possess power that is perceived as a potential threat to what they believe and thus become easily "demonizable" in the fearful person's mind. The radicalized person feels, in a way, victimized and this in turn supports their rationalization of becoming a "perpetrator" in order to protect themselves or those they love. They feel vulnerable and powerless in some way and choose radicalization, hatred and destructiveness as a supposed strategy of solution.

   OR the radicalizable person may feel fearful, insecure, powerless, have low self-esteem, feel they have little social-worth and are angry about this situation. They may also perceive that they have no more effective way to manage their emotions and perceived life situation. For these reasons, they will seek some form of simplistic, extreme and judgment based, punitive and destructive life strategy to resolve their perceived situation. They may hope that they can empower and redeem themselves, and feel better about themselves, socially and personally via the strategy of radicalization.

2. Simplistically and thus blindly "buy into" the belief that killing or harming others, or some nation or institution, is the only or best solution to their perceived problems. They may also buy into the belief that the "enemy nation or religious or social group" is the source of their perceived problem and threat to themselves or those they care about OR that destroying the enemy will give them the power, control and the self-worth and group acceptance, validation and recognition they seek.

3. **Feel** that by joining a radical group and adopting an extreme ideology that they will gain:
    a. Self-empowerment
    b. Self-importance
    c. Improve their feelings of self-worth and self-validation
    d. "Redeem themselves"
    e. Give them social-worth and a feeling of being accepted within the group

Thus, their choice to radicalize will solve their perceived life and emotional problems by killing the enemy and by being part of the group that does the killing. This process of killing the enemy is assumed to potentially lead to attaining a feeling of emotional safety through heroic social and personal value. In essence, they assume that by following this path they will in a way "become somebody that matters". And that the somebody they will become will be above and better than other people, and thus they will be safe from the subconscious potential abandonment they fear.

This life strategy of radicalism is the result of wanting to be, and choosing to be, part of something "bigger and thus more important than oneself". To a degree this dynamic could be seen as participation in a form of social or cultural narcissism. Narcissism itself is just an extreme form of ego-identity defense and self-worth redemption strategy. In these people, their self-perceived ego-identity is (often subconsciously) one of low value, low status, and low power, and they resent the seemingly unresolvable emotional state. Becoming radicalized is therefore in part a coping mechanism for low self-esteem.

In positive situations, becoming part of something bigger than ourselves, (i.e. such as taking part in making the NASA moon landing happen, or being part of a disaster relief effort after an earthquake, or helping to cure cancer) leads to profound loving and extreme self-less efforts. In negative situations, this same process leads to lack of conscious discernment, and thus blind self-less allegiance to terrorism, extreme forms of competition of various kinds (i.e. social, economic, religious, cultural, political, etc.), nationalism and even participation in war.

4. Feel they can "believe in" and trust the radical group's intentions, beliefs, values, rules and goals, and that the group will then value and support them in turn. They come to believe that they are safer and more powerful with the radical group than without them, and that they can trust the group consciousness more than their own personal consciousness and discernment. So in essence they choose to "trade up" for a better ego-identity than they previously had.

5. Buy into the Victim/Perpetrator/Rescuer paradigm, the Judgement Cycle and/or the Hatred Cycle. (All these are safety and control strategies).

All the previously described elements of radicalism are only maladaptive reactions to and coping strategies for unresolved fear, lack of feeling in control of one's life, and lack of perceived self or social value. It is primally felt by the insecure person that if they had social value, power, status and control that their fear would go away, and that they would be protected from potential abandonment and death. At the level of un-consciousness, they are operating at, they cannot reason well, love all of humanity, and cannot truly and accurately understand the likely negative and dysfunctional results of their choices and actions. This is especially true if they are told by an authority figure that if they die in the process of battle, that they will then feel better and be rewarded in heaven. It is this misapprehension of reality, and of supposed cause-and-effect relationships that leads to maladaptive life strategies.

These strategies are then constantly re-rationalized to be necessary after they are initially bought into. To change these tendencies, after one has already operated in a destructive manner could lead to unacceptable levels of guilt and shame, which they would want to avoid. Therefore, guilt and shame can hold one in the extreme state of mind. This process occurs because fear blinds us to our other more loving, peaceful and creative options and

263

solutions. Once locked into fear, people become "frozen" in a static belief state, and a limiting set of life options and strategies that block them from empathizing with or loving those they hate.

Anti-Abandonment Strategies:

(These strategies are designed to avoid mental, emotional or relationship abandonment by self or others of all kinds). We apply these strategies to make sure we are not abandoned by the people we are in relationship with. These strategies can include trying to become indispensable or codependent in a relationship. They can also include tendencies to try to remain very attractive physically. Paradoxically they can even include a tendency to claim to be a victim in order to create guilt in a spouse, so that they will not abandon us, or so that they will give us what we want in a relationship. In essence we hold our spouse emotionally hostage to the threat of guilt and our claiming victimhood in order for us not to be abandoned or to empower us in the relationship.

Self-Worth Attainment & Self-Redemption Strategies:

These strategies are designed to help us feel good or better about ourselves in various ways. These strategies are often reactively created and then applied to our lives when we have previously recorded simulacra feelings of having been bad, wrong, socially or interpersonally unacceptable or imperfect (i.e. potentially abandonable).

These negative mis-interpretations of ourselves and our life experiences can lead to deep feelings of inadequacy, guilt and shame, or even self-hatred or self-loathing without a path to resolution. Therefore, when we begin to feel so very badly about ourselves, we then seek to develop self-worth attainment and self-redemption strategies, in order to escape from our pain and cope with these unresolved negative emotions. This creates a cycle of constantly feeling bad about ourselves at one level of our system, and of constantly trying to make up for feeling badly at another level. This way of trying to deal with our emotions is almost never successful. This cyclic process only distracts us from doing what is truly necessary to resolve our emotional difficulties. Meaning that the self-worth development strategies and redemption strategies do not effectively change the root negative feelings we hold about ourselves, so we remain in unresolved pain.

By following these strategies, we have no way to know when we have done "enough good" to be redeemed for having been "bad or wrong", because we remain perpetually in judgment of ourselves. The reactive and disempowering impotency of these control strategies is vital to understand, as well as their tendency to create further self-distrust when we realize that they do not work. The best solution is to consciously map the maladaptive decision-making dynamics of these strategies, and then directly work with and resolve the core fears, limiting beliefs and negative emotions that drive the strategies.

We all want to feel "good" about ourselves, and these types of redemption strategies, often codependency oriented in nature, falsely appear to help us to feel and believe that we are "good people". We feel that by applying strategies, such as a "rescuer strategy", that we can redeem ourselves for our past misdeeds by operating in a mode of "saving others, people pleasing and meeting other's expectations". This dynamic undermines our fundamental sovereign process of free-will, self-empowerment and self-sovereignty. Another main problem occurs when we try to apply these strategies, in order to redeem a part of ourselves that feels *fundamentally unredeemable,* for example in the case of one person murdering another person. Such a situation is often deemed unforgivable by society, various religions and the consensus consciousness of humanity. In this situation, we experience constant and frustrating inner emotional conflict, as nothing we do seems to reduce the negative feelings about ourselves. In such a situation, a person can primally feel that the only solution to their tremendous feeling of being judged and of judging themselves is to destroy themselves, (i.e. self-hatred). In this situation literal self-destruction is erroneously seen as the only way of controlling one's life circumstances and of redeeming oneself, (i.e. an eye for an eye thinking).

In all of these strategies we have a tendency to constantly output a tremendous effort without adequate positive result. We only find the potential for resolving these conundrums when we first recognize and accept how we truly feel about ourselves. Then we can make real progress working with these troubled emotions and working to forgive ourselves and others.

Attention Seeking/Recognition Seeking/Drama and Controversy Creating Strategies:

From birth, we are instinctively motivated to seek other's attention, starting with that of our parents. Then throughout our lives, as we develop we live out many strategies to attain this desired attention in relationships and social situations. Many of us associate having other's attention as a way to get our needs understood and met, and therefore social recognition in all its forms is generally deemed desirable. Some of our attention and recognition seeking strategies are constructive, caring and beneficial. While others are destructive or harmful to ourselves, other people or the world. "Success at any price" is an example of one of the more destructive strategies.

The attention/recognition/drama seeking set of ego-strategies are, like all other safety and control strategies, driven by safety seeking, emotional pain avoidance and emotional abandonment avoidance. We can record <u>any sort</u> of belief in our recorded simulacra, no matter how unrealistic, inaccurate or maladaptive. These beliefs can include, for example, that "attention of any kind equals love". To the subconscious primal emotional process, having attention of <u>any kind</u> focused on oneself can, (via this misguided recorded belief process), be literally be felt and interpreted, via the lenses of our beliefs, as "love, safety and security". How we interpret the attention we receive is largely determined by which of our subconscious simulacra lenses we view the attention through in any given moment. Even if the attention we receive is detrimental or in some way pain producing, there can be parts of ourselves (our recorded simulacra) that interpret the attention as useful, necessary or potentially security producing. This tendency to misinterpret the "dynamics of attention", often occurs in a dysfunctionally generalized way. Meaning that we interpret our experiences without conscious discernment.

This generalized mode of mis-interpretation of reality can be seen in situations such as:

- ❖ "If I am a success other's will respect me"
- ❖ "If I am not a success no one will want me or love me"
- ❖ "If someone smiles at me they must like or care about me"
- ❖ "If someone is angry with me I <u>must have</u> done something wrong"
- ❖ "If someone is attracted to me physically they must love me"
- ❖ "If I fail in my job I am a complete loser"
- ❖ "If I am a male and I am not competitive then I am not manly"
- ❖ "If someone has sex with me that means they love me"

All of these mis-interpretations are very general in nature, all are inaccurate or untrue in many situations, and if inaccurately believed to be true, all have the potential to influence our decision-making to our detriment. Still these interpretive lenses or our simulacra may form the foundation of our attention seeking and recognition seeking strategies, and therefore influence our lives and relationships fundamentally. All of this tends to go on in our lives below the radar of our consciousness.

A "mass example" of this dynamic of attention seeking can be seen when children invariably seek and want attention from their parents, even if it is

266

negative attention. The results of receiving negative or abusive attention by a child are profound. Meaning that when grownup, children of abusive parents may then seek a spouse that is abusive in the way they offer their attention in the relationship. To a child, attention of any kind is felt to be better than no attention at all. This is especially true if the child was told by their parents that the abusive attention they displayed toward the child was justified, necessary to make them a better child, or because they were in some way "bad". The developing child may assume that if they believe in these judgmental stories told by the parent (i.e. accept them to be true and agree with them), that they are less likely to be emotionally abandoned by the parent. The child may even assume that there is some potential for them to be redeemed, fully accepted and loved by the parent if they believe the messages from the parent. Then they may assume, subconsciously, that in order to receive positive attention in future relationships that they must arrive at it via first receiving negative attention. Of course, the negative interactions the child gets involved in when they are adults usually do not get better, no matter how much effort is applied.

These maladaptive child-self oriented simulacra "live on" in our subconscious, into our adulthood. Because of their influence we continue to operate and make decisions at subconscious levels, in these simple, child-like and maladaptive attention seeking ways, without our realizing it. If we have learned to influence others via attention seeking behaviors, then attention itself can be seen by each of our primal child-ego simulacra as a kind of power over others and our environment. Meaning that if we can supposedly "command the attention" of others, via any attention seeking behavior or medium, this result is seen as proof of our ability to control or influence others. If we find that we can get other things in life (money, sex, security, etc.) via attention seeking behaviors, then these results tend to hold the maladaptive strategies in place. Attention seeking behaviors, although potentially influential socially, are ultimately disempowering, and undermine our attainment of conscious self-sovereignty.

Subconsciously believing that we have "workable strategies" to move others to give us attention then leads our subconscious to feel safer, because we feel we have a sort of control over others. Receiving attention from others by these recorded simulacra parts is also seen as "proof" that we exist socially and interpersonally, and that our control strategies are working. Peripheral problems caused by these strategies tend to be ignored, since we have essentially gotten the result we want by applying the strategy. This received attention is felt to be especially important to those of us who have had negative relationships with our parents, or who have felt socially ignored, disempowered or left out. Therefore, this attention can literally be felt to be life bringing to the parts of ourselves (recorded simulacra) that have thirsted for it.

The realization of ourselves as part of the social group via attention or recognition seeking strategies, even in dysfunctional ways, is felt to be security producing. Even aberrant negative behavior that leads to significant problems and negative social results, can be seen (through the lens of the recorded simulacra in our systems) as proof of empowerment and safety. The dynamic of attention seeking, is driven by a mis-interpretation of what attention itself really means in our lives. Some people live their lives chasing after this attention and recognition in all its many forms (i.e. success, fame, money, sex, power, status, relationships, social position, authority, etc.). The attainment of this focus of attention on themselves is so addictively motivating to some as to undermine all positive spiritual, moral and social values.

What determines how humans focus their attention from moment-to-moment is often a very instinctive and primal process, (i.e. often based on safety, survival and control motivations and strategies). When we focus on someone around us who is creating drama we are reactively motivated to focus on their behaviors, often by subconscious fear. On the other side of the coin. When we are focused on our own internal feelings of inadequacy or lack that then lead to our desiring attention, we often focus on ways of acting and behaving that will supposedly lead to creating some sort of drama. These are the two sides of the attention seeking and control seeking dynamic.

It is often our most deeply fear based emotions that determine many of our tendencies to focus on specific aspects of our lives and relationships, and this focus then drives our decisions. Since the decision-making strategy is driven by fear, this type of subconscious attention seeking, and social validation seeking behavior, can be both voracious and insatiable, especially if our control strategies have appeared to work in the past. In these cases, we can become addicted to receiving attention in various forms, (i.e. receiving money, fame, status, more "Tweets", etc.). At the same time, we can become addicted to watching other's attempts to receive attention, (i.e. through their dramas, attempts to purposefully create controversy, social media, news, their "Tweets", etc.).

Our attention seeking strategies can work and give us desired results for a time, and then fail to have affect. (i.e. What happens emotionally to a famous and successful actor, actress or entertainer when their success ceases?). The

268

unconscious attention/recognition/security seeking strategies within us are the key motivations that are feeding today's frenzied on-line social media behaviors and dynamics. Attention itself, in addition to leading us to feel more connected with others, is seen as a form of power and success. Greed and competition, which are often associated with this attention seeking behavior are both driven by fear. This subconscious fear and innate insecurity is the fuel that feeds the rampant negative aspects of social media and its misuse by many.

In social media, it is true that the desire to be connected and to feel connected to others is highly motivating, still our fear of not being successful in this process creates great stress and insecurity, and is therefore also highly motivating. One example of this stress is the fear that many people experience if they are "unfriended" on social media. There are many ways that the growing and often turbulent phenomenon of social media is currently being misused. These include it use are as a mechanism of manipulating large groups of people, and of affecting their perceptions, decisions, feelings of self-worth and their perceived social image(s). This turbulent process is creating chaos in many people's lives.

This misuse of social media can be seen in:

* Cyber bullying and "Trolling", (criticizing, shaming, blaming, threatening and devaluing others)
* Blackmailing of individuals by governments or criminal groups in order to support political, nationalistic or criminal agendas
* Sexting
* Use of Twitter and other on-line social media systems by political candidates to drive public opinion via:
    * Innuendo
    * Misinformation
    * Half-truths
    * Hate speech
    * Judgmental and critical statements
    * Racist statements, propaganda, intentions and agendas
    * Dramatic and negative statements whose truth and accuracy cannot be verified in a timely manner, and therefore have effect without a mechanism to correct the false information
* False news stories that are intentionally created in order to purposefully produce misunderstanding in the public by corporations

or political groups, and many of which have lately been utilized to influence voting in elections in the U.S.

❖ Hacking of emails that are then dumped into social media venues in order to distort the public's decision-making processes and to keep them from realizing truths

❖ Harmful gossip

❖ Baseless conspiracy theories

❖ Social media battles, sometimes for no other reason than to create more empty drama and to purposefully distract people from far more important issues

❖ Publishing of sexually explicit pictures and movies of x-spouses to cause emotional harm or distress

The above list of social media abuses are actually abuses of information and communication. When, where, how and why we choose to focus our attention, in every moment of every day or our lives, literally defines our experience of life, and many of our life choices. Human beings often focus their attention on whatever drama they perceive to be going on in their environment, and often without discerning filters. The drama itself is often felt to have a sort of power over us, or can even appear to represent a potential threat. Then we feel that this threat must be "constantly watched" in order for us to remain safe or to feel safe. This is a main reason why people continually and mindlessly watch the latest dramatic news stories or listen to extreme talk shows.

Human beings often tend to focus on:

❖ The flashing lights at a traffic accident

❖ Dramatic news on the television (if it bleeds it leads types of news)

❖ Drama filled and negative radio talk shows pushing political, economic or social agendas

❖ Conspiracy theorists

❖ Social squabbles

❖ The latest celebrity conflicts, scandals or dysfunctions

This process of literally working to grab our attention, via verbal and visual manipulation, can be used as a way of controlling how we spend our time, how we think and feel, how we vote, how we spend our money, how we see our relationships, and how we look at the world around us. The process of applying political and financial competition to these strategies of holding our attention is creating ever more virulent forms of attention seeking on the part of those who gain from holding our attention. This dynamic could be seen as a sort of "drama hypnosis and attempted drama programming" of us as individuals and as a society.

The effect of this drama oriented misinformation on individuals is especially potent if we do not first purposely choose to seek out information that conflicts with the sources of information we regularly tend to listen to. If we only listen to information that agrees with the drama we have become entrained in, then we will remain unable to see the bigger, truer picture, no matter what the truth really is. By becoming focused only on one sort or source of "trusted drama speak information" we lose the capacity to be independently and consciously discerning.

Whenever we choose to focus on any experience of life, we then create more referential simulacra (memories), which, as we stated previously, are often later referred to as if they were true, accurate or believable. What does this profound dynamic mean in regard to the influence of the streams of misinformation we are constantly being inundated with? What influence does this process of recording misinformation in our systems, day after day, via manipulative mass media have on our children's development? What influence will this recorded misinformation have in the long-term development of humanity's societies? It is important to understand that these described dynamics are right now having constant global influence. How important is conscious discernment, and the ability to learn the truth for ourselves, in such a rapidly evolving world with so many unmanageable influences and conflicting information sources?

A key part of this attention dynamic is experienced when we have the attention of others focused on us as individuals. In this process, we are receiving subtle energy from others, whether the energy is felt to be positive or negative. It is the feeling of experiencing their energetic focus on us, and of receiving their associated emotional energies, that we are often subconsciously seeking, through this strategy of wanting to be the center of their attention. Feeling ourselves receive these energies validates that "we still exist in the world", and that we are in some way important (even if it is in a negative way), and that we are thus "a relevant part of the social environment". This attention seeking mode of interacting with others is often designed to distract ourselves from our deep personal feelings of emotional emptiness, pain, inadequacy, self-judgments and fear of abandonment.

On a global scale, strategies have already been developed to use this process of triggering our focus of attention for profit and marketing, as well as for the purposes of indoctrination into nationalist, populist or radical

271

agendas. These are control strategies, no different than the control strategies used by individuals attempting to control each other as individuals, in order to achieve goals of individual safety, security or empowerment. The only difference is that these strategies are being affected by large groups, political parties, corporations and governments. This book is about developing, attaining and maintaining conscious self-sovereignty in an increasingly complex world. In order to accomplish this goal for ourselves, how important is it to recognize these growing and increasingly subtle trends, dynamics and influences?

A "mass control strategy" is now being tried via mass collection of information about us as individuals by governments and corporations. This mass of information is assumed by those who are collecting it to be the foundation fuel that is necessary to supply numerous current and future control strategies. These strategies are being developed by corporations and governments, whether their goals are to get us to buy a product or a political agenda.

As previously stated, no one can ever truly control anyone else, because we all have free-will, and our free-will cannot be taken from us by anyone, via any manipulative mechanism. Any attempt to control anyone else is <u>always driven by fear</u>, even if the control strategy is being applied by an authority, a government or a corporation. Therefore it can be seen that it is fear, and only fear, rather than wisdom or intelligence, that is driving the collection of our information by various groups. Again, control cannot be achieved by anyone, and the unwise attempt to do so can only end in more global problems.

Another mass attention control strategy (i.e. controlling the perceptions of large groups of people) is the utilization of consistently focused attention itself as a method of attempted control and influence. Some people work very hard to remain consistently in the public eye and thus "apparently relevant", and just their successfully doing so can create the appearance of power, credibility, success, affluence and influence. They then use their "manufactured celebrity image and seeming importance" to make money from the process of people focusing their attention on them, through various types of marketing or monetizing schemes. The power they attempt to appear to have, can be interpreted by those of us who do not see through the dynamic as "real power", which they supposedly could apply in our lives, if they so chose.

These people have the supposed power to influence each of us to "watch and resonate with them, their beliefs, values, biases and emotions", whether positively or negatively. It has gotten to the point that it does not matter to many of us how negatively they operate socially, in that our desire for safety or power by participating in their dramas overrides our moral interpretive capacities. Some examples of seemingly powerful or charismatic people are: "The Khardahsians", Donald Trump, Vladimir Putin, and numerous other celebrities. These people may be using social media and news organizations as an attention and perception influencing mechanism, as a social image creation mechanism, and as a way to attempt to wield power of various sorts in society and the world.

Clever individuals tend to use the news systems as their tools, and as leverage to attain goals, rather than the news systems operating as integrous reporting systems, that are necessary to consistently inform the public of the truth. The desire by the various aspects of the news media to hold our attention (to attain ratings), has become in many cases a higher priority than offering quality news. This conflict of interest between profit and truth tends to undermine the news media's integrity. These attention influencing are almost invariably self-serving. Anyone who truly has our best interest at heart will tend not to use such strategies to try to influence us, without fully and truly informing us in a balanced way. To those who are narcissistically inclined, the supposed power to "draw and govern our attention" can be mistaken for the capacity to wisely influence, lead, inform or govern us.

This primal subconscious dynamic can lead subconscious parts of ourselves to see anyone who creates enough drama and attention seeking dynamics as in some way powerful or in authority, and thus to be feared, respected or emulated (i.e. see the influence of Stockholm Syndrome on human beings described earlier in the book). Of course, not all people can be influenced in this way, still a significant portion of the population can be influenced enough to confuse them and entrain them in detrimental behaviors and choices. Up until this time in history, much of governance and leadership have depended upon these simple dynamics of attention and fear management strategies to move large groups of people, and thereby to wield power in hierarchical social systems. It could be seen as sort of magic trick, where the attention of the crowd is influenced in order that the magician can make us see whatever they want.

We, as individuals, often buy into the false power of those who appear to have the capacity to demand or command our attention, though they may have no real power or integrity at all. The "Mass Media Machine", in all its forms, is exacerbating this maladaptive social dynamic, without adequate oversight or insight. The same is true of some aspects of governance. Therefore, we vote for whoever supposedly has the most power, (i.e. the most capacity to hold our attention, and thus supposedly the ability to wield this "attention power", and thus supposedly they would then have the power to give us what we want and <u>keep us safe</u>). This is invalid reasoning. This whole process occurs without regard to their true spiritual, mental, philosophical or emotional leanings or capabilities. In this way "social media might, is seen to make right". There are child parts of all of us that want a strong parental figure to "make us feel safe" and to place responsibility for our lives in their hands. Many of us want to do this, rather than choosing to be self-accountable, self-sovereignly mature, discerning, conscious.

In the evolving social media jungle, "power acquisition via attention seeking" and power wielding via management of others tendency to pay attention to one's communications is seen as all important. In effect our focused attention means "money" to them. In today's world many people's importance is even being gauged by the Twitter following they have as a social and financial metric.

Social media strategies are often driven by the desire for:

- ❖ Money
- ❖ Power
- ❖ Glamour
- ❖ The capacity to draw and enjoy attention of all kinds
- ❖ Status
- ❖ Sex appeal
- ❖ Gender dynamics
- ❖ Purposely created controversy
- ❖ Safety
- ❖ Control and Influence
- ❖ The factor of time (if we have more power and money we supposedly can make more time to enjoy them both)

These factors and dynamics are operating within the social hierarchies of all human societies constantly. In the social hierarchy of a society these values can, in a way, be seen as equal to each other in their influence. Each can be seen as a form of energy, and each supports and feeds the others. One can even be transformed into the other. For example, to advertisers, the capacity for a person they have a legal agreement with to draw the public's attention equals marketing opportunities, which then equals money. (i.e. Attention is transformed into money). The list above are all social values and factors we have been conditioned to "believe in" and to operate with socially and

274

interpersonally. They also form the basis of many exchange and transaction based human interactions and relationships. These types of interactions (exchange and transaction based relationships) are discussed further later in this book).

Therefore:

* ❖ Having attention focused on us personally seemingly leads to power and status
* ❖ Power supposedly leads to safety and security
* ❖ Attained status and ability to draw attention then supposedly leads to power and money
* ❖ Money and power supposedly lead to status and more free time to enjoy various aspects of life
* ❖ Money supposedly leads to safety, security and power
* ❖ Sex appeal supposedly leads to attention, money and power
* ❖ Money and power supposedly leads to more sex or sex appeal
* ❖ More time supposedly leads to more opportunity to get attention and to then amass more money, power, status, etc.

These dynamics can be seen as a sort of "circle of interdependent components" that are used by individuals, groups and even nations to manufacture, support and implement their safety and control strategies. These strategies are self-serving and often involve utilization of misinformation, distraction, misdirection and manipulation of others.

Safety and control strategies that make use of the values listed above (values which are stored in our recorded simulacra as beliefs) can be "pieced together" in innumerable ways to support attainment of one's goals and personal agendas. These safety, survival, attainment of goals via attention seeking, and control strategies, have been governing humanity and social dynamics for a very long time. It is time for us to transcend this set of unconscious problem generating dynamics in their entirety. Within the social media process, they are fast becoming a mechanism of greed, manipulation of society, and of undermining self-empowerment and self-sovereignty in individuals, in the guise of "feeling connected".

Social Value Creation Strategies:

(These are strategies we apply to create and consistently prove our value to others whom we are in relationship with, to those we work with, and to society in general. This type of strategy is based upon the erroneous view of there being a hierarchy of human beings, (i.e. Some people are better, more valuable, more acceptable, more powerful, more desirable or more deserving than others, which is of course only an illusion that many buy into, and sometimes in a self-serving manner). These same emotional drives can also be exhibited in strategies of ruthless competition with others, with a goal achievement focus. They can be exhibited in dynamics of social attention seeking as a method of using drama to empower ourselves socially. These strategies can also be seen in people who are constantly comparing themselves, their behavior and self-perceived value to others, in order to prove themselves better in some way, in order to feel emotionally and socially safe.

Our other subconscious purposes in applying these strategies is to achieve social and relationship power, leverage, status and thereby have social-value to exchange with others). These strategies can include tendencies to acquire whatever resources we can in life, that we feel we can then exchange with others, in order to get from them what we want. These strategies therefore tend to lead to relationships of conditional love and **transaction and exchange based relationship dynamics**. Transaction based relationship strategies are not supportive of unconditional love, because the condition is the process of exchange, and whether the exchange is deemed fair, desirable, worthwhile or supportive of what we want and of our personal life goals. These strategies are all manifestations of ego-identities, rather than conscious self-aware heart to heart interaction.

These relationship strategies are generally based upon and motivated by one or more of the following values or priorities (simulacra) that are obtained or supported via exchange in the relationship:

- Safety, security, stability and consistency
- Attention seeking and recognition
- Sex and beauty
- Power
- Status
- Money
- Time (i.e. more time to live a healthy life and to live, experience and enjoy life)
- Control
- Freedom
- Self-worth we derive from the relationship
- Social-worth we derive from the relationship

- ❖ In general, how we feel about ourselves by participating in the relationship
- ❖ Feelings of "need, self-perceived in adequacy or lack"
- ❖ Helping to avoid some of the various kinds of pain and insecurity that life invariably brings
- ❖ Fear of some aspect of life that the relationship helps us avoid
- ❖ The way the relationship supports our personal gender identification and definition

I did not add the word love in the above list of values as something that could be exchanged, since unconditional love is only something that can be given freely, without expectation or remuneration. Transaction or exchange based relationships do not tend to culminate in unconditional love, because they are fundamentally based upon numerous requirements and conditions being met. These relationship strategies are always dependent upon a tendency to interact interpersonally, via some particular social-value or personal-value value based paradigm or model. When the transactions or exchange dynamics are no longer deemed adequate the relationship then has fundamental problems or disintegrates.

Examples of social value creation strategies that would support us in transaction and exchange based relationships include:

- ❖ Attaining a lot of money in order to prove ourselves better than others, show us to be a good provider, or to keep another person financially dependent upon us in a marriage.
- ❖ Trying to be physically more attractive or interpersonally attractive (i.e. Sexy), (including physical augmentations of various kinds, such as the way we dress, or getting face lifts or breast augmentations).
- ❖ Working to attain social power, status or fame.
- ❖ Working to attain power in business, that we can then use in an exchange oriented manner and to feel more in control of our lives.
- ❖ A self-worth development strategy of codependent rescuing of others. These strategies are often applied in personal relationships, (i.e. Emotionally rescuing our partner, including one who is stuck in any sort of addiction).

Other rescuer strategies can be seen when people choose to become spiritual leaders, doctors, teachers, or even military personnel. Meaning that some of these people derive self-perceived social value from rescuing others. On the flip side, these rescuing strategies can be applied quite ruthlessly and unconsciously as in the case of cult-leaders, seeming or claiming to rescue the people in their spiritual group. Of course, not all spiritual leaders or doctors function in this rescuer strategy mode, and many are operating with a focus on love. Still the strategy <u>can be</u> a motivation for these less optimal reasons.

Oddly enough we can even choose to apply social value creation strategies that are designed to lower other's value in order to raise our own social value, status, power or prestige. This type of strategy is seen in social situations when one person attempts to demean, negatively label, judge, criticize or socially diminish the other's social value and thus their social status. This dynamic is seen clearly in competitive political battles, competitive business situations, and it even happens far more often in marriages. Living by this strategy means living from a point of view of social hierarchy. Meaning that the person following the strategy fundamentally believes there are those who are in some way either better or less than others, and they want to make sure they are higher than others.

By lowering the perceived social value of others and invalidating their opinions, beliefs, values, behaviors or views we become "heroes and heroines". (For example, this is how the enemy is "demonized" in fiction, the news, war, political battles and in divorces). The judgment based and fear driven Cycle of Hatred is the source of all political hate speech and criticism, whether by politicians or citizens. Even while hatred is seen and rationalized by many as:

- ❖ "Seeking or effecting justice"
- ❖ Attacking our enemies "justly"
- ❖ Fundamentally empowering
- ❖ An effective and efficient method of influencing and controlling others and controlling social situations
- ❖ "Fighting fire with fire"
- ❖ Necessary to achieve competitive goals
- ❖ As a way to prove one candidate is "stronger or better" than the other or conversely as a way to prove that a candidate is "bad, incapable and unacceptable"
- ❖ A valid expression of either "masculine or feminine power" (whether it is being employed as a strategy by a man or a woman in any social context)

Agenda Setting Strategies (Trying to willfully define reality for ourselves and others):

This set of strategies is designed to give us the power to define the reality, parameters and dynamics of any situation, group or relationship, via setting or defining life or situational agendas, goals, fundamental beliefs and priorities. Agenda Setting Strategies are all control and competition based strategies that are based in exchange and transaction dynamics. They therefore have similarities to the Social Value Creation Strategies we just reviewed above. Setting agendas means setting the goals, priorities, values, requirements, direction, beliefs and timetables for groups of people, or those we are in personal relationship with, including our spouses and families.

Agenda control strategies can paradoxically be disguised as "good leadership". We subconsciously assume that if we (the leader) can be the one who defines the reality/agenda, that we can then control others within the context of the agenda, since we were the one who defined it. We assume that we must "define the reality we experience", (both personally and socially), in order to then be able to control it and have maximum power in regard to it. Undefined reality, situations, relationships and undefined agendas are, from the vantage point of this strategy, therefore seen as unsafe and disempowering. This type of strategy, like all strategies does not allow for our just happily and lovingly "being in the world". This agenda setting strategy is supportive of the next set two strategies that we will discuss, (i.e. "The Competitive Strategies" and "The Victim, Perpetrator and Rescuer Strategies").

Competitive Strategies:

Competitive strategies (i.e. trying to conquer, exploit, undermine, surpass, negate others, and prove oneself superior to others) are all driven by fear of vulnerability of all kinds and the fear of powerlessness. They are also driven by desire for control and power of various sorts and do not incorporate higher consciousness perspectives, spirituality or loving philosophy. Like many fears, the fear that drives competitive strategies is usually subconscious and are often purposely repressed. The influence of these strategies are therefore antithetical to authentic emotional intimacy, integrous relationships, unconditional love and human evolution in general. Competitive strategies are also a type of life control strategy. In other words, we cannot be operating in a competitive mode and simultaneously be emotionally open and emotionally vulnerable.

279

At the subconscious primal emotional levels of human being's, competition and being competitive, has historically been seen as "good and necessary" by many people, and has also been seen to be literally equal survival and safety. Competitive intentions, behaviors and motivations often "trump" people's focus on being kind, loving and humane to one another. A prime example of this dynamic is our human competitive tendency to be "super predators" within our ecosystem, which has been exhibited for thousands of years. Meaning that there are primal aspects of humanity that take it for granted that we have the right to dominate, consume, fundamentally change and even destroy any aspect of our world, our ecosystem, and all its lifeforms, including ourselves. Even greed and desire are often, at their roots, driven by this same fear dynamic, as a way to cope with our underlying fear. Stunningly, we are even extending this presumptuous attitude to other planets, (i.e. one "minor example" would be the talk of terraforming Mars and creating outposts on the Moon).

All forms of predation are competition and survival based and are simply reflections of this blindingly unconscious competitive dynamic, it is just a matter of degrees as to how destructive they are. We humans, due to the myopic influence of our fear for our own survival, and our fear of being disempowered and unsafe in comparison to other people, can in certain situations rationalize any form of destruction or killing, whether personally or internationally. Our competitive tendencies can be channeled, (i.e. competing in physical sports, etc.), still doing so does not eliminate its non-optimal uses. Part of the process of competition can be the vilification of those we are competing against, (i.e. politics, war and terrorism). Another detrimental aspect of competition is the emotional motivation of hatred that results and is often unrealized when we feel vulnerable, powerless, angry and blaming toward those we are competing against. In these situations, competition can turn deadly.

These competitive predatory strategies are consistently applied not only to the planet; we also, to one degree or another, apply them to each other as individuals daily. We could look at some aspects of managed intra and international economics as managed predation, rather than merely as competition. Predation can take the form of manipulating others, controlling others, using our positions of knowledge, power or authority in a corrupt manner, using other's energies and efforts to attain our goals, and dominating others into submitting to our beliefs, values, or religious or political agendas. There is of course constant competition between various groups, many unseen by the public, that attempt to influence the operation of all aspects of the U.S. Government, we could refer to some of this as "lobbying". In these cases, competition leads to corruption.

Some human beings also act in emotionally and sexually predatory ways, even toward their own children. On a global level, any nation intentionally and purposely keeping its population disempowered, ignorant and uneducated, and thus more controllable could be seen as predatory. I am not condemning people, any group, nation or humanity as a whole with these words. I am doing my best to non-judgmentally and unconditionally lovingly describe a very natural species dynamic that is best fully understood, so that it can ultimately be fully transcended by humanity. We cannot compete our way to world peace. It is vital to understand that competition cannot be regulated via traditional law, since technology is outstripping the laws capacity to regulate its uses in competitive processes.

Competition can also be seen in dynamics of social comparison for the purposes of personal empowerment or status seeking. Competition via social comparison based strategies, whether exhibited in men or women, is a key source of gender related problems between men and women in relationships. It is often this emotionally blinding dynamic of competition that keeps people in relationships from experiencing peaceful and consistent mutual emotional trust, respect, intimacy and safe open communication. In a rapidly changing world this dynamic is important to understand.

Some of the more extreme forms of competitive strategies and tendencies can be supported in men, by the women they are in relationship with. Meaning that some women can feel safer or more secure if they perceive that they have a highly competitive spouse. Even though operating via this type of competitive strategy and life orientation may keep their men emotionally closed and guarded, focused on career and financial gain more than on love and family, and therefore seemingly emotionally unavailable. This dynamic is a fundamental reason some women feel they are not emotionally resonated with and understood in their relationships and personal emotional dynamics.

Therefore, any competitive strategy, whether exhibited by men or women, in any relationship, is a double-edged sword in relation to its effect on our relationship quality. Though these strategies may meet some people's expectations of a mate, they are ultimately emotionally detrimental. Competitive strategies are not the sole reason that men and women do not emotionally communicate well, still they are a part of the picture. Competitive strategies in all areas of life, have been lauded socially and interpersonally, and have often been seen as unquestionably necessary and security producing

281

ways of life. Still the strategies always lead to unresolved fear and mistrust of authentic, intimate and vulnerable interpersonal emotional dynamics.

The primal fear that drives competitive strategies in both men and women affects all social venues and relationships. This is true because all competition and comparison strategies are exchange and transaction based in nature. Therefore, the focus on exchange and equity tends to overshadow authentic emotions and unconditional love in the relationships these strategies are operating in. The fear of potential abandonment for not meeting the exchange based expectations of the other is always looming in exchange based relationships. Not meeting the other's expectations, or our own expectations not being met by our partner, is seen as relationship failure that could lead to abandonment. If this is so, how can we trust someone we constantly fear either abandoning us, punishing us for failing to meet their expectations, or that we fear not meeting our perceived exchange based needs or wants?

Unfortunately, these primal, fear driven, and dysfunctional competitive strategy dynamics are also supported and bought into by both the global masculine and feminine consensus consciousnesses. The male and female consensus consciousnesses are often fundamentally in direct competition with each other, for raw power in the world and in the process of evolving the species. What the root chakra most wants our expectations to be met, our beliefs to be proven true, and to achieve as much control as we can attain, which it sees as safety. These competitive dynamics create significant misunderstanding, conflict and suffering in many relationships, and have been the key reason for male domination in many societies in the past. These competitive strategies are so primal as to be fundamentally indistinguishable from the competitive energies of animals in the wild, fighting to try to prove they are the best mate and to dominate the herd. Competition is a global issue that has fundamentally fragmented humanity, and is at the same time a fundamental process of the dynamic of tribalism at every scale.

Global threats and drama are being experienced by all populations (i.e. via wars, terrorism, social and economic distrust and uncertainty, etc.). These situations are emotionally triggering for many people. As individuals become more emotionally triggered, the motivation to fall back on and operate in these fear driven competitive ways is amplified. Therefore, the supposed need for these strategies are seemingly further validated. Because of this fearful reactive tendency and feedback loop, there is not yet a conscious willingness within enough of the world's populations to truly peacefully balance power between the genders and between all groups and nations.

282

This social division creating dynamic of competition is fragmenting humanity at all levels and in all areas, (i.e. national competition, religious competition, economic competition, gender competition, technological competition, etc.). Competition is looked upon as a solution to many of life's problems, especially economically and politically. In truth competition is a slow poison, that humanity is consuming, and participating in it keeps us distracted and blinded to the problems that competition itself creates.

Tribalism, as defined earlier in this text, is a foundational motivator for and support mechanism to competition, and it keeps the fear that drives competition from being directly faced, addressed and comprehensively invalidated and then transcended. Competition is a fear management and coping strategy. Life issues and need fulfillment can be achieved through cooperation, teamwork and collaboration. Until competition as a "go to social strategy" is transcended there cannot truly be consistent peace on earth or between any two people.

It is useful to realize that the most intense and detrimental form of competition is the act of killing others. This method of "solving perceived life and social problems via killing" (including via murder, war, terrorism and anti-terrorist drone strikes) has been used by human beings for a very long time. The same myopic dynamic of social and business competition is even now fueling corporations rationalizing choices that will literally and directly lead to the deaths of human beings by various means, in various parts of the world, including via political influence, pollution and global warming. Nations are doing the same thing. I am not condemning any group; I am suggesting that we can adopt more optimal ways of making decisions and developing our world. Where does the dysfunctional dynamic of competition end? Why praise or practice a way of life that is in some ways destroying our world?

Victim, Perpetrator and Rescuer Strategies:

Many people see life and relationships through the lenses of these three simple perspectives. Some see themselves as innocent powerless victims and others as powerful and "bad" perpetrators of their emotional pain, their life limitations and therefore their self-perceived state of victimhood. Others see themselves as rescuers of the innocent victims and as such are validated as being "pure and good people" for having rescued others. The rescuers also may feel socially and emotionally validated in punishing or killing the supposed perpetrators (i.e. police personnel, military personnel, lawyers and judges etc., may feel validated in punishing "the bad people" rather than understanding them and working with them in more constructive ways).

Paradoxically people who have felt victimized in the past often feel validated in punishing the people that they perceive as the perpetrators of their pain and suffering. In this way, victims can unwittingly become perpetrators themselves and can feel very self-righteous in doing so.

These three life strategies, (victim/perpetrator/rescuer strategies or V/P/R) are all dysfunctional and can operate in very subtle ways, in any area of our lives and relationships. They are also paradoxically very gross, simplistic and even barbaric strategies in their various forms of interpersonal application. Applying them creates over simplification of the nature and dynamics of relationships, that ultimately creates misunderstanding and conflict that is then difficult to resolve. If we hold onto these illusionary polarizing perspectives, they will continue to create drama, feelings of persecution and powerlessness, and validate our seeing ourselves or our positions and behaviors as being "more right, righteous or better" than other's positions or behaviors. Conversely, they can support us in feeling disempowered, wronged, wounded and incapable of changing our lives for the better. They can also give us a false sense of self-worth, if we are operating as a rescuer. Even rescuers can become perpetrators or victims in certain circumstances.

The V/P/R dynamics can be seen at all levels of society, business and in fundamental interactions between nations. These strategies and their associated dynamics can only lead to misunderstanding, mis-communication and ultimately conflict. All three of these states are supported by the ongoing and unresolved Cycle of Judgmentalness that holds them in place. All three of these strategies are often cycled through by individuals each day, in their day-to-day decision-making processes. Meaning at one moment we can act as perpetrator, in the next feel victimized and moments later can then shift right into rescuing someone.

The V/P/R strategies, for many of us, become the foundation of our interpretive and decision-making values and points of view. The V/P/R strategies are also another form of Control Strategy, in that their intention is invariably to control or have power over someone or some situation that we see as detrimental. Even "playing the victim" can in some ways be socially empowering. The V/P/R strategies are also Self-Value Attainment and Management Strategies; in that they help us to avoid our own self-judgmental tendencies, by giving us someone else to blame or condemn for our life situations, choices and results.

So, the V/P/R strategies are actually a blend of several of the strategies mentioned in this sections listing of fear driven control strategies. We could

284

say that all of the strategies listed here are all representations of living in a fear reaction mode and a process of projecting negative possibilities onto life and relationships. Thus, none of these strategies can ever fully support present moment consciousness or inner peace. Therefore, they represent a sort of anti-consciousness process and anti-human evolutionary process. A question I would ask the reader is this. How many people perceive themselves to be victims, and use this self-perception as a rational to then be dominated by those they are rescued by? How many rescuers want to be subtly dominant in their relationships with those they rescue?

By judgmental criticism alone some people have actually been flogged publicly, often without merit, and as a result are emotionally and physically destroyed. If we feel our self-worth threatened or our social value threatened, we quite often lash out in terrible ways at the supposed perpetrator of the attack. The truth is that when we feel or rationalize ourselves to be an "innocent victim" we often unintentionally become a ruthless perpetrator.

Conscious and subconscious beliefs (though often bought into in an unquestioning manner) are often counterproductive, yet are still believed in wholeheartedly. They also tend to fundamentally and detrimentally affect our decision-making processes and our emotional processes at both conscious and subconscious levels. We can acquire and hold any type of dysfunctional belief in any lifetime. The most deeply held core beliefs are driven by fear and are often acquired in our early childhood.

We often hear the echoes of our core beliefs expressed in our internal dialog. Many of them may start with the phrase "I have to do…" or "I have to be…" or "I have to feel …". We may also say "I need to". Examples of these internal dialog statements would be "I have to succeed or win" or "I have to be a good mother or father" or "I have to be perfect". In these situations, we actually do have the freewill not to do or be whatever we feel so emotionally driven to do, be or achieve. Still we can easily tell ourselves, by our internal dialog, that we do not have freewill in these specific "I have to" type of fear driven emotional situations. If we do operate from I have to perspectives, then we will automatically drop into feelings of hatred if we feel thwarted in our effort to accomplish that which we feel we <u>have to</u> accomplish.

"I have to" is, by default, an often-subconscious fear driven victim state of mind and emotion, and a state of complete refusal to be self-accountable for our having free-will and personal power. In addition, when in this mode, we also tend to fall into blame mode of self or others, and are potentially willing to act aggressively toward self or others, if we fail. Changing this limited perspective is often deeply feared and avoided.

Some example "I have to" statements we may hold in our system's, and that affect us, our emotions and our decisions profoundly are, "I have to":

❖ Be right
❖ Tell the truth
❖ Fear what others think or feel about me
❖ Make others "like me"
❖ Obey the law
❖ Be authentically "who I am"
❖ Watch out for those who might harm me
❖ Make others do the right thing (as far as I as an individual can know the right thing)
❖ Prove I am better, stronger or smarter than others
❖ Remain invulnerable to others
❖ Remain safe
❖ Remain in control
❖ Control my emotions
❖ Be perfect
❖ Remain true to what I feel or believe
❖ Be willing to destroy anyone who might try to harm me
❖ Protect myself at all times, even if means killing others
❖ Be a perfect parent or spouse
❖ Be free to do as I want
❖ Keep others from controlling me
❖ Make sure I don't make a mistake
❖ Avoid being abandoned
❖ Take care of my family
❖ Redeem myself
❖ Regain my honor and integrity

These internal dialog statements of "I have to" are very different than, for example, saying to ourselves "I want to be a good mother or father". Operating on internal decision-making statements of "**I want to or I choose to**" allows us to always recognize our personal power of free-will, and thus not to operate from fear. Doing so also gives us room and permission to be imperfect, human, to periodically fail, and to constructively learn to improve from our choices that we perceive to be failures as we go through life. In a way, it is sovereignly empowering to say "I want to or I choose to" in our internal dialog. To reduce life stress and internal emotional conflict we can remove the phrase "I have to" from our personal vocabularies. I also suggest removing any statements of "I should...", "I shouldn't..." and "I can't", all of which are veiled and potential self-judgments.

It is time that we choose, as a species, to evolve and develop more sophisticated decision-making and interpretive strategies, which are not based on recorded beliefs/simulacra or subconscious primal fear. In so doing we can shift to a mode of learning from life via conscious discernment-driven self-sovereignty. We can choose to learn via strategies based upon self-trust and evolvable and transformable ego-identities, rather than fixed and constantly defended ego-identities. We can eventually learn to transcend ego-identity in all its forms and thus its limitations. We can learn to make decisions based on love for all and for the intended good of all. Teaching divine love and sophisticated conscious discerning decision-making strategies to ourselves and our children is a key to humanity achieving our most positive potential. We can thereby leave behind all detrimental tendencies.

The achievement of divine love as the foundation of our interpretive and decision-making processes requires a significant personal commitment. It also requires consistent conscious emotional self-monitoring and a conscious willful intention to hold this space of consciousness. It also requires us to be willing to look at ourselves and all our decisions and behaviors with a forgiving, compassionate and divinely loving eye.

Each of our choices across our lifetime has culminated in our current moment of conscious awareness and quality of understanding. If we had not made our past choices just as we did, (no matter how seemingly detrimental) we would not have achieved the level of insight, understanding and wisdom that we now have. In fact, you probably would not be reading this book at this moment if it weren't for your past choices, whether positive or negative. Each of our past choices is ultimately a step on the path to our growing closer to God. I would suggest that judging any of our past choices or behaviors inhibits us from understanding all we can from them, rather than motivating us to understand them and grow from and past them.

Whenever we gain a new insight we could take a judgmental look at ourselves and say "why didn't I know this before?" OR, "I should have realized it sooner!" OR "what is wrong with me that led to this situation?". Instead we could choose to congratulate ourselves for our achievement of new understanding from our experience. It is our choice of approach in regard to attaining understanding and wisdom that determines how positively we feel about ourselves and how much we learn from every moment of life.

Shifting From Judgmentalness and Control Seeking To Self-Sovereignty:

To live a sovereign and conscious life means living in unconditionally loving regard for ALL human beings. It requires us to become self-aware enough to stand on our own (not influenced by the consensus consciousness) in our decision-making and in the developed discernment and insight which supports our decisions. For this process to fully come to fruition we must first trust ourselves, our self-sovereignty, and be willing to accept the importance of, and validity of, other's sovereignty. Therefore, if we do judge or blame we can choose to IMMEDIATELY forgive and thereby release the negative emotional energy involved in the judgment. In this way we do not hold onto or live in resentment, and our acquired resentments do not last, fester, grow or result in future conflict.

Next, we can proactively release all our expectations of others and of ourselves. This is beneficial since expectations can only lead to judgments and thus further attempts to control self or others in order to get ourselves or others to conform to our expectations. I would suggest that it is useful to work through any and all fears that could lead to judgmentalness, controlling choices or behaviors. There are many methods available to heal the fears that drive judgmental and controlling tendencies, and they are all worthwhile to apply to our lives.

If we do become hung up on any past judgments, tendency to blame or any mis-interpretations of events, actions, decisions, relationships or situations, then we are stuck in the past. If we become stuck, and emotionally focused on the past, we become ineffective, disempowered and conflicted. If we are in judgment of any emotion that we personally feel, then we will be unwilling to constructively work with it and ultimately to heal it. Choosing to completely forgive and to cease blaming ourselves or others is not always easy. It is important to realize that forgiving others does not equal tolerating negative treatment or forgetting what occurred in the past. Still we can creatively manage our interactions with others without judging them, becoming angry at them, controlling them or hating them.

We all have warring aspects of ourselves, many of which we are not fully aware of, so that when we do choose to forgive we usually unknowingly only do a partial or incomplete job of it. Many people feel they have forgiven others or themselves long ago, and yet they still have aspects of themselves

288

that hold onto perceived wrongs, slights or unresolved situations. These emotions must be lovingly, diligently and thoroughly "dug up" and released if we want to live in a state of consistent inner peace and empowerment. Therefore, whatever technique or method we choose to apply to our emotional system in order to achieve forgiveness, must be applied in a thorough manner.

Some suggested techniques which can help us to forgive are:

- ❖ Prayer to spirit for help in forgiveness.
- ❖ The Sedona Method.
- ❖ The Ho' Oponopono (a highly recommended Hawaiian healing method—see the book "Zero Limits" by Joe Vitale and Ihaleakala Hew Len).
- ❖ The Emotional Freedom Technique (EFT), also known as "tapping".
- ❖ Mindfulness meditation while focusing on our negative emotions related to the past.
- ❖ Sanskrit mantras that heal fear and anger which can be found in the book "Healing Mantras" by Thomas Ashley-Farrand.
- ❖ An Ayurvedic healing exercise that can be found on my web site KarmicHealer.com called "The Forgive and Forget Self-Healing Process".
- ❖ Voice Dialog Therapy.

To be human is to love, and it is also just as human to judge, fear or hate; still we always have a choice to take the higher road. Our lives can be filled with peace and love, and ensuring that this is the case often means hard work, yet it is always worth it. We always get back what we put in.

Effects of Our Beliefs and Assumptions On Our Process of Discernment:

Experiences are sources of information which we acquire through making choices, interacting with others and participation in life. These experiences are, at their foundation, made up of the information we receive through our various senses. Our senses are fed by the energy that our chakras receive and process. For example, there is a chakra in each of our eyes, ears, our hearts and even in each of our hands. We make interpretations of the information we acquire through each of our senses, which we collectively see as experiences, and we then record these interpretations in our memories. Then when we reflect upon these recorded interpretations we draw conclusions about their meaning and implication, and these conclusions we would call beliefs. These recordings are of course simulacra. This process is how we formulate our beliefs and perspectives about life, ourselves, society and the world.

Once we formulate our beliefs about ourselves and others, we then record these beliefs into our memories and in our chakras. Each of the beliefs and simulacra we have recorded into our chakras become a lens through which we interpret future life experiences. These lenses operate at each chakra level in different ways. Therefore, we can have many different lenses through which we simultaneously perceive any future experience. From the point of the original recording of our beliefs onward we tend to hold these beliefs to be accurately representative of reality and even project them onto reality, rather than seeing what is really happening around us without the filter of previously acquired beliefs.

Once we have created our internal map of our external reality in this way, we then become so sure our map is accurate that we often look to it as being more accurate than any external perspective, situation, information source or reality. We often feel safer making decisions based upon what we internally believe about life and relationships, than trusting and making decisions based upon external information from the environment. Perceived safety itself being the determining factor or the "believability switch" that is thrown within us to tell us to record the interpretation of the experience as a belief.

In this way, we often subconsciously choose to project our recorded simulacra and their associated beliefs onto our lives and relationships, similar to projecting a movie onto a blank movie screen. Beliefs then lead to assumptions, which lead to expectations, which then lead to misinterpretations, which then lead to disappointment, anger, control, judgment and punishment. None of these steps lead to divine love. Therefore, beliefs themselves can be seen both as developmental stepping stones and as spiritual learning disabilities.

We look at the information we project onto the "screen" of life, which is colored by our beliefs, and assume what we see is true. Then, based upon this erroneous source of information, we draw conclusions and extrapolate meanings about our reality, situations, events and relationships. This is neither a conscious process nor a pure mode of learning, yet it is a habitual human process of learning from experience as we compare and reflect upon previously acquired beliefs. Quite often we project fearful imagined futures and then act from our reactive fear to these internal projects as if they were external realities.

We acquire most of our deeply held and fundamental beliefs in our childhood. These beliefs are imprinted as energy patterns in our lower chakras (1st and 2nd chakras). Our interpretations of our later life experiences and of all our relationships are strongly influenced by what we are taught and learn when we are children. Whatever interpretations we make of what we see through the cloudy lenses of our childhood beliefs become the information we base our later life decisions and actions upon. This is a key reason for relationship drama, conflict, misunderstandings and miscommunications, and lack of emotional fulfillment. This process is also fueling dynamics of global conflict.

Our beliefs become a filter on what we see, experience, learn and understand from life. Therefore, the mechanism of our beliefs governs what we think and do, and what we allow ourselves to experience and thus come to learn and understand. It could be said that our beliefs color and limit everything we learn after we acquire them. So our beliefs are a direct governing mechanism of our future life choices, actions, emotions, behaviors relationship dynamics, and thus influence our degree of sovereign use of our power in every moment.

How we choose what to believe in the present moment is profoundly influenced by many aspects of our existence. Some of these influences are our subconscious memories of past-life experiences. These memories of past-life experiences contain karmic patterns, old beliefs, emotions and energies. These patterns, emotions and energies are constantly coloring our process of choosing what to believe, value and achieve in our current lifetime. We are constantly adding to our storehouse of past-life experiences and achieving new understandings as we move through our current life.

This process of constantly adding new memories to our storehouse goes on moment-by-moment and year by year as we live our lives. From this newly acquired information we then create new interpretations and beliefs about life and relationships. Then based upon these new interpretations and beliefs we attribute specific meaning and implication to our future life experiences. So the process of belief can be seen as a slow and potentially non-optimal process of species evolution. For example, we may fundamentally believe that "all men are bad" or "all people are selfish". If we hold these beliefs and look at the world through the lens of these beliefs, then we will make misinterpretations of other's behaviors.

For example, if we see a man yelling at a woman and we cannot hear what he is saying, we may interpret that he is treating her badly her. We might then attribute the meaning of the situation to be one of male abuse of a woman. If we attribute this meaning to the situation we might walk up and strike the man in order to rescue the woman. Only then might we come to understand that he was yelling at the woman because her hearing aid battery had failed. The result is that we acted upon assumption and projection of subconscious belief to our detriment and to the detriment of others.

This multifaceted cognitive and emotional dynamic is a key part of how and what quality of wisdom and understanding we ultimately gain through and from our experiences. Belief based interpretation of life is a practice of habitual experiential information intake. This information intake and its associated steps of interpretation and belief creation is part of the way we manage our recorded storehouses of personal information across lifetimes and within lifetimes.

Once we have attributed meaning to the situations and relationships we experience, we then use our attributions of meaning as a basis for the creation of our personal life rules, values and codes of conduct. These chosen life rules and values are often specifically selected to protect us or those we love in some way. For example, the rule we record of "look both ways before crossing a busy street" is recorded to keep us safe. These life rules could also be seen as acquired habits of decision-making. In like manner, we may create life rules to protect our egos, to maintain our physical and emotional safety, our social status, our social or self-images, our perceived reality and what we value.

These life rules and values spread from parent to child across generations, and from society to individual, and from person-to-person in day-to-day life. In this way life rules move from person-to-person across cultures (not unlike viruses). Eventually if these rules and values spread to enough people in a society or culture they may be adopted as either social norms or even become the law of the land. This developmental cycle is important to understand, since it determines the limiting dynamics of the development of societies and cultures. It also makes it difficult for them to assimilate the rapid change of all kinds that we are experiencing globally, and this limitation causes vast stress and conflict.

As we live our lives, all of this personal experiential information is recorded within various parts and levels of our energy systems (not only in our physical brains). Each piece of information is given a certain level of value and priority, and its relationship to other pieces of information is determined, defined and recorded. Each of our beliefs have different levels of priority in our lives. For example, the belief that "the sky is blue" is probably not as high a priority to us as "I have to eat, breathe and have shelter from

292

the elements in order to remain alive". The priority we place on any particular belief is often directly affected by the circumstances of the experience that originally created it.

In any life experience, we may feel varying emotional reactions to events and situations. The quality and intensity of our emotional reactions to our life experiences imprints our beliefs with greater or lesser intensity within the holographic constructs of simulacra. The interpretation of the original experience determines the intensity of the emotional reaction. It does not matter what actually occurred in any experience, what matters is how we interpreted what occurred. This is because it is the interpretation which creates the emotional reaction, which then defines the depth and intensity of the imprint made upon our subconscious, and thus the priority and tenacity of the recorded belief. Which then directly further affects our later interpretations and decisions.

Our beliefs directly affect our personal sovereignty and ownership of our power. If we hold disempowering beliefs such as "I am worthless" or "I am weak," or "I am not good enough" then we will function as if these beliefs were true. What is true is that we are all powerful, all the time, we simply need to recognize and remember this.

If we hold non-sovereign beliefs or codependent beliefs such as "I am worthless unless I have a relationship" or "I cannot stand on my own" or "I have to take care of others", then we will again function as if these beliefs were true. Thus, our beliefs can define the boundaries of our perceived power and sovereignty, and therefore our perceived ability to wield our power freely and in an independent and self-reliant manner. Our beliefs also tell us, usually erroneously, whether we are safe in any situation or relationship or not. If we disempower ourselves via choosing to hold to limiting or distorted beliefs, we will likely be unwilling to strongly manage our relationship boundaries. If so we may become less sovereign, perhaps to the point of allowing others to dictate our lives or even abuse us. If we are less sovereign we are literally less conscious, free, powerful and creative.

The life experience interpretations and beliefs which previously appeared to be most relevant to us, are later relied upon, focused upon and monitored more closely than others. This process is for most people subconscious and automatic. This process of belief management is deemed necessary because "beliefs are believed in" by the subconscious mind to not only be a map of our reality, but to be reality itself.

However, these recordings are all just abstractions of our basic experience of reality, rather than the experience itself. When we analyze and intellectualize what we experience, it then becomes more abstract and complex. So "over-thinking" rather than feeling about our understandings of life can actually lead to less practically useful and applicable results. In fact, some people have learned to live in a strictly intellectual fashion (for example, a person who, practically speaking, lives "in their head" rather than from their emotions). These intellectualized people are usually men rather than women. Through their intellectualization of the world they have disassociated from their essential emotional nature and from their own most basic emotions and levels of emotional awareness and thus from their emotional power and intimacy. Although basic primal emotions are often a cause of many problems, they are also our initial reference points that tell us how our subconscious and egos are operating. Our basic emotions are also a fundamental part of our social and interpersonal decision-making processes. These emotions are constantly being expressed in work environments, under the veneer and guise of professionalism.

Working with our first and second chakra level emotions is necessary if we want to balance our male and female energies and work through our detrimental subconscious tendencies and karmic patterns. In effect, we cannot heal within ourselves that which we cannot or are unwilling to feel. So initially these lower chakra emotions, patterns and processes represent part of our process of transcending egoic tendencies and attaining sagacious consciousness.

If we try to skip this step of emotional self-understanding and go straight to some form of "analytical or intellectual intelligence" as a supposed antidote for all of humanity's and life's issues, we leave behind key elements of what makes us human. So, in a paradoxical manner our primal emotions, lower chakra awareness and subconscious patterns, once transformed and integrated with our upper level chakra awareness and understandings become a key source of our personal power and wisdom. Suppressing our emotional process also generally results in a person who is extremely limited in what they can learn from life, their experiences and relationships. Our emotions teach us so much; it is a shame to waste them through judgmentalness of them, fear of them, or through emotional suppression.

The practice of monitoring our highest priority beliefs and assumptions related to our prior experiences of reality is usually subconscious. Depending upon the level of priority we have placed on a specific belief, we may at some point unknowingly become reactively tunnel-visioned in on it. This occurs when we are triggered by similar current life circumstances to focus on and project the old experience, beliefs and associated reactive emotions. This

294

focus then leads us to see the present through the distorting lens of the prior experience rather than as new and fresh.

When we become tunnel-visioned in on any previously arrived at belief and assumption, along with its associated emotional charge and attribution of meaning, we project it onto our current reality and our relationships. We literally become partially blind to all other incoming situational information and interpersonal considerations that are occurring in the now. The old recording of experience in the subconscious becomes the lens through which our conscious mind views the world. This way of functioning creates a limited and distorted perspective from which to see and interpret our current moments of life. In these situations, we become instantly unable to learn certain things from our current life experience. This is because we are internally and emotionally re-living and reprocessing the prior recorded experience over again, rather than processing the current experience in a clean or pure manner. Most of humanity shares this reactive tendency to project the perceived past onto the present. Thus, as an evolving species, humanity is encumbered by it.

The assumptions we hold about life are based upon our beliefs. For example, if I believe that "men are dangerous" then I might assume that "men can hurt me". Assumptions then in turn create expectations of life which we then project onto life. For example, if I assume that "men can hurt me" then I might expect that "men will hurt me if I interact with them". Assumptions and expectations are often more highly emotionally charged and action oriented in nature than their underlying beliefs. Expectations are simultaneously a projection outward onto our environment and inward onto the internal reality of our underlying beliefs. Beliefs may or may not be emotionally charged. Non-emotionally charged beliefs may just be related to information we accept as true or accurate about reality or our lives. Emotionally charged beliefs may be those we base our life view and motivations, emotional self-worth, emotional reactions or our relationship decisions upon. We record our beliefs like "bookmarks in our book of life" so that we can make decisions based on what was previously perceived to be accurate and useful information. This whole mental and emotional process is supposed to guide us in a proper and safe way to live life.

A simple example of this internal dynamic and how it directly affects key aspects of our lives is on the following pages.

(Note: I suggest proactively "mapping" your core beliefs using this structured method in order to effectively understand and transcend them, as consciousness is always better than operating upon belief).

By the way we could just as easily have mapped the beliefs:

❖ "Men are all bad."

❖ "Women are too emotional."

❖ "No one will ever love me."

❖ "I am not good enough."

❖ "I will never find happiness."

❖ "Terrorists are all evil".

The Mapping a Core Belief Chart on the following pages provides a more detailed description of the Cycle of Beliefs.

Mapping a Core Belief:

Situation:

Someone we perceive to be in authority tells us that democracy is the foundation of freedom and that it is necessary to be willing to fight, kill or die for it.

Our Recorded Interpretation:

"The person in authority knows better than I do. Since they are in authority, they have the power to punish or devalue me if I do not agree with them, therefore I should listen carefully, and what they are saying is probably relevant and true. I will accept my best interpretation of what they are saying as true and record it in my memory as such."

Actual Belief Recorded in Our Subconscious:

Democracy is necessary in order to be safe and to have freedom and it is necessary and honorable to fight or die for it.

Assumption That is Projected and Then Recorded in Our subconscious:

If I am not willing to fight to defend democracy, I may be socially and emotionally abandoned or even punished by those in authority and by other people I know, depend upon and love. (This is obviously a fear-inducing assumption; therefore, fear is the emotional charge associated with this assumption. This fear can later drive the formulation of the emotions of anger and hatred, which when enacted destructively on a battlefield, or in any

296

other context, can create results which can then lead to guilt, shame, PTSD and depression).

Meaning Is Attributed To The Belief, and Its Associated Assumptions Are Then Recorded In Our Subconscious:

It is therefore okay, necessary and expected by those in my society that I kill other people who do not agree with or value democracy, in order to defend democracy, and to keep myself or others safe from the enemy and from my own countries authorities. (Note: The fear from these underlying assumptions is still the driving motivation which makes us willing to kill others, rather than love of others or of our country. Yet this dynamic is subconscious to most of us and we rationalize that we are motivated by patriotism or nationalism).

Rule We Create For This Situation:

I must always uphold democracy, even if I must use force and /or kill.

Thoughts Form As a Result Of Beliefs, Assumptions, Attributions of Meaning, and We Then Create Rules:

❖ Those who do not support democracy are not like me and are not trustworthy, are bad, wrong, misguided or even evil.

❖ Those who do support democracy can be trusted and are like me and are good, right, just and acceptable.

❖ Other forms of government are inherently "less good" than democracy, or are flawed, wrong or dangerous. (Can you see how such perspectives undermine world peace and acceptance of other culture's ways, beliefs, values and perspectives?)

Expectations We Formulate In Regard To Others:

❖ That good citizens will publicly uphold democracy.

❖ That good citizens will not question the validity or value or correctness of our current form of democracy or those in authority.

❖ That good citizens will fight those who question or do not uphold our version of democracy.

❖ That people who kill in the name of democracy are good people and patriots.

❖ That those in authority in a democracy are probably right or in integrity in their decisions in regard to the democracy.

Conclusions Reached As a Result of All of the Above:

- ❖ I must be a good citizen and uphold democracy.
- ❖ I must not question our fundamental style of government or its mode of operation.
- ❖ I must be willing to fight those who do not agree with our style of government.

Prioritization Of The Importance of Our Created Beliefs:

- ❖ We associate the belief that "democracy must be supported" with our personal survival and the survival of our families and nation. So we prioritize this belief very highly in comparison to our other beliefs, consciously or not. For example, this belief is prioritized more highly than "I believe the sky is blue or that a good cake contains eggs, sugar and flour".
- ❖ The result is more conflict and war and a continuation of the support for the belief that we must be willing to fight to uphold democracy, since we are in effect subverting the safety of democracy by continually fighting, killing and inciting others who do not agree with it.

Actions Taken After Acquiring The Belief That Democracy is Necessary In Order to Have Freedom:

- ❖ Sign up with the military in your country or in a foreign country.
- ❖ Die as a result of the conflict, kill other human beings, or both.
- ❖ Increase the level of negativity, misunderstanding and conflict in the world.
- ❖ Trigger other nations and their people to hate, vilify and fear democracy and democratic nations.
- ❖ Trigger other nations and their people to attempt to subvert democracy, through drastic methods, including terrorism.

Dysfunctional beliefs are often created due to misinterpretations or limited interpretations of our early life experiences. These beliefs are the foundation of our relationships, life and emotional coping mechanisms, and they were the best understandings we could produce at that point in time. The original misinterpretation usually occurs due to a lack of sophisticated interpretative capacity at the root chakra level of our system in our youth.

Recorded misunderstandings can also be created by choosing to model ourselves after dysfunctional parental patterns and their relationship dynamics. The recorded belief at the subconscious level is generally significantly limiting in some way as in "I am only safe if I am perfect" or "I am only safe if I am in control". Often groups of aligned detrimental beliefs support the formation of dysfunctional life strategies and painful relationship dynamics. To resolve such situations, the group of aligned beliefs or simulacra must be individually deconstructed, resulting in the detrimental life strategy or relationship dynamic dissolving. It is then necessary to replace these previously unconscious belief processes and recorded simulacra with consciously chosen behaviors.

Beliefs and simulacra form the basis of our ego-identity(s), self-image and social-image(s), whether they are based in reality or not. The beliefs that we create become the filters that we interpret life, relationships and events through, though these beliefs have often become transparent to our consciousness.

On the next page, we describe the step-by-step process by which beliefs are actually created, and how they then create the realities that we experience in our day-to-day life. We refer to this process as the:

Belief-Based Reality Creation Process Defined On The Next Page:

Belief-Based Reality Creation Process:

BELIEF-BASED REALITY CREATION PROCESS

SELF-DEFINED BELIEF / REALITY ADDICTIONS

1. Recorded Beliefs, Roles, Rules, Priorities and Values Based Upon Interpreted Life Experiences (Often Generalized)

The generalization of root chakra beliefs occurs when we record generalized beliefs about the world from our experiences, rather than a specific belief. We do this because the root chakra assumes that the more general the belief, the "safer" we will be. For example, rather than recording that a specific man or woman who hurt us at some point in our lives is dangerous, we tend to record a belief something like either "men are dangerous" or "women are dangerous." (Both men and women follow this subconscious belief creation process in a similar manner. For this particular example we are showing the results of a woman having recorded the original belief that "men do not care.")

2. Assumptions Made Based Upon the Previously Acquired Belief

Assumptions could be "my husband will be insensitive or emotionally unavailable," "I cannot trust men to care," or in this particular example, "He probably won't remember or care what is important to me, his wife, in regard to Valentine's Day."

BELIEF-BASED REALITY CREATION PROCESS (CONTINUED)

SELF-DEFINED BELIEF / REALITY ADDICTIONS

3. Projections, Associations and Expectations

We project the energy of our expectations which stem from our assumptions through our chakras and onto reality and our relationships. In effect "telling" those we interact with and/or love how to act in order to please our subconscious beliefs and by doing so keeping us feeling "safer." We also record associations in our systems, (sometimes these associations are rather random in nature) related to our assumptions and expectations, for example, "Receiving flowers on Valentine's Day means my husband loves me." Yet, since the original belief we have stored in our root chakra, based upon our early life experiences of having an emotionally unavailable father is that "men do not care" the expectation and projection onto our husband is "He will probably forget to get me flowers on Valentine's Day."

4. Misinterpretations and Inaccurate Attributions of Meaning

We create misinterpretations of our experienced reality due to the distortions in our perceptions created by our projections onto life and relationships. Once we project misinformation onto reality we then arrive at inaccurate attributions of the meaning of what we have misinterpreted to be occurring. This process then triggers reactive emotions to the misinterpretations we have made. "I did not receive flowers today by 4:00 p.m., therefore my husband does not love me and I am angry about his lack of caring." (Even though the flowers are just late arriving this year and they will actually arrive by 7:00 p.m.)

5. Emotional Programming is Triggered Leading to the Formulation of Emotional Motivations and Intentions

We misinterpret situations and then we assign inaccurate meaning to them and then we emotionally react to our misinterpreted meaning. Our reactive emotions then support the creation of emotion-driven intentions. "My husband forgot the flowers on Valentine's Day, I am angry, my anger then motivates me to intend to try to make him feel badly in some way for having emotionally abandoned me."

BELIEF-BASED REALITY CREATION PROCESS (CONTINUED)

6. Unwise or Misinformed Decisions and Actions

When we arrive at misinterpretations and we then base our decisions upon them in an emotionally reactive way, we then tend to make unwise or misinformed decisions and actions. "I start an argument with my husband when he gets home at 5:00 p.m., which then escalates and we both attack each other ruthlessly about all sorts of other preexisting relationship issues."

7. Unexpected Negative, Unsatisfying and Disappointing Results and Emotional Pain

Once we take action and make decisions based upon misinformation, it leads to these unwanted results. "We argued and then decided that the only solution was to get a divorce." (The flowers then arrive at 7:00 p.m. and the husband angrily throws them into the trash, feeling his wife does not deserve them.)

8. Negative Emotions, Controlling and Dominating Behaviors, Ego Self-Defense Mechanisms Triggered, Justification, Resentment, Denial, Bias, Rationalizations, Contempt, Prejudice, Self-Righteousness, Judgments, Punishments, Hatred, Conflict and Aggression

We then fight and argue and judge and blame each other self-righteously as we go through the long and painful divorce process.

9. Often Negative Results REVALIDATE the Original Belief

The painful results of this overall cyclic process support my original belief that "men do not care" even more than before, since I have associated this preexisting belief with far more emotional pain and suffering than it originally had when it was first recorded in my root chakra. Therefore in future relationships I distrust men even more and tend to "lead" with this detrimental belief in my relationships even more strongly and thus refuse to be emotionally vulnerable and intimate in my future relationships.

SELF-DEFINED BELIEF / REALITY ADDICTIONS

Although later in life we may consciously learn better ways to see our lives, this level of our system (our root chakra) is often unable to reinterpret past situations in a new and clearer manner once we have grown up. So, in spite of our later learning, we retain the negative and dysfunctional patterns of youth and they tend to aggressively resurface when we feel insecure or threatened. When they do, they quite often overwhelm what we would refer to as our conscious mind. It is simply true that our conscious understanding is constantly in a tug of war with our subconscious beliefs and emotions.

The previously diagrammed process describes the cyclic and self-reinforcing method of acquiring beliefs about life and then attempting to re-apply them over and over as we live our lives. In effect, we are trying to determine through this experiential practice the truth, falsehood and practical applicability of various states of perspective, awareness, consciousness, focus, value, decision-making and basic information about life and relationships. We first record the belief information, and then we attempt to apply it to reality. If it does not fit reality we eventually will modify it, yet we may also stubbornly hold onto specific beliefs because we have come to associate them with our physical, mental, emotional, spiritual or social safety. When this happens, we experience limitation in the speed of our overall mental and emotional development of understanding as people and souls.

Whenever we hold subconscious beliefs that we associate with mental, physical, emotional or spiritual safety, they tend to more strongly color our vision and significantly undermine precise and accurate discernment of situational interpretations. In fact, holding these erroneous beliefs tends to manifest results and situations which are just the opposite of what we consciously want. (For example, the fear of not being cared for literally tends to manifest the reality of not being cared for as seen in the example above). Thus, they directly affect our decisions and actions and life results. Thus, they directly affect how we learn to apply our personal power, and when, where, how and why we wield it, as well as the results we get by doing so.

By mapping our beliefs in a methodical way, we are empowered by our understanding of their influences, costs and benefits in our lives. This mapping method supports our process of willfully changing our core beliefs in constructive ways. It also helps us dis-identify with detrimental simulacra recordings. If we have not clearly and comprehensively discerned the implications of our beliefs on our lives, careers and relationships it is difficult to become motivated to change for the better.

We all face the challenges of managing our ego-identities, our social identities, our tendencies to judge self and others, and our vulnerabilities to

303

old influences or models of seeing life. We all have a "ghost in our psychological machine" made up of our subconscious simulacras, as well as the profound influences of our karmic patterns. We are also all significantly influenced by what we consciously or subconscious choose to believe at every moment of our lives.

These influences, although pervasive, persuasive and sometimes detrimental are key elements of our process of living life and ultimately of our attaining transcendent understanding, discernment and ultimately enlightenment. In the long run these elements of our being and their influence on our developmental path will ultimately culminate in our becoming more conscious, sovereign and self-aware, and thus prepare us to master and own our personal power. In the end our capacity to achieve and maintain a discerning state of consciousness positively affects every area of our lives and empowers us to build a world of love that works.

Chapter Nine
The Human Chakra System and the Importance of the Root Chakra in Today's World

THOUGH WE ARE NOT ALWAYS AWARE OF IT, WE EACH LIVE in our own personal bubbles of energy consciousness, and these bubbles of energy are called our **auras**. Auras are the layered energetic extension of our physical and spiritual being, and emanate from our main chakra centers. Our main chakra centers are energy vortices which manage the information and energy of all aspects of our lives and relationships. It is the aura which gives us the sense experience of other's physical closeness to us or our own proximity to physical objects. For example, when we close our eyes we still tend to sense the presence of a wall in front of us when we are close to it. We also tend to feel and perceive other's emotional proximity and some of the emotions that others are feeling through our auras. This is experienced when we "feel in our gut" that someone is angry or upset, although they may show no outward physical sign of being distressed.

We have seven main "in body" chakras. We also have many other chakras and the actual number is debatable, although there are ancient sages who have recorded their perception that there are upwards of 188,000 greater or lesser chakras. Each of these chakras helps us to process some aspect of our life experience at all levels of subtlety. Understanding the specific functions of our seven main "in body" chakras can help us to better manage our process of consciousness and our personal power, attain higher consciousness and thus maintain our personal sovereignty. Most of our main "in body" chakras emanate from the spine. Knowledge of our chakras can significantly improve our lives, our emotional and spiritual health, and our relationships.

Information and Sensory Processing:

This subtle energy system of chakras provides us with information and sensory experience processing capabilities as individuals and as groups. This subtle energy is an expression of the soul as it moves through the chakras and into this physical world and between people. This energy is often called Qi or life force, and has also been described as electromagnetic energy, yet it has not yet been proven to exist by mainstream science. This subtle energy creates a constant and dynamic network of communications between all humans and even all living things. This energy network is literally visible, can be accurately sensed and is very real for those attuned to perceive and work with it. Although subtle, it can be felt very keenly by those practiced in feeling and working with it, either in spiritual healing work or via Qi Gong practice.

One example of how this subtle energy works can be seen in the chakras and energy systems of birds that allow them to energetically communicate in a real time manner and sense one another. This communication allows flocks of birds to basically "move as one" when they fly without running into one another. The same is true of schools of fish. This energetic interaction facilitates group decision-making and has its corollaries in human group decision-making. For example, it can be seen in the ways that well-honed athletic teams learn to work together without verbal communication. It can also be seen in close personal relationships where couples can finish each other's sentences.

Some people experience this energy as simply either a "good vibe or a bad vibe" when they first meet someone or interact in a new group situation. Our inter-connectedness as a species via these chakra energies creates and supports the ongoing manifestation and educational process of the collective consciousness. The operation of humanity's ongoing interactive network of subtle energy communications at both conscious and subconscious levels makes our incarnate state of physical existence a vehicle for spiritual evolution and eventual attainment of enlightenment via experience based evolution. Our main purpose for being human, in my view, is to experience life in this physically incarnate state and in this rich socially interactive and educational environment we call earth. In this way, we evolve from having attained a multitude of insights and understandings from our experiences and from our perception of other's experiences. In effect, we are all here to learn, to teach and to grow from these activities and interactions.

Enlightenment is an ongoing process of achieving complete spiritual understanding and resonance with God. Full God consciousness and harmony with God and the universe through the accumulation of educational life experiences over the course of many incarnations is the goal. In effect, our bodies and chakra-based energy systems are designed to allow us to construct, manifest and experience reality on this physical plane that we then learn from. We all process energy, experiences and information through our chakras that are related to our soul's intentions. We acquire this information as a result of the sensory input related to our physical, mental and emotional body's activities.

This ongoing process of social energetic interaction is in many ways driven by human thoughts, emotions, decisions and motivations. Then we each experience the resulting physical and energetic reality which we have created and learn from it in a variety of different ways. Thus, we are empowered through this activity of first manifesting and then experiencing our creations to learn and develop alongside other human beings. It is the chakra-based energy system of the whole of humanity that is fed by the information and energy of acquired experiences of each of our individual human systems and vice versa. This reflective, cyclic and interactive dynamic is a key support system to the development, learning and evolution of our species. It is also a support system to basic social, economic and technological development and progress.

Our emotional reactions, thoughts, interpretations of our lives and relationships, actions and choices are directly affected by the information and energy we receive, send and process through our chakras. Within our chakras and auras, our karmic patterns, belief patterns and subconscious parts, such as our child selves, are stored and constantly operate. These elements of our systems are stored along with the emotional charges and perspectives that we recorded at the time of creation of each of these aspects of our subconscious and our ego-identities. All of these patterns work together like a sort of interwoven tapestry to create our comprehensive interpretations of reality that we refer to as "consciousness". The triggering of these developed subconscious elements of our systems are the sources of our emotional reactions to our relationships and experience of life.

Chakras and Interpersonal Interactions:

A simple way we can become more aware of this energetic extension of ourselves (the aura) and its interactions with other's auras is through the activity of close interpersonal interaction. A real-life example can be seen if we are sitting on a bus or riding in an elevator and there is someone next to us whose energy we are not harmonious with. In this situation, we may begin to feel uncomfortable, irritable or even aggressive toward the other person. In this situation the other person's "energy bubble" has, to a degree, interacted directly with our own and has crossed our personal energetic boundaries in a somewhat disruptive or non-harmonious manner. In this circumstance, we may find ourselves leaning away from the person or we may even choose to change seats or move away from them in order to avoid their energy.

This dynamic of interactive auric energies can trigger a sort of primal territorial response in us and also simultaneously in other people. In effect, we are competing for energetic space and control of our perceived reality, often without realizing this is happening. Oddly enough, many of us react to such situations by sending messages of threat from our root chakras, whether we consciously intend them or not. Meaning we can subconsciously be sending the message "stay away from me or I will kill you" or "If you come near me I will hurt you". When we do this, other people feel it and react to such intimidating energetic messages. This is not just body language that transmits these messages; this is "energy language". People who abuse their authority in <u>any kind of relationship</u>, including parents, politicians and CEO's often send these messages to intimidate others into acquiescing to their intentions, via these threatening messages. Some religions send the energetic double message of "if you do not agree with our beliefs, values or dogma that you will go to hell", while simultaneously sending the double message that if you submit you will be "loved and be safe". In these situations, people often do not recognize their own conflicted emotional reactive dynamic and choose apparent safety through submission. I do by the way suggest surrendering to God, I do not suggest surrendering your conscious self-sovereignty to anyone else.

The bottom line is that at some level of our energetic being, we sense that other's personal energies. Thus, we know when they are either not harmonious with our own, are in conflict with us, or are in some way perceived as "not good for us or not in agreement with us". In a very practical sense, until we learn to accept everyone and ourselves from a standpoint of divine love and compassion, our primal reactions to each other's energetic and emotional states can keep us out of disharmonious and potentially detrimental situations that we are not yet prepared to consciously manage.

With the attainment of enough conscious divine love and compassion, we gain the ability to perceive and love the soul (and all of the energy) of whomever we are interactive with and thus have no negative or uncomfortable reaction to their presence. Thus, we can learn to choose to love and enjoy each other "warts and all". The more energetically sensitive we are, or become, as we develop our energy systems, the more vulnerable we may feel ourselves to be in regard to other's energy systems, disharmonious energetic interactions in social situations, and other's energetic projections. I suggest consciously practicing with increasing your awareness of this energy sensory process in order to enhance your personal awareness of how you interact with others around you.

The opposite situation is also true, meaning that in loving and intimate situations it is our subtle energy system which allows us to feel the positive and harmonious energetic interactions with others with whom we are in close relationship. Their energy in turn triggers our positive emotional and physical responses. We can feel the energy from the other person quite clearly if we choose to focus on it. It is through this intimate energetic interaction that our emotions and our emotional decisions in relationships are guided. In this way, we can experience feelings of trust, security, warmth and passion from others and offer the same to them in a well synchronized manner. Without the subtler elements of our energy systems, our experience of intimacy would be limited to only direct tactile sensation, which by itself is a somewhat empty experience, and which is not otherwise integrated with emotional process. The combination of the various energetic senses we possess and the heartfelt emotions they trigger is necessary for the multidimensional experience we call life and true intimacy.

The Seven Main Chakras:

Our auric energy layers emanate from the seven main in-body chakra centers. Chakra energy centers are spinning vortices of subtle spiritual energy and six of the seven we are speaking of emanate from various levels of our spinal columns. Various systems have been developed to describe, open, develop and work with the chakras, including the Hindu systems of Yoga, the Chinese system of Qi Gong, Western New Age chakra development systems or Tibetan spiritual systems.

All of these chakras based spiritual systems have their differences, even though the differences may be subtle. There are even some differences among the various Hindu systems. For the purposes of this discussion we will focus only on the general Western New Age chakra system of seven main in-body chakras. Even Christian systems of belief have representations of halos on top of the heads of saints. This location just happens to be the location of the crown chakra, which is the main chakral connection to spirit.

By the way, you need not be a Buddhist, Hindu, Qi Gong practitioner or participate in any religion to believe in or constructively work with your chakras. Chakra consciousness is available to all. One easy way of starting to work with your chakras is through simple meditation on the thoughts, feelings and internal dialog that can be perceived when we focus on any single chakra.

The Seven Major Chakras diagram below shows the positions of the seven main "in body" chakras starting with the 1st, the root chakra, which emanates from the tail bone and counting to the 7th, the crown chakra, located on top of the head. There are many more chakras, many of which are located outside the physical body.

The Seven Major Chakras

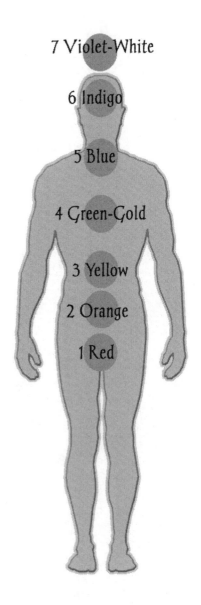

7 Violet-White

6 Indigo

5 Blue

4 Green-Gold

3 Yellow

2 Orange

1 Red

The colors of the individual chakras are listed inside the figure in the diagram above. Each chakra operates within a certain light energy frequency which is reflected in the color of each chakra's energy. Those who are psychically gifted, particularly if they have their 6th chakras open, can actually see the colors of the chakras and the surrounding aura and the energies that move through them. Energy healers and spiritual practitioners can work with these energies in either healing activities or for the purpose of spiritual development.

The chakras, for those who can see them, appear as a series of colored funnels or small tornados of energy extending both forward and backward from the spine. Each of the main chakras relates to a specific layer of the aura; the closest layer being associated with the root chakra and the furthest layer is associated with the seventh chakra. The energetic layer associated with the root chakra extends only a few inches outward from the surface of our bodies, with the subsequent layers of the aura each extending farther and farther from our bodies, for most of us to a distance of several feet. The aura of a highly spiritually developed individual can radiate out powerfully for literally miles in every direction.

Chakras 2 through 7 start out at birth in a non-functional dormant state. When we are born only our root chakra is open and operating. It is during the first three years of life that we store some of our most profound core beliefs in the root chakra, which will then shape our lives, emotions, relationships and decisions throughout our lives. These core beliefs become filters on our developmental interpretive processes and thus become the sources of the information we use to make key life decisions. As we continue to age, our other chakras gradually and naturally open as they are nourished by the world's life force energy which flows upward from the planet, and by the universal life force which flows downward to us all from spirit, the planets and the universe.

Chakra development, especially the root chakra, is profoundly influenced, either positively or negatively by parental energies and the family karmic patterning information that those parental energies carry and transmit to us during our formative years. Root chakra development is also profoundly influenced by any early life traumas we may experience and more generally by the influence of the surrounding cultural consensus consciousness.

With the opening and development of our higher chakras we attain the ability to:

❖ think new and more complex thoughts

❖ feel more complex emotions

❖ understand ourselves and others

❖ express and communicate in sophisticated ways

❖ become conscious of all aspects of life and relationships

❖ become spiritually evolved

This ongoing chakra development also means that we literally gain the ability to learn and understand more about ourselves, the world and our relationships faster and more accurately. Due to the influence of our karma, some of us develop our chakras in a limited way. We may have seen a person who was always in their head, so to speak, and seemed only able to think about life and was incapable of feeling about life. If so we might have been seeing someone whose heart chakra and second chakra were blocked or had not yet fully opened and developed. Our chakra development therefore determines our quality of consciousness. The development of our chakra system can be the defining aspect of our spiritual path and associated attainments; it can also allow us to more fully mentally and emotionally live life.

Development of Our Chakra Energy Centers:

I have worked with tens of thousands of people and their individual energy systems, either directly or through family members or loved ones. From this work I have learned a great deal about how people can and do develop emotionally, spiritually and energetically. I have also seen how their chakra development either facilitates or undermines their achievement of spiritual consciousness, wisdom and personal power. If a person does not have their chakras open, clear and functioning there are many things they cannot do or achieve in life that others can, including processing emotions, reaching intuitive understandings and exhibiting psychic abilities. Without our chakras open we simply cannot know what we do not know.

There are many children in the world who, due to lack of proper food, social facilitation and education, are in a difficult developmental situation. If a child grows up homeless and on the street, uneducated and living in constant fear and insecurity, and in fear of starving or being harmed or killed, then they may well only have their root chakra open in later life. They may thereby be comprehensively impaired in their development as a person throughout their lifetime.

Usually our chakras develop best as a result of:

1. Good personal and family past life karma.

2. A positive social culture to participate in.
3. Good nutrition and available health care.
4. Supportive, loving and positive family energies. (Note: Family patterns of judgmentalness, domination, criticism and negative energies can limit these openings).
5. Available and utilized higher education.
6. Available and utilized spiritual education, guidance and support.
7. Direct interaction with highly energetically or spiritually developed people.

For these listed reasons children born into industrialized and affluent nations have an edge in chakra development over non-industrialized nations. A caveat to this situation are those children who purposefully and intentionally choose focused and long-term spiritual development paths, which are available even in non-industrialized nations. In these cases, they may live their entire lives in a monastery and work diligently every day to achieve astute levels of spiritual consciousness and ultimately even enlightenment.

For those in industrialized nations with sufficient food, education, and free time to develop themselves spiritually there is much more room for rapid spiritual achievement. Especially in these days of freely available spiritual information. That said, we get out of our spiritual efforts that which we put into them. I have experienced the blessing of doing "hands-on" spiritual healing work on six highly developed Buddhist lamas from Tibet, some who had been following their spiritual path for over sixty years and managing large ashrams. I have also worked on many very evolved Buddhist monks. I can tell you that the Lamas' energy systems are the most pristine, clear, loving, kind, conscious, non-conflicted and sophisticated systems I have ever seen.

Through the eyes of these spiritual adepts (energetically speaking) I was given glimpses of states of consciousness, inner peace and tranquility few experience. In effect their systems were completely and highly congruently attuned to loving kindness, conscious self-awareness and loving spiritual focus. Working with them is like breathing clean fresh air in the mountains. It is useful to note that even in these wonderfully evolved human beings there are still (although much harder to find) karmic patterns, energy blockages and belief patterns that benefit from energy healing. I am not professing Buddhism as the best spiritual path, only doing my best to illustrate the results of lifelong spiritual focus, practice, method and effort.

These spiritual people worked long and hard for their attainments, and as previously stated it usually does take hard work for most of us to achieve these states. Still, spontaneous opening of chakras, attainments of spiritual awareness or even manifestation of powerful psychic abilities do occur regularly around the world at this time. It is my perception that these spiritual leaps are due to these individual's prior life spiritual efforts coming to current life fruition. These attainments are all steps on the road to spiritual mastery and the attainment of comprehensive wisdom or enlightenment. As the collective consciousness of humanity moves forward there will come a time when the "100th monkey effect" takes hold and these states of being will become the norm rather than the exception. (See internet sources for more information on the 100th Monkey Theory).

Examples of people who have made significant investment in their spiritual path are Christian or Jewish mystics, Hindu Yogis, Tibetan Lamas, South American shamans and Muslim Sufi mystics. These people generally exist in a very different ongoing state of conscious awareness and in a more positive emotional state than most of us.

Traditionally these adepts have likely developed in the following ways:

❖ All seven of their in-body chakras and several out-of-body chakras will be open and mostly clear of blockages or conflicts (karmas) and all are functioning well.

❖ All their main chakras would be consistently energized, highly developed, balanced and integrated with all their other chakras.

❖ Much of their personal karma will have been burned away through their spiritual efforts.

❖ They may exist in a generalized state of divine love and compassion for all of humanity and themselves, and have high self-esteem and exhibit grace-filled humility.

❖ They exhibit strong personal discipline, willpower and determination, personal integrity and impeccability in their worldly and spiritual decisions and dealings.

❖ They have reconciled the differences, imbalances and conflicts between their masculine and feminine natures, as well as their worldly and spiritual natures, and past-life and present-life perspectives, values, beliefs and motivations, and have highly integrated energy systems.

❖ They tend to exhibit good physical health, a very clear and precise mind and memory, keen intuition, a high degree of emotional intelligence, unshakable calm and inner peace, and they also "age well".

316

❖ They have consciousness of the quality of function of each part of their bodies from moment-to-moment, including their internal organs and their chakras.

❖ They may also exhibit one or several Siddhis or attained psychic abilities (for example clairvoyance, clairaudience, clairsentience, telepathy and self-healing).

Many self-development methods (Yoga, meditation, Qi-Gong) can be applied to develop one's chakra system and subsequently one's degree of consciousness and the quality of our mental, emotional, physical and spiritual function. I suggest using the methods that personally intuitively resonate best with each of us as individuals.

There are several Westernized methods of energetic self-healing that are being developed and applied which can facilitate clearing of our chakras and emotional systems and open us to spiritual consciousness. These include the Sedona Method, hypnosis, and the karmic release work described in the "Essential Energy Balancing" series of books by Diane Stein. In the past this spiritual developmental work tended to occur in a gradual fashion, over the course of entire lifetimes, yet time and human transformation is speeding up now, for many reasons.

Mastering The Root Chakra:

For the purpose of this book we will mainly only discuss the first chakra or "root chakra", as this is one of the most influential chakras in terms of world transformation and evolution at this time. Mastering this chakra is a key step in the development of self-sovereignty as well as optimally owning and consciously mastering our personal power.

1ST CHAKRA
ROOT CHAKRA
PRIMAL ENERGY
(FOUR PETALS)

Relates to survival, security and self-preservation instincts. A key component of being grounded. Supports the ability to live on the physical plane. Associated with our spinal column, kidneys and bones. Ruled by Saturn and Pluto. Associated element is earth. Located just below the genitals. Associated with the physical body auric layer which extends about four inches around the body. Also associated with the etheric body auric layer.

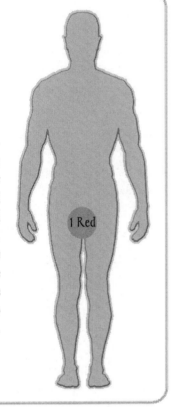

ROOT CHAKRA: The root chakra's main function is to keep us physically alive, safe and incarnate. It helps us manage our boundaries and personal territory, and it is also central to our process of threat management and pain avoidance. This chakra is the source of our primal energy, our ability to act assertively, and paradoxically also the source of dysfunctional fear, destructiveness and primal aggression. It is at this level that we manage our perceived power within our relationships and the surrounding society. This chakra is simple in its function and capabilities and has only four energy channels or petals. Its energetic color frequency is deep red, and it directly affects the adrenal glands. The root chakra is about self-preservation; it manages our fight-or-flight instinct and our motivations to remain safe and secure in any social situation. This chakra is also the source of our competitive and predatory nature, meaning that we humans are and have ever been predators. Still this ultimately ecologically detrimental tendency can be transcended.

318

The root chakra is associated with the reproductive organs in males and females and their sex drive. It is also where we manage our hierarchical power relationships with others, and perceive our position and status within the society and the groups we belong to, including our family. It is also potentially the foundation of our process of attaining and maintaining self-sovereignty via wise and discerning application of our personal power. Yet this can only happen if we attain consciousness at this root chakra level.

Until our root chakra's function is brought to a state of consciousness it may not congruently support us in functioning in an effectively sovereign manner. This can be due to low self-esteem, negative early life conditioning, fear of another's power, or self-judgments or self-hatred at subconscious levels. In these cases, we will be rendered unable to stand up for ourselves, feel confident, fully own our personal power, accept accountability for our own lives and choose to function independently from the influence of others and society.

One other key function of the root chakra is to help us to be mentally and emotionally grounded. Complete integrated groundedness is achieved with the help of our conscious intention and willpower via transcendence of fear. The main reason for being ungrounded is unresolved conscious or subconscious fear. After we resolve our fears and are well grounded, the root chakra provides us with fundamental experiential information and energy related to physical existence and life that is necessary to support wise decisions in day-to-day life. If ungrounded we may be rendered incapable of deeply understanding the fundamentals of life situations. If ungrounded we may be unable to take care of necessary yet mundane life tasks in a timely manner (for example, pay our bills on time, or keep and fulfill on agreements). If ungrounded we tend to function in a disorganized and unfocused manner. Common states of ungrounded function are states of perceived victimhood.

The root chakra's perspective is very limited and from this level of consciousness we can only perceive life from the level of physical existence and safety management. The root chakra does not have the capacity to understand existence beyond the physical, to love or experience compassion, or to realize that we are immortal spiritual beings who cannot truly die. Therefore, when functioning at the level of the root chakra we fear both death and abandonment.

The root chakra lacks the ability to realize the existence of God and aspects of spiritual existence beyond the physical realm. This is why the root chakra generates and feels fear, since from its perspective (and in a strictly physical way) we can cease to exist (die) at any time. So, the root chakra's fear tends to motivate and color many of our life interpretations, emotions, decisions and actions. It also keeps our minds focused on worldly rather than spiritual values and ways of making decisions.

As discussed earlier, the root chakra feels only two fears (all other life fears are just distorted reflections of these two). These are fear of death and its associated physical pain and suffering and feelings of loss, and the fear of abandonment with its associated pain of emotional loss. These two fear states actually shape much of our interpersonal and social behavior, as well as the structure of all societies, laws, economics and politics. This chakra even significantly affects the direction and development of science and technology.

The root chakra is so simplistic in its operation that it acts as a sort of "decision-making switch" that then determines our life options. Meaning that at the subconscious root chakra level we make decisions whether to love or to kill. For example, most of us "love" or at least feel positively toward puppies or kittens or other small cute cuddly animals and children. Many of us would not hesitate to kill a snake, a spider or a cockroach, or any other entity that we felt fundamentally threatened by. This decision is usually made reactively, subconsciously and out of fear. It is this same process which "turns off" our process of caring for others or the environment, when we see a chance for personal profit.

The root chakra is the mechanism that motivates us to opportunistically and blindly "capitalize" on any situation, whether financially, socially or interpersonally, without discerning regard for the consequences of doing so. The root chakra is also the source of all hierarchical views of society and relationship, tribal dynamics, prejudice, bias, and social or cultural exclusionary tendencies. It is this fundamental primal and simple mechanism that determines the decision as to whether an average person in the street, or a police officer, or a military person chooses whether or not to kill someone. When threatened, many of us will literally "switch off" our positive emotional processes, via the action of the root chakra, (i.e. our capacity for love, forgiveness, compassion, emotional understanding, sympathy or empathy). This decision is generally made without our even realizing that this process has taken place. Simultaneously we become open to fear, anger, jealousy and hatred, without understanding that this is happening. We will then be required to deal with the results of such choices, whether these effects are karmic, social or emotional in nature. We also tend to rationalize these choices as valid or necessary after making them and acting on them, since they were originally determined at the subconscious level.

320

It is useful to understand that there is a "gap of consciousness" that has existed within all of humanity for a very long time. This gap is seen between our conscious loving spiritual nature, (which if followed can ultimately result in enlightened God consciousness), and our often subconscious ego-identity based primal natures. This gap exists due to the tug of war between these two main unresolved and non-integrated aspects of our beings. Our root chakra is the main driver behind all ego-identity dynamics. These two key influences on our consciousness, our choices, our emotions and our process of learning as human beings are not truly at odds with each other. At the same time, these two motivating tendencies (Godliness and worldliness) act to pull our focus of consciousness and with it our free-will power to choose in two basically different directions. (i.e. When we are focused on spirituality we are often not well grounded in practical daily realities and thus not empowered to deal effectively with many of the negative conflicted and competitive dynamics of human existence. At the same time, when we are focused on the practical daily realities of survival, holding down a job, raising a family, etc. we have a difficult time living in a spiritually conscious state of unconditional love.

This is not a simple battle between "good and evil", and it is not just a polarized difference in perspective on life, value and relationship. This gap of consciousness represents a fundamental difference in what is valued, focused on and utilized as decision-making criteria, from moment-to-moment by all human beings. Therefore, the interactive dynamic between these two influences represents the main or key influencing factors on the destiny of this planet and its occupants. It is the lack of reconciling and fully integrating these main human motivations that has kept humanity from evolving more rapidly.

It is the lack of humanity's having consciously chosen to "peacefully close this overall gap of perspective, value and consciousness" that has brought us to this point in history. This situation must be transcended if humanity is to evolve further without massive conflict occurring. To close this gap there is a great deal of learning that needs to occur within the consensus consciousness of humanity, and this learning is to a degree being held back by the spiritual consciousness undermining influences of ego-identity focus.

In order to optimally evolve as a species, we must resolve this developmental discontinuity and fundamental competition between our worldly and spiritual aspects. Thus, we human beings will be required to more fully realize ourselves as spiritual beings. This is the only solution to the ongoing internal tug of war each of us faces between these fundamental aspects of our being. Most of us are not taught any sophisticated or complete method of reconciling these conflicted motivations in constructive ways. Therefore, we tend to express these unresolved conflicts at various levels of our systems in dysfunctional and non-constructive ways, and often in social situations.

The unreconciled gap within the larger spiritual consciousness of humanity and the larger primal nature of humanity leads to a sort of blindness on the part of each. Meaning that our spiritual nature is unable to fully grasp and integrate with the primal and often negative aspects of our systems and thus constructively heal and evolve them. In contrast our fear driven primal natures are often unmotivated and for this reason unable to grasp the more abstract nature and truths of our spiritual essence and reality. It is vital, for the future of all of humanity, that this gap be resolved, and for these seemingly disparate parts of our larger nature to be fully reconciled and integrated, if we want peace to prevail in all of humanity. This evolution of conscious perspective must occur not only in individuals, it must also be resolved in all religions, cultures, groups and nations. On the next page is a diagram depicting this conflicted evolutionary dynamic.

The root chakra is a part of our foundational subconscious cognitive and decision-making functions and is key to defining our perceived identity, social worth and self-worth, so it is very important to keep it clear and functioning properly. Yet currently everyone's negative karma (i.e. the cause and effect results of their prior choices) is bubbling up into their root chakras faster than in the past, and these energy patterns, along with the consensus consciousness karmic influences tend to "clog" our individual root chakras. Therefore, most people's lower chakras are impaired to some degree, which in turn affects their decisions, emotions, general outlook on life, feelings about themselves and their relationships.

Each of our chakras functions as a lens through which we perceive various aspects of our lives. Each chakra represents a specific level of consciousness and energy frequency. Each of our main chakras processes a specific level and type of energy and associated information about our lives and interpersonal experiences.

The root chakra is the least sophisticated, simplest and least positively oriented chakra for most people. As our higher chakras open (4th 5th, 6th and 7th), our sophistication of consciousness increases as well as our ability to love more deeply and unconditionally. Still even with our higher chakras open, our consciousness constantly and dynamically moves up and down through our chakras in reaction to life experiences and relationship dynamics. Therefore, our focus of consciousness often temporarily drops to the level of the root chakra (often due to fearful reactions to perceived life situations). When this occurs, we tend to lose sight of more positive and wise options and opportunities. We also lose the ability to choose and hold a loving and creative attitude as we become more primal, aggressive and personal safety focused.

During our day-to-day activities, we focus on life through one chakra lens at one moment and then on another aspect of life through another chakra. We are generally unaware of these transitions of consciousness, or the influence they have on our interpretations of life experiences, our relationships or our learning. It is possible however to consciously, wisely and intentionally manage our chakra systems and to willfully choose which chakra we view life through at any given moment. In this way we can become empowered to choose to apply the conscious viewpoint of a higher chakra to a situation where most people would usually react in a knee jerk manner with a lower chakra interpretation. This is an example of how subconscious reactions and impulses can be overcome to our benefit, and where, when and how the power of conscious willful intention can be wisely applied.

324

An example of this activity of consciously managing our chosen point of consciousness, in action, could be seen in the case of our losing a job that we and our family financially depended upon. In this situation, many of us would allow our level of consciousness to immediately drop to viewing life through our root chakra. (For example, we would tend to focus on the survival and social status aspects of our situation. We might interpret ourselves as a failure. We might even go into a state of fear for our safety and security). In this way, we might suddenly render ourselves emotionally unavailable to our spouse or our children, or become angry as our fear turns to frustration and desire for control over our lives. Although most of us would not act upon it, we might still angrily consider or fanaticize about vengeful actions toward the organization we previously worked for, especially if we felt betrayed or victimized by them. This is because our positive emotions and sophisticated relationship management functions are located and managed at higher levels of our chakra systems and are taken "off-line" by root chakra interference.

In these negatively emotionally charged situations, our point of consciousness is generally focused in our first or second chakra. This situation may only last for a moment, yet it still occurs in most of us and it influences our decisions, our life choice results and our potential for happiness. For some of us, these negative emotional states can go on for a lifetime. Learning to consciously, willfully and consistently manage our point of consciousness is one of the most empowering steps one can take to make their lives better and to function in a positive and sovereign manner.

There are wars and conflicts occurring on several continents at this time. We can choose to unconsciously react to these situations instinctively (meaning that we can let our fear driven root chakra rule our emotions and our point of view) and thereby hold a limiting root chakra view of these occurrences. This leads to fear and focus on our personal safety and security and that of our families or our nation and we may even hate the "enemy". If we react unconsciously in this way, we will effectively be rendered blind, defenseless, powerless and afraid to do anything creative, constructive, loving, forgiving and positive. True, we might be willing to fight and die for any of these causes, yet I would say this choice would be limiting, destructive, and will, in the end, not serve the collective good.

Rather than view world conflict from the point of fear we could just as easily choose to manage our focus of consciousness and raise it to the level of our hearts. In this way we can forgive our enemies, retain a clear perspective, and be empowered to create positive solutions to world challenges that do not involve emotional ego dynamics, fear or violence. If we all choose to function in this self-empowering way, then ultimately all of humanity can effectively climb out of the lower realms of unconsciousness forever. This is and has always been a choice that we all have the power to make or unmake at any moment of our lives.

A limitation in the root chakra's function is that it is simple and unconscious in its interpretive capacity, decision-making and cognitive ability. Therefore, it can inadvertently and literally work against our personal survival and safety in its attempts to achieve what it believes to be its purpose. These subconscious and unrealized influences of the root chakra create a tug of war between our positive and intelligent conscious intentions and unwanted subconscious negative emotions and behaviors. These internal battles can go on for years and create duplicitous dynamics.

In effect, we store a belief in our root chakra such as "I am only safe if I am perfect" or "I am only safe if I am accepted by everyone". Neither of these beliefs can truly and completely be fulfilled in reality. Therefore, they create ongoing stresses in life as we unsuccessfully try harder and harder to be perfect or to be accepted. This activity is literally an expression of addiction; in that we may feel we cannot stop operating in this way. The pain of this addiction then leads to other reactive stresses which can then lead to other types of addiction, such as drugs and alcohol, in order to reduce or manage the stress and pain of our internal conflict.

Sages from the ancient past have said that all attachment or aversion to anything in life limits our spiritual evolution and consciousness. Addictions can be seen as forms of attachment to desires or attempts to avoid something painful. It could be said that we are all addicted to something, to some degree, and to our detriment, even if it is a seemingly innocuous habit. Application of personal power can be best achieved without addictive attachment to any specific life results or desired emotional states. Habits of all kinds undermine consciousness. The numerous conflict-producing attachments to aspects of life each of us have are a key reason why the techniques in the book "The Secret" have not had total immediate effect in creating desired worldly realities, because while we want change we simultaneously fear losing the status quo. They are also reasons it is difficult for most of us to live in the "now".

The influences of the consensus consciousness, created from the history of humankind, could be seen as a giant form of addiction to the past and past ways of believing. For example, stubborn and detrimental attachments to traditional cultural or religious beliefs. If what we consciously want is in conflict with our preexisting beliefs then we will receive conflicted, diluted or limited results.

I perceive that most addictions are driven at their subconscious roots by:

❖ Recorded subconscious pain-producing misunderstandings, beliefs or expectations about life.

❖ A desire for, and a dysfunctional attempt to, escape or control some perceived threat, stress, problem, fear, or life/relationship pain or trauma (often subconscious and root chakra oriented in nature).

❖ Generational family patterns of addiction or family karmas. As in the children of alcoholics being more likely to themselves become alcoholics.

❖ Preexisting personal patterns of addiction from past-life karma (many of us have been addicted to various substances or relationships in past lives).

Beliefs Are Stored In Our Chakras:

We all have recorded beliefs stored in various parts of our systems and in every level of our chakras. Each of these beliefs usually has an emotional charge stored with it that drives us, and often the emotional charge is rooted in fear. These beliefs can either be consciously or subconsciously held. Oddly enough what we consciously believe can be directly opposed to what we subconsciously believe, then our beliefs generate resulting realities that are aligned with the conflicted beliefs. This dynamic creates a discontinuity between what we consciously think should happen in life and what actually does due to the influence of our subconscious beliefs. This happens because our subconsciously influenced choices undermine our conscious intentions. Attaining congruity between our conscious intentions and our subconscious beliefs brings personal power to manifest what we truly want to experience.

Once beliefs are recorded in our chakras, (especially our lower chakras), they influence the energy and function of these chakras profoundly. The importance of understanding this situation is that we tend to project onto the world what we believe to be true, through the energy of our chakras, even if what we believe is not good for us or others. When this happens, we influence and interpret the outer world to be more like we subconsciously believe it "should be", rather than it really is. If we have limiting or negative subconscious beliefs about life or relationships, then we tend to manifest those realities in our lives.

In relationships we actually attract others whose beliefs are in agreement with our own at subconscious beliefs. For example, I have seen situations in which a woman had the subconscious belief that she deserved nothing in a relationship. Yet she was at the time in an unhappy relationship with a man. This man had a subconscious belief that he was worth nothing. In this strange way they were in basic agreement with each other's beliefs and therefore subconsciously speaking "perfect for each other". Like or compatible beliefs and energies attract like beliefs and energies. This matching of subconscious beliefs does not mean we will be happy with each other; it only means that we are in agreement at a foundational level because we feel safe with those who agree with our beliefs. As stated earlier, each belief is directly related to a recorded simulacrum. We attract others if we have beliefs in common with and we then act as mirrors for each other in order to enhance our mutual spiritual evolution and learning from each other. Often without realizing the nature of this dynamic.

There are an infinite variety of matching and yet dysfunctional beliefs we can base relationships upon. I would suggest that it is important to identify our core relationship beliefs and that we then positively shift them to the point that they actually serve us well. Our beliefs also similarly affect what we manifest in regard to our work, our finances, and our dreams. Thus by changing our beliefs we can literally build the lives we want by changing our energy, emotions, decisions and ways of thinking for the better.

Root chakra reactions can be triggered, and this is what happens when someone "pushes our emotional buttons". It is useful to realize that just as individual humans have a trigger-able root chakra, the same is true of corporations, religions and nations. Americans, just like the citizens of all nations, are directly connected to and interactive with the root chakra of their nation. American citizens each constantly feed the national root chakra energy and belief information, and reciprocally the nation's root chakra constantly sends information and energy to its citizens.

When the 9/11 terrorist attacks happened, the root chakra of the American nation was traumatized. In like manner, the root chakra of each person in the United States was interactively affected and many were ultimately entrained by the fear and anger that built up in the nation's root chakra. This process led to unwise and costly war or attempt to "control that which we feared". This connection between our individual energy systems and the consensus consciousness energy system is always a two-way street. We citizens affect the nation's root chakra and it affects ours constantly.

This reflective dynamic is a key element of the evolution of individuals and that of the collective consciousness of nations. Unfortunately, few nations, corporations or religions have developed much more than their first or second chakra level of consciousness. So the group consciousness of all of these national and corporate entities is still unable to consistently function from a spiritual perspective or from divinely loving compassion, or even for the common global good. If groups have only the root chakra functioning they are systemically limited and therefore can always advocate judgmental violence of some form.

Most human organizations function only from the standpoint of organizational ego, control orientation, focus on continuous growth and increased power, the "financial bottom line", and organizational survival and security. This is why some of the most loving and sage efforts by individuals in these organizations often fall on deaf ears and are not translated directly and efficiently into improvements in organizational culture, policy, structure or decisions. The same is to some extent true of all human organizations and nations, and a main reason why they do not take environmental concerns into account until they themselves are directly threatened by them. Simply focusing on "growth or profit" no longer works as an organizational strategy or a national economic strategy when global resources become scarce and the environment is toxified. I have faith and hope that this situation will rapidly change for the better in the near future. At this time, this dynamic is representative of another learning disability.

Only through the process of consciously and systematically mapping our personal and social beliefs, interpersonal dynamics, control strategies, and subconscious agendas can we hope to become conscious enough to manage them. Each of these aspects of our mental and emotional systems creates a sort of self-perpetuating inertia or momentum, that also creates reflections of them in the physical world around us and in our relationships.

So, it is our internal map of the world that we constantly reference that creates our outer world situations. Therefore, our internal maps themselves are the source of the continuation of external detrimental world dynamics, such as continuing to pollute the world, even after we recognize that damage done by pollution. "Map inertia" and the social inertial dynamics of fear control strategies are the sources of most human ills and the reasons we do not effectively and constructively act to cure those ills.

We each enjoy a different quality and degree of consciousness, and due to the influence of subconscious beliefs, and chakra functions, our quality of consciousness is constantly changing. This dynamic has its benefits and yet remaining optimally conscious is always the better option. Clearing our systems of detrimental subconscious influences and developing our chakra system, opens new worlds of understanding which cannot be reached in any other manner. Having a fully developed energy system also gives us the opportunity to better enjoy life as well as to create life in ways we could previously not have conceived of. These self-developmental accomplishments ultimately support all phases of learning to own our personal power. This process can be a great adventure; I hope you enjoy it.

Humans as Super Predators:

Humans have many good qualities, not the least of which are empathy, sympathy, compassion, capacity to surrender to God and in doing so to exhibit the capacity to love unconditionally. That said, not all human beings consistently exhibit these good quality traits. One aspect of humanity that is often exhibited in various forms is that of a tendency to act in a predatory manner towards other human beings, or toward all of the other inhabitants of this planet. This tendency has become deeply engrained in the psyche of humanity and shows itself in many of our habits and behaviors. Predatory tendencies are taken in some venues to be a requirement for success and achievement, or can even be associated in some people's minds with personal or group safety.

In essence, predatory behaviors are a primal survival strategy that we need to outgrow as a species. I would suggest that ultimately filtering this detrimental tendency out of the human population is to our benefit. It is regrettably a "costly package deal" to participate in this primal and loveless mode. Meaning that we cannot function as a predator in some situations and assume that these habits, choices and tendencies will not detrimentally affect other aspects of our lives, our relationships and our world.

Human beings have been seen by some as "super predators", meaning that the process of predation that occurs constantly in our world's ecosystem, by humans, is seen to have in some way been better mastered than by us than by other species. This unbalancing mastery then creates imbalances throughout our world's ecosystem. This unbalanced predation dynamic leads to many downline domino effects, unforeseen and unintended consequences and potential long term down sides. Predation itself is instinctive, primal, opportunistic and personal survival oriented, it is also a state of perceived self-importance. A self-importance that outweighs all other considerations in our decision-making.

Therefore, predation, it is not a process of conscious intention, love or compassion, even if rationalized to be so. It is also not driven by a long-term view or understanding of reality, or our eco-system's health, or the implications of our choices. Therefore, predation is not a process of wisdom or discernment. One example of this type of the problematic aspects of the prey instinct is seen in the animal world in the regard to "tamed tigers" that have been raised by humans. Meaning that even a tiger that has been raised from birth, with constant love, to be tame, may in certain circumstances act in a predatory reactive and destructive manner toward humans. Traditionally conditioned "civilized humans and nations" can, in certain situations, be just as coldly predatory in their actions, decisions and viewpoints. Predation is unconscious violence in action, and humans have more capacity to be violent than any other species.

Predatory dynamics in human beings, and their implications and effects, are vital to understand if we want to live loving self-sovereign lives and ultimately to achieve world peace. There are blindly opportunistic aspects to the process of predation, which operate despite our best attempts to consciously harness and channel this dynamic in various ways. One way we have tried to channel predatory aggression and survival instinct is via tribalism and an outgrowth of it which we call the economic model of competitive capitalism. Making a living via competition in any form can be seen as a watered-down form social aggression. These influences are often rationalized as necessary, just or proper, _after_ the predatory dynamic has occurred. Therefore, predatory influences in human beings are inherently self-blinding and obscuring. Our ego-identities prefer to remain unaware of our competitive and predatory tendencies. If our ego-identities do realize these tendencies, we can self-judgmentally turn on ourselves for our own behaviors. Thus, we do not learn to function in more peaceful and constructive ways because we choose not to. Therefore, we do not learn easily or directly to fully transcend them.

When we operate in a predatory manner, our root chakra takes over our thinking and decision-making, and blinds us to the spiritual, emotional and moral truth and implications of our actions. Thus, when operating this way, we can harm, manipulate or even kill without remorse or clear understanding of our behaviors or actions and their karmic costs. Consciously recognizing these influences in our systems from moment-to-moment is crucial to their transcendence, both personally and globally.

Some examples of human predatory characteristics and dynamics are:

❖ A selfish or self-centered perspective toward benefitting oneself in any given situation or relationship.

❖ Being willing to opportunistically or ruthlessly use, exploit, manipulate, take advantage of, undermine or control any:

- Situation
- Relationship
- Person
- Group of people
- Aspect of our world including any facet of our ecosystem. Operating in a predatory manner includes the literal enslavement of human beings, including children, which is still going on in various parts of the world.

❖ Not consciously and with conscience recognizing the implications of our actions or choices.

❖ Not being in touch with our spiritual nature or our hearts when we make our decisions or take action.

❖ Powerful and blinding primal motivations "to get", to take, to achieve or "to have any specific experience of life" (i.e. to have what we want or desire, without regard to the influence of doing so on others or the world around us).

❖ An often cold and intellectualized perception or rationalization of the necessity of any action, choice, behavior or style of decision-making. This can include prioritizing the "bottom line" in business situations above the value or situations of all employees. It can also include making scientific research decisions without regard to potential harm.

❖ A tendency to rationalize one's choices without deep introspection as to their moral or spiritual meaning or implication, this includes all acts of physical, social or emotional violence.

❖ Attempting to damage, destroy or manipulate other people's reputations, self-esteem, personal power or freedoms. Therefore, predation can be exhibited emotionally, socially, physically, psychologically and even spiritually, (i.e. as in cults and destructive religions).

Predation is a core element of the human consensus consciousness that has evolved via the social dynamic of tribalism. Tribalism has over time become somewhat more complex in its operation as humans have evolved socially, philosophically, politically and technologically. Tribalism is still a main influence on how societies and cultures develop, operate and evolve. It is important to recognize that tribalism is, at its core, highly resonant with instinctive predatory tendencies. Therefore, tribalism is a form of social organization and management and its dynamics are therefore a form of social technology designed to enhance the potential for survival.

By social technology I am not speaking of "social media softwares" like Facebook.com, Twitter.com, Snapchat.com or Instagram.com, although these computerized technologies are fundamentally changing how society operates in their own ways. Still we can see the predatory instincts of humanity played out in these technological arenas, (i.e. cyber bullying and aggression in all of its forms). I am speaking of new social technologies and models of social evolution, social education, social interaction and engagement, social transformation, development and ways of managing organizations, cultures and societies. We need better social technologies than tribal based technologies. New forms of social technology can be supported by computer technology and the internet and already has been shown to perform this function. By developing and applying new social technologies we can gain the capacity to intelligently engineer the evolution of humanity, not to control its development, only to facilitate it in an optimally wise, informed and empowered manner.

The tendency toward social violence and judgmentalism of all kinds is built right into our language(s), and we often use language to exact this violence. Language is our default mechanism of condemnation, criticism, social and interpersonal abandonment, judgment and punishment.

Fear and its domino effect emotion of hatred generates feelings of "I have to" in our internal dialog and emotions, as in "I have to protect myself" or "I have to survive". This reactive dynamic creates an internalized perspective of there being no other option other than that of harming, destroying or killing others, self or aspects of the world, and our ecosystem. This is just another facet of human's predatory dynamic.

Paradoxically, being on the winning side in elections is seen by some as being directly associated with survival of various kinds, (i.e. our jobs, our values and beliefs, and our social agendas. Thus, when this misunderstanding of life occurs we may react with hatred of the perceived enemy, political group or mode of governance. Thus, we cannot see from the vantage point of unconditional love in our hearts, and therefore cannot realize that our spiritual nature has effectively been shut down by our fear.

This primal predatory fear dynamic drove the decision to drop atomic bombs on perhaps hundreds of thousands of <u>non-combatant Japanese citizens</u> living in the cities of Hiroshima and Nagasaki. Today the United States has still not apologized for this action, and many people see no reason to do so and that nothing "wrong" was done. If we as a nation feel guilt or shame for this prior choice we tend to suppress it, and this suppression can manifest as unreconciled and irreconcilable self-hatred. When we cannot learn or understand our way out of any situation detrimental situation or prior choice it can lead to the emotion of hatred. We also hate ourselves and others when our safety strategies don't "control" perceived threats and the problems we perceive cannot be resolved via control. Such conflicted situations can only be transcended spirituality. The emotion of hatred just wants to reactively destroy those it cannot deal with, understand or work with safely. Inability to deal constructively with complex social issues often generates hatred. This profound dynamic can even include parents hating their children if they cannot control or understand them. Parents can hate themselves for not knowing how to be a "good parent" when they have unreconciled conflict with their children. For all of the above reasons I would suggest that predatory tendencies of all kinds be transcended. We can achieve this, we need only choose to, and commit to, doing so. We are all worth it.

Fear leads to the desire for control so that we can feel safe. We judge others in order to give us the rational to control and punish those who we fear. Still this dynamic does not lead to being able to truly control perceived threats. When threats don't go away due to our judgmental efforts, then we feel we must hate, in order to effect control, in order to then be safe. Predation and hatred are self-reinforcing, self-validating and self-rationalizing processes. Which has created a sort of indelible tendency in the human consensus consciousness, which is resonated with by individuals, to validate the supposed usefulness of hatred. Hatred has been human's default safety strategy. We tend to hold onto our hatred for long periods of time, and we fear others holding onto their hatred. So, you may ask yourself, how can I give up hating as a defensive option if no one else is giving up their hatred? My answer is that it must start somewhere, with someone if we want to transcend it. Christ was a very good example of this loving way of life.

Hatred is often used to punish those we perceive to be "bad". Acting in violence and destructiveness and <u>thus hatred</u> toward those who are perceived to be bad or evil is, in a distorted way, seen as goodness and a necessary way to remain safe. Global problems that seem too big to deal with and thus threatening, can therefore lead to the most destructive emotions, energies and judgmentalness. Condemnation of others is often used as the go to method of expressing hatred, in order to be seen as good or better than others. All predatory tendencies and hatred are the enemy of love and compassion.

Chapter Ten
The Aspects of Human Transformation

HUMANITY'S HISTORIC MODE OF LEARNING IS ONE OF - recording in our memories the ongoing interpretations, related emotions and basic information from our day-to-day individual experiences (simulacra). When I speak of learning I am not merely referring to the learning that occurs when we are taught by a teacher, read a book or watch a new television show, although these can be sources of significant insight. What we learn from our life experiences and relationships is different in many ways from institutionalized learning because experiences tend to deeply, foundationally and subconsciously affect and imprint us over the course of a lifetime. These imprints can support and lead us to the eventual attainment of wisdom, understanding, deep insight, capacity to create and personal power. Conversely, they can create fundamental limitations in belief, consciousness and capacity to understand any situation.

Experiential learning is powerful and occurs as the result of multilevel chakra processing of information and energy. Making the most of our experiential learning opportunities helps us to see deeply into ourselves and others at all levels of our being. In the process of interpreting and working with our experiences we can gain great insights into our own unique ways of assimilating information. Technology today is directly affecting how and what we learn, yet even our most advanced technology cannot replace experience-based modes of attaining comprehensive astute understanding. Yet there are other "technologies" available that facilitate learning, such as yoga and meditation, which can improve the efficacy of this system of experience-based development.

Oddly enough, experiential learning is often so subtle and transparent to our consciousness that we do not always realize learning is occurring. Many of us simply live our lives without carefully or comprehensively examining the inner workings of our lives and emotions, and thereby miss out on a fantastic opportunity. I suggest that proactively, methodically, efficiently and constructively "connecting the dots" or linking our experiences and associated knowing that comes from them can assist in the achievement of deep understanding of self and life. Despite our often-disjointed process of learning from life experiences they can still be cathartic. If we wish to own our personal power, let's consciously understand the nature of our power and how it is created via learning from experience. Then we can begin to understand how our power works, what supports its function and how it can be constructively focused and applied in our lives.

A useful quote for this point in our discussion was inscribed long ago on the entrance to the temple of Apollo at Delphi; it reads simply "Know Thyself". If we unconsciously experience life, then we can easily miss the sometimes-subtle influences of our preexisting karmic patterns and the various influences of aspects of our ego-identities and subconscious parts. If these influences occur without our awareness we will not optimally utilize them for our learning or also fully transcend them. All of these recorded patterns and what we can understand from their existence in our lives, similar to the influence of our chakras, form a ladder we can climb to sagacious consciousness.

If we choose to remain unconscious, we may not grow to understand how we can proactively and willfully heal ourselves, and then reorganize and integrate ourselves and the various aspects of our being. Thus we cannot transform into sovereign, discerning, self-reliant individuals, who consciously own and discerningly wield our power. Experimenting with new ways of thinking, interpreting, deciding, managing our life information and experiences in order to more readily learn from our lives, ahead of the world's change curve, can be quite productive, enjoyable and satisfying. It can also serve the greater good, as we can become optimally prepared service-oriented contributors to the global transformational dynamic.

For most of us our day-to-day life experiences occur in repetitive and cyclic manners. We go to work, day after day. We interact with family members, day-after-day, and we have repeatedly triggered emotional reactions to all of these situations. In each of these repeated life situations we also repeat our personal interactive patterns and behavioral tendencies such as being kind and empathetic or angry and judgmental. In this way, we tend to reactively move in and out of our unconscious ego-identity parts. This constantly influences our chosen point of consciousness, thus our point of understanding, interpretation and decision-making fluctuates from chakra to chakra and level of consciousness to level of consciousness continually.

When we are in our ego-identity strategies and parts we often literally become less intelligent, in that our ego function directly shuts down our upper level chakra functions. This process undermines more astute or sophisticated states of consciousness that our upper chakras are capable of. What most people experience as their "conscious mind," is, for most of us, a

338

constantly fluctuating and limited state and degree of reactive mental, emotional and energetic function. This dynamic limits our personal power and practical capability as we move from our ego-identity parts to higher degrees of consciousness at upper level chakras, and then back to ego. The quality of mind we experience from moment-to-moment, and its associated capabilities, become the determining factor in the degree and quality of the personal power we have available to apply to any situation. Then this power defines the quality of our results. Our quality of mind and emotion also then determines our degree of self-sovereignty, moment-by-moment and the way we choose to apply our freewill.

And so, the quality of our freewill and personal empowerment is simultaneously based upon:

* Our quality of chakra function and development at each level of our chakra system.
* How much balanced male and female energy our root chakra allows to flow to our higher chakras.
* What limiting karmic patterns are currently in place in our systems.
* What subconscious beliefs, subconscious personality parts, emotions and patterns are currently triggered and influencing our consciousness, and what we are focused on now.
* How capable we are of consciously and intentionally managing the chakra level of our moment-by-moment point of consciousness. This is because the level of our point of consciousness determines which chakra lens we look at any situation or relationship through.
* Our consciously chosen and willful intention in the moment.
* What lens of identity, self-image or social image identity we are viewing the situation through.
* How sovereignly centered within ourselves we are and non-influenced by other's beliefs, expectations and desires we are.
* How much discernment, capacity to focus and discipline we have acquired up until this point in our lives.
* How grounded we are in the present moment.

What in an optimally functioning and clear human being would be termed sage mental function can in some cases become significantly diminished, distorted, negative and limited in certain cases. For example, in situations where we feel, interpret and act on anger, control, fear or jealousy, we act to our detriment. In addition, we hold ourselves back by our tendency to repeatedly project onto all aspects of our lives and our relationships what we subconsciously believe, assume and expect, although we usually do not consciously realize we are doing so.

We can unknowingly and subconsciously misdirect ourselves and simultaneously do not see or experience all of what is happening in the present moment. Thus many of us tend to live out much of our lives with the behavior patterns, habits, emotional tendencies and information that we learned as children. We acquire many of these attributes or tendencies directly from our parents or primary caregivers. We then tend to repeat the same behaviors because we make the same misinterpretations of our life experiences that our parents did. We operate this way even if our behaviors are repeatedly proven to be interpersonally or financially costly, inaccurate, detrimental, non-applicable or socially inappropriate.

This same detrimental dynamic occurs in many marriages. In these relationships, we draw to us someone that is similar to one of our parents and then project onto them, over and over, our subconscious beliefs and unresolved detrimental emotional patterns. We do this to someone we consciously love, to the detriment of the relationship. In this way we continually try to "cookie cut" our spouse to fit our subconscious preconceptions of life. We may also unknowingly project these patterns onto teachers, bosses, friends or coworkers. Therefore, although the players in our personal karmic plays are different at various stages of our lives, the plot remains the same.

This activity of projecting the past onto the present can reinforce those previously learned interpretations as being more true (even if they are patently false). This intensification of subconscious belief can tend to have even more limiting effect on our overall perspectives on life, how we make our decisions and how we apply our personal power. In effect the repeated misinterpretations that we record in our memories become deeply engrained subconscious interpretive habits. These interpretive habits therefore become addictions to our own habitual detrimental thought patterns and inaccurate map of reality. All of these individual belief systems and interpersonal/social constructs are of course artificial. Meaning we each construct them via our life choices and often our interpretations and recordings of our parents' choices rather than their being created by nature or based upon any more accurate, valid, constructive or useful interpretation of reality.

Nothing that we record in our memories or learn from life is either right or wrong, nor is it either good or bad per se. It is simply either more or less useful or supportive of our personal and collective understanding, attainment

340

of power and co-creative capacities, joy and our capacity to love divinely. It is also more or less useful in our soul's ultimate attainment of enlightenment.

In the past, the truth or validity of conditioned social and mental constructs such as cultural traditions, was rarely questioned. Even today this tendency to suppress questioning the basic beliefs of culture, political systems, educational systems and even family values is widespread in all human populations. We are simply expected take them to be true, and these beliefs and patterns in turn affect our decision-making at subconscious levels, often with great intensity. This creates strong yet limited emotional motivations and associated actions and results. Because of these dynamics there is a tendency among human beings to try to retain the status quo, no matter how dysfunctional the situation. Although it tends to feel safer for individuals and groups to retain the status quo, it is ultimately a key limitation on the global transformational process.

Many beliefs, values and traditions are wonderful, yet if the implications of holding to them is not well understood and managed, their existence can hobble our development as a species. It is a challenge to recognize when we are making our daily life choices based upon these underlying mental and emotional constructs. It is also worthwhile.

These subconscious constructs are in many cases nothing more than simple recordings of our parents' best guesses, assumptions or beliefs about how to live life, and to interact in relationships. These constructs accumulate in a layered manner, within each individual, as we grow up, and through our experiences we continually add to our subconscious store house of information or misinformation. This activity is often equated with acquiring wisdom, truth and knowledge although it often does not fulfill that function.

We often consciously forget our most fundamental or influential childhood learning and decisions and push them down into the subconscious, where they continue to powerfully affect our life interpretations and decisions. This is especially true with unresolved traumatic experiences that we do not want to re-experience through memory, thus they remain unresolved.

It is these patterns that fundamentally affect the degree of happiness we enjoy later in life as well as our most key life decisions, emotions, experiential interpretations and perspectives. Like the air around us, which we move through every moment of the day, these subconscious activities have become transparent to our conscious minds and most of us like to keep it that way. This is how and why people's ego-identity elements have such strong influence on their life actions and decisions. The ego-being made up of all this "recorded stuff" which we assume to be accurate, transcendently important, useful and unquestionable and which we then project onto our lives and relationships. We even develop elaborate ego-identity perspective self-defense mechanisms, designed to keep the misinformation we have recorded active, unchanged, in place and unquestioned.

In this way we feel the safety of continuity of ego-identity and life perspective, even though what we have recorded and continually apply to our life decisions can actually wreak havoc on our lives. Yet even in the face of vast mental, emotional or financial difficulties, we usually don't choose to realize we are engaged in this activity even as it is happening.

Moving Beyond the Seduction of Perceived Safety:

As individuals and as groups we continually attempt to apply our belief constructs to our decisions, relationships, careers and life experience as we grow older. We often try to make our present reality submit to our early life beliefs rather than formulating new and more accurate and functional interpretations and/or beliefs based upon new experiences of the present moment. A similar dynamic occurs when scientists try to make the facts they are studying fit their theories rather than their theories fit the facts. This tendency inhibits our process of learning. It is useful to note that individuals, organizations and even nations learn in a similar fashion. This is because all national cultures and all organizational cultures have a group consciousness which has absorbed information, beliefs and misinformation since their inception. Then any misinformation and misperceptions that have been recorded are worked with as if they were true, to the organization's collective detriment.

WINGED STATE OF FREEDOM

LIBERATION FROM HUMAN DRAMA

LEVEL 10	self-sovereignty
LEVEL 9	authentic personal power
LEVEL 8	shift in consciousness
LEVEL 7	personal authenticity established

NEW PHASE BEGINS

| LEVEL 6 | a breakthrough of surface illusions occurs |

BREAKOUT PHASE

LEVEL 5	uses conditioned social and mental constructs of cultural traditions to define or describe life
LEVEL 4	ignorant of collective illusions
LEVEL 3	accept perceived limitations
LEVEL 2	governed by safety/control mechanisms
LEVEL 1	subconscious, primal function

THE PROCESS WE EXPERIENCE WHEN WE "WAKE UP" IS SIMILAR TO AN INSECT THAT FIRST EXPERIENCES A LARVAL STAGE UNDER WATER, THEN MUST FIGHT TO BREAKTHROUGH THE SURFACE TENSION OF THE WATER, AND THEN EXPERIENCES A WINGED STATE OF FREEDOM.

We as individuals may work to validate or even fight for our recorded belief constructs, even if it means physically attacking or invalidating someone else's beliefs, decisions or ways of living. Our underlying motivations for functioning in this manner are rarely conscious, positive, beneficial or even truly moral. When this activity occurs, we do so because we feel fundamentally unsafe, threatened, and we desire to validate our feeling of safety (not the reality of safety) by refusing to accept new information. It is useful to be aware that we are most negatively emotionally triggered and impacted when our false or inaccurate beliefs are exposed publicly as clearly false. This emotionally conflicted state often leads to the reaction of denial of the new information that is invalidating our previously held belief.

Still we do not usually mind invalidating other's beliefs and perspectives on life, and may even do so with a certain self-righteous zeal. (As in "I feel good about myself because I have set them right or fixed their wrong perspective"). In this way our personal ego self-defense mechanisms blind us to the pain we cause others, and from seeing their perspectives clearly, and thus validating them to be equal to our own. When it comes to beliefs, it does not have to be a win/lose situation, though we often feel that in a fundamental or primal way that it does, in order for us to feel safe, and thus we try to make it so. If we believe that others must change their beliefs to match ours then we will attempt to control, influence, manipulate or even force them to do so. This type of approach does not respect other's God-given right of freewill. Rather than educating others, it creates conflict, mistrust, miscommunication, misunderstanding, low self-esteem and fragments relationships and society.

In our attempts to apply the preconceptions we acquired in our youth, to our current lives, the lives of others and to our environment, we often find that our preconceptions do not exactly "fit", and thus we may try even harder to "shave off the corners of reality" to match our preconceptions. In this way we may work to force our beliefs onto others, our relationships or onto our perceived social situations. This detrimental yet seductive tendency often takes place in a manner that motivates us to completely and purposely ignore key elements of situations or relationships. In these situations, we intently and sometimes righteously project our expectations onto the world.

This process occurs when we try to help someone with advice which does not actually fit their situation, yet we can get trapped by pushing our idea despite our growing realization that it was not a truly beneficial idea to begin with. Or when we are managing other people in an organization and run into difficulties. Then rather than listening to other's ideas on a topic we continue to push harder to make our way of approaching the situation "work". We may continue to push even if it costs more, causes conflict, decreases interpersonal trust, and diminishes teamwork and the other's self-esteem, and thus organizational function.

This dynamic also occurs when children witness a cherished parental belief or perspective proven invalid or inaccurate, and openly state so to their parent, which then leads to conflict. Then, rather than accepting the child's clearer insights, adults may react with the desire to control them and prove them wrong. The parent may even get angry and tell the child that they are wrong or that since they are not an adult they cannot really understand what adults go through or understand, (i.e. "do as I say, not as I do"). In effect our ego self-defense mechanisms deny and obstruct our own learning and acquisition of new understanding, and we pass those attributes on to our children.

The silver lining to attempting to project our preconceptions onto reality is that the attempt to project always brings with it some degree of reflective insight, via conflict, though this result may not be our conscious intention at the time. Our awareness of the aspects of reality that do not fit our preconceptions always cause us some degree of internal reactive unease, conflict, pain, disharmony or perceivable imbalance. It is these uncomfortable experiential fragments that we may partially notice, though we rarely initially fully grasp their relevance, and thus we tend not to initially completely understand their meaning. Therefore, despite our best subconscious efforts at denying that which doesn't fit our preconceptions, we do acquire an ongoing database of new and increasingly conflict producing information.

Although this newly acquired information is recorded in our systems at some level we still tend to invalidate or ignore it. We do this because acceptance of the pieces of the puzzle of reality that do not fit our preconceptions would tend to directly invalidate our cherished beliefs, assumptions and preconceptions. This situation would then result in fear, uncertainty and insecurity and potential self-judgment for having been "wrong" about our prior beliefs. Again, the innate primal desire to feel safe seduces us and tends to trump conscious awareness and acquisition of deep understanding that might lead to actually being *more safe* via wise, accurate understanding.

Eventually we do acquire sage conscious understandings and new ways of interpreting and understanding self, others and life from the process of reflection upon that which we experience in life that does not fit our preconceptions. This gradual dynamic of achieving new understanding then eventually trumps the previous non-optimal subconscious emotional drives and beliefs, and supports foundational change in perspective and behavior.

Still this attained state of conscious awareness of our underlying motivations and beliefs and the attained willful intention to transcend them usually occurs only after repeatedly going through the same non-adaptive and often painful cycle of trying to apply our preconceptions onto reality. One additional result of these shifts in consciousness is that life and relationship information that previously was denied, ignored, filtered, devalued or not effectively acted upon suddenly tends to take on new meaning. Like the gears lining up inside a clock, our decision-making and behaviors related to this information also shift and we are freed from our prior state of ignorance.

This process is of course not a simple process of "learning lessons", though I do see it as part of a larger form of integrative gestalt learning. This is a process of gradual acquisition of understanding and enlightenment from many often-disparate experiences and influences. To go about it optimally and proactively, and with intention, requires conscious, comprehensive, coordinated, analyzed self-evaluation. It also requires collection of interpretations from potentially years of self-observation in interaction with other people, and the acquisition of a good bit of environmental and interpersonal feedback. It then culminates in our finally coming to the point where we exact our conscious will on our process of perceiving our situation in order to see it differently than we previously have, and then to act in a different manner.

The long-term result of these gradual shifts in consciousness would typically be a fundamental shift in perspective about life and relationships. If we go about this activity in an unconscious and reactive manner the shifts may take years, and yet they can appear to be instantaneous moments of transcendent understanding or ascensions, as people have cathartic shifts in understanding. Still many of us may not realize the multitude of steps that brought us to that transcendent moment of powerful insight.

I have developed methods of rapidly facilitating this cathartic shifting of consciousness and changing behavior in others. I do understand that many of us may equate learning with the simple acquisition of pieces of information or concepts (as in learning lessons in the traditional institutionalized educational sense) yet this is not what I am referring to.

346

This overall consciousness development process could just as easily be described as:

- ❖ Attainment of accurate and comprehensive awareness
- ❖ A foundational shift in consciousness
- ❖ Evolution of consciousness
- ❖ Release of illusionary states of mind
- ❖ Transcendence of limiting karmic patterns of consciousness
- ❖ Transcendence of limiting beliefs or limiting habitual mental or emotional states
- ❖ Dismantling simulacra constructs

I would describe the attainment of discerning and astute understanding as a very multidimensional and multifaceted form of organized learning from all aspects of life. This path of attainment ultimately leads to comprehensive shifts in what we could refer to as consciousness or perspective in all fundamental aspects of life.

In this consciousness building endeavor, we are required to become aware that some portion of our internal construct or map of reality has not been working as well as it could, or is not balanced or aligned. For example, we may have come to believe that we lack power in life or in our relationships due to our early life experiences of other's successfully applying their power toward us (such as parents, teachers, those in authority, etc.). So, some of us may adopt a consistent and generalized perception of personal powerlessness and low self-esteem. Later we may find this perspective does not serve us in attaining our goals, and thus we may eventually learn enough to realize that this perspective of powerlessness is false and only a chosen belief. We may then gradually begin to notice just how much power we really do have, and may then choose to use our power more wisely and compassionately than we felt others did to us. We may even eventually choose to change all of our patterns of thought and belief, and thus re-write our life story in a more functional, self-empowering manner that actually does serve our perceived needs and desires. Optimally acquiring these new states of functional understanding requires them to then be integrated into all levels of our daily life, decision strategies and levels of our chakras. When this result occurs in a comprehensive manner we become able to proactively and consciously mold our lives to meet our consciously perceived needs and desires.

This cyclic activity of attempting to apply our internal reality construct to life will be repeated over and over until we consciously and willfully choose to rewrite our internal map of reality in a more accurate and empowering way. It is therefore useful to see this manner of acquiring more functional understandings about life as an ongoing method of mapping and re-mapping our recorded reality in ever more accurate ways, and documenting what we learn from this action in our conscious memories.

Intentionally Creating Beneficial Patterns:

We may fear changing our beliefs and methods of decision-making because we have nothing better with which to replace them. We may resist change because we fear change in general, or we fear the specific change may be disempowering, or we may not believe we deserve better than we have. However, we do eventually become increasingly aware of how non-constructive the beliefs, roles or values we have been working with are as we continue to erroneously apply them. We tend to reach this awareness of non-applicability of our roles or beliefs and their associated decisions, behaviors and emotions ever more quickly with each cyclic repetition. This ongoing repetitive cycle gradually results in a reduction in cycle time of our developing awareness that the old pattern does not work.

Of course, reaching this realization of a belief or pattern's dysfunction can be repeatedly emotionally stressful or frustrating, yet it is ultimately beneficial. Meaning our emotional pain ultimately creates awareness of our dysfunction. Speeding up our attainment of the understanding the dysfunction of the particular belief (simulacra), value or role is necessary so that we may more quickly discard it, and choose to create a new and beneficial pattern.

By repetitively practicing what does not work, we gain the ability to put the pieces of the subconscious process together ever more quickly and thus consciously and more rapidly reach and change the understanding that it is not working. This process will continue until we learn to immediately recognize the whole dysfunctional cyclic pattern with all of its detrimental aspects and implications, and are then empowered and motivated to instantly and comprehensively choose to do something else. At this point we could say that the cycle time of our understanding that the old pattern does not work reaches zero. Meaning we reach a point where we comprehensively understand the pattern in terms of its overall characteristics, sequence of steps, usual results and the detrimental implications of those results.

At this point we feel adequately confident and motivated in choosing to consciously and willfully intervene in our own life cycle and override the old pattern, role, rule or belief, before it has an opportunity to be played out again to our detriment. In doing so we move off the wheel of karma in regard to that specific pattern and can access new choices and thus create new and more positive resulting experiences. We then feel confident in choosing to define and apply a more functional or useful role, rule, belief or behavior.

This newly defined and potentially more positive pattern will then eventually become more and more habitual and unconscious through repeated use. A better way to proceed in life would be to simply choose to remain pattern-less and belief-less by choosing to remain consistently conscious in our interpretations and decision-making from moment-to-moment. We would thereby be divested of the need to subconsciously react in accordance with a set of predetermined patterns, rules, roles, interpretive lenses or beliefs.

The method of efficiently reaching the zero point in the cycle in each of our subconscious patterns is the essence of quality human experiential learning. Until the zero point is reached, major and lasting life change often does not occur, as we continue to cyclically repeat the same old patterns over and over, even in completely new situations. This learning process applies in the same way to individuals, groups, corporations and nations.

Reaching the zero point in regard to understanding the dysfunctionality of any of our patterns can be achieved either through persistent trial and error, or through proactive, conscious, disciplined and even meditative effort. In effect more positive results can be arrived at by consciously choosing to map, reevaluate and positively redefine our beliefs from moment-to-moment, via the belief mapping process defined in Chapter Eight. To achieve this useful goal, we must consciously formulate and maintain a disciplined intention to do so. In addition, we must apply effective methods, such as analytical meditation, mindfulness meditation, and emotional introspection to facilitate ourselves in better understanding our subconscious patterns.

This learning dynamic affects our learning as children and as adults. Everything we learn in a lifetime, via institutions of higher learning, may at some point be found to be false, inaccurate, obsolete or non-applicable to our reality. Though if openly expressed, this understanding of the limitations of the educational institutions could produce conflict when interacting with existing educational authority. Educational authority traditionally and culturally does not tend to enjoy being openly questioned regarding its fundamental usefulness, method, accuracy or validity. This is an example of institutional ego-dynamics in action.

Yet in our current experience-based model of acquiring understanding and wisdom, until we reach the zero point in any particular learning cycle, we tend to refuse to acknowledge the inconsistencies of our recorded patterns with reality. We also tend to deny or minimize their associated negative results or influences, and thus we may live with the less than optimal results in all areas of life and relationships until the pain of doing so eventually motivates us to change.

Learning What To Be By First Learning What Not To Be:

Do we learn best by making mistakes? My perspective is that learning via the self-defeating tendency to interpret our life choices as mistakes is not learning at all. Yet many of us have been trained to interpret even our most well intentioned life choices, which then do not turn out as desired or expected, as mistakes. When we do so we unknowingly turn against ourselves to our detriment. We may even see parts of ourselves as "problems" to be fixed, rather than as lovable aspects of ourselves that we just need to understand better. When we do arrive at conscious understanding of our subconscious parts we become empowered to change and optimize their functionality.

A more accurate way of expressing this aspect of the human learning process (meaning attaining understanding via evaluating the results of our choices) would be to see it as a cyclic activity of learning what not to do or be. In human learning and evolution there are no mistakes; we are simply all experiencing a continual refinement of our understanding, values, wisdom, consciousness and intention via interpreted and recorded life experiences via trial and error. From this perspective we could say there is no true right or wrong, only our experience-based spiritual evolutionary process, which is constantly in a process of unfoldment and coming to fruition.

Certainly, each of us explores many blind alleys in our attainment of sagacious understanding, meaning we try out non-adaptive or non-constructive ways of being, acting, making decisions, feeling or interpreting life. However, we would not have made these supposedly wrong choices if we had already known better. Once we understand better, via the catalytic and gestalt educational influence of acquired experience, we cease to make negative or unfruitful choices, and we can cease to react to life with negative emotion. This is a process of growing discernment and a method by which people eventually attain enlightenment.

Enlightenment has been defined in many ways throughout history; here it is defined as the achievement of a state of:

1. Conscious oneness and resonance with God and all of humanity at all levels of our chakras and being.

2. Full conscious self-awareness and inner peace, including freedom from all suffering.

3. Unconditional, pristine or pure divine love and respect for all aspects and levels of ourselves and all other beings. (transcendence of all negative emotion, fear judgmentalness and desire for control).

4. Consistent joy.

5. Conscious understanding and acceptance of all aspects of life, evolution and God (meaning a state of realization of ultimate spiritual truth).

6. Transcendence of all simplistic dualistic or polarized thinking (i.e. right/wrong, true/false, safe/unsafe, male/female, us/them, better than/less than others, etc.).

7. Freedom from the karmic cycle and the need to reincarnate in order to learn or evolve. (By this statement, I do not mean that human beings are required to, in any way, transcend an inherently flawed nature, as we are all perfect as we are, all the time, at every step of our soul's evolution. I do mean that the system of soul education we have chosen and refer to as karma either must run its course or be transcended in some manner for enlightenment to occur).

All of us have experienced seemingly unfortunate aspects of our lives. We may have felt abandoned, abused, misunderstood, wounded, victimized, hurt, judged or disempowered in some way or to some degree. We could look at these experiences as the process of our karma unfolding. As stated previously, karma is never about punishment, karma is about setting up challenging circumstances that we then grow and evolve from by transcending them. Paradoxically each of these experiences is a fantastic opportunity for personal development and achievement of understanding and empowerment if we are just willing to interpret and work with them as such.

The eventual result of all our perceived suffering is to learn how to divinely love. Just as a grain of sand irritates an oyster to create a pearl, our remembered negative experiences and emotional suffering eventually motivates us to become the conscious beautiful beings we all have the potential to be. In these lives it has never been about who we were or what we have done or experienced, it has always been about who we have the potential to become. For example, if we are the child of angry, blaming alcoholics, then we are provided with a huge opportunity to learn to how not

351

to treat others, how <u>not</u> to see or interact in relationships, the ultimate emptiness of drama, and how <u>not</u> to make life choices.

In the process of transcending life's challenges, we have the potential to achieve self-mastery, to develop self-discipline, to forgive and to focus on developing our personal sovereign nature. We are also required by this process to delve deeply into our emotional processes, to transcend our own addictive and codependent tendencies, to constructively work with our negative emotions and to better understand many foundational aspects of relationships. We may also ultimately become motivated to create a very powerful capacity to divinely love and trust ourselves, and to hold this state of consciousness, in spite of any negative relationship or social circumstance. Had our soul not chosen to be born into challenging conditions, we would not have been motivated by circumstance to achieve empowering understandings, and thereby attain the courage and strength that comes with them. Though our souls may choose immense life challenges, that does not mean we are ever "victims of ourselves". It only means that our souls know how strong we really are, the value of achieving profound understanding, and what we are really capable of achieving and transcending our goals.

If we were orphaned and then lived a youth of perceived abandonment, or were abandoned by our parents early in life, we might be required to learn a great deal about self-reliance and independence, personal sovereignty, and management of our emotions and courage. I have repeatedly worked with people in this circumstance and found that some have, due to their pain, chosen to deeply value their personal relationships with great dignity, integrity, and consistent focus, and also to be great parents to their own children. In this way, through transcending our painful life experiences, we come to see the value of more loving ways of being and of caring about others.

To create positive relationships, we might be required to work with the wounded aspects of ourselves, and in this way to achieve wisdom, discernment, understanding of ourselves and compassion for others. It could be argued that in order to truly help anyone else we must first deeply understand ourselves and our own pain. Therefore, painful circumstances can be very beneficially motivating. Had we not had these experiential reference points for orientation and interpretation there are many deeper aspects of life we would not come to understand. In fact, our sometimes painful life experiences literally guide us in our attainment of understanding.

There are those of us who were physically, emotionally or sexually abused as children. As far as I have determined, from my work with clients, this type of abuse is the most difficult hurdle for anyone to transcend, and is simultaneously a very common occurrence around the world. Paradoxically the people I work with who have had these experiences are often the most emotionally self-aware and motivated to heal and grow. I have also seen a profound spiritual seeking and tendency for self-development in them. It could therefore be said that even in these most dire circumstances there is opportunity for profound spiritual development. I have worked with many people who experienced literally unimaginable childhood abuses and I have been inspired by their courage and self-healing achievements.

When children are abused in these ways they are presented with a great deal of misinformation, false intentions, twisted emotional relationship models, lies, and negative energies which imprint and damage their chakras. In situations of abuse these children are often even blamed by the person abusing them for the occurrence as a method of controlling them. (As in, "Look what you made me do to you"). If abused by the person they most trusted, such as a parent, they experience the most profound feelings of abandonment, betrayal, confusion and vulnerability. They may also have been threatened by the parental abuser with the possibility that the parent could be taken away if the child communicates what has occurred, thus triggering a seemingly endless cycle of crippling fear of abandonment and shame in the child.

Abusive experiences result in our recording often repressed subconscious fear, trauma, unresolved conflicts and profound misinterpretations and misunderstandings of ourselves and our relationships. All of these emotions are magnified if the abuser was our parent. We are also essentially told by the actions of the abuser that we do not deserve to have any personal boundaries, and that our bodies are not our own, that we are fundamentally not valued or safe, that we are under the complete control of someone else, and that we have no personal power. Those of us who have experienced these tremendously damaging and emotionally conflicting situations are later required by our emotional pain and by the demands of life to eventually heal from it. We are also required to re-understand our experiences in a complete and transcendent way, in order to leave them behind. Until we do so we may be unable to have healthy relationships and to feel good about life and themselves.

The experience of child abuse strips away every feeling of safety, security and personal value. It can occur in a profound, unexpected and traumatic way, and at a time in our lives where we have very little understanding with which to accurately interpret or effectively emotionally face the situation.

353

This being the case, the only way out of the recorded and unresolved trauma is to consciously work through it all and to thereby heal it, by making peace with it. In doing so we become strong and self-aware, we learn to discern reality from the projected illusions and influences of others, and we learn to sovereignly manage our power and boundaries. We also learn to forgive ourselves and others in the process and this is necessary since we often blame both ourselves and the abuser. Although tremendously painful and seemingly wrong and terrible, it is often from such traumatic motivations that we grow self-aware and powerful. Through the transcendence of the experience we conquer fear and gain vast understanding of ourselves, relationships and life that would never have been available to us otherwise.

We gain much from the experience of learning not to be like those who hurt us, and to not allow their influence in our lives. To those who have experienced such dire and abusive life circumstances I can say only that although your experiences have been terrible beyond knowing, the understandings you have or will attain from the process will serve your soul for eternity. They will also potentially empower you to help others who have traveled the same path. Those who have experienced situations of abuse have the potential to understand more about love, more deeply, than many of us can imagine. Many who have had these experiences have eventually developed wisdom, sensitivity, determination, discipline, and have chosen to look with understanding, forgiveness, compassion and discernment upon every human being.

Although the karmic system of soul development does have some seemingly obvious temporary drawbacks, it does not benefit us to either judge or fight the system of karma. It does however benefit us to improve and evolve our learning processes, and our karma, as gracefully and rapidly as we can, and to integrate the results, and thus experience less pain and suffering.

In the activity of repeated physical incarnations, we may choose to be what some would call "bad people". We may choose to participate in war, abuse, greed, being judgmental, destructiveness, self-centeredness, etc. rather than generosity, love, compassion, acceptance and consideration of others. Some might assume that the reason for these seemingly negative choices is simple ignorance or worse yet an innate human tendency to gravitate toward the negative. However, I might suggest another perspective, which I believe can bring greater illumination to the deep, complex and ultimately beneficial system of reincarnation and thus how to better live our current lives.

When we choose negative or destructive lifetimes and life strategies we learn from them and acquire information about what does and does not either optimally work, or serve us, and others, in regard to that specific type of lifetime, lifestyle or life strategy. Certainly, by applying certain negative or non-optimal life strategies we may attain wealth, temporary security of a sort, power and the freedom to negatively affect others whom we are in conflict with. Some would see these detrimental dynamics, strategies and results as pluses. These dynamics could be demonstrated in the situation of a successful businessperson who sees himself/herself as a tough smart deal maker, rather than as a greedy self-centered and emotionally insensitive and emotionally unavailable individual.

However, applying these non-optimal strategies, choices and actions might lead to:

- ❖ Unknowingly harm those we love.
- ❖ Cause us to lose the capacity to love ourselves and others.
- ❖ Create bitter enemies and thus great personal and interpersonal suffering.
- ❖ Cause us to disconnect emotionally at multiple levels of our emotions from ourselves and others.
- ❖ Fragment our overall consciousness into many suppressed and compartmentalized and incongruent "parts".
- ❖ Motivate us to become so focused on achieving our goals or specific material results, that we miss out on opportunities to love, to be loved or to learn.

These results could be seen as minuses as well as representing some of the roots of what is termed negative karma. Consciously and positively managing ourselves in all life situations and relationships is necessary. Yet we often cannot fathom all of the reasons not to do something, until we have actually done it. Just as a young child does not know why it is detrimental to touch a hot stove until they do so. This is because we are souls on a quest to eventually make wise and balanced choices. Therefore, we may have no better route to attaining true understanding as to why certain life choices simply do not work better than initially blindly chosen personal experience. We often cannot get to a point of consciousness, wisdom, understanding and compassion without first personally going through certain negative experiences. Until this experiential process occurs we cannot understand other's suffering, and therefore cannot formulate the intention to feel

355

compassion and unconditional love for them or act with the self-discipline necessary to not strike back at them, when they strike us.

For some of us, who in a freewill manner, choose this unrefined path of self-development, (i.e. learning via trial and error experiences) it may appear that we can acquire understanding only by trying out different life strategies, beliefs and values. Then, after finding them lacking in some fundamental way, we then attain the conscious motivation to change to a more positive and balanced state of being and way of life. Trial and error is not the most direct path to enlightenment. However, it can ultimately be a sure way to proceed, in that once we have acquired these experiences we then have a very meaningful and motivating experience base with which to support our developmental path to enlightenment. If we have learned wise lessons via our experiences, we may be less likely to fall backward in our evolutionary process.

In the long run, as we evolve, we achieve finer and finer balance in perspective and in our methods of making life choices, as well as greater clarity of consciousness. Therefore, through the act of making apparently negative choices, we are eventually enabled to make better and better decisions, and thus end up with much better long term life results. If our mind is not yet clear of karmic influences we may see life situations in a distorted way, similar to a person wearing a set of glasses with an incorrect prescription. As such we tend to misinterpret and thus misunderstand the meaning and implications of experiences, sometimes in significant ways. We then make decisions based upon this erroneous information to our detriment and the detriment of others. This downward spiraling tendency can go on for a long time (many lifetimes for some) before we choose to learn to spiral upward in our soul's evolution through positive love-based choices.

If we look at human history from this standpoint, especially the most seemingly negative examples of cruel or merciless humans, we may be able to accept that they too were simply ignorant of fundamental spiritual and humanistic understandings. Like all of us, they were involved in a soul learning process of what not to be, albeit in their lives it may have been via a very destructive path and sometimes on a massive scale. (i.e. Genghis Khan, Hitler, Mussolini, Saddam Hussein, Bashar al-Assad, etc.). In my work, I have found many people like this, though they mostly function on a smaller scale of perceivable damage. In almost all cases I have found that these people were themselves emotionally damaged, angry or fearful, to the point that they lost emotional perspective, and thus were both unable and unwilling to positively manage themselves and their choices. What are the implications of

356

these understandings regarding all the people we heartlessly "warehouse" in prisons without significant effort to rehabilitate, educate and positively empower them?

I make no excuses for anyone's destructive choices or behaviors nor do I condone them. I also do not claim that ignorance is an excuse to avoid being accountable for one's actions or choices. I will say that the process of karma (learning via cause-and-effect) will likely place these destructively oriented people in circumstances that will allow them to learn how to transcend these negative tendencies and life strategies. Again, karma is not designed to punish them, it exists only because they would not otherwise have a way to be motivated to change, were they not placed "in the other person's shoes" by the process of karma. So yes, in future lives (if not sooner) these same people may live the life experiences of victims of abusers, simply and only for the necessity of attaining soul understanding.

We humans learn via experience. If we do not know how to work and play well together then we tend to be placed in circumstances that will facilitate our learning to do so. Yes, sometimes these are difficult or painful circumstances, yet they are also what we most need. All of us cause one degree or another of destruction to ourselves, the world and those we live with, and even to those we love most, throughout the course of our lives. Like all of us, detrimental historical figures were somewhat blindly learning through trial and error how not to function, and of how not to apply their personal power. In so doing, though they likely did not realize it at the time, they were also teaching all of us what not to allow and how not to be. In later incarnations, these detrimental and negative choices and associated experiences could ultimately serve their soul's highest good as well as the greater good of humanity. This may seem an overtly bold or even unwarranted statement in the face of terrible historical events, and certainly I am as fallible as every other human being. Still this is what I perceive to be true, and of course what I hope most in my heart to be true, as it describes a process of human evolution, that ultimately leads to better situations for everyone. It is important to realize we can speed up this process of learning and by doing so reduce our pain.

Extreme examples of negative behavior of all kinds move the collective of souls to say "no more of this" and to ensure that future social situations develop in a more constructive manner. Negative people function as models and examples of what not to be for the rest of the world. These people also show us what to avoid in terms of destructive leadership qualities and destructive societal developments, as well as what to put a stop to before it can take root. These negative examples bring about important understandings and we tend to remember them clearly. These experiences make humanity less vulnerable to manipulation and control by harmful nations, groups or individuals who, at their heart, conspire to harm because they do not yet know any better. These understandings and historical reference points guide our present and future political decision-making. For example, in democracies we become willing and empowered by the past to use our democratic power to oust those in leadership positions who do not truly serve the common good.

In the past, we could, as a world, "afford" to have these types of large-scale negative learning experiences, such as world wars, because at that time we were not technically or militarily capable of destroying ourselves or the world. We were also not as internationally economically interdependent as we are today. However, that time has passed and we must all hope that we have learned well enough from the past to not allow leadership decisions to be made in such a way that any nation misuses its power to our extreme or irreversible global detriment.

A useful metaphor of how humanity is evolving is that of a simple rock tumbler. A rock tumbler is a device for polishing rough stones. A rock tumbler is a rotating metal drum in which a group of rocks are contained and constantly tumbled, causing them to repeatedly crash into one another. In this activity, the sharp or jagged edges of each of the rocks are eventually worn away and we end up with a group of beautiful well rounded and polished stones. We could see this planet and the progress of humanity, as we reincarnate over and over with various levels of achieved understanding—as an immense rock tumbler (or a soul tumbler). Imagine a situation in which billions of humans are constantly somewhat blindly, and often negatively, bumping into one another in their various states of unconscious or negative behavior. First they learn how not to be or how not to function. Then slowly, through the action of responding to and learning from their own pain and suffering they evolve and become more conscious and sophisticated. Then the next step, learning by comparison and contrast, they come to understand how to function in more and more healthy, balanced and loving ways.

It is important to note that as some souls come to more astute understandings they can, and often choose to lovingly help the younger less experienced souls to understand the developmental process sooner and better, and with less pain and suffering. Examples of these types of souls would be Jesus Christ, Buddha, Muhammad, Gandhi, Nelson Mandela, Mother Teresa, Jiddu Krishnamurti, Ramana Maharshi, etc.

358

Adjusting and Adapting to Change:

Each person reacts to and adjusts to any life or relationship change in a unique manner. Some people are very easy going and have learned to effectively roll with the punches that life throws their way. These people have learned not to be too attached to any expectation, life result or desire. They are also less likely to be in judgment or hold onto a perspective of aversion to any life situation or relationship. Others may be less flexible and less open to seeing the benefits of change and may even try to force their previously acquired expectations and ways of seeing life onto their changing situation, usually bringing less themselves than optimal results.

This polarized situation can be seen in the current battle between those who want society to return to traditional values of various types and those who want to evolve societal, technological and political function to meet the world's budding complexity and changing needs. Other people react to perceived change with open fear, drama or violence, though they often do not truly understand the true nature of the change that is occurring or its true implications in their lives. Whatever the nature of the specific change and whoever is experiencing it, we can be sure it will always bring with it some degree of mental, emotional or energetic reaction, whether this reaction is resistance or inspiration. Fundamental change always requires significant effort, management, thought, acceptance, decisions and learning on the part of the person experiencing it.

In addition to change directly perceived by the individual, there are always domino effects of change that are often obscured or not understood. Meaning that if anything significantly changes in our lives it tends to bring about many other down-line changes or ripples as a result. This happens whether we realize it has happened or not. Trying to avoid understanding and refusing to accept the fact of these dynamics out of stubbornness, selfishness, fear, laziness or lack of discipline usually leads to several potential problems and much re-work.

Most of the pain associated with significant change is usually unnecessary, and any life change can be navigated and managed consciously and gracefully. Even if we are talking about a key personal change in our life. (For example, losing a job, changing jobs, getting married, getting divorced, having a child or moving to a new city). If we choose to be proactive, and preemptively manage the changes in our lives, we will usually be better off. This requires conscious self-discipline. If we just let life happen to us we will usually not be as happy, fulfilled or satisfied. We may even see ourselves as

359

victims of the changes we experience and feel ourselves to be disempowered by them.

I would suggest that there are many positive, effective and useful ways we can help ourselves and those we love to adjust to rapid change and even benefit by it. The first thing to do in any change activity is to choose to realize our power to navigate it, manage it, learn from it and positively influence it. We can then consciously choose, and willfully intend, to work with the change in a positive, sovereign and functional way, with gratitude for all aspects of it, and see it as an opportunity in disguise.

"Change Grief" as a Result of Change Shock:

We have previously defined and spoken of Change Shock and its influences on our processing of our moment-by-moment experiences of life. In these times of rapid and fundamental world change and transformation we can also experience "Change Grief". In a very fine book written by Elizabeth Kubler-Ross, called "On Death and Dying", the author defines 5 stages of grief that most people tend to go through. These stages are:

- ❖ Denial
- ❖ Anger
- ❖ Bargaining
- ❖ Depression
- ❖ Acceptance

This model, although simple, can be a very useful way of interpreting and managing one's process of grieving the loss that rapid change and the current world transformation invariably is, and will continue to bring. This process of grief includes loss of tradition, old ways of relating and believing, and for some of us the loss of our personal hope for the world becoming that which we have desired it to be. That said, I would suggest that the above listed model, as initially defined, is incomplete. Meaning that there are many potential negative emotional states and control seeking dynamics that are often a part of the process of grief and it is important that they be fully understood.

I would suggest that along with these 5 initial basic steps of grief that we can also experience:

- ❖ Judgmentalness and blame of self, others, groups, nations, institutions and life in general.
- ❖ Hatred of self and/or others and of the changes themselves.

❖ Guilt, Shame, Jealousy, Fear, Worry, Emotional Agony, Anxiety, Confusion, Depression, Despair and Disillusionment, Revenge Seeking, Resentment and Violence.

❖ Various distinct feelings of what we tend to interpret as loss.

❖ Internal mental, emotional and spiritual conflict.

❖ Projections onto the future of possible re-occurrence of the loss or change we are grieving as well as potential negative effects that the past change could bring about.

❖ Desire to control many aspects of the present and the future, including our relationships. This reaction can then trigger any number of control or safety strategies we have previously recorded in our systems and practiced in the past.

❖ Fundamental changes in our self-image, our social-images and our general world view, including the loss of our sense of identity, social status, security and self-worth, which can bring about states of shock, fear, pain, etc.

It is useful to understand that all of these reactive grief related dynamics are normal, natural and to a degree even necessary in order for us to learn all that we need to learn from the experiences of loss, profound change and from the grieving process itself. In effect, as painful as loss and grieving are, they can teach us important spiritual lessons. It is also useful to recognize that if we remain consciously, willfully and mindfully diligent we have the power to move through these often painful dynamics far more quickly and with far less discomfort. I am not suggesting repressing any of our emotions in our process of grief, I am suggesting working with them more consciously and constructively.

The release process listed in Chapter 11 and in Appendix 1 can be very helpful in accomplishing this worthwhile task of mindfully relieving our personal suffering and that of those we love. We can even learn to love and thrive in situations of profound change, if we first choose to change our fundamental perspective on its meaning and implication in all aspects of our lives and relationships. Change is here to stay; therefore, I suggest we can get better at managing it.

The Management of Increasing Global Complexity:

There is a useful dynamic to understand when we are discussing global transformation and change management, in all of its dimensions. This concept is the evolution of, and increasing complexity of, operations of corporations and nations, that are changing more rapidly than those governing them can effectively manage. This capacity to manage the growth of complexity directly effects how they interact with other corporations and nations. This is an issue of fundamental capacity to govern future societies.

The capacity of any corporation, organization or any nation to manage themselves wisely is constantly changing as they grow, evolve, become more complex and integrate technology into their core operations. With today's technology, we have the power to do incredible things. We also have the potential to cause great harm. My statement is this: Our world continues to become more and more complex, without significantly greater education being simultaneously available to, and infused into all of humanity. Which leads to my question: At what point of societal and technological complexity and speed of change do we become, as groups of human beings, unable to wisely and discerningly manage our societies? Is there is a "top end" of complexity that humans can successfully manage? If so, what are the implications for our future as nations and as a world? Is there valid reason, based upon these questions, to develop more sophisticated strategies and methods of managing the change and growth of our nations and our societies in the very near future?

Rapid change is difficult to manage on any scale, and in any situation. The current speed of change, and the scope of change, in our world is unimaginable. It is not a widely known fact that most of the major change initiatives in large corporations tend to fail, for a wide variety of reasons. Change in the bureaucracies of nations is even more difficult to effect, still it can be done and it is what must occur if we are to squarely and effectively face the challenges that we are currently presented with in a timely manner.

This process of successfully managing rapid world change cannot be accomplished via technology alone, though certainly technology is part of the answer. Successful management of the change requires the careful, mindful and knowledgeable management of the change of human cultures within the nations. This is true no matter what size group of human beings we are speaking of, from corporations to nations. The tribal and egoic tendencies of all groups of human beings tend to complicate the process of managed change. Clearly better understanding these dynamics will allow us to intelligently manage the unfoldment of the changes that must occur in our world in the very near future, in a manner that minimizes stress and conflict. Recognizing that there could be degrees of complexity associated with rapid change that we simply cannot handle with our current methods of management is crucial to our successfully achieving our goals. By doing so,

362

we open the door to new and creative solutions and ways of operating that have never existed before.

The Dynamics of Perception vs. Interpretation vs. Bias

Whenever we see any life event or relationship situation in our lives we immediately form a basic perception of what has occurred through our senses. Next, we <u>interpret</u> the event and assign our imagined projection of the supposed meaning and implication of the event or situation. These projections are often inaccurate, and to some degree dysfunctional in nature, especially if we believe our interpretation to be completely accurate and true. Last, we record our interpretations of events and experiences in our memories.

After we record our interpretations of events, they later become referred to in our memory as facts, which we then base life decisions on. These recordings are created by seeing the situation, relationship or event through the lens of at least one <u>previously recorded</u> simulacra. (i.e. Through the lenses of our earlier life experiences). What this often leads to is the application of a "judgmental and biasing step" to our interpretation of the nature and meaning of the recorded experience. This process can take the form of interpreting the situation or event we are experiencing as either in conflict with our values or beliefs, or as unfair, undesirable, wrong, victimizing, unloving or simply bad. None of these biased interpretations is ever fully true, and all of which can feel fundamentally and unquestionably true. This being the case, we are constantly recording new experiences through the biasing lenses of the past, no matter how dysfunctional those lenses may be. Essentially, we are constantly recording misinformation, usually without realizing it is happening.

This dynamic of "adding misinformation or a story" to the otherwise "clean interpretations and recordings of our life experiences" often leads to conflict with others. This happens because others tend to interpret these same instances in time quite differently, and in their own unique ways, that are often not in alignment with our own. It is this ongoing dynamic of adding biasing misinformation to any situation interpretation that leads to conflict, misunderstandings and arguments in relationships.

You could say that to an extent we are all prisoners of our recorded past. Meaning that our past determines (i.e. biases) how we will choose to interpret the present and how we will then project the future. All of our past memory recordings are simulacra through which the "movie of our lives" is viewed, and therefore all can lead to inaccurate conclusions as to what is happening in the present moment.

It is better to interpret and record our experiences without dualistic bias, and this is a practice that we can all become far better at if we choose to. If we simply focus on perceptions of events and situations, without then adding a "good or bad, right or wrong, or safe or unsafe" dualistic interpretation to our experiential recordings, then we can more easily see things in a way that is nonbiased. It is also important to understand that we can change our prior interpretations of experience if we choose to willfully do so. If we make this choice then we can literally in effect our past and by doing so become empowered to change our present and our future. This process of "scrubbing our biased memories" can be accomplished via meditation and through a variety of other methods.

Chapter Eleven
Self-Sovereignty and Empowerment:

Once we become self-aware of all of the elements of our mental, emotional and energetic systems and their tendencies and dynamics, we become empowered by this realization. Through working with our systems in a constructive manner we can then attain the state of conscious self-sovereignty. With this attainment, we become not only capable of owning our personal power, we become capable of shifting our consciousness to more and more astute levels of unified, aligned, harmonious understanding and function, and thus become more creative and effective. In this way, we become more capable of aligning with God, more capable of facilitating humanity as a whole in its transformational process, and more empowered to manifest lives that are constantly fulfilling and meaningful. This is an option available to all of us, as long as we set and consistently hold to the conscious intention to achieve it.

Conscious intention is a congruent state of willful, highly motivated and discerning focus of our energies, mind, attention, skills, knowledge and emotions in a constructive, organized manner on the attainment of any desired state or goal. Conscious intention is a self-aware insight guided process of sovereign discipline, meaning that it includes the consistent capability of independent and self-reliant wise, mature, grounded and balanced decision-making. This is a type of intention which is based upon sage understanding of self, personal and spiritual dynamics, values, life and relationships. There is requisite quality and degree of understanding that must be achieved in order to have powerful motivations in the attainment of our intentions. Intentionality is not merely willful self-control or suppression of negative or conflicted emotions or motivations.

Intentionality is a process of maintained resolute goal focused certainty which is continually enhanced by what we learn from the results of every decision we make. Intentionality is also a method of conscious mental, emotional, energetic, ego-identity and even spiritual self-management in all life situations, while on the path of goal attainment and manifestation. In essence, it is a process of being unwilling to be distracted from our intention by any life influence. Therefore, conscious intention is a fundamental requirement in the dynamic of wisely manifesting and maintaining the life we want through the application of our personal power. We cannot own our power in a sovereign manner without it.

Without conscious intention, we tend to remain unaware, without actionable understanding, unfocused, ineffective, indecisive, conflicted, ego-identity driven, without resolve and unable to apply our personal will or achieve our most significant life goals. Without defined intentions and life strategies our life energies tend to remain incongruent, blocked, diffuse and not optimally consistently, efficiently and constructively applied at every moment of our lives. Setting conscious intentions supports us in developing sophisticated and comprehensive life strategies, which we can then powerfully apply to achieve our goals.

Remember: What we focus our attention on is what we tend to feed, move toward or manifest. If our attention wanders, or we become distracted or confused, then this choice will work against attainment of our goals. If someone else, either through manipulation, creation of drama or negative intention determines the focus of our conscious attention "for us" then our sovereignty is fundamentally hijacked. It is our conscious process of attention management that empowers us to discerningly, comprehensively and accurately evaluate and map the parameters of relationships and situations in a way that supports our intentions. Once this is accomplished we then understand what we must understand in order to make wise and empowered decisions and navigate relationships.

Development of conscious situational awareness and managing this focused and attention-driven awareness is a discipline in itself. Learning to disassociate and dis-identify from our distracting, limiting and thus undermining ego-identity elements, reactive emotions and internal dialog of all kinds empowers us to make situational awareness a sovereign process. In this way we literally define and create new cognitive, mental and decision-making technology, which we can then apply to our lives and our creative process. An example of this process would be our learning to develop, design and work from our own sovereign principle-driven, fact-based decision-making strategies.

When we are fully focused on the attainment of a conscious intention in life, we are more focused, self-aware, confident, congruent, efficient, effective, well organized, well prepared and methodical, disciplined, empowered and are thus generally much more successful. Thus, we tend to be more satisfied with our lives and the results of our choices. Without willfully developing our conscious intentions we tend to languish in mediocrity, and in a state of ongoing distraction and distractibility from our

368

intentions, and are therefore vulnerable to being tossed about by whatever life situations and influences seem to "happen to us". We also tend to live our lives without experiencing life's deeper meanings or awareness of our own intrinsic spiritual and emotional nature, essence, worth and substance. Yet in the application of conscious intention neither victimhood nor any other state of disempowerment can ever really exist to deter our progress.

Some synonyms of intention that illuminate various facets of it are:

- ❖ Meaning
- ❖ Purpose
- ❖ Objective
- ❖ Target
- ❖ Plan
- ❖ Intent
- ❖ Goal
- ❖ Aim

Powerful intentions are always associated with a consciously chosen and precisely crafted vision of some desired life, relationship state or situation, and are based upon quality values and conscious motivations. The challenge is to first choose wisely and discerningly what we desire to achieve and to know **why we have chosen it**, and to thereby fully understand our underlying motivations in the process of achieving our goals.

Our motivations must evolve with our understandings, and great motivations stem from great understandings. Motivations of fear, desire, ego-identity, blind curiosity (the unfettered process of science?), greed, pleasure or sense gratification, pain, anger or hatred achieve little. The reason is that these non-optimal motivations are often unknowingly driven by subconscious feelings of powerlessness, lack and desire for control. Whereas motivations resulting from the abundant state of divine unconditional love and compassion have the real power to achieve a great deal that is truly of value.

Motivations of merely chasing "good feelings or avoiding bad feelings" are usually driven by subconscious insecurity, feelings of not being fundamentally safe in the world, or the lack of a sense of our own self-worth. Many people assume that the process of chasing after good feelings equals the process of attaining happiness, yet this process often does not attain the desired result because these motivations are usually driven by unresolved ego-identity states of lack. We cannot find happiness working from a mindset of lack.

369

For these reasons, I suggest developing as many of the following facets of intention as we can, as they are all directly supportive of achieving and maintaining what we consciously intend. In this way we are most likely to attain what we most want in life, with the least effort and in the shortest amount of time.

Facets of Conscious Intention:

❖ Core motivations of unconditional self-love and positive self-worth.

❖ In order to achieve any chosen intention, it is necessary to have a clear definition of what you want to achieve, including when, where, why and how you can achieve it, and for what purpose.

❖ Recognize that you will likely be required to fundamentally change yourself or some aspect(s) of your life or relationship situation, in order to attain the intention. Therefore, it is necessary to be at peace with this understanding. If you are conflicted about what you intend to accomplish your emotional or mental incongruity will create internal conflict, that then diminishes focus and waters down results.

❖ Remain self-aware at all levels of your system regarding your intention, while on the way to achieving your intention (meaning in all situations, all relationships and in all interactions).

❖ Understand that a truly conscious intention is based upon a profound decision, one you make and that you hold to with potentially ultimate commitment. Therefore, your intention must transcend all other life priorities.

❖ Being consistent and persistent in working toward your intention is a requirement. At the same time remaining open to unforeseen opportunity and remaining flexible and willing to learn from your path of intention is also optimal.

Requirements of Intention:

Intention is about creating and manifesting what we love most, personally evolving in our act of creation, and then experiencing the wonderful results of our achieved intention. We can be motivated in life by either fear or love, it is always our choice which emotion rules our intention selection process, and which fuels our intentions. All other negative emotions stem from underlying fear, (i.e. anger, jealousy, hatred, etc.) and like fear, they do not make quality fuel for motivation.

Intention is also about the manifestation within ourselves of the knowledge, understandings and wisdom, or the "necessary support system," for the attainment of our intentions at all phases of their fruition. The whole act of creating and achieving our intention requires us to walk a path of ever increasing understanding in order to manifest quality lives. Therefore, we must do so consciously, discerningly, wisely and with love. Living our highest intention is both an act of attainment and of accepting full ownership of our personal power.

On this path I suggest focusing only on positive motivations, while working toward our chosen intentions. Thus, in terms of all aspects of our intentions we remain for everything positive and against nothing at all. If our intention is to "stop" anything from happening or to control anything in our lives, then we are not in a creative manifesting mode. Positive proactive intentional states support a mode of thriving and not modes of reactive surviving. Defining oneself as a "survivor," though sometimes temporarily useful, is to limit one's greater potential and power with this limiting ego-identity. The root chakra's fight-or-flight mode may be useful in emergencies, yet in most other situations it functions in a negative, limited and thus limiting manner. Therefore, the root chakra's influence is only useful to those who have not yet found a better way.

Our conscious intention can be both the main driver and guidance system for all of our life choices if we choose to build our lives around our deepest intentions. In this way we come to understand well, and to refine the process of implementing our most foundational motivations. We can dynamically and consistently organize and structure our lives around and through our chosen intentions. This does not mean we are ruled by our intentions, nor stifled or limited by any chosen process of organization or structure necessary to achieve them.

Still sophisticated and well managed organization of our lives is a keystone of sophisticated achievement and significant life evolution. In this pursuit of intention, the acquisition of knowledge, skills and information are key steps to self-mastery. This is especially true since in the process of achieving our goals we may be called upon to literally create from the ground up the developmental methods necessary to manifest our chosen intentions in the "real world".

In the act of manifesting our intentions we need not allow our environment to detrimentally influence the achievement of our intentions. If we consistently reduce all environmental, relationship and social "friction", limitations, and undermining influences related to achieving our intentions we will move toward them faster! In this process, I suggest identifying and awakening the "numbed," incongruent, conflicted or unconscious aspects of our systems that are currently running on "automatic" and in a less than functional manner. If you are a male these conflicted aspects of your being may emanate from your feminine energy side (which all men have, although they often suppress it). If you are female these conflicted aspects of your being may emanate from your incompletely accepted masculine energy side. We all have both energies in our systems, and both are good and necessary for us to balance, harmonize and integrate in order to fully empower ourselves and to become fully conscious.

SUBCONSCIOUS VERSUS EMPOWERED HUMAN RESPONSE SYSTEMS

SUBCONSCIOUS AUTOMATIC REACTIONS	CONSCIOUS EMPOWERED DISCERNING RESPONSES
reactive	contemplative
protective of immediate survival often with long-term repercussions	panoramic vision, accountability
easily distracted	conscious focus
childlike manipulative behaviors	mature intentions
stubborn	determination
protect perceived status	protect personal ethics

IF WE CONSISTENTLY REDUCE OUR UNDERMINING REACTIVE INFLUENCES, WE CAN MOVE TOWARD OR ACHIEVE OUR INTENTIONS FASTER!

From the moment we first choose and commit to our intention we are choosing to be willing to acquire important understandings from every experience we subsequently have. We can then directly and constructively apply these insights to all aspects of our lives, as well as to the long-term achievement of our intention. Conscious awareness, study and refinement of our decision-making, analytical and interpretive methods, skills and tendencies are imperative in achieving our intentions. This is necessary because the way we live our lives must be foundationally and comprehensively congruent with our intentions. Otherwise we will not be optimally empowered to achieve them. This process requires us to remain in a stance of consistent openness to acquiring new understandings, abilities, skills and knowledge. I suggest maintaining a steady positive intensity in the attainment of our intention. This consistency of purpose and productive activity can, over time, move mountains.

Managing Our Mental and Emotional Systems:

There are many dimensions and aspects of refined and evolved intention, they are all of value, and understanding them well can help you manifest your intentions in the world. Passion is helpful to fuel any powerful intention we truly desire to accomplish. In the achievement of our intentions, our positive emotions and passion are excellent fuel, so I suggest you use them! In order to achieve any intention, we must have "the emotional want to", and it needs to be properly, optimally and consistently channeled, focused and managed. When we are in a higher state of consciousness than our simple primal negative levels of emotion then our positive emotions become our allies. Learning to manage and release our negative emotions and to align our positive emotions with our conscious intention is empowering.

Of course, there are other types of energy at our disposal that can support attaining our intentions, including developing our physical vitality, receiving energy from spirit by choosing to align with spirit, and developing our personal life force or Qi. Effectively building, maintaining, managing, harnessing and consciously mastering our life force resources empowers us at all steps of our path of intention. When we are good managers of our mental and emotional resources we will not waste them or apply them unnecessarily. If we do waste our resources, we may then unwittingly and unexpectedly reach a point of incapacity to continue on our path of intention and development.

From the moment we set any intention there is the potential and even the likelihood for us to encounter social resistance to our plans or goals.

When we manage and consistently resolve and harmonize this social resistance, we tend to use fewer resources since we are not wasting energy fighting resistance. All aspects of this resistance must ultimately be transcended, and this can usually be done by harmonizing with the resistance or healing some aspect of ourselves related to the resistance. It is generally not the case that we would be required to conquer the resistance, though many take this socially conflict-ridden path, to their detriment and the detriment of society. This conflicted path could be termed competition and although lauded by many as necessary to achieving goals it is a root of social and relationship conflict and division. Therefore, in the long term, it undermines our achievement of our chosen intentions.

Still in a practical sense we live in a world populated by many unconscious conflicted and competitive people, therefore it is important to be willing to shield and protect ourselves, our life vision and our precious intentions, while retaining our personal and spiritual integrity and impeccability. There is a degree and element of risk in all human endeavors; and managing risk is part of life, still this activity need not become an unbalancing preoccupation.

We all have individual priorities in life and a unique personal nature which influences how we arrive at our goals, and we have each been taught to prioritize specific aspects of our lives in different ways. If we want to manifest an intention, then learning to shift our priorities fundamentally and dynamically as we travel our life path is necessary. If we have "sacred cow" priorities, based upon erroneous subconscious beliefs, feelings, values or unresolved karmic patterns, they will limit our self-awareness, and thus limit our top end potential of achievement. Courageously reevaluating and reorganizing our priorities in an ongoing manner as we progress along our paths of intention is suggested for best results.

For those of us who choose very positive, high and powerful intentions, our intentions become the highest priorities of our lives, and in effect the cornerstones of and reason for our existence. As we develop and evolve we will become more and more empowered to choose and affect more powerful and sophisticated intentions, and in doing so create even more wonderful realities. In this practice it is essential to learn to balance and rebalance our priorities continually, patiently and flexibly. Retaining balance in all areas of our lives supports us in remaining less stressed and thus optimally effective and efficient in achieving our goals for the long run. For example, it is good to retain balance in regard to health, mind, body, spirit, emotions, relationships, work and recreation.

374

When we work to consistently balance our lives, then we are also on the road to the attainment of consistent internal harmony, inner peace and congruent alignment. This means we are learning not to allow any internal competition, conflict or friction between our priorities, emotions, values, beliefs, or our various subconscious ego-identity "parts". In this way, we are actively learning to reconcile conflict in all of these areas. We accomplish this via consciously understanding, integrating, re-balancing and managing these components of our systems. Meditation is a great and necessary way to achieve this. In this way, we can proactively and preemptively manage life stress before it becomes a limitation, a problem, a resource drain, a distraction or an illness. (For example, we can make the positive choice to cease trying to either please or control anyone else. This choice tends to directly diminish our stress. We can choose to manage or eliminate our own self-expectations and expectations of others and thereby reduce the potential of "overwhelm syndrome" that is causing so many people life stress these days).

When we are focused, centered within ourselves (not self-centered) and grounded in this material world, we then gain the ability to make wise decisions and hold clear, constructive perspectives at every level of our perception and consciousness. Disciplined focus on our intention is crucial as it eliminates distractions and thus waste. People who are not well grounded and integrated at each level of their systems tend to, in some area of their lives, be unclear, flighty, unrealistic, unorganized, and incomplete in their understanding of self and life. So they are unable to move the mountains they want to move in a powerful and internally unified manner.

Remaining grounded requires self-awareness and discipline, plus basic understanding of the benefit of being grounded and specific meditative methods of grounding oneself. Many ungrounded people do not even realize they are ungrounded. Paradoxically optimal groundedness requires understanding the negative consequences of not being grounded. People who are not optimally grounded often have mental or emotional blocks, non-optimal beliefs or energy patterns in their root chakras, that they are unaware of. Many ungrounded people also operate from unrecognized subconscious fear or unresolved emotional pain or trauma. Yet these influences can be effectively identified and cleared.

In the act of attaining our intentions it is useful to be patient with ourselves. If we want to achieve extraordinary goals, we must patiently formulate and take the wisest steps and be willing to wait for necessary conditions of opportunities to ripen. Patience is not a condition of repressing any of our motivations or our negative emotions. Patience is a state of clearly understanding the benefit of only acting when we are fully prepared to act and when it is optimal to act, and thereby remaining at peace with ourselves in both action and inaction. Simultaneously it is also good to be courageous and even bold in the attainment of our intentions when it is time to take action. Both action and inaction are often driven by fear and this motivation undermines conscious attainment of goals. Managing our tendency to be patient with wisdom rather than fear is necessary. If we choose to continually transcend fear of all kinds, then we will move toward our goals more quickly and positively.

As we move along our paths of intention we can benefit by being willing to evolve, develop and consistently apply a conscious method or system of self-integration in relation to the various subconscious simulacra or "parts" of our systems. Integration of the many parts of your subconscious into a unified and aligned consciousness can be achieved via a mechanism called "Anchoring and Integration", which is a Neurolinguistic Programming or NLP technique. There are numerous other methods I teach to achieve this internally integrated and harmonious state; however, they are outside the scope of this text.

High internal integration, alignment and congruency of the various levels of chakra consciousness in regard to our intentions empowers us. It is a support requirement of highly sophisticated intention and thus to high accomplishment. You cannot be or remain self-aware, holistically determined, centered, balanced, focused, and harmonious and grounded unless you are well integrated.

Our intentions work best when they resonate with our soul's essence and therefore with God, since our souls are direct expressions of God. In their most refined forms our intentions represent pure expressions of our deepest personal soul essence and our resonance with spirit. In this way, we move in an internally unified and congruent manner, with ultimate power, determination and commitment to ourselves and to our chosen intention. Our intention need not be something we want just for ourselves; however, it must be something we care deeply about attaining or achieving and find meaning in. This is true even if our intention is solely and unconditionally for the benefit of others or of the world.

The wisest intentions serve ourselves and humanity at the same time in a balanced way because we are all one and thus all beautiful, perfect and of value, all the time. Meaning you the reader matter far more in the grand scheme of the universe than you probably realize. You are a child of God, so how could the situation be otherwise? In order to choose and affect these types and qualities of highest intention we must choose to apply discerning willpower in all of the choices we make on the path to attainment of our goals. If we do not put our personal will behind what we want to do or manifest, then other influencing social and environmental factors in the world may distract or impede us. We must be willing to stand up for our most heartfelt intentions, and our personal will is the "backbone" of this process.

We all have some degree of innate creativity though we do not all recognize it, value it or know how to apply it. This creativity is the source of our greatest power, since it occurs most potently when we are in complete alignment with spirit. Applying flexible creativity and artistry to all moments of our lives means being willing to draw upon all aspects of our being, including both our male and female energies, all aspects of our worldly selves, and our "left and right brain" skills, abilities and perspectives. To create anything in life requires a blended balance of both male and female energies, whether we are creating a baby, a book, a company or a space shuttle.

Creativity occurs via the congruent, intentional consistent and dynamic interplay of our conscious and subconscious mind, and spirit. The creative process is fueled by our own positive emotions and the energy, power and love of spirit. Acting creatively in every moment of our lives is our natural and most optimal state and is the direct and simultaneous expression of God's love for us and our own love for ourselves and each other. Self-love and profound and complete self-trust-driven decision-making, and intention building, are both healthy and fulfilling.

If we do not choose to love ourselves, we will not treat ourselves or others well on the journey to achieving our intentions. We may not even allow ourselves to achieve our intentions due to subconscious self-sabotage. If we do not fundamentally trust ourselves, our love motivated process of intention attainment, and all of our decisions and actions on our journey, then we will continually doubt or second guess ourselves. Self-doubt does not support taking decisive, effective, bold and consistent action.

It is useful for us to choose to be optimally self-supporting, self-reliant, self-accountable and self-aware. We are all, to a degree, interdependent (not co-dependent). Yet if we rely on others in an unbalanced way we may find too late that they will not support the achievement of our intentions exactly as we would prefer, and thus again we may reach a point of limitation in our journey. We must be willing to be self-accountable and to manage our interpersonal boundaries or we will not diligently hold our choices and actions to the standards and requirements which are necessary to achieve our goals. If we are not self-aware and discerning as we walk down our soul's path of life creation, we will not even realize we are making unwise choices. Until it is too late. Nor will we accurately perceive the negative results of those choices and thus not learn the most that we can from our chosen experiences.

There are many tools we can utilize along the way to positively affect our intentions more directly; these include affirmations, mantras, meditation and prayers which can all facilitate the manifestation of our intentions. Another way to achieve this goal is to consciously and methodically design, construct and refine strategies of goal attainment which are action oriented and efficacious. However, I suggest being careful what we wish for and understanding well beforehand what we are working toward, because we may well get it. Therefore, I suggest we proactively evaluate and extrapolate what our life will be like after we achieve our intentions, before we actually begin our efforts to achieve them. Many people have won the lottery and then found themselves penniless, miserable and stripped of their most valued relationships within a year or two. If we intend to manifest more money I suggest we first insure we are prepared to manage that much money energy consistently and constructively, otherwise it may overwhelm us. The same is true in the process of acquiring power of all kinds. Power magnifies the positive aspects of our nature as well as the negative, i.e. addictions, negative emotions, drama, karma, etc.).

Along the path of our intentions we must be willing to become aware of, consciously map and constructively confront and work with elements of our ego-identities. Our ego-identities and the simulacra recordings that make them up may not yet be prepared to support either the process of attaining our conscious intentions or living with our achieved intentions. If this is the case, and we do not know it ahead of time, we may spin our wheels for a very long time, not realizing how or why it is happening. We may also end up in a situation that is not felt to be as wonderful as we originally hoped. If this turns out to be the case I suggest forgiving ourselves immediately and acknowledging all that we have come to learn and understand on our previous path of intention. Then simply move on more wisely to achieve our next intention.

One potentially limiting facet of our ego-identity is the "recipe" or set of standards we each subconsciously hold to in regard to what it means to be a "good or nice person". By the way, all of the standards we live by are in essence "artificial" in that we have made them all up as we go through life.

378

None of our standards are any "more right", real or better than anyone else's. Of course, there are many other aspects of our ego-identities that are beneficial to become aware of and to manage in relation to our intentions. The reason I mention this one issue is because if our conscious intention violates our personal subconscious definition of goodness or does not support our self-worth or self-image, and we do not realize it, then we will tend to fight ourselves unknowingly and we may even unconsciously defeat our own wisest intentions. At the very least we will slow our progress toward our achievements. Sage intention could be said to be an expression of spiritual maturity. Spiritual maturity is built upon a foundation of balanced mental, emotional, energetic and physical maturity, all of which require conscious effort and awareness to attain.

It is crucial to be willing to put an end to existing ego-identity and fear-motivated intentions and reactive decision-making styles. When this is achieved, we attain a state of conscious, graceful humility, calm and balance. Decisions made in fear are rarely optimal and often hinder significant progress. Therefore, I suggest rooting out those tendencies in our systems in a diligent, methodical, patient and determined manner. Methods of clearing fear and other non-optimal emotional states are listed at various points in this book. (A complete discussion of fear, and how to fully transcend its effects on your life and relationships, is available in a book titled "A World Without Fear, By: John Jones").

If we choose to release these unnecessary emotional tendencies, we become capable of living in a sovereign manner in the now and can be fully consciously present at all times. (For example, we don't get lost in other "time zones" such as focusing on the past or the future to our detriment. Nor do we become lost in in any of the various aspects or projections of our child-selves which can powerfully influence attainment of our goals). If we live in fear, then we cannot be sovereign and access and apply own our power; these are mutually exclusive states.

Only by living in a self-sovereign manner in the now do we have true power and thereby optimally grow in our understanding of our experiences. Through monitoring and managing our thoughts, internal dialogue and emotional states we can determine which time zone we are subconsciously choosing to be in from moment-to-moment and make corrections. Setting and consciously managing our personal, emotional, social and energetic boundaries is also a key element of sovereignty. Whether we are talking about boundaries in the context of business, close personal relationships or any life or social situation, boundary management is key to staying on course to achieve our intentions.

We must willfully set and hold our own boundaries; otherwise others will tend to ignore them and potentially undermine our life efforts. This is not always done out of spite, it is often out of ignorance, their subconscious patterning or competitive zeal. However, none of these detrimental influences will serve the optimal attainment of our intentions. Paradoxically, although we are all spiritually one and cannot be otherwise, it is still possible, and best for our spiritual development, to function in this sovereign manner. Conscious boundary management makes this possible.

Accurately understanding the most likely implications of our choices, all along the way toward achieving our intention, is useful. This means analyzing, envisioning and projecting what these likely implications are, prior to making our choices, which then helps us to "precisely craft" optimal choices. If we have no willingness to "look before we leap" we could end up in either the frying pan or the fire. Clear awareness of these implications requires us to be mentally and emotionally clear so that unhealed elements of our systems do not distort or block our vision. In achieving this state, it is useful to let go of all past hurts, pain, jealousy, betrayals, desires for revenge and fears of all kinds. These unhealthy states will only slow us down or distract us. Ultimately none of these negative states will help us reach our chosen goals.

Precision, clarity and focus in execution of all steps and actions related to our intention is fundamental to our success. If we do a sloppy job of working toward our intention there is likely to be a lot of unnecessary re-working and back tracking, or we may "completely miss the mark" in attaining our intention all together. We could look at this mindfulness process as a sort of "quality assurance" in regard to one's life. In order for us to be very precise, we must first cultivate and attain clarity of consciousness. Meaning that we must be clear about what our intention is and remain clear in our own minds and hearts about who we are and where we are at every moment in relation to the achievement of our intention. Optimally understanding what we are doing, why we are doing it, and remaining focused at every step of the way is key to achieving our intentions.

Intentions we choose when we are younger tend to evolve over time and this is as it should be, since we are all constantly growing in our understanding, knowledge and sophistication. Being willing to continually and consciously refine and evolve our understanding of our intentions is important. Doing so allows us to take advantage of changing conditions, such as new environmental resources, evolving technologies, and changing social

380

situations and relationships. If we are learning constantly, and if we apply our innate personal style of learning to achieving our intentions, we will usually manifest them much easier and faster.

It is good to remember that intention is something that must be "formulated". Intention formulas, like recipes, require forethought and ongoing refinement based upon evaluation of results, in order to achieve the best and most palatable outcomes, and they can always be creatively improved. Therefore, I suggest being willing to accept and adopt new and ever more pristine habits, methods, behaviors and values. In this way, we constantly unlearn and deconstruct old and no longer useful tendencies and transform ourselves in new ways. It may help to realize that most of us are, to one degree or another, trapped within prisons of old and non-adaptive beliefs, life stories, methods, expectations, emotions and lower states of consciousness, behaviors, habits, etc. Our freewill intentions and consciously applied personal power are the keys which can free us at any time. Constructive and timely adaptation to changing circumstances is therefore wise.

It is useful to realize that our souls have likely spent a long time on this planet, living many diverse lives. In that time, we have each grown in understanding, and while on our paths we have each developed a sort of "evolving soul guidance system" within ourselves. This guidance system is directly reflected in the karmic patterns generated from this and past lives. Meaning that our karmic process (or our current understanding of cause-and-effect dynamics) is simultaneously the map, the path and the vehicle of our life and spiritual development. This remains true as long as we remain unconscious to the process of karma. Meaning that there are ways of living life that transcend the somewhat simple cause-and-effect dynamics of karma. These attainable states of consciousness are beyond the scope of this book.

We can, on our path of life exploration, refine the accuracy of our karmic map. We can also add to the map by coming to more sage understandings that are only available as the result of healing wounded, ignorant or dysfunctional karmic aspects of our being. If we do so our karmic map and patterns will better support our chosen life intentions. Our karma can thereby effectively become the crucible within which our soul's intentions are developed, evolved and ultimately achieved. In this way we can transcend karma as our soul's developmental process.

A Process of Dismantling the Ego-Identity, In Spite of All Our Ego Defenses:

All individual human beings have many subconscious parts of themselves that we do not usually recognize the existence of in their day-to-day lives. For example, we can have a part of ourselves that feels that it needs attention from others or one that wants to avoid embarrassment or criticism. The operation of each of these parts of ourselves tends to occur separately from other parts of ourselves. For example, our desire for attention operates separately from the part of ourselves that feels that it is necessary to fight in order to protect ourselves from other people. Other separate subconscious parts of ourselves may have other intentions, such as to achieve success or to control others or to make sure we remain free of other's controlling tendencies.

These subconscious parts influence our decisions, our interpretations of life from moment-to-moment and our emotional reactions to events. These parts are often in conflict with each other, making it difficult to navigate our lives and relationships. This situation can be seen in situations where we want something in life very much and **at the same time** we feel guilty or selfish for wanting it and **at the same time** resent others for "making us feel guilty". These conflicted reactive emotional dynamics between our subconscious parts are a significant source of life stress. This is true since most people do not know how to fully understand and thereby be empowered to resolve the conflicts between their parts in a constructive way. It is necessary to dismantle these subconscious parts in order to attain inner peace and to transcend their undermining influence.

One of the main reasons these disparate parts create problems is that we often become highly identified with the feelings that each of these parts generates, and so we assume it is necessary for us to continue to feel what "they feel". The important thing to take away from this discussion is that although you may feel (often intensely) that these parts "are you" and that "you" are feeling a certain way, in regard to a certain situation, that this is not precisely what is occurring. It is your subconscious parts that are generating these feelings, that the conscious you then accept as yours, and then you live by them.

The composite of all of these subconscious parts and the dynamics of their interactions with each other and with other people's subconscious parts create what I would call social ego-identity dynamics. Until these parts are cleared from your system they will continue to create internal negative emotional reactions and interpersonal dynamics of drama and conflict. In

382

order to clear them from your system you must make a conscious and determined decision to do so, and then work methodically to dismantle them.

There is a well-developed system of therapy called "Voice Therapy", which seeks to harmonize these conflicted or negative subconscious parts, by giving conscious voice to them. This therapy is not designed, in my understanding to clear these parts permanently and consciously. I suggest that the Voice Therapy technique can bring emotional relief. That said, only by completely clearing these parts from our systems will they cease to either limit or detrimentally affect you, your relationships and your future. Therefore, I offer the method of clearing subconscious parts of your mental or emotional system (simulacra recordings) and their associated beliefs described later in this chapter. It is very empowering to realize that you can clear any belief you have been holding very rapidly with this method. All that is required is to choose to and be motivated to accomplish this.

It is vital not to let any aspects of our ego-identity "regrow" once we have worked to transcend them. This is especially true if we have emotionally conflicted subconscious parts that keep us internally at odds with ourselves, and thus create indecision and inability to take constructive action on our own behalf. Therefore, we must keep at the process of clearing these aspects of our systems consistently, so that we breakdown our ego-identity(s) rapidly enough that it cannot re-grow faster than we dismantle them. This process requires absolute willful intentionality, focus, consistent effort and discipline to recognize and dismantle all of the seeds of ego-identity, many of which we have been continually referencing in our interpretation of our life and relationship experiences.

It is useful to clear all simplistic, limiting and polarizing identity elements. (i.e. Any parts of ourselves that look at life in polarized ways. Such as safe and unsafe, right and wrong, win and lose, true or false, or parts that see ourselves as either good rescuers, bad perpetrators or innocent victims). These polarized parts support living life in a state of ongoing internal conflicted division of consciousness or "duality".

These subconscious parts are constantly influencing our decisions, and thus directly creating our life results. These parts each have their own agendas, values, goals and beliefs and they are almost never aligned with each other in their goals, values, etc. These parts also have situations they want to avoid due to their fears or insecurities. Meaning we can have a part of ourselves that wants to avoid abandonment, and a separate part that wants to be in control of our lives. These parts can hijack our decision-making at any moment of our lives, if we allow them to.

We all reference the personal values that we each hold in our systems when we make decisions. In fact, we tend to directly base many of our decisions on these personal values. These values may be spiritual values or worldly values. We all tend to carry a mixture of both. Many of us hold values of:

Spiritual Values and Intentions of:

- ❖ Integrity and Truthfulness
- ❖ Spiritual purity
- ❖ Being consciously resonant with and surrendered to God
- ❖ Spiritual states of joy, bliss or inner peace
- ❖ Spiritual states of unconditional love for God and all of humanity
- ❖ Religious values, such as Godliness, being Christ like or Buddha like, or other specific values of our specific religion holds most sacred
- ❖ Non-dualistic consciousness
- ❖ Living in a state of consciousness in which we have released all attachment and aversion to all aspects of life and relationship

Worldly Values and Intentions of:

- ❖ Our family's and our own personal happiness, safety and security
- ❖ Money
- ❖ Social Status and Relationship Status
- ❖ Security
- ❖ Control
- ❖ Power
- ❖ Sex
- ❖ Safety
- ❖ Personal self-worth and deservedness
- ❖ Time (having enough time and meeting our own and other's expectations of timely achieving goals)
- ❖ Beliefs we hold (it could be said that values, rules, roles and priorities are only specific types of beliefs about life that we have recorded)

It is true that holding and making decisions based upon positive values is important and in a very practical way useful in managing our lives. Still holding these values alone is not the answer to making wise decisions. Many of our values can be in conflict with each other, even the positive ones. Other values must be balanced, such as spending time with family and the time it takes to attain money and security. At the same time, there are many things that we either fear happening, or feel insecure about. Each of these feared

384

events, situations or circumstances creates a fear motivation within us, that then influences our perspective on life and our decisions. These fear motivations become <u>a literal value</u> (though not a constructive one) that we then balance against our other values, often without realizing we are doing so, in our decision-making processes.

These fear driven parts constantly influence our decisions, even more than our conscious set of values do. Therefore, our day-to-day decisions reflect a composite or mixture of what we want to happen, and what we don't want to happen or fear happening, simultaneously. This conflicted dynamic creates a great deal of internal stress, confusion, complexity and turmoil when we try to make decisions. It is all a result of fragmented consciousness. This state of fragmentation can be resolved if we work to clear these subconscious parts and their influence from our systems.

It is the process of fully dis-identifying with these parts, and the fears that are often associated them that ultimately frees you. Again it is not the wanting of anything in life that creates problems. Still it is often the attachment to wanting what we want that causes pain and suffering. Meaning that there is an ongoing fear stress of not having what we want, until we actually achieve it or gain it. The problems we experience are the result of the fear drive that underlies many of what we assume to be our conscious motivations.

Below is a method of permanently releasing these subconscious parts (or simulacra recordings, as defined earlier in the book) and their ongoing influence. This method requires us to ask ourselves a series of questions. The list of questions shown below are only example questions. They are designed to help you learn to find and then work with the parts of yourself that limit you, cause you difficulties, and that you want to clear, in order to bring peace and consciousness to your life. These questions all start with the three words "who is it".

When you ask yourself these questions you are realizing that it is not "the conscious spiritually aware you" that wants, or feels whatever is being wanted or felt. It is a part of your subconscious that either feels, believes, fears or wants something, whatever that "something" is. Whoever the part of you is, that you are questioning in this process, is not the "true you". This process is designed to help you fully realize this truth and thereby to free you to resonate directly with your soul and God. The complete process is described after this listing of example questions.

Please review the list below. It can help you to get in touch with aspects (or parts) of yourself that you may not have realized existed or that were influencing your life results. These subconscious "selves" often run most people's lives, without their realizing it is occurring. In **Appendix 1** of this book you will find a categorized listing of these types of questions that may help you identify and resolve specific problems in various areas of your life.

Who is it that:

- ❖ Feels victimized?
- ❖ Feels misunderstood?
- ❖ Feels I am failure?
- ❖ Feels confused at this moment?
- ❖ Feels small and powerless?
- ❖ Feels empty and worthless?
- ❖ Feels lost and alone?
- ❖ Feels my grief will never end?
- ❖ Feels trapped in my life, career or relationship?
- ❖ Wants money, power, control, status, sex, success, attention, etc.?
- ❖ Fears not having money, power, control, status, sex, success, attention, etc.?
- ❖ Is confused about my sexuality?
- ❖ Worries about my future?
- ❖ Cannot let go of the past?
- ❖ Feels I have made many mistakes in my life?
- ❖ Feels I am always wrong?
- ❖ Wants to rescue others?
- ❖ Wants to be rescued?
- ❖ Worries about my children?
- ❖ Fears abandonment?
- ❖ Feels that safety equals power or control?
- ❖ Feels I cannot trust myself or others?
- ❖ Fears for the safety of my family?
- ❖ Feels I am only safe if others understand me?
- ❖ Feels that no one is listening to me?
- ❖ Feels my needs are not being met?
- ❖ Fears my needs will not be met in my relationship?
- ❖ Feels I am only safe if I remain dependent in my relationships?
- ❖ Wants to feel or be "special"?
- ❖ Wants to "be somebody" or that feels I am not already somebody?
- ❖ Feels uncertain in this present moment?
- ❖ Fears change, uncertainty or the unknown?

- ❖ Feels that it is unsafe to freely live my life?
- ❖ Feels it can only make decisions when it is completely certain of the outcome?
- ❖ Feels stressed in this present moment?
- ❖ Feels I am only safe if I perform well in my life roles (husband, wife, man, woman, teacher, worker, etc.)?
- ❖ Feels that I literally "am what I do" for a job or career (i.e. I am a plumber, a doctor, a manager, a teacher, a housewife / househusband, etc.)?
- ❖ Feels that I am my identity?
- ❖ Feels I am not the person that other people perceive me to be?
- ❖ Feels I am only the person that other people perceive me to be?
- ❖ Feels that I have to be what others want me to be?
- ❖ Feels I only have value, and am only safe, if I meet other's expectations?
- ❖ Feels I have to be like others in order to be safe?
- ❖ Has an agenda?
- ❖ Feels abandoned by god?
- ❖ Does not know what I want from life or my relationships?
- ❖ Feels that I can never have the love and happiness I want, because I am bad, wrong, broken, imperfect and unredeemable?
- ❖ Feels that I can only be happy if I have what I want (i.e. The relationship, the job, the amount of money, the security, the status, the control, etc.)?
- ❖ That has regrets or is ashamed of my past?
- ❖ Feels they need to redeem themselves for past deeds, behaviors of feelings by being a "good person" or by helping other people?
- ❖ Fears misusing my own power?
- ❖ Fears other's judgments of how I use my power?
- ❖ Worries and feels that I am not good enough and never will be?
- ❖ Feels I will never get to where I want to be?
- ❖ Feels I will never have what I want most?
- ❖ Sees this current moment as a problem?
- ❖ Sees my relationship as a problem?
- ❖ Is unwilling to forgive myself or others?
- ❖ Feels righteous judging and punishing others?
- ❖ Feels I do not have enough time?
- ❖ Feels I do not have enough money, and never will?

❖ Feels I can only be safe if I have provable value to others?

❖ Wants to present a social image of perfection?

❖ Fears not being perfect?

❖ Wants to be perfect?

❖ Feels that being perfect is the only solution to my problems?

❖ Holds ideals about self, relationships or life?

❖ Feels I do not truly know who I am?

❖ Feels that I am "my mind"?

❖ Prioritizes myself above others?

❖ Uses the appearance of being a spiritual person as social validation and a way of achieving social acceptance?

❖ Feels "this way" ... (whatever we may be feeling in the current moment, including anger, hatred, fear, shame, worry and guilt)?

❖ Believes or thinks that I am ... (good, bad, lovable, unworthy, not good enough, etc.)?

❖ Believes or thinks that other people, are ... (bad, against me, hate me, do not understand me, untrustworthy, will betray me, etc.)?

❖ Believes that I cannot ... (achieve my goals, face my fears, make a decision, understand myself, set a clear and effective intention, etc.)?

❖ Believes that I or others should not ... (behave as they are or I am, make choices as I do or they do, believe as I do or they do, wants what I want or wants what they want, etc.)?

❖ Wants this (whatever "this" is) ... (to hurt others, to become wealthy at the cost of my relationships, to control others, to live in fear, to be somebody, etc.)?

❖ Gets angry at seemingly minor and ultimately unimportant social or interpersonal slights, criticisms, insults or when I do not get my way?

❖ Feels I am right and good and that others are all wrong or bad?

❖ Fears that I do not really exist to others, and am not important?

❖ Fears being destroyed by others?

❖ Fears death?

❖ Fears being nothing and thus having no value?

❖ Feels it is necessary to give up your personal power to anyone for any reason?

❖ Feels I "have to" be afraid and worry in order to remain safe?

It is not always comfortable to face these parts of ourselves, and fully process them out; still it is vital to constructively deal with them in order to live fulfilled peaceful lives. Remaining limited or trapped by these internal influences, negative emotions and internal dialog is not freedom, nor is it a road to happiness or inner peace. It is useful to realize that if you choose not to work with these ego-identity elements, they will just continue to define your perception of reality, influence your choices, and create problems, pain and suffering. In fact, it is these patterns that hold suffering in place year after year.

The process of resolving and releasing all of these limiting feelings is simple, direct and effective:

Step 1:

Focus your conscious mind in the area of your body that "feels" whatever feeling it is that you want to clear and process out. For example, if you feel anger or fear, you will usually feel the feeling in a specific part in your body. You may even feel it in multiple parts of your body. If you feel it in various parts of your body or emotional system, then just focus on where you feel it most strongly. I would also suggest initially evaluating the intensity of the feeling or belief, and specifically rate its intensity, on a scale of 1 to 10. At the end of the process it is then good to re-evaluate the intensity of the feeling, and perceive the degree of reduction in the intensity you experience. For example, after applying the process you may experience that the emotional intensity has diminished from a level of "8" down to a "4". In this way you can prove for yourself that you are making progress and better manage your process. You can continue the applying the process until you no longer have the feeling or belief at all.

A concrete example of this process would be seen if you feel anger, guilt, and shame in your system and you focus on where you feel it most in your body and rate its intensity level. Other examples you could experience would be if you hear your internal dialog or self-talk that tells you that you are not good enough, or that you are worthless or that others are bad and untrustworthy. If so, then focus on where you feel this internal dialog coming from in your system and initially rate the intensity of the feeling.

Step 2:

Next: Form a sentence in your mind that clearly reflects whatever the part of your system is "saying or feeling", and that you want to clear. For example, form a sentence similar to: "Who is it that feels that I am worthless?" OR "Who is it that feels controlled by my mother/father?" OR "Who is it that fears being abandoned by my husband or wife?" or "Who is it that feels trapped in my life", etc.

Step 3:

While focusing on the part of yourself that you want to clear or heal, begin repeating the statement you have formulated to yourself, over and over. It is your choice whether you vocalize the statement or simply repeat it to yourself. If you want to get optimal results you must focus **absolutely** on where you feel the feeling in your body as you repeat the question. This is necessary because the part of your subconscious will often try to hide from or escape your conscious questioning and focus. This is because each of our subconscious simulacra/parts has a self-defense system of sorts that tries to keep us from changing it. For example, if we are holding a fear that we want to clear we often feel safer living with the fear than clearing it. If we are angry at others we may feel safer remaining angry, or may feel better about ourselves remaining self-righteously angry, than releasing the anger and forgiving. It is common for parts of us to feel unsafe forgiving ourselves and others. We feel that if we do forgive, that we will no longer have the supposed control that judgmentalness gives us. So, please continue repeating the question until the emotion is fully processed out of your system.

To fully succeed you must face the feeling with as much intention as you can. If you do so, the part of your subconscious that feels negatively will process out of your system permanently. If you feel any resistance to repeating the statement, simply override it with complete focused determination. This experienced resistance is only your subconscious resistance to changing your old beliefs or habits of thought, feeling and decision-making. Therefore resistance is actually a good sign of progress. Keep going!!!

Step 4:

Continue repeating the "who is it" question until you feel that the emotional part of yourself that you wanted to reconcile has fully changed and processed out of your system. (i.e. You no longer feel what you felt). Again, listen to any emotional or internal dialog responses you get as repeat the question, as these answers can be informative. That said, even if you get an answer to your questioning such as "me" or "my mother", or "it's all their fault", do not stop repeating the question. It is the energy you want to process out fully. Simply getting an internal answer of any sort does not fully accomplish this goal. When the feeling is fully resolved, you will know it because you will no longer be able to feel it.

390

Step 5:

Check in with your system to see if there is any residue of the old feeling, internal dialog or belief left in <u>any part</u> of your system. If you find any residue of the part, then again determine what level of intensity it is operating at in your system and where it is now most intensely located in your system. Then <u>continue</u> repeating the statement until the belief, feeling or internal dialog is fully gone. If you are satisfied with the results of your process, then go onto the next belief or feeling you want to positively change.

In this process you may get many different internal dialog answers to the "who is it …"question. For example, you could get the answer back in your internal dialog of "it's my mother's or it's my father's fault", or you could hear the word "me" or you could hear "it's all my fault". You may also get no answer at all, and this is completely fine. In that the process works, and the processing occurs, whether you get responses to your questions or not. The reactive answers you do tend to get from your internal dialog are just bits of old recordings generated by the subconscious. Therefore, these answers are not always important.

One way these internal dialog responses can be useful is if they inform us in some new way about our past experiences or relationships. In this way they can help us to better understand ourselves, our lives and our relationships. It is common when clearing our most wounded or conflicted aspects of ourselves that our defenses to processing them out can even repeatedly scream the word "No!!!", at the moment we begin repeating the "who is it" statement. This reaction is only part of the clearing, it is not "real", nor is it a problem. Resistance is in effect a sign of progress in the processing of the emotions we most want to be rid of.

It is vital to continue working on whatever stuck feelings you are working to release until they are fully resolved. Though these parts may do everything in their power to distract you from facing and completely resolving them. In essence their fear driven defense systems only feel safe when they are operating in the previous dysfunctional manner that has become a habit. If you allow this fear driven process of distraction to keep you from focusing on the detrimental feeling or belief, then it will simply remain and continue operating in the previous manner.

Paradoxically there are emotional parts of us that can feel safer by continuing to feel bad, unhappy and wrong. They may even feel it is appropriate for us to remain timelessly in an unredeemable state of self-punishment or self-loathing, and of not having what we want in life. These feelings, although sometimes intense and detrimental, are only old recordings, and do not and cannot truly define us. Holding onto them for even a moment is not beneficial.

The result we are seeking by asking any "who is it…" question is the complete clearing of the prior detrimental behavioral tendency, negative belief, thought process, negative internal dialog, debilitating perspective or emotional state. It is useful to understand that the "who is it" method can be used to clear even our most deeply entrenched beliefs. Including beliefs that have been holding us back from achieving our most cherished goals. Beliefs tend to manifest reality, and positive empowering beliefs can help you to some extent. Limiting fear driven beliefs tend to hold you back from creating the life you want. So, if you clear all of the limiting beliefs that you hold (whether positive or negative), then you are immediately empowered to consciously improve your life and to attain your goals. You are left with only consciousness, without the filter of any beliefs. Acting from any state of belief is to act unconsciously. Acting in a fully conscious manner is always our most empowered state.

This method of clearing ego-identity elements is very effective and works to process out any part of our systems that is conflicted or operating in a judgmental, dysfunctional or emotionally negative manner. It does not matter when, where, how or why the old emotion or belief was created and recorded in our systems. As long as we can either feel it as a feeling in our body, or hear it in our internal dialog, and truly want to process it out, it can be resolved in this manner. If you feel resistance to releasing the feeling they you can ask yourself "who is it that is resisting releasing this feeling or belief?".

In applying this release method, we are required to put some distance between our consciousness and the dysfunctional or negative feelings that we have become highly identified with during the course of our lives. Once this distance is consciously perceived and it is understood that these feelings and beliefs are not ourselves, we become empowered to process out the recorded identity element that has been causing difficulties.

In effect this process helps and guides us to effectively and permanently dis-identify from perceived elements of our personality or ego-identity. Once this happens these elements cease to influence our decisions, emotions and interpretations of life events and relationships. This release process is derived from the work of the highly spiritually realized Indian teacher Ramana Maharshi. Ramana basically stated that we can ultimately achieve enlightenment by continually asking and ever more deeply answering the basic question "Who am I?".

392

By asking "who is it that feels this or believes this?" we recognize that it is not our consciousness that is holding onto this feeling or belief. It is often a "child-self" or a misinterpretation of past experience which we have recorded.

Of course, who we truly are is an infinitely powerful child of God and aspect of God. Fully realizing this truth brings our ultimate empowerment, as well as our ultimate state of inner peace and joy. Clearing each subconscious ego-identity element is simply a step on this spiritually developmental path.

Chapter Twelve
Integrating Our New Insights:

WHENEVER WE ACQUIRE NEW INSIGHTS WE TEND TO EXPERIENCE them in various areas of our lives and to apply them at various levels of our systems, yet often not at all levels simultaneously. From a metaphysical standpoint, we could say it is best to implement, integrate and align the understandings we have gathered on our life paths at all the levels of our chakras and consciousness. These chakra levels are each a window on the world through which we see, experience, interpret, decide upon, act out and also record our life and relationship experiences. Our chakras are also exit points for the energies we send out to effect and manifest our reality, intentions and relationships, whether these energies are positive or negative. So, there is a constant interplay of energies between all of the parts of ourselves, all other human beings, the world, spirit and the universe via our chakras.

In this process, we first record our new interpretations of our experiences, integrate them into our energy consciousness and perceived identity, and then we apply our newly acquired insights from those experiences to our present lives. Yet due to the lack of early life awareness of this process many of us unintentionally go about this fundamental developmental effort in a somewhat distorted, incomplete, incongruent, non-methodical, non-comprehensive or disjointed manner. Thus, we do not tend to consistently ensure, with discerning intent, that we have fully grasped, understood and integrated each "new understanding" at every level of our systems. The reason for this incomplete process is simply inexperience and ignorance of the option, and of the benefit and the process of doing so. This process is just not currently taught by parents or standard educational systems.

This incomplete dynamic of learning and incompletely applying what we learn in our lives is especially true in the mental and emotional processes of children who have not been taught advanced interpretive skills. By "interpretive skills" I mean the capacity to discerningly and accurately become aware of all key facets of any social situation, process or relationship. Therefore, they have difficulty in successfully navigating their life situations and arriving at clear and precise understandings of their nature, workings and parameters. Therefore, they have fewer catalytic or gestalt attainments of clear profound multidimensional understanding to base their later experiential interpretations and decisions upon.

The attainment of this sagacious and non-linear and more complete interpretive method of learning must be accomplished in a manner which supports positive discerning decision-making and decisive constructive action in regard to the situations we encounter.

In these transformational and rapidly changing times, integrating the various aspects of our being, faster, better, and on more levels is becoming ever more important in order to be able to successfully process the complex aspects of our reality and life experience. By levels of our systems I mean the range of chakra levels contained within our energy systems which manage the various aspects of our lives and information related to them. These chakra levels manage everything from survival, to emotions, relationships, sex, money, power, analytical thought, compassion, wisdom, discernment, creativity, decision-making, energy, personal will and our connection to God. Therefore, learning to manage them consciously is vital to humanity's evolution.

Human beings tend to learn or acquire a large amount of new knowledge, experience and raw information as we reach out into the world of both human and spiritual experience. This acquired learning is initially often very cognitive, conceptual, abstract or mental, such as might be acquired in reading a book, or it may be strictly emotional or kinesthetic in nature. Therefore, the new information is initially often only available to either their upper or lower level chakras, without our realizing this to be the case. So, the new information is neither well-integrated nor well-grounded into all levels of our systems.

For this reason, the new information is not yet optimally applicable to our process of managing all aspects of our mental, physical and emotional reality. Therefore, it is only useful to a limited degree and may not significantly or directly improve our overall life performance. An example of this non-optimal process would be seen if we did not know how to swim and then read a book on swimming. Reading a book on swimming does not mean we mentally or physically truly understand how to swim. We must integrate the information we have read in the book with the actual physical experience and practice of swimming. It is the combination of basic information, experience, cognitive processing and practice that helps us integrate the information more fully throughout our system. Therefore, we must in some way integrate our upper and lower level chakra energies and information in order to perform optimally in any area of life.

Most people's paths of acquiring new states of conscious understanding, in a way, inherently lack optimal integration and "grounding". This is because our traditional learning practices are initially an upper chakra and mental or cognitive learning practice (3rd, 4th, 5th and 6th chakras). This method of learning often does not optimally and directly include and affect developmental changes in the lower chakras (1st and 2nd). In this situation people "get" the understanding conceptually, logically or in a mental way. Yet it does not fundamentally change their core beliefs stored in their lower chakras, their fundamental emotional dynamics and point of view, their habits or their basic behavior. Most of us are willing to learn, yet most of us also fear and resist foundational change in our lives, especially in our core subconscious beliefs and emotions. Learning new concepts does not equal a foundational change in emotion, belief, behavior or decision-making. Recognizing the incompleteness of this process of learning is vital if we want optimal results.

The flip side of the chakra learning process is seen when we experience lower chakra learning which does not directly involve the upper chakras, and it can be somewhat disconcerting to have such an internal discontinuity of perspective. A common circumstance where this occurs is when we become involved rapidly and passionately in a personal sexual relationship. In these cases, we may soon afterward realize that despite all our intense and seemingly "real and relevant" lower chakra feelings of desire and sexual motivations that we are fundamentally incompatible with the person we shared the experience with. These situations are brought about by our consciousness not being optimally integrated and aware, yet the initial "blindly chosen" experience is often necessary to motivate us to become more integrated and self-aware. If we have an experience which brings about a rapid and foundational shift in our core beliefs or emotions, then we will of course have significant change in our systems. Yet we may not have full cognitive understanding of what is occurring, and thus may not have as profound a shift in our conscious thinking, strategizing and decision-making.

Our conscious awareness of our internal multi-level incongruity of thought and feeling occurs when we realize our upper and lower chakras are out of sync or are not aligned with our chosen life path or experience of life. An example of this is when we work for years to become spiritual and then find ourselves suddenly and surprisingly triggered to act out in ego self-defense, primal rage, greed, jealousy, selfishness or fear. This type of situation occurs when our lower chakra patterns and quality of function have not been raised to the level of understanding and energetic frequency of our upper chakras. (These upper level chakras are designed to function at higher frequencies of spirituality, energy, complexity, sophistication of thought and emotion than our lower chakras, so they can effectively be utilized to diagnose and improve our lower chakra dysfunctions).

Eventually we are usually motivated by the discomfort, dysfunction and limitation of these differences in development, awareness and understanding of the various levels of our chakra systems to work to update our lower chakras to the level of understanding that our upper chakras have achieved. We therefore integrate the newly acquired knowledge into the lower frequency chakras of our system, and in so doing we pragmatically and optimally become able to better apply the achieved capability of understanding to our day-to-day lives. Then we mentally and spiritually reach out to learn more, and again we eventually filter this new knowledge downward into and throughout our lower chakras. So, we are constantly overwriting and evolving our old recorded patterns of thought, emotion, belief and behavior that we have stored in the simulacra of our lower chakras at earlier points in our lives with new understandings.

Through the development of improved upper chakra function, we are empowered to attain new conscious awareness in our upper level chakras, and then learn to see life through the lenses of our upper chakras more often. We can also attain increased conscious awareness of our lower chakras in this way (in effect we can look at our lower chakras through the lenses of our upper level chakras) and can then see how they may be acting out in non-optimal ways. Through this path of developed understanding via reconciling incongruous levels of self-awareness, we gradually and eventually gain the ability to effectively manage our negative or non-optimal emotions, patterns and behaviors. In this way, we ultimately achieve peace and enlightenment.

If our chakras function in an incongruous or non-aligned manner we continually learn and understand life differently at the different levels of our chakras (with each chakra's associated simulacra, emotions, and interpretive and decision-making mechanisms). So, for most of us our chakra's functions are continually out of sync with each other to one degree or another. We are, through this non-optimized and non-synchronized chakra development cycle, simultaneously and constantly working to reconcile conflicts and re-synchronize the various levels and internal views of reality (mental, spiritual, emotional, physical and social) with all that is happening around us. This instinctive style of gaining and understanding life experience can be made more conscious, methodical, efficient, systematized, and planned rather than reactive. Doing so creates a more effective and useful method of acquiring knowledge, understanding and wisdom about life in general. Doing so also effectively streamlines the process of self-integration and tends to result in very rapid acquisition of knowledge and wisdom, while simultaneously giving us the ability to practically apply it in all areas of our lives. It certainly empowers us to apply the newly acquired information, knowledge and experience in more areas and levels of our lives than we otherwise would.

There is more than one way to achieve this integrated way of optimal mental, emotional and spiritual function. One of them is through a practice of analytical meditation or mindfulness meditation (information on these practices is readily available on the internet). These methods help us to more clearly evaluate our internal quality of function in a meditative state, at each chakra level, in order to become aware of any disparities, blind spots or conflicts between the levels of our systems or our subconscious parts. In this way we can more optimally and consciously keep our systems synchronized and harmonized in their development and thus at peace.

Again, it is important to recognize that if our lower chakras are not clear of early life negative conditioning, or if we are dealing with a significant upwelling of un-reconciled negative karmic patterns, that these factors can significantly impede our function and thus the achievement of our life goals until they are effectively and completely resolved. We cannot be fully sovereign, nor own our power if we are not integrated. The instinctive reactive process of integration described above, that most human beings to some degree follow, though less efficient, is still valid and ongoing, even in emotionally difficult circumstances. However due to the ongoing conflicts it creates, it requires a greater degree of discipline, self-management and effort to ultimately achieve full integration. It also requires us to live our lives in a disjointed, internally conflicted mode of semi-consciousness and reactive negative emotions, with much less power to consciously and positively influence our own lives and the lives of those we love. Therefore, I suggest the more conscious, methodical and efficient approach.

Divine Love of Self and Others:

There is a type of love called divine love that is the foundation of all truly sage attainments of spiritual consciousness. A brief working definition of this type of love is that it is pure, it is free to all, no one has to do anything to deserve it, and it need not be worked for or striven for. Divine love is given without attachment or expectation of any kind, including not expecting to be loved in return for having given our love. Giving love freely means exactly that, freely. Divine love is within all of us and it is, like all love, sourced from God, and it shines through our heart chakras, like light through a clean window.

This type of love asks nothing whatsoever in order to be given in limitless quantities because it understands that this process of giving is all that truly matters. This love is given in complete sovereign independence of anything others may do, believe, think, say, want or feel. This love could also be seen as the "willfully channeled love of spirit" which we can all access, if we choose to. Paradoxically we must actively choose to divinely love before we are able to feel and express divine love. Love, just like hatred, anger, fear, guilt or shame are all choices that we make every day. We all have the right to love and be loved as freely and completely as God loves us. Still many of us are caught up in an ongoing struggle within ourselves to determine whether we deserve happiness and love or not, and whether others deserve it from us. Often we lose in this unnecessary internal debate. The concept of deservedness itself is not truly valid, because it often functions as nothing more than a socially conditioned mask for the cycle of self-judgment. We all deserve love, all the time, no matter who we are, and no matter what our past choices or experiences.

It might seem too many of us that we feel divine love for family members, our spouses or children. Yet this is most often not precisely the case; in fact, it is quite the opposite for many of us. We may choose to withhold love, appreciation, attention, affection or approval based upon a set of conscious or subconscious conditions. These conditions can be traditions, rules, roles, requirements, values and judgments of ourselves and others. Once these judgments have been made and impede our open expressions of love, we then tend to rationalize why it is not appropriate to completely, freely and consistently love either ourselves or others. In addition, we tend to rationalize why it is appropriate to abandon, criticize, punish, control, devalue and ostracize others. In doing so we may feel somewhat comfortable in the apparent safety of our self-justification (or ego justification) and yet we are rendered less able to emotionally and mentally live with ourselves and others in peace.

The obvious contradiction between the supposed intention to divinely love as compared to our actual choice and resultant behavior of not doing so eludes many of us. If we do become aware of it we may then feel lost in feelings of inadequacy, guilt or shame. Often we use the withholding of approval, trust, attention, acceptance and love as relationship leverage, and as a threat or bargaining chip to obtain something we want, (i.e. some emotion, some kind of attention or some behavior from someone else). This is not an expression of love in its most evolved form. The greatest difficulty with this process is that we also unknowingly withhold this quality of love from ourselves, through our own feelings of guilt, shame, anger and fear.

Complete and total forgiveness of self and others is the cure (see the Ho' Oponopono healing method). In the practice of divine love, it is suggested that we continually forgive others for their actions, emotions and life choices no matter what they do. By so doing we learn to see beyond our judgments of them, to let go of the past and are thereby empowered to see the soul within the person. I am not suggesting by saying this that we allow ourselves to be abused or walked upon. If this occurs repeatedly and cannot be reconciled I suggest disconnecting from those types of relationships for our own wellbeing, yet still fully forgiving.

Any judgment we hold of anyone (including of ourselves) is a burden we carry. Thus, we are empowered by forgiveness to live more freely and lovingly, in the now, and in all our relationships. Forgiveness is a great and necessary practice, however I might suggest that there is an even more effective and useful approach to life. This is because in order to forgive we must first have judged either another person or ourselves or both. Then we must retroactively work to "un-judge" them or ourselves via the willful practice of forgiveness. So in effect we allow ourselves to become stuck temporarily in judgment (sometimes for years or lifetimes), then we un-stick ourselves at some point in the future "when we are ready" to forgive, and come to understand the benefit of doing so. What this tends to do is to allow the negative, punishing and judgmental parts of ourselves to continue to be fed regularly through our ongoing judgments, and then it may just "put them on a diet" when we eventually choose to forgive. Therefore, the basic judgmental tendency remains in place.

This practice of delayed forgiveness is still judgmental; therefore it is still a life and relationship limiting and damaging process. We are just eventually letting go, and then congratulating ourselves for being a loving and forgiving person, after we have first judged. I would suggest that not judging in the first place is the only way to delete the whole negative cycle from our lives and from the world. In order to attain this perspective, we first need to understand that there is nothing at all that is appropriate to judge in anyone, as we are all children of God with pure souls, therefore there is nothing that needs forgiving. What is required in order to achieve this conscious and optimal state of consciousness is to willfully and consciously choose to love first and always, rather than to ever fall into the trap of judgment.

To truly divinely love another person means to have all levels of our hearts and minds open to them at all times in a constant state of compassion, without requirement or expectation of them, of any kind. It means to be unwilling to judge their actions, thoughts, beliefs, behaviors, decisions, values, point of view, opinions, religion, race, politics, nationality or emotions in any way. It means fully respecting their choices as being the result of their God-given freewill, no matter how seemingly destructive, negative or short-sighted they may appear to us in the moment. It does not however mean submitting to abuse or negative treatment in any relationship or situation, or placing our personal safety at risk to any degree. Loving unconditionally means that we have consciously chosen to raise the other person, our interpretations of them, and their true spiritual value to us, above all mundane or temporal considerations. In effect, it means to see them as the children of God that they truly are without condition, expectation, question, hesitation, interpretive filters, distortion or interruption.

In my personal experience, few people are yet willing to make the personal commitment necessary to love everyone they know, or interact with, in this manner on a consistent basis, still it can be done and eventually we all will. I believe the statement by Jesus Christ sums it up, "Do unto others as you would have done unto yourself". I would add here though that many people are, due to their impairments of consciousness, emotion and understanding currently cruel, critical and judgmental toward themselves as well as others. Yet the reason for this is usually that someone has taught them not to love and accept themselves and others without condition. They may also be unknowingly acting under the influence of some very heavy past-life karmic patterns. Therefore, their choice to act in these ways has been made in misunderstanding or ignorance and subconscious impairment. They simply need time, facilitation and opportunity to unlearn this type of detrimental behavior. In our life paths we can either choose to love them and help them develop or we can judge, punish and hate them (which does not work); it is all our choice. I suggest loving them.

Divine love means loving without any requirement of possession or control over those we love. In the case of possessive love, possession and control over another's emotional and relationship choices, behaviors, attention and physical presence is often the condition for continued love. In today's world most of us take possessive love for granted, and even see it as the best way or the only way to "really love". Possessive love is even supported by our current legal systems. We may look at anyone who does not love "possessively enough" as wrong in some way, or cold or as not being "truly loving or committed" or we may feel they are not deeply or passionately involved in the relationship.

Possessive love and resulting drama tend to go hand in hand. Possessive love is simply the result of fear driven control strategies, in the guise of true love. Non-possessive love is even seen by some as an aberration, rather than something to be esteemed. As if these subconscious and socially conditioned states of fear, insecurity, attention seeking and relationship control seeking, which are the underlying motivations for possessive love, were actually good and necessary in some way. As if the only way for love to be "real and fulfilling" is to have our love based in fear and insecurity, and to have it be constantly and exclusively expressed to one person and then tested and re-proven daily.

There is an assumption that what we give in relationships we should receive in equal and like measure, which then often leads to feelings of unfairness and even betrayal. This assumption of required balance in relationships also creates a constant process of comparison in our relationships to determine if our love is balanced with another's. This is of course just another way of trying to control others, and can even turn into emotional blackmail in order to achieve the type of relationship behavior we desire from others. Putting guilt trips on others or threatening them with abandonment is often how this is accomplished. (For example, "Look how much I have given to you" or "Why aren't you as loving as I am?")

This type of exchange oriented interaction leads to emotional extortion, hurt feelings, conflict, forced relationship behavior, resentment, fear, drama, and further imprinting of these unhealed states of insecurity. If we do not feel the exchange is balanced, then we tend to claim victimhood and feel betrayed. Submitting to this exchange dynamic or being overtly tolerant of this style of ego-centric love is a type of enabling behavior. Oddly enough it has become a cultural norm for many and has even become institutionalized in and supported by the legal system.

No relationship will always be completely fair or balanced for any length of time, and to try to force it to be so will only cause further and ongoing stress, misunderstanding and conflict. I would offer here, as a suggested solution to this social problem, our biblically recorded knowledge of the life of Christ, as a fine example of divine and non-possessive love.

In today's world we are often taught to derive our self-worth and self-esteem from and through external conditions and relationships, rather than from internal self-awareness, realization of our connection to spirit, self-acceptance and sovereign freewill choice. We are thus being taught not to accept, trust and approve of ourselves or others as we are or as they are without condition. Thus, we are being taught conditional love. We are also taught to compare our personal situation to other's situations, and this comparison usually results in unhappiness. Due to these limiting and conflict producing tendencies many people are constantly unhappy, seeking short-term happiness in dysfunctional ways or are lost in social or relationship approval seeking. We literally do not know how to, and are not usually taught to, consistently feel good about ourselves just as we are. Meaning that happiness and feeling good is usually considered secondary to many other social expectations and priorities in life.

The reason for this detrimental situation is that as a species we have adopted the philosophy that we cannot fundamentally trust each other or ourselves and that we must be willing to control each other and ourselves into living via "good beliefs, and right behaviors and choices". This process cannot lead to happiness, since it is based at its foundation upon control, expectation, distrust of self and others, projected fears, judgment and threat of punishment, non-acceptance, rejection or abandonment. We have been raised in this environment for so long that it has become transparent to our consciousness and seemingly acceptable or even necessary to us. We are like fish in an aquarium that have ceased to be able to perceive the water we live and function in from moment-to-moment.

We may not realize our own expectations of ourselves or others, and our judgmental reactions to these expectations not being met, until someone else points them out. Many of us literally believe that if our expectations are not being met that we are not being loved by others or those we are in relationship with. This detrimental tendency to remain unconscious to our personal judgmental dynamics has become as much a part of us as our breathing. Thus, we just tend to accept it as necessary until the dynamic itself leads to a problem that is perceived to be so great that we can no longer ignore it. Then we are forced by circumstance to learn, change and grow (reactively rather than developing proactively). That time is now and today, the problems of our world are now too great to be ignored.

We must learn to see the value of vast and foundational change in how we as individuals, and all of us as a species, love ourselves, each other and our world. We all have power and can change how we choose to love now! We are all fully deserving of this joyful experience. We need to teach each other to love without requirement or condition and actively model this behavior.

Divine love of self and others is attainable; however it does not just happen, it must be built, owned and willfully and consciously refined and maintained from day-to-day. The key to starting on this path, which will ultimately culminate in an ongoing state of divine self-love, is to first make the decision and set the intention to achieve it. From this decisive developmental point in your soul's journey it is only a matter of time, (though it may be lifetimes for some of us), until you achieve it for yourself and thus offer it to those you love.

Living Consciously In an Unconscious World:

For those of you who are reading this and who perceive yourself to be either a little or a lot more self-aware than many of the people around you, life is probably difficult in many ways. Looking at the world around you, you might see what appear to be a multitude of unnecessary problems, tragedies, dramas, distractions and dysfunctions. These situations may cause a number of disconcerting mental and emotional reactions within you, including sadness, heartache, anxiety, depression, fear, stress or in some cases even temporary panic. There are many reasons why you might react in these ways, although I would suggest that none of them, no matter how apparently reasonable, will truly serve either you or those you love.

As has been previously stated you can be pretty sure that more of these types of situations will be occurring in the world's near future. However, please trust me when I say that you do not deserve to be unhappy or your life made more difficult. What is happening around the world, as painful as it may sometimes be, is in many ways necessary and even beneficial for all of humanity. We humans have <u>thus far</u> chosen to attain understanding and to evolve via cause-and-effect, and trial and error, and sometimes via negative reactions to chosen life experiences, rather than through loving, conscious wisdom. This style and method of development is gradually changing and improving, and ultimately the previous cloud of unconsciousness will be seen to have a silver lining.

If we are on the path of consciousness and spiritual development, then we have probably grown in regard to how much we can love and care about ourselves and others. This means our heart chakras are opening and developing, and we are learning to see life through our hearts, rather than just through our desires, goals, minds, our survival instincts, our beliefs, or our sometimes negatively patterned emotional reactions. If this is the case then we may indeed be uncomfortable in the current world environment of stress, conflict, confusion and suffering. It is not necessary for this to be so, however.

We can live in an ongoing and significant degree of love, inner peace, faith and equanimity in spite of any environmental or relationship conditions. We can learn to love being conscious, and choose to leave behind any pain that being conscious may initially create. In order for this to occur, we must first learn why we have been choosing to feel and experience this pain, and how our subconscious may still be making some detrimental decisions for us. Then we must choose to change how various parts of ourselves operate, so that we no longer interpret our life as wrong and pain producing. If we do this, then we can change life into a creative adventure and a process of sovereign self-empowerment as the world transformation continues to unfold around us.

We live in a beautiful world and we all have the right and the potential to live powerful wonderful lives of continual joy and divine love. It is our birthright, our opportunity and our responsibility to be who and what we choose to be and become. In this path we all influence each other and we all influence the world with everything we feel or believe, every choice we make, every thought we think and every action we take. This is a wonderful and awesome opportunity, power and responsibility. Becoming more conscious, healed, integrated and whole, day-by-day will eventually bring us to the levels of understanding we desire and that the world needs from us.

The universe and God are continually helping us to achieve this state, and continued unflinching faith in that fact is necessary and optimal. If we choose to make this personal developmental commitment, then we can all make the future world an even more beautiful place for ourselves and our children. In these challenging times nothing less will do.

Thank you for kindly and compassionately accompanying me on this journey.

Appendix 1:

Comprehensive Ego-Identity Deconstruction Listing

This listing cannot be fully comprehensive, because there are literally an unending number of potential simulacra and ego-identity parts that people can record and then re-experience. This listing is meant to get you started in your own process of ego-identity deconstruction and process of healing your conflicted simulacra or subconscious parts. Some may be easily related to in the beginning of your work; others may not become visible to your consciousness until you have cleared the more conscious layers of your ego-identity. All of these listed questions begin with the words, "Who is it …?". It is useful to realize that once we have effectively dropped all elements of ego-identity, and all the subconscious fear drives that create them, then what is left is simply love and compassion. You don't need an ego-identity to live and work in this world. I would suggest that you and everyone else only need love. Any tendency to continue to resonate with ego-identity can only eventually drag us back down into negative fear drive emotional dynamics and strategies.

❖ **Relationships:**

- ▪ Feels unlovable
- ▪ Fears rejection, being judged and criticism
- ▪ Fears conflict in my relationships
- ▪ Feels I am not understood or accepted
- ▪ Feels I cannot trust my emotions in a relationship
- ▪ Fears what others think or feel about me
- ▪ Fears being emotionally vulnerable in my relationship
- ▪ Fears emotional intimacy in my relationship
- ▪ Fears physical or sexual intimacy in my relationship
- ▪ Wants to be in control of my relationship(s)
- ▪ Feels I can only be happy if my romantic expectations are met by my spouse
- ▪ Feels I "have to" have others make decisions for me
- ▪ Feels I cannot make decisions by myself and for myself
- ▪ Feels I can only be happy if I am in control of my future relationship
- ▪ Feels I can only be happy if I am married
- ▪ Feels I will never have the love I want in life
- ▪ Fears not being in control of my relationships

- Feels unable to satisfy my spouse
- Fears my spouse leaving me
- Feels I am nothing without a relationship
- Fears losing the social status of being a (wife, husband or married person)
- Feels that no one loves me or wants me
- Worries that I am not meeting my spouse's expectations
- Feels I have to prove my worth to my spouse
- Fears failing as a wife, mother, husband or father
- I angry at my spouse
- Blames myself for the way my relationship is going
- Blames my spouse for the way our relationship is going
- Feels unattractive (not pretty or handsome or sexy enough)
- Fears I am not wanted by those I love
- Hates my spouse
- Fears that my spouse hates me
- Fears that I am only wanted by my spouse for sex
- Fears I am only wanted by my spouse for my ability to financially support them or the family
- Feels I am not good enough to be wanted
- Fears I will fail in my relationship
- Fears my spouse will cheat on me
- Fears my spouse will fail me in our relationship
- Fears that I am not giving enough in my relationships
- Feels guilty about my relationship
- Feels guilty about my not being emotionally available to my spouse
- Feels that relationships are about exchange
- Feels not getting equally in relation to what it has given
- Resents my parents or spouse for controlling me
- Feels I have to do what my mother or father tell me to
- Feels guilty about my emotions and what I feel toward my spouse
- Constantly judges how I feel and what I feel
- Feels I should not feel what I do feel in my relationship(s)
- Feels I should have been there for someone who passed away
- Feels I cannot let go of my grief in regard to the loss of a relationship, spouse, child or parent
- Worries constantly about my children, spouse or parents
- Hates that I cannot control my emotions in my relationship
- Hates that my spouse cannot control their emotions in our relationship
- Hates myself for hating others

- ❖ **Career:**
  - Does not feel confident
  - Feels I am a failure
  - Feels I will never reach my goals
  - Feels others do not appreciate me or my skills or ability
  - Fears I will not be promoted
  - Fears I may lose my job
  - Hates my boss
  - Feels my boss hates me
  - Worries about my future
  - Is unhappy in my job or career
  - Cannot make a decision as to what to do or where to work
  - Feels I made a mistake in my career path
  - Wants to impress my boss
  - Feels my self-worth is defined by my boss or my successes
  - Feels that if I am not a success that I am a failure
  - Cannot let go of past negative feelings related to past places of employment
  - Feels I don't know what I want to do with my life
  - Worries that I may be fired
  - Feels I am not good enough to be promoted
  - Feels I am not worthy of success
  - Feels I cannot accept myself unless others do so first

- ❖ **Addiction:**
  - Cannot cease drinking, smoking, taking drugs, eating, etc.
  - Hates myself for my addiction
  - Judges myself for my addiction
  - Feels others judge me for my addiction
  - Feels I cannot break my addiction
  - Fears other's judgments of my addiction
  - Fears being abandoned because I am an addict
  - Fears my addiction will destroy my life and relationships
  - Feels my addiction is stronger than I am
  - Feels that my addiction means I am bad, wrong, weak, unacceptable, broken, worthless, etc.
  - Judges other addicts
  - Feels that I have to redeem myself for my addictive tendencies
  - Feels I cannot be redeemed from my addictive tendencies
  - Feels or fears that I will always be lost in addiction
  - Feels I will always be an addict
  - Feels that being addicted is wrong and bad

- ❖ **Trust and Betrayal:**
  - Feels I cannot trust myself
  - Feels I cannot trust others or anyone
  - Fears being betrayed
  - Fears I will betray those I love
  - Fears the pain of being betrayed
  - Wants to punish those who have betrayed me
  - Wants to punish myself for betraying those I love
  - Hates those who I feel have betrayed me
  - Hates myself for betraying those I love
  - Feels I am not in integrity with others
  - Feels I do not know how to be authentic in relationships with others
  - Fears others will not be in integrity with me
  - Feels others are not authentic in their interactions with me
  - Feels that I have no intimacy in my life
  - Feels that my spouse is emotionally unavailable

- ❖ **Dualistic Thinking, (Right and Wrong / Good and Bad / Safe and Unsafe):**
  - Feels I am wrong or bad
  - Feels I have to prove I am right and others are wrong
  - Fears I am not good enough
  - Fears being wrong or imperfect, broken or incomplete
  - That feels I am not safe unless I can prove I am good enough
  - Fears being unsafe
  - Wants to be safe
  - Wants to be right all the time
  - Fears being wrong
  - Wants to be good
  - Fears being bad
  - Fears letting go of what I have believed in the past

- ❖ **Ego-Identity (Dissolving the Ego-Identity and Narcissism)**
  - Hates my life
  - Doesn't feel I am good enough
  - Doesn't like myself
  - Feels that I am my work or my career
  - Feels I am only good if I meet other's expectations
  - Fears not being understood
  - Fears not being recognized and rewarded
  - Feels I have to prove I am better or higher than others
  - Feels that I cannot allow anyone to be equal to me

- Feels I have to have other's attention
- Feels I am better than everyone else
- Feels I am smarter than everyone else
- Feel I know more than everyone else
- Feels I have to be recognized and rewarded in order to have or be in "control"
- Fears not being powerful
- Not being in control
- Feels it must overcome or defeat others in order to be in control and safe
- Feels others do not know I exist
- Fears that I do not exist
- Feels that I have to compete against others in order to be safe
- Feels I have to conquer or defeat others in order to be safe
- Feels that I am not safe
- I can only be safe if I compete against and conquer others
- Hates and wants to destroy those I feel vulnerable toward
- Wants to get everyone's attention
- Feels I am only safe if I am a somebody
- Feels I have to be somebody
- Fears just being
- Fears not being or not existing
- Feels I have to prove I am important
- Feels I have to prove I know more than others or am smarter than they are
- Fears not knowing as much as others or not being as smart as they are
- Fears being seen as less than others
- Feels I have to prove my worth to others
- Sees relationships as a process of exchange
- Feels I have to have something to exchange with others to remain safe and in control
- Fears being nothing and no one
- Fears not being understood
- Feels I have to be understood in order to be safe

❖ **Conflict:**

- Fears conflict with others
- Feels I am in conflict with others
- Feels that others are in conflict with me
- Wants to be in conflict with others
- Feels I can only be safe if I am in conflict with others

❖ **Safety and Survival:**

- Wants to be safe
- Wants to survive
- Fears for my safety
- Fears for my survival
- Fears others hurting me, abandoning me or criticizing me
- Fears dying
- Fears others hurting me
- Fears being hurt or physically or emotionally wounded
- Hates not having what I want
- Hates not having my way
- Hates not having what I need

❖ **Control:**

- Feels I have to have things my way
- Feels that my way is the only acceptable way
- Feels that I am right and others are wrong
- Fears losing control
- Fears others controlling my life
- Wants to be in control
- Feels unsafe unless I am in control
- Hates it when others try to control me

❖ **Power:**

- Feels trapped in disempowerment
- Feels disempowered
- Feels that I am right and my way is the right way
- Feels I have to have things my way
- Hates other's tendencies to apply their power to me
- Feels I have to have power in order to be safe and feel safe
- Feels I have misused my power
- Feels guilt or ashamed of my use of my power
- Fears other's applying their power to me or my life or relationships
- Feels that having power equals having status
- Feels I have to have power or be in power
- Feels that if I do not have power over others that they will over power me
- Still feels I have to do what my mother or father tell me to
- Still feels I always have to please my mother or father

❖ **Competition, Status and Ambition:**

- Wants to be better than others

- Feels I must prove myself to others
- Feels I must prove myself better than others
- Want to dominate others
- Hates it when anyone does better than I do
- Wants to attain a position of high status in regard to others
- That wants to be in control of others
- Feels that if I make a lot of money I will be a success
- Feels that I have to be a success or I will be a loser or worthless
- Hates being looked down on by others
- Feels that I am better than others
- Feels I will never be anything until I succeed or am a success
- Fears social embarrassment
- Fears being criticized or judged by others
- Feels that I only have value if I have more or am more than other people
- That I want to be or appear to be special
- Fears not being seen as perfect
- Fears social vulnerability or abandonment
- Feels righteous or better when criticizing or judging or punishing others
- Feels it is right to tell others what to do
- Feels I can only be accepted if I prove myself better than other people
- Worries about what other people think or say about me

❖ Money:

- Feels I will never have enough money
- Fears not having enough money
- Feels that the amount of money I have defines my personal worth or social worth
- Feels that it is unfair that others have more money than I do
- Feels victimized by those with more money than I have
- Fears losing all of my money
- Feels that without my money I am nothing
- Feels that without my money I have no power
- Feels that power equals money and money equals power
- Fears my spouse making more money than I do
- Fears my spouse spending all of my money
- Fears being too focused on money or being greedy
- Feels that I am greedy or financially selfish
- Fears conflict with my spouse about money
- Feels I must be the decision-maker in regard to money matters
- Feels I must control my money

- Fears others taking my money
- Feels that others want me only for my money
- Feels that my money equals my social status

❖ **Time:**

- Feels that there is never enough time
- Feels that I need more time
- Feels that time is money
- Fears others controlling my time or taking my time
- Fears time, aging and ultimately death

❖ **Recognition and Attention:**

- Wants attention and recognition
- Wants everybody's attention
- Feels I am nothing unless I have other's attention and recognition
- Fears that without attention, I am unsafe
- Feels I deserve recognition
- Resents that I have not gotten the attention I deserve
- Wants to control others via attention seeking
- Feels that if I have recognition that I am loved and accepted
- Feels that if I have recognition, that I have power
- Fears not having other's attention
- Fears not being recognized
- Fears that if I am not recognized then I am unsafe or do not really socially exist or have value

❖ **Negative Emotions of All Kinds (Fear, Anger, Hatred, Guilt, Shame):**

- That feels hatred, fear, anger, guilt, shame, jealousy, anxiety, stress, etc.
- That feels others hate me, are angry at me, are jealous of me, etc.
- Feels I am only safe if I am angry
- Feels I am only powerful if I am angry
- Feels my hatred or anger is justified
- Fears other's hatred, anger, jealousy, etc.
- Judges my own negative emotions
- Judges other's negative emotions

❖ **Fear, Worry, Stress, Tension and Anxiety:**

- Feels fear, worry, stress or anxiety in this present moment
- Feels that I am only safe if I worry
- Feels that worry will keep me safe

- Feels that fear will keep me safe
- Feels that being in control will keep me safe
- Fears my feelings of fear
- Worries about my future
- Worries about my children, parents or my spouse
- Worries about my past
- Feels uncertain in this present moment
- Feels that I can only make a decision if I am certain of the result or outcome of doing so

❖ **Confidence:**

- Feels non-confident
- Feels uncertain what to do
- Feels others have more confidence than I do
- Feels I have no power
- Feels others have more power than I do
- Feels I have no control over my life
- Feels I will probably fail
- Feels I cannot accomplish what I most want in life
- Compares myself to others constantly
- Fears others will see that I am not really confident
- Fears that others will take my confidence or power

❖ **Self-Worth and Social-Worth:**

- Feels unworthy
- Has no self-worth
- Does not know how to feel good or better about myself
- Feels I am not good enough
- Feels I will never be good enough
- Feels that others are better than I am
- Feels that others have greater worth than I do
- Feels others determine my social worth or self-worth
- Feels I have no power over my social or self-worth
- Hates myself
- Feels I have no worth unless others constantly give me attention

❖ **Selfishness, Self-Centeredness, Pride and Arrogance:**

- Feels that I am selfish
- Fears that I will be seen as selfish or self-centered
- Feels that others are self-centered or selfish
- Hates selfish people
- Resents selfish people
- Judges selfish people

- "Knows" that I am better than everybody else
- Wants to be better than everybody else
- Wants to have power over other people
- Feels I can only be happy if I always get what I want
- Feels I deserve to have power over or control other people
- Feels that others are less than me or not as good
- Feels that people are not all equal
- Feels that my pride will make me better than others
- Feels that pride is beneficial and will lead me to success
- Believes that pride and arrogance equal self-confidence
- Feels that I can only be safe if I prove myself better than others

❖ **Integrity and Honesty:**

- Believes no one is trustworthy or acts in integrity
- Feels that no one is honest
- Fears that others I am in relationship are not honest
- Fears that others will not act in integrity with me
- Feels that honesty is weakness
- Fears being found out to be non-integrous
- Feels that if people are not honest that they are bad
- Feels that I cannot be safely honest with anyone

❖ **Victims, Perpetrators and Rescuers:**

- Feels I am a victim
- Feels that I have been victimized
- Feels that (whoever) has victimized me
- Fears others hurting me
- Feels that others have more power than I do
- Feels that others have power over me
- Feels wounded by someone else's choices, feelings, actions or behaviors
- Feels that there are "bad people" in the world
- Feels that I am a bad person
- Feels that I have to rescue those in need
- Feels that I have to take care of my spouse
- Feels that I have to take care of or am responsible for others
- Feels I have the right to punish others who have hurt me
- Feels that others deserve punishment
- Feels that I deserve punishment

❖ **Judgment and Forgiveness of Self and Others:**

- Feels I must judge and punish myself in order to then feel I am a good person

- Feels I can never forgive myself
- Feels I am always doing everything wrong
- Feels I can never do anything right
- Feels everyone else is a problem
- Feels I am messed up or broken
- Hates myself
- Feels I am bad
- Feels I can never forgive my (spouse, mother, father, or other family member)
- Fears forgiving my (spouse, mother, father, or other family member)
- Fears forgiving myself for my past choices or behaviors
- Feels that if I do not continue to judge and punish that I will not be safe or in control
- Feels that others never meet my needs or expectations
- Feels that no one ever listens to me and is angry about it
- Feels that on one cares about me and is angry about it

❖ Spiritual Development:

- Feels I am not spiritual enough
- Feels I am unworthy of God's love
- Feels judged and abandoned by God
- Feels I am "my mind"
- Fears being abandoned by God
- Judges myself for my non-spiritual behaviors, emotions or choices
- Feels I am not a child of God
- Feels that I am unredeemable
- Feels I can never be forgiven by God
- Feels I must judge myself in order to be holy, spiritual or accepted by God
- Fears not being accepted by my spiritual congregation
- Fears being abandoned by my spiritual congregation

Acknowledgements

I want to acknowledge and thank the following people for their contributions to this book: My wife Lynn, my mother, my family and especially my sister for their love, patience and support in this often challenging process. Max my best friend. All the people who have graciously allowed me to work with them to help heal their lives and in the process and through their courage have given me the perspective needed to write this book. Ja-lene Clark and Jo Ann P. Deck, who have inspired me to reach higher than I realized I could. Thanks also to Ja-lene for her excellent artistic expressions in regard to the book's graphics and cover. Thanks to Dr. Ginger Grancanola Ed.D. for their willingness to read early revisions of this book and for providing her insights. Thanks to the people in my working group who have supported my work for years, for their technological and artistic expertise, their transcription efforts and for teaching me so much. I also thank those of you who helped to start me on my spiritual path, you know who you are.

I thank God and all the angels and ascended masters who have graciously and patiently worked with me each day for their support, and without whom I would understand nothing of value.

About John Jones

Psychic, life coach, spiritual teacher, reader of past lives and healer of Karmic patterns, and a channel for spirit guides and those who have crossed over. John Jones has offered his expert services to enhance the lives of people in 28 countries.

For the last 33 years John has devoted himself to deep meditation and working with his Kundalini energy in order to clear, heal, develop and fine-tune his energy reading and psychic abilities. He conducts all of his healing work with the constant channeled guidance of spirit, angels, ascended masters and his client's guides. His accurate readings of the human energy system lead him to the energetic and karmic roots of mental, emotional, spiritual and relationship issues and conflicts so that he can help his clients release their related energy blocks. His ability to read and comprehensively and methodically map the conscious and subconsciously recorded beliefs of his clients offers illumination of the fundamental influences that have created the client's life situations and experiences. His clients are respectfully guided through a detailed progression that facilitates the healing and transformation of the client and their relationships at all levels—spiritual, mental, emotional, energetic and physical.

In his spiritual teaching practice, John focuses on teaching methods of self-awareness, self-evaluation, self-healing, self-empowerment and self-sovereignty, attaining higher levels of spiritual consciousness and improved self-awareness.

He is a graduate of Missouri State University in Springfield Missouri, with a Bachelor of Science in Sociology/Anthropology and a Minor in History. His studies in the humanities and the social sciences have merged with his spiritual insights to provide the foundation for *Enter the Era of Empowerment.*

John provides his personal and professional consulting services to corporations, doctors, psychologists, lawyers, actors and directors, chiropractors, human resources management personnel, executives and a wide-variety of other individuals. As a result of this work, his clients have gained important insights and communicated their experiences of life-enhancing results including increased self-esteem, self-empowerment, heightened spiritual consciousness, feelings of inner peace, decreased physical and emotional pain, and significant improvements in all of their key relationships.

Resources:

Farrand, Thomas Ashley, "Healing Mantras, Using sound affirmations for personal power, creativity and healing", Published by Ballantine Wellspring, The Random House Publishing Group, New York. Copyright 1999

Maharshi, Ramana, "The Spiritual Teaching of Ramana Maharshi". Copyright 1972, Sri Ramanasramam, Shambala Publications Inc., 1998

Karpman, Stephen, M.D., "Drama Triangle" entitled "Fairy Tales and Script Drama Analysis", http://www.karpmandramatriangle.com/pdf/DramaTriangle.pdf

Krishnamurti, Jiddhu, "The Awakening of Intelligence", HarperSanFrancisco, A division of HarperCollinsPublishers. 1973, by Krishnamurti Foundation Trust Ltd., London

Jones, John B., "A World Without Fear: Release Your Fears & Reclaim You Joy.", 2015 Published by Karmic Communications, LLC

Jones, John B., "Navigating Your Life", 3 DVD Visual Educational Series, Copyright Karmic Communications, LLC, 2008, ISBN 978-0-9817641-0-8

Jung, Carl, "The Portable Jung", Edited by Joseph Campbell, The Viking Portable Library, Published By the Penguin Group 1976

Gardner, Dr. Howard, "Frames of Mind: The Theory of Multiple Intelligences", Publisher: Basic Books; 3rd edition (March 29, 2011)

Ocean Fish Populations Cut in Half Since the 1970's:
By: Andy Campbell, Huffington Post 09/16/2015
http://www.huffingtonpost.com/entry/crucial-marine-populations-cut-in-half-since-the-1970s-report_us_55f9ecd2e4b00310edf5b1b2

Elizabeth Korbert, "The 6th Extinction, An Unnatural History", Published by: Henry Holt and Company, LLC, Copyright 2014

Elizabeth Kubler-Ross, M.D., "On Death and Dying, What the Dying Have to Teach Doctors, Nurses, Clergy and Their Own Family", Published in New York, The Macmillan Company, 1969

http://247wallst.com/technology-3/2016/12/03/us-needs-to-train-100000-cybersecurity-experts-by-2020/

US Needs to Train 100,000 Cybersecurity Experts by 2020

By Douglas A. McIntyre   December 3, 2016 8:45 am EST

Published on Monday, June 20, 2016 by Common Dreams

Refugee Planet: There Have Never Been This Many Displaced People on Earth, Half of refugees worldwide are children, new United Nations report finds, by Nadia Prupis, staff writer

http://fortune.com/2016/06/24/brexit-david-cameron-eu/

Brexit Just Made All of Britain's Problems Worse, commentary by James P. Moore Jr., JUNE 24, 2016, 12:54 PM EST

http://thenextweb.com/artificial-intelligence/2016/10/17/deepmind-ai-platform-can-now-learn-without-human-input/

Google's 'DeepMind' AI platform can now learn without human input by BRYAN CLARK — 8 weeks ago in ARTIFICIAL INTELLIGENCE

http://www.theverge.com/2015/7/2/8885845/bmw-toyota-hydrogen-fuel-cell-cars **Some of the biggest automakers are taking hydrogen seriously. What now?** by Chris Ziegler Jul 2, 2015, 3:04pm EDT

http://www.forbes.com/sites/michaellynch/2016/10/04/shale-oil-didnt-kill-off-peak-oil/#71b0454d5509

OCT 4, 2016 @ 06:58 PM 4,061 VIEWS12 Stocks to Buy for 2017, Shale Oil Didn't Kill Off Peak Oil, Michael Lynch , **contributor**

http://www.reuters.com/article/us-iraq-war-anniversary-idUSBRE92D0PG20130314

WORLD NEWS **| Thu Mar 14, 2013 | 12:53pm EDT**

Iraq war costs U.S. more than $2 trillion: study

https://en.wikipedia.org/wiki/Shallow_water_blackout

Shallow Water Blackout

http://dpeaflcio.org/programs-publications/issue-fact-sheets/the-u-s-health-care-system-an-international-perspective/

The U.S. Health Care System: An International Perspective, Fact Sheet 2016, Source: DPE Research Department

Made in the USA
Middletown, DE
14 September 2020